Surprising
Marriages

25 *Surprising* Marriages

Faith-Building Stories from the Lives
of Famous Christians

William J. Petersen

 Baker Books

A Division of Baker Book House Co
Grand Rapids, Michigan 49516

Published by Baker Books
a division of Baker Book House Company
P.O. Box 6287, Grand Rapids, MI 49516-6287

This book contains material from *Martin Luther Had a Wife* (© 1983), *Harriet Beecher Stowe Had a Husband* (© 1983), *C. S. Lewis Had a Wife* (© 1985), *Catherine Marshall Had a Husband* (© 1986), *Johann Sebastian Bach Had a Wife* (© 1987), and *Husbands and Wives* (© 1989) published by Tyndale House.

Printed in the United States of America

Library of Congress Cataloging-in-Publication Data

Petersen, William J., 1929
    25 surprising marriages : faith-building stories from the lives of famous Christians / William J. Petersen.
        p.   cm.
    Includes bibliographical references.
    ISBN 0-8010-5753-1 (paper)
    1. Protestants—Biography. 2. Spouses—Biography. 3. Evangelicalism—History. 4. Marriage—Religious aspects—Christianity—Case studies. 5. Spouses—Religious life. I. Title.
BX4825.P48   1997
270'.092'2—dc21   96-45565

Contents

Introduction

This is a book about marriage, not about church history. You might learn a bit about church history in the process of reading these pages, but that's not the primary purpose of the book.

When you focus on the marriage of a person, you look beyond his or her greatness and you see his or her humanity. I certainly don't want to debase these men and women whom God has used in spectacular ways. But it is good to see them as mortals with shortcomings and foibles. It is good to see Francis Schaeffer smashing the pot of ivy and Polly Newton biting her fingernails when her husband is late in coming home. It is good to hear Catherine Marshall unable to understand why her husband had to travel so much. It is good to hear Ruth Graham complaining that her husband seemed to be taking her for granted, and to find Katie Luther taking the hinges off the door of her husband's study after he had locked himself in.

As you read this book, you will discover that the marriages of these Christian leaders are made out of the same stuff that composes all marriages. The marital problems they face are problems you face as well. And some of these great Christians didn't do as good a job with their marriages as you are doing with yours.

You might think that Christian leaders would have exemplary marriages, and that the Lord has chosen them because they are models of virtue and victory at home. The fact is, they struggle to make their marriages what they should be, just as the rest of us do.

In fact, the marriages of Christian leaders seem to be more fraught with clogs and bogs than the average Christian marriage. When you think about it carefully, this is not surprising. Greatness, like genius, places unusual stress on marriage. For one thing, leaders are in the spotlight, and nothing grows normally under such conditions. For another thing, the very gifts and character traits that make a person stand out as a leader may make him or her a challenge as a marriage partner.

In this book you will not find extended treatment of the spiritual accomplishments of these men and women. There are many excellent biographies available, and I hope that the brief treatments in this book will whet your appetite to learn more of these choice servants of God. A short bibliography at the end of each chapter lists some excellent biographies.

I am more interested in the ingredients of their marriages. So I am emphasizing family backgrounds, courtships, early adjustments, family relationships, and the blending of strong personalities. Sometimes you might think that I have failed to have a proper appreciation for the spiritual accomplishments of a particular Christian leader, and I apologize for this beforehand. Space has limited me. It may seem that I have failed to extol some giants of the faith like John Wesley, whose marriage was extremely difficult. But my purpose has been to look at the marriage and the home life, not the public ministry.

God has a knack for using the struggles of married life and the tensions of raising a family to make us what he wants us to become.

The process isn't always easy.

Catherine Marshall once wrote, "Husbands and wives are basically incompatible." Fortunately, incompatibility hasn't always stood in the way of a good marriage.

You will learn one other thing from this book, and that is this: No one set pattern for marriage makes a marriage work.

As you read about these marriages, I hope that you will receive some insight into your own marriage, for it is often easier to get insight into your own problems when you see them in the lives of others. And that is my prayer, that your own marriage will be strengthened as you take a close look at the marriages of others.

Romancing
the Rough Diamonds

In the musical *My Fair Lady*, Professor Henry Higgins boasts that he could transform any woman of the street into a lady. Then he meets a flower girl named Eliza Doolittle.

Miss Doolittle is a challenge indeed for "'enry 'iggins." But of course, since *My Fair Lady* was a box-office hit, Mr. Higgins had to be successful in transforming Eliza into a lady. In addition, much to his chagrin, he finds himself falling in love with her.

Without a doubt, Eliza Doolittle was a rough diamond.

Many a marriage has begun with a man or maid attempting to work a similar miraculous transformation in a spouse. Usually the attempt is unsuccessful.

Hewing rough diamonds is a perilous business, especially in marriage.

Sometimes, it is the roughness itself that provided the romance, and when it is polished, the romance has disappeared. Sometimes the process of polishing, or, more often, of chiseling the rough edges, destroys the relationship.

But sometimes, especially if the polishing is done unconsciously, it works—just as in the Broadway musical.

The three marriages in this section are textbook cases of rough diamonds being polished, but you will find other examples as well in the pages of this book. In many ways, Martin Luther was a rough diamond, smoothed through the years by Katie. Billy Sunday and Billy Graham, two evangelists, married young women from more cultured backgrounds than their own and greatly benefited from the relationships.

But the three in this section are noteworthy: John Newton, the sea captain whose conversation was peppered with swearing; Dwight Moody, the poorly educated son of a whiskey-sotted stonemason; Charles Spurgeon, the brash country boy who didn't know how to dress properly.

As you read the following pages, ask yourself questions about why these marriages seemed to work so well. Why was it that these men who married "up" did not resent the greater education and culture that their wives possessed?

D. L. Moody once said, "I have never ceased to wonder at . . . the miracle of having won the love of a woman who is so completely my superior with such a different temperament and background." Emma Moody, like Henry Higgins, had succeeded in romancing a rough diamond.

My Judicious Counselor

John and Polly Newton

You wouldn't think that a slave trader would make an ideal husband, would you?

He was away from home for months, sometimes years, treating slaves as if they were animals and hoping that most of them would stay alive during the crossing of the Atlantic.

On the other hand, you might think that a minister might make a better husband, especially a warmhearted minister who delighted in counseling and wrote touching hymns like "Amazing Grace."

Polly was married to both the slave trader and the minister, and they were both John Newton. Once a promiscuous, filthy-mouthed sailor and an atheist, John became a sympathizing pastor, an inveterate letter writer, and a close friend of one of England's most famous poets.

The story of their courtship and marriage is one of the warmest love stories in all of church history. It's one of the most surprising as well, for John and Polly were so different.

On the surface John seemed to be the man of the world who had experienced everything; but in the presence of women of class and culture he was out of his league. That was Polly's milieu. Unlike John, she always knew exactly the proper thing to say and when to say it.

On the surface Polly seemed calm, cool, and collected, but inside she was fearful and flustered.

He loved her dearly, and their marriage was a happy one.

11

Hollywood hasn't discovered the life story of John Newton yet. But it's a great love story, full of delightful twists and turns and always full of God's amazing grace.

John was seventeen and dreaming of an exciting future. His sea captain father had charted a very workable plan for his son's life. If John followed it, he could be independently prosperous before he was thirty and could become a member of Parliament by the time he was forty.

John liked the idea, too.

Here was the plan: John would sail from England to Jamaica and work on a plantation as an overseer of slaves. In a few years he would amass enough money to buy a plantation for himself. Then in a few more years he could return to England, buy a country estate, and enter Parliament.

It sounded simple enough.

But then, only a few days before his scheduled departure, he received an unexpected letter. It came from a friend of John's mother. Since John's mother had died a decade earlier and this friend had never written before, it was certainly unusual.

In the letter Elizabeth Catlett invited John to visit her and her family if he ever was in the area. Since the Catletts lived in Essex and since John was about to travel in the opposite direction to Liverpool and then to Jamaica, it seemed unlikely that he would ever accept Mrs. Catlett's invitation, even if he wanted to. Because he was much more excited about going to Jamaica than about visiting an old friend of his mother's, he really didn't want to accept the invitation.

But then his father asked him to run an errand for him, and the errand, by a strange coincidence, took him within a half mile of where the Catletts lived. So John decided to take a brief detour to see his mother's old friend.

The Catletts had six children, ranging in age from thirteen-year-old Mary (who was called Polly) to a baby in the cradle. John felt at home immediately; it was an enjoyable family. And he found Polly the most enjoyable of all.

She seemed older than thirteen, maybe because she was the oldest of the children and often managed the household. She was either a bit bashful or reserved—John couldn't tell which—but she was a lady already. She was not a great beauty, but when she smiled—which was often—she winsomely displayed her dimples.

John was smitten. He had never been in love before, and he hardly recognized what had come over him. In her presence, he was tongue-tied. It seemed ridiculous that a girl of thirteen should so affect a young man of seventeen, a young man on his way to the other side of the world to make his fortune.

He never told the Catletts that he was supposed to be packing his bags for Jamaica, so they asked him to be their houseguest for a few more days. Almost mesmerized by the sight of Polly, John readily consented.

Nine years later, he recalled his first meeting in a letter to her: "I knew not at first what ailed me. I was uneasy when you were absent, yet when you were present I scarcely durst look at you. If I attempted to speak, I trembled and was confused. My love made me stupid at first. I could not bear to leave you."

Three weeks after he had arrived, John continued his journey homeward. His father and stepmother had been worried about him; John had never written to explain to them where he was nor why he was staying so long. He himself hardly knew what made him stay so long.

The ship for Jamaica had long since sailed, and John's sea captain father was understandably irate. He couldn't figure out the irresponsibility of his son, who seemed to be throwing away a future for what seemed to be a spell of puppy love.

John couldn't forget Polly. He wrote to her, "When I first loved you, I dreamed of you night after night for nearly three months successively."

At the time of John's first meeting with Polly there was little in his life that would seem to be a preparation for life with Polly Catlett. And by the time John and Polly met, he had already experienced more of life than most seventeen-year-olds.

Born in 1725, John was the only child of Captain John and Elizabeth Newton. Captain Newton was a mariner of the old school, respected among his peers and feared by his subordinates, and that included his wife and son.

He liked the role of sea captain and he played it to the hilt. At times pompous because he thought a sea captain should have a bit of strut and swagger about him, he didn't display emotion either aboard ship or at home. Undeniably he loved his wife and son, though he apparently never wanted them to know it.

He felt a bit guilty about spending so much time away from home, especially because his wife was sickly. So year after year when he went on his lengthy voyages into the Mediterranean, he brought home trinkets for his family from the Middle East, along with his cargo of spices and silks.

Though not a man of religious conviction, he was a man of principle. Elizabeth was devout, tender, and somewhat intellectual. Her friends called her "a pious, experienced Christian." But she suffered from tuberculosis and spent much of each day on a couch coughing while wrapped up in a Spanish shawl that her husband had given her.

While she was wrapped up physically in a Spanish shawl, she was wrapped up emotionally in her son. "Almost her whole employment," John wrote later, "was the care of my education."

"When I was four years old," John recalled, "I could read with propriety in any common book. She stored my memory . . . with many valuable pieces, chapters, and portions of Scripture, catechisms, hymns, and poems." When he turned six, she thought it was time for him to learn Latin.

She had dreams that he would become a preacher, just as her husband had dreams that John would become a Mediterranean sea captain like himself.

But in the spring of 1732, Elizabeth's physical condition worsened. Her husband was at sea and there was no way to send him word, so neighbors took care of six-year-old John, and Elizabeth, only thirty, went to stay with Elizabeth and George Catlett, who had a home in the country.

John never saw his mother again. She died a few weeks later.

His father soon remarried, and John was sent away to a private school whose headmaster was a "tyrant of the cane and birch rod."

John's formal education didn't last long. On the day he turned eleven, he was taken by his father aboard his ship to get another kind of edu-

14

cation—seamanship. During the next six years he took five Mediterranean voyages with his father, who kept trying to make a first-class mariner out of his son.

Despite the fact that his father was a strict disciplinarian and set high standards for his son, John didn't apply himself seriously to the job. When John was sixteen, his father sent him out with another sea captain. That captain confirmed the father's fears. John was too much of a dreamer to become a good sea captain. He liked to read and discuss. In John's words, "I was fond of a visionary contemplative life, and was quite averse to the thought of industrious application to business." His father thought him either absentminded or lazy, and maybe a little bit of both.

That's when his father thought that the best alternative for his son was to get him into Parliament, via a plantation in Jamaica.

Once again the father's plans went awry. John took a detour to the Catlett home that lasted three weeks instead of three days.

When John returned from the Catlett's, his father punished him by dispatching him, as a common sailor, on another Mediterranean voyage. This time, John handled the trip quite well. In fact, when he returned, his father felt confident that his son was finally maturing. Captain Newton got an officer's berth for John on another outbound vessel.

Before leaving for the sea again, John had just enough time to pay another visit to Polly. Like the previous time, however, he could not tear himself away. Polly's attraction was stronger than the attraction of becoming an officer on a ship.

This time when John returned home, his father almost disowned him. He believed his son was throwing away his future.

For John it turned out to be more serious than simply losing the opportunity to be an officer on board ship. Rather than sailing the Mediterranean, he found himself pressed into service as a common seaman in the British navy, serving on a man-of-war. England was at war with France, and naval battles were high-risk ventures.

Because of his previous knowledge of the sea, John worked his way up to the rank of midshipman in a few months. At the same time he seemed to take as much delight in working his way down morally. "My delight and habitual practice was wickedness," he admitted. Gradually, he moved away from the religious convictions of his mother and soon became an avowed atheist who took pleasure in convincing others to turn from the Christian faith.

John took part in only one wartime battle, and when Christmas came again, he found himself back in an English port. That was the good news. The bad news was that his ship would be leaving in a few days for the East Indies, and that would mean five years away from home. For John that meant five years away from Polly, and he had not as yet had a good chance to tell her what she meant to him. So John asked for liberty to go on shore for the day.

Of course, whenever he visited Polly, a day usually expanded into a week. But even if he had suddenly become conscientious about meeting his naval obligations, it would have been impossible for him to make the trip to the Catlett's and back again in twenty-four hours.

This time the Catletts became very much aware—and quite concerned—that John was getting serious about their daughter. John was nineteen now; Polly was fifteen. It wasn't that the Catletts disliked John; it was that they had twice witnessed his irresponsibility. He had not shown the maturity that they would want in a son-in-law. Besides, he was a sailor who seemed to be increasingly irreligious with each visit, even though he tried to be on his best behavior in the Catlett home.

John knew that if he was at sea for five years, Polly would certainly be taken by the time he returned, so this was a crucial visit.

The visit was disappointing to John. "I had little satisfaction," John commented later. He never felt he communicated to Polly how deeply he loved her. She always seemed to keep him at a distance. When he hinted about his love for her, she "could neither understand my hints nor give me room to come to a direct explanation." She gave him neither "positive encouragement nor absolute refusal."

What actually happened was that George Catlett finally ordered him out of the house and told him not to try to see his daughter again until he gave his permission. Elizabeth Catlett, though agreeing with her husband, said that if John ever settled down and could promise a future for their daughter, she and her husband would not object to an engagement. But until then, he shouldn't even correspond with Polly. John and Polly worked out a secret arrangement by which they could see each other.

John's twenty-four-hour leave turned into a week, which was not too surprising. Perhaps what was more surprising was the fact that he was not severely punished by the ship's captain.

Perhaps John was hoping that the ship would leave for the East Indies without him, but that didn't happen. Instead, a storm delayed their journey for several more weeks. Each day he thought more of Polly and the gloomy prospect of five years away from her.

Finally, just as the ship was preparing to set sail from England, John walked away. More technically, he deserted. He couldn't bear being separated from Polly for all that time. Perhaps if he could get to his father, his father could figure out some solution. His father always seemed to be able to work out difficult problems.

But two days later, before John could reach his father, soldiers spotted him trudging through the Devon countryside. He was arrested as a deserter, and the normal penalty for desertion during wartime was death.

His punishment was not death, however. "I was confined two days in the guardhouse," John later recalled, "then sent on board my ship, kept a while in irons, then publicly stripped and whipped, after which I was degraded from my office. All my former companions were forbidden to show me the least favor, or even to speak to me."

John thought death would have been preferable. In fact, he seriously contemplated suicide. "The evils I suffered were likely to grow heavier every day." Not only was he facing separation from Polly for five years, he was sure he would never see her again.

"Inward or outward I could perceive nothing but darkness and misery. . . . I cannot express with what wishfulness and regret I cast my last look upon the English shore. I kept my eyes upon it till it disappeared. When I could see it no longer, I was tempted to throw myself into the sea."

Suicide, he thought, was the only thing left for him. "This would put a period to all my sorrows at once."

John didn't know why he couldn't go through with a suicide attempt. Later he reflected, "The secret hand of God restrained me."

About a month later, a slave ship bound for Africa sailed near the British man-of-war. The captain of Newton's ship ordered the slave ship to supply him with two men, and the captain of the slave ship boldly asked for two men in return. Hearing this, John ran and pleaded to be exchanged. Within a half hour, he was out of the navy and into the slave trade.

Slave ships came from England with cloth, firearms, and trinkets, which were traded for slaves on the West African coast. The slaves were transported to the West Indies for sale in the slave markets. Then a cargo of sugar and rum was loaded on board to be taken back for sale in England. The triangular trade route brought a good living for many ship captains, as well as prosperity for some Englishmen who set up slave warehouses in Africa.

In the process, John Newton, not yet twenty, sank to new depths of immorality. He shared in the brutality against the blacks. Usually about a third of the slaves were women, and as biographer John Pollock reports, "John Newton let lust run unchecked." John himself put it this way: "I rejoiced . . . that I now might be as abandoned as I pleased, without any restraint. . . . I not only sinned with a high hand myself but made it my study to tempt and seduce others upon every occasion."

When John began to incite the other sailors to disobedience, he once again became a liability. His conduct meant that most likely he would be traded back to the next British man-of-war that the slave ship encountered. It was a prospect that John didn't relish.

So he went ashore in Africa and took a position as manager of a slave warehouse in Sierra Leone on Africa's west coast. On paper, it looked as if it might bring prosperity to John. But what John thought would be a move for the better turned out to be for the worse.

The man who owned the slave warehouse had a black common-law wife. She hated the new white man who had come to share her husband's wealth. Whenever her husband left the area, she did all she could to abuse John. When a tropical fever struck John, she considered it her chance to be rid of him forever.

18

Carried to a slave hut, he was frequently deprived of both food and drink. At night he crept outside and pulled up roots to eat. Often the raw roots made him sicker.

But eventually John recuperated. When the owner returned and John related all that had happened, the owner refused to believe him. Instead, he turned against John. Soon John found himself in ankle irons, a servant of slaves.

At first he was in "floating captivity," chained on the ship's deck, "exposed for twenty, thirty, perhaps near forty hours together in incessant rains, accompanied with strong gales of wind without the least shelter, when my master was on shore." Then he was taken ashore to plant a lime grove under the watchful eye of a slave.

At first, the slaves mocked him; then they began to pity him. One house slave even smuggled writing materials to him. This gave him a chance to write letters to his father (actually it was an SOS) and to Polly, whom he could not forget. The slave that had given him the paper then slipped the letters in the middle of the stack of the owner's outgoing mail pouch.

At best, it would be several months before any help could come to John in Sierra Leone. He knew that. He also knew that prospects of rescue were slim.

Before help came from England, however, help came from a neighboring slave trader, who asked for Newton's services. It was another "we-don't-want-him, you-can-have-him" situation for John.

This time, however, John became a good friend of the slave trader for whom he worked. Stationed a hundred miles away, "we lived as we pleased, business flourished, and our employer was satisfied." He slept with African women as he wished and began adopting local manners and customs. Within three months he had renounced any thought of returning to England.

And it was just about the same time that a rescue ship, sent by his father, was cruising the coast trying to find him.

John had been planning an inland journey but had been delayed a few days. The captain of the rescue ship was also on the verge of turning back. Later, John recognized that the hand of God was in this fortuitous meeting.

But at the time he wasn't so sure. He wasn't sure he wanted to go back to England now. "Had an invitation from home reached me when I was sick and starving at the Plantanes, I should have received it as life from the dead, but now, I heard it with indifference."

To entice him to return, the ship's captain invented a story of how a distant relative of John had left him a huge estate.

John wasn't so sure he could believe him. Even if he did believe him, he didn't know that he wanted to go back to England. He was starting to enjoy his circumstances in Africa. He lived almost like a prince, he had a mistress, he had a life of ease.

Then he thought of Polly. If it were true—even in part—that he had inherited an estate, he would be able to marry Polly and live in comfort with her.

His memory of Polly made him accept the offer of the captain of the rescue ship. Later he wrote Polly: "If I had not known you, perhaps I should never have seen the coast of Guinea. But it seems more certain that if I had not known you, I should never have returned from it."

Though John was on his way back to England and to Polly, he was still the same John. "I was no further changed than a tiger who has been tamed by hunger."

Since the rescue ship was also seeking gold, ivory, dyers' wood, and beeswax, it continued down the coast of Africa for almost a year before turning around toward the British Isles. During those twelve months John fouled the ship with his presence. His filthy language shocked even the roughest of sailors. If any of the crew had a semblance of Christian belief, John sought to shred it. He mocked the gospel and derided Jesus Christ. When in a drunken stupor he nearly plunged overboard into the Atlantic, the ship's captain wondered if maybe John was a Jonah who should be thrown to the whales in order to preserve the lives of the other crew members.

Then one evening as the ship began heading north, John picked up a translation of Thomas à Kempis's *The Imitation of Christ* and read the words, "Life is of short and uncertain continuance. . . . Today the man is vigorous . . . and tomorrow he is cut down, withered and gone."

The words clung to him, no matter how much he tried to shrug them off. That night a fierce storm struck. John heard the screams of a sailor as he lost his life. "The ship is sinking," voices shouted in the dark. John, along with the others, manned the pumps and plugged the leaks. For hours they labored, seeking to save their lives and salvage what remained of the ship.

Exhausted by his toils and despairing that there was anything else he could do, John muttered, "If this will not do, the Lord have mercy on us." Then he thought about what he had said. It startled him. When he had nowhere else to turn, he had actually acknowledged God and had asked for mercy.

The next day no one else knew what was going on in John's mind. For most of the day he stood at the helm of the ship, exhausted from manning the pumps the night before and steering as best he could. He mused over the question whether such a profane sinner as he could obtain mercy from God. When he tried to recall Scripture verses that spoke of pardon and forgiveness, all that came to his mind were passages that reminded him of judgment. "I waited with fear and impatience to receive my inevitable doom."

Gradually, however, his thoughts turned to Jesus Christ and to the crucifixion. He recalled that Jesus Christ did not die for his own sins; Jesus died for the sins of others. The only question that John now had was whether he had gone too far to be included with the "others."

Those eleven hours at the helm were decisive hours for John. Later he wrote, "March 21 is a day to be remembered by me. I have never suffered it to pass wholly unnoticed since the year 1748." He was not yet twenty-three.

As the ship struggled back to England, John began reading the New Testament and was especially heartened by the story of the prodigal son, "The prodigal had never been so exemplified as by myself."

There was no euphoria, no delirious heights of joy as he entered the kingdom. He was still wrestling, trying to understand, trying to see how he fit into God's scheme of mercy. But there was no doubt in his mind that God had hold of him. "I see no reason why the Lord singled me out for mercy . . . unless it was to show, by one astonishing instance, that with Him 'nothing is impossible.'"

Blown off course and almost impossible to steer, the ship finally landed in Northern Ireland. Ashore, John wanted to write to Polly immediately, but he hesitated. He had lived so lewdly in Africa that he wondered if he could ever be worthy of the girl about whom he had dreamed for so many years.

Instead he wrote first to his father, asking for forgiveness. The reply came quickly. Captain Newton rejoiced both in John's survival and in his turn from evil.

Rather than write to Polly, John decided to write to Polly's aunt, who had long been a useful intermediary for the correspondence which Polly's parents had forbidden. He asked the aunt to determine whether it would be permissible for him to visit Polly.

While waiting for repairs to be completed on the ship, John got a second letter from his father. Captain Newton, who had been appointed governor of Fort York in Hudson Bay, would be sailing from London shortly to assume his new position. Since he realized that he wouldn't be returning to England for another three years, and since he thought his son might be thinking of marriage during that period, he dropped in on the Catletts to talk to them about a possible match between his son and their daughter. He thought that John would be pleased to know that they had no objection.

Yes, he was certainly pleased to know it. The last time he had seen the Catletts they had forbidden any correspondence.

So it was good news indeed. Yet as John reports in his autobiography, "I found I had only the consent of one person to obtain; with her I stood at as great an uncertainty as the first day I saw her."

He waited to hear from Polly's aunt, but no reply came. It meant little to have the approval of Polly's parents if Polly herself was opposed. He could interpret the lack of a reply in no other way but that Polly was no longer interested in him. He decided to try to divert his thoughts from her as much as possible, so he wrote tearfully to the aunt, "Though I do not expect to be ever able wholly to conquer my passion, I will endeavor . . . never to trouble either her or you any more with it."

"I thought it best for both of us to break it off," he wrote later.

But shortly after he had sent the letter, he heard from Polly's aunt. The Catlett family was temporarily in London, and Polly would be happy to see him there if he wanted.

John's ship had finally limped back to his home port of Liverpool, so John didn't hesitate to accept the invitation. Quickly he found a coach bound for London.

The meeting in London was surprising in many ways. Polly hadn't changed much in the four years since John had last seen her. She was still, as Pollock puts it, "a young woman of poise and charm and good nature, with the same simplicity which had captured his heart long ago." And on the surface, John hadn't changed much either; he was still just as flustered and tongue-tied in her presence.

Of course, he had wallowed through a muck of experiences in Africa. He had been wracked with disease, had been wasted by near starvation, and had participated in every type of sordid activity imaginable. He had kept a native mistress. Death had seemed commonplace; life had been cheapened; cruelty, brutality, and rape were daily occurrences. And he had gone from the depths of despair and contemplation of suicide to a redeeming relationship with God through Jesus Christ.

But in front of Polly he was tongue-tied. Not only was he tongue-tied, but—in spite of all his experiences—he was somewhat boring.

In fact, people even said to him, "Polly is cheerful and sprightly; you are heavy and dull."

Despite all her cheerfulness and sprightliness, Polly had a reserve about her that made it difficult for John to know what she was really thinking. She was pleasant enough, but that didn't really mean that she was pleased with his company—or did it? He simply didn't know how to read her. "I was always exceedingly awkward in pleading my own cause in our conversation," he stated. At the unsatisfactory conclusion of his London visit he asked her if she minded if he continued to write to her.

She gave her consent, but nothing more.

A few days later he wrote her a touching letter. He reminded her of how frequently he had written her when he was in the navy and when he was in Africa, and she had never written back. He asked for only "a crumb" in return. He begged for "a little of your charity, one morsel for God's sake, before I am quite starved."

Penniless, John couldn't afford a coach back to Liverpool, so he trudged the 150 miles, mulling over the question of whether Polly loved him or not.

He had already accepted a position as first mate on another slave ship (because he didn't think he was qualified for any other line of work), and he resolved that, if he didn't hear from Polly before sailing, he would try to forget her.

But he did hear from her. "Her answer, though cautious, satisfied me." Frankly, it didn't take much from Polly to satisfy John, but it was "a crumb," and the more he read over the short, cautious note, the more he transformed the crumb into a whole loaf.

A few weeks later, when his ship set sail from Liverpool, John felt things were under control. He felt reasonably good about life. Romantically, he was communicating with Polly, and spiritually, he was in touch with God. Vocationally, he was first mate on a slave ship and had been promised the opportunity of becoming a sea captain his next time out. What more could a young Christian ask? For a young man in his twenties, who as yet had no compunctions against slavery, the future looked promising.

But the rosy outlook lasted only a few weeks. By the time the ship had landed on Africa's west coast, as John puts it, "I was almost as bad as before." He had stopped reading his Bible, had become careless in prayer, and had no Christian fellowship. "The enemy prepared a train of temptations and I became his easy prey. For about a month, he lulled me asleep in a course of evil, of which a few months before, I could not have supposed myself any longer capable."

What kind of evil?

Well, down in the hold of the ship were naked slave girls. It was customary for the officers to have their pick. Momentarily he pushed away the temptation, but then, "I was now fast bound in chains; I had little desire and no power to free myself." So he descended into the hold, picked out a girl, and raped her.

Off the boat he was provided "a black girl for his pleasure." His lifestyle reverted to his old patterns. "If I attempted to struggle, it was in vain."

Then illness struck. He was reminded of his previous illness in Sierra Leone and the depths into which he had sunk at that time. Would this be the pattern again?

At first, he despaired of finding divine forgiveness; the "door of hope" seemed to be shut. Then in desperation, while very weak and almost delirious, "I made no more resolves, but cast myself upon the Lord to do with me as He should please." Forgiveness came; peace returned. "Though I have often grieved His Spirit and foolishly wandered from Him since (when, alas, shall I be more wise?), His powerful grace has preserved me from such black declensions as this I have last recorded."

That was another turning point in John's life.

After setting sail from Africa and delivering his cargo of slaves to the slave market in Charleston, South Carolina, John returned to England and to Polly after an absence of a little more than a year.

John had served well as first mate, so the ship's owner confirmed his previous offer of the command of a slave ship when John was ready to go out again. Though beginning to recognize the cruelty of the slave traffic, he still didn't see the inherent evil in it. What he saw was a job that might guarantee enough income so he and Polly could get married and he could support her in the manner in which she was accustomed to live.

He was twenty-four now, and she was twenty. During the latter half of his recent voyage, he had written her faithfully. When he was separated from her, his love for her grew strongest. Pollock puts it this way: "In Polly he saw innocence and gentleness in a world which, for him, as a slave trader, was filled with violence and deceit. She was pure; only for Polly could he conquer lust. Her love would be his calm harbor in which his restless, homeless spirit could anchor."

On this visit to Polly, John hemmed and hawed his way to a marriage proposal. He had hinted at it in his letters, but he still wasn't sure how she would respond.

But it still stunned him when she said, "No, and don't ask me again."

Few of Polly's letters are available, so it is difficult to know what was going through her mind, but probably several factors contributed to her refusal of his proposal of marriage.

She cared for him—there was no doubt in her mind about that—but being married to a sea captain was not a life that she might relish. John's life was dangerous; she worried about him when he was at sea. She knew about the life that John's own mother had experienced.

Her friends all advised her against it. They felt that she and John were such opposites that though they might be attracted to each other, a marriage between them would be disastrous.

But there was something else. She recognized John's brilliant mind. He was a voracious reader. Though his education had been brief, he had learned ancient languages on his own. He not only read but enjoyed the philosophical writings in Roman and Greek literature. She didn't write him often because she felt he was superior intellectually. She could make pleasant conversation on the surface, but she had a hard time communicating intelligently in a letter.

While John was stunned by her rejection, he was surprisingly not disheartened. After retreating to a nearby woods, he rehearsed his lines and determined to try again. He consulted his closest ally in his matrimonial venture, Polly's aunt. Then he talked to Polly's mother. Both of them gave him their support.

So he tried again.

Once again she said no, but this time John felt she wasn't as adamant.

So he broached the matter a third time. She listened, then argued, then conversed more rationally. She had enjoyed a happy family life, she said; her friends called her "happy Polly Catlett." Wouldn't marriage to a sea captain mean the end of happiness for her?

John tried to convince her that the two of them could find happiness together. They talked on and on. Finally she slipped her hand in his. It was his answer.

Later he recalled the moment: "I sat stupid and speechless for some minutes, and I believe I embarrassed you a little by my awkwardness. My heart was so full that I knew not how to get a word out."

The engagement was short. A month later they were married, the day before Polly's twenty-first birthday.

It was not an exciting honeymoon. They continued to live at her parents' home, and as Pollock says, "Polly was so cautious and reserved that she seemed hardly the Polly of his dreams." As for John, he didn't experience any emotional highs either. But love grew. And as she began to express her love for him, he was no longer tongue-tied in expressing his love for her.

But there was a problem in their relationship, one that John hardly wanted to face. He had come into a vital relationship with Jesus Christ, but Polly's religion was formal and polite. Though he admitted that spiritually he was still a babe, he wasn't sure that she had even come that far.

This bothered him, and he didn't know what it meant for the future. There was a danger, he felt, that he might love her even more than he loved God himself. "I rested in the gift and forgot the Giver." How could his intense love for her coexist with his love for God?

He wished that there was some other way he could provide for her besides going to sea as a slave captain. But he wasn't qualified to do anything else. At one point he hoped that he might inherit some money from a distant relative, but that didn't work out. Then he went into debt to buy tickets in the National Lottery, hoping that by winning it, he and Polly would not have to separate. As he says, "The prospect of the separation was as terrible to me as death."

There was no other way. He would have to return to Liverpool and take command of the slave ship that had been offered him.

It was a difficult departure; he didn't want to leave, and she didn't want him to leave. Both feared that he might never return. "It was hard, very hard to part, especially as conscience suggested how little I deserved that we should be spared to meet again."

A week later, he wrote requesting her daily schedule: "When you write next, let me know at what hours you usually rise, breakfast, dine, sup, and go to bed, that I may keep time with you, or at least attend you with my thoughts."

In her reply she assured him of her love, and he was elated to acknowledge: "I have now the same confidence that you love me, as that I love you."

On this trip, John didn't succumb to the debauchery that had characterized his previous slave trips. "I was once no less eager after their pleasures than they [his crew members] are now," he admitted to Polly. "But you have so refined my taste since, that nothing short of yourself can thoroughly please me." Though he was offered female slaves to sleep with, the thought of Polly made him refuse.

He wrote her two or three letters a week. Most of the time his letters revealed how much he loved her and how he basked in her love.

After fourteen months at sea, he returned to Polly and the Catlett home for six months before setting sail on another voyage.

On her birthday he wrote to say, "I rose before the sun to pray and give thanks for you."

A typical comment in another letter was, "I find some new cause of endearment in you every day."

He carried a pencil drawing of her with him: "I frequently look at it and talk to it."

John kept hoping that the next slave voyage would be his last, but none of his trips were overly successful financially. He wrote Polly: "Perhaps we may not be rich—no matter. We are rich in love. We are rich indeed, if the promises and providence of God are our inheritance."

John was twenty-nine, Polly twenty-five, when he completed his third voyage as captain of a slaver. Each separation from Polly seemed harder than the one before; each time that the slaves were herded into the hold of his ship, it distressed him more. "I was sometimes shocked with an employment that was perpetually connected with chains, bolts, and shackles." And he prayed "that the Lord in His own time would be pleased to place me in a more humane calling."

He was ready now for his next voyage. At least, outwardly he seemed to be ready. His crew had been selected; his cargo had been put aboard. In only two more days, his ship was scheduled to set sail.

John and Polly were chatting over afternoon tea. It all seemed quite normal. But suddenly John collapsed, sprawling almost lifeless at Polly's feet.

She screamed for help. A landlady rushed in; a doctor was called.

For about an hour, John remained unconscious. Then, finally, he blinked his eyes and regained his senses.

A headache lingered; and at times without provocation he seemed to be swirling in dizziness. Doctors told him not to venture out to sea until the symptoms totally disappeared, so John had to resign his command. (Incidentally, the next voyage of what had been John's ship was disastrous. His replacement, most of the officers, and many of his hand-picked crew perished at sea.)

What precipitated John's seizure was never diagnosed. Some of his biographers have suggested that it might have resulted from a buildup of psychological tensions.

For a recuperation period, John and Polly returned to her parents' home. But shortly after they arrived there, Polly herself became strangely ill. Physicians were unable to diagnose it. John felt it must be a delayed shock. All the worry she had experienced during John's voyages culminated when she witnessed the collapse of her husband at her feet. She had managed to cope until she was safely back at her parents' home. Then she caved in. "She decayed almost visibly," John reported. "She became so weak that she could hardly bear anyone to walk across the room she was in." For eleven months she was bedridden.

It was an agonizing time for John in several ways. Not only was he deeply concerned about the health of his wife, but he was also concerned about how he would provide for her. He had no idea what God had for him in the future, but he hoped and prayed it wouldn't be separation from Polly. To prepare himself for whatever it might be, he studied Latin, French, and mathematics and immersed himself in his Bible.

What was so mysterious about Polly's condition was that at times she seemed as if she was almost completely recovered and he would be very encouraged by her progress. Then in a few days, her situation would change drastically, and it seemed as if she were dying.

He felt well enough to go back to sea, but he would never go while Polly was so ill. So he didn't know what to do. But as he prayed about the matter, he received a message from the Liverpool ship owner for whom he had previously been working. The message informed John that the position of tide surveyor in the customs department at Liverpool would soon be available. The ship owner urged John to apply for it.

He got the job. As tide surveyor, he supervised about fifty people, boarded ships as they arrived in Liverpool, searched for smuggled goods, and assessed excise taxes. Until Polly recovered completely, he had to leave her at home with her parents, but he was only on the other side of England, not on the other side of the world.

Whenever he had time and money, he crossed the country to be with her. "I left London on Saturday about ten," he wrote her, "but soon found I had a very indifferent horse. And though I tell him how impatient I am to see my dear Polly, he will not move one foot the faster."

In Liverpool John was stirred by the preaching of the great evangelist George Whitefield. In a letter to Polly he tried to share his excitement with her. Not long afterwards, John got a reply. Polly told him not only that she was feeling better, but that she had prayed from her heart for the first time, and that she felt that God had delivered her.

It was the best news that John could imagine.

Polly's growing faith, in spite of nagging doubts, is evidenced in her correspondence. When she said she was afraid that she was a hypocrite, he replied, "It is a good sign that you are not." And she responded, "I delight, admire, and hang upon every sentence and every action of my dearest John, and yet how wanting and how cold am I to the gracious Author of all our mercies to whom we owe each other."

Finally, Polly was well enough to join John in Liverpool. It would be their first home together after nearly six years of marriage. However, she had some reservations about setting up housekeeping in Liverpool. Having been accustomed to upper-middle-class living, she feared that in Liverpool she would be expected to keep company with washerwomen. Besides the fact that Liverpool was not noted for its culture or people of social standing, it was rumored that John was keeping company with Methodists, and Polly's aunt despised Methodists.

But Polly was ready to make the move to Liverpool even if it meant meeting some Methodists. She still wasn't sure, however, about hobnobbing with washerwomen.

Now past thirty, John still was undecided about a career. There was nothing wrong with being a tide surveyor; in fact, it was a respected job in the community. Yet he didn't feel that God wanted him to be a tide surveyor all his life. He recalled that his mother had hoped he would enter the ministry. But he had never preached a sermon, although once he had tried to give a testimony. After that single experience, he concluded that God probably didn't want him in a pulpit after all.

But when he and Polly traveled to the rural hamlets of Yorkshire and people asked him to tell his life story, he felt he couldn't refuse. The more often he gave the story, the more he felt at home as a preacher.

After spending his thirty-third birthday in prayer and fasting, John decided to become a minister. As difficult as that decision was, it was simple compared to the soul-searching involved in whether to join with the Dissenters (with whom his mother had fellowshiped) or with the official Church of England (with which the Catletts were associated).

He leaned toward the Dissenters. He had been impressed with many of the independent churches he had visited, and he felt that ordination might be easier to obtain following that route.

However, if he wanted to influence people, the best way would be in the Church of England. So, after an inward struggle, he applied to the archbishop of York for ordination. Because he did not hold a degree from Oxford or Cambridge, he was refused ordination.

An independent church in Yorkshire offered him a pastorate; he turned it down. John Wesley wanted him to enlist as a Methodist lay preacher; he said no. But when friends urged him to start his own independent chapel in Liverpool, he was tempted to say yes.

Already he and Polly had been holding Sunday evening services in their home. To expand the evening ministry into an independent church would not be a big step. John liked the idea, but Polly didn't. And because Polly didn't like it, he didn't go ahead with it. Later he commented, "I believe no arguments but hers could have restrained me for almost two years from taking a rash step, of which I should perhaps have soon repented."

At another time he said, "She kept me quiet until the Lord's time came when I should have the desire of my heart. The Lord's time is like the time of the tide, which no human presence can either accelerate or retard. Though it tarry, wait for it."

He waited and waited. In fact, he waited until 1764, more than five years after he had made his decision to enter the ministry, before the Church of England finally consented to ordain him. He was nearly thirty-nine years old when the parish church in the small market town of Olney was offered to him.

Perhaps other ministers wouldn't have considered the parish of Olney much of a prize at all. Its parishioners were poor, and many suffered from lung ailments. Located halfway between Liverpool and London, the most that could be said for it was that it was a convenient stopping point.

But John and Polly were elated.

For John a new career was beginning. And for the next sixteen years, perhaps the most satisfying years of their lives, the Newtons served the Olney parish.

He visited the sick and elderly and shared their woes with them. Only on Sundays did he wear his clerical garb; otherwise he wore his old sea jacket, which became his trademark.

At a time when special services for youngsters were virtually unheard of, John launched weekly children's meetings. He said what he wanted to do was "talk, preach, and reason with them, and explain Scriptures to them in their own little way."

About the time he was beginning his pulpit ministry, he was persuaded to put the story of his early life in writing. When it was published as *Out of the Depths,* he became a celebrity. "The people stare at me and well they may. I am indeed a wonder to many, a wonder to myself; especially I wonder that I wonder no more."

His book brought him mail from all across the country, but most notable was the letter received from a thirty-two-year-old poet, William Cowper, who had suffered two mental breakdowns and had three times attempted suicide. In deep depression, he had convinced himself that God's salvation could not extend to him. However, as he read John's testimony he found hope.

John and Polly invited him to Olney, and for five months he stayed in their home. Then he got his own house nearby.

Like John, Cowper (whose name is pronounced like Cooper) enjoyed writing poetry, hiking, and jokes. Like Polly, he enjoyed gardening. Cowper's garden practically bumped up against Polly's patch, so they exchanged horticultural tips quite frequently.

John thought it would be good therapy for his friend to write hymns; before long they were stimulating each other, honing one another's talents, though John never considered his attempts at poetry to come close to Cowper's in quality.

Soon Olney became famous for the hymns written by the two friends, and of course the Olney congregation enjoyed the opportunity to be the first to sing them.

William Cowper wrote such hymns as "There Is a Fountain Filled with Blood," "O For a Closer Walk with God," "Jesus, Where'er Thy People Meet," and "God Moves in a Mysterious Way," while John contributed such hymns as "How Sweet the Name of Jesus Sounds," "Come My Soul Thy Suit Prepare," "How Tedious and Tasteless the Hours," "Safely Through Another Week," "Glorious Things of Thee Are Spoken," and, of course, "Amazing Grace."

Eventually, when John published their songs in a hymnal called *Olney Hymns*, he said he did it "as a monument to perpetuate the remembrance of an intimate and endeared friendship."

But despite the hymn-writing therapy, Cowper's mental derangement returned. John and Polly took turns staying with him to make sure he wouldn't try suicide again. He moved back into the parsonage, so John could try his jokes and comic verses on him. But nothing seemed to work.

It was a heavy strain on both John and Polly. John wasn't in the mood to write hymns with Cowper afflicted so seriously. John writes, "My grief and disappointment were great; I hung my harp upon the willows, and for some time thought myself determined to proceed no further without him." After about a year of severe depression, Cowper smiled at one of John's jokes; his recovery came rapidly after that.

Though the years passed, the love between John and Polly did not diminish. Polly was sometimes needed to care for her aging and ailing father, and these separations stimulated frequent letters from her husband.

His letters combined bits of biblical observations, humor, news, passionate love, and warm concern.

Consider, for example, these excerpts from various letters, written over a thirty-five-year period:

33

Love at first is a child and grows stronger by age.

I feel your headache at this distance.

The house looks unfurnished without you, and I miss you in every room.

I am always a little awkward without you. It is not a humble servant who says this, but a husband, and he says it, not in what is called the honeymoon, but in the twenty-third year of marriage.

I cannot wish you to love me less, but I often wish you could be less anxious about me.

You certainly have been my idol, and I often fear, you are too much so still. Alas, how difficult it is to draw the line exactly between undervaluing and overvaluing the gifts of God.

The blessing of the Lord has in the course of thirty-five years ripened the passion of love into a solid and inexpressibly tender friendship. I shall never find words fully to tell you how much I owe you, how truly I love you, nor the one half of what my heart means when I subscribe myself.

Your most affectionate
and obliged husband.

Polly's health—both physical and emotional—was always precarious. Ever since her reactive illness early in their marriage, she suffered from periods of sickness. Several times she was "confined for five or six months" and sometimes she seemed at death's door. John said she was sick about a fourth of the time; when she was well, however, she carried on a very normal schedule.

Both John and Polly thought they would live the rest of their lives in Olney. He had turned down invitations from other churches and had even rejected the presidency of a college in Savannah, Georgia.

However, as a neighboring cleric put it, "Too much familiarity cost him the estimation of the people." Divisions threatened to tear the church apart, and John seemed powerless to stop them.

After a disastrous fire had burned a good section of Olney, John suggested to town officials that bonfires be banned from holiday celebrations. Though the town fathers agreed, the drunken revelers on Guy Fawkes Day felt that the Newtons had spoiled their fun. After parading raucously down Main Street, they veered toward the parsonage. When a friend saw what was happening, he ran to warn John. He said that forty or fifty men "full of fury and liquor" were coming down the street and anything might happen when they arrived at the parsonage.

Polly was terrified; she began to panic. John didn't want to give in to the mob, but he knew that Polly couldn't be reasoned with either. So he approached the ringleader of the mob and bribed him to halt their advances. John said, "I am ashamed of the story."

Not long afterwards, when a church in London, St. Mary Woolnoth, invited him to come, he accepted. "London is the last situation I would have chosen for myself," he admitted. But he recognized that his ministry in Olney was finished.

In London, as in Olney, the home of the Newtons became a center for ministry. "My time is divided between running about to look on other people," he wrote his friend Cowper, "and sitting at home like a tame elephant . . . for other people to come and look at me."

In 1788 when Polly was fifty-nine, new pains beset her. Without John knowing about it, she consulted a doctor, who diagnosed it as breast cancer. She was not surprised.

Her first concern was John; such news would be devastating to him. So she thought it best to try to arrange an operation while John was away on a trip. In that way he wouldn't know anything about it until the operation was over.

But the doctor said no. The cancer was too far advanced; the tumor was too large. The truth was, he said, that Polly had less than two years to live.

At first, John seemed to take it harder than Polly. Trying to submit to God's will in the matter, he confessed that he tossed "like a wild bull in a net." Meanwhile, Polly handled it stoically for a while.

But only for a while.

As Polly's malady increased and her pains became more intense, John watched helplessly. In times of remission, Polly studied the Bible vigorously. Later John wrote, "I have her Bible by me (which I would not part with, for half the manuscripts in the Vatican) in which almost every principal text from the beginning to the end of the book is marked in the margin, with a pencil, by her own hand." John was proud of her.

Then in the fall "her thoughts became clouded and confused; and she gradually lost, not only the comfortable evidence of her own interest in the previous truths of the Bible, but she lost all hold of the truth itself. And together with this, she expressed an extreme reluctance to death. . . . This was hard to bear indeed."

Besides that, "her attachment to me abated. She spoke to me with indifference."

Though this change was difficult for John, he didn't despair about either her love for God or for himself. "To say that she had no faith in God would be like saying she had not loved her husband for the previous forty years."

After about two weeks in such "conflict and dismay," Polly regained her normal disposition. But her health was continually sliding downward.

Shortly before Christmas in 1790, Polly died. She was sixty-one.

John wrote, "When my wife died, the world seemed to die with her."

Even before her passing, John had struggled with his grief and emotional agony. He tells about it: "About two or three months before her death, when I was walking up and down the room, offering disjointed prayers, from a heart torn by distress, a thought suddenly struck me. 'Surely the Lord will help me if I am willing to be helped.'" He feared being plunged into a long period of "unprofitable grief."

So after her death he made himself busier than ever. He added to his schedule. "I was afraid of sitting at home and indulging myself by poring over my loss. Therefore I was seen in the street and visited some of my serious friends the very next day."

"I had no right . . . to complain. I considered her as a loan, which He who lent her to me had a right to resume whenever He pleased."

John continued preaching in his London church until he was past eighty. A friend suggested to him that he halt his pulpit ministry, but John responded, "I cannot stop. What! Shall the old African blasphemer stop while he can speak?"

In 1807 John died, seventeen years after Polly. He wrote his own epitaph: "John Newton . . . once an infidel and libertine, a servant of slaves in Africa, was, by the rich mercy of our Lord and Savior, Jesus Christ, preserved, restored, pardoned, and appointed to preach the faith he had long labored to destroy."

The former infidel and libertine had been blessed with a great marriage. After Polly's death John published his *Letters to a Wife*. In it he stated, "She was my pleasing companion, my most affectionate friend, my judicious counselor. I seldom, if ever, repented of acting according to her advice. And I seldom acted against it without being convinced by the event that I was wrong."

Bibliography

Newton, John. *Cardiphonia*. Philadelphia: Presbyterian Board of Education, n.d.

———. *Letters of John Newton*. Edinburgh: Banner of Truth, 1960.

———. *Letters to a Wife*. London: W. Oliver, 1793.

———. *Out of the Depths*. Reprint. New Canaan, Conn.: Keats, 1981.

———. *The Works of John Newton*. New Haven: Nathan Whiting, 1826.

Pollock, John. *Amazing Grace*. San Francisco: Harper and Row, 1981.

So Completely My Superior
Dwight and Emma Moody

Many of you know Dwight L. Moody, the Billy Graham of the nineteenth century. An amazing, seemingly tireless evangelist, he crisscrossed the Atlantic winning hundreds of thousands for Jesus Christ.

Yes, you probably know Dwight L. Moody, but I don't think you've ever heard of Emma Moody, his wife, who liked to stay in the background.

I think you should get to know both of them better. You might be surprised at the kind of man Dwight was at home; you might also be surprised at Emma. Just when you think you have her pegged, you find something about her that amazes you.

But what kind of a marriage would this be between this Martin Luther-like man and this "shy and reserved" woman? You might be surprised at that, too.

"The only person in all the world who really knew D. L. Moody was his wife," writes biographer J. C. Pollock.

Maybe that's true, but it is doubtful if anyone—even D. L. Moody himself—really knew Emma Moody.

DL (he seldom used his given name Dwight Lyman) and Emma were opposites. In fact, their son Paul said, "No two people were ever more in contrast. . . . He was impulsive, outspoken, dominant, informal, and with little education at the time they met. She was intensely conventional and conservative, far better educated, fond of reading, with a discriminating taste, and self-effacing to the last degree."

It was a good thing that they were different. No home would have been big enough for two people like D. L. Moody.

But don't get the idea that Emma Moody was a pushover. She had a mind of her own.

D. L. Moody never put her in her place; she made a place for herself. It was a behind-the-scenes place that she enjoyed, out of the limelight. For instance, she refused to appear on the platform during her husband's evangelistic campaigns—and she faced criticism for it. Yet early in his evangelistic meetings, she was his prize worker in the inquiry room. "When I have an especially hard case," DL once said, "I turn him over to my wife. She can bring a man to a decision for Christ where I cannot touch him." One of Moody's most famous converts, E. P. Brown, a magazine editor and notorious infidel, was led to Jesus Christ by "shy and reserved" Emma Moody.

Moody's accomplishments as an evangelist on both sides of the Atlantic are legendary. He traveled a million miles, preached to 100 million people, and saw 750,000 respond to a gospel invitation. He revolutionized mass evangelism and founded what is known today as the Moody Bible Institute, the first Bible school of its kind.

A big man, five-ten and more than 250 pounds, he grew bigger and broader over the years of his ministry, not merely in physical size but also in the scope and character of his ministry. Emma had a lot to do with that.

Born in Northfield, Massachusetts, in 1837, Dwight Moody had no easy time of it. His father, a whiskey-drinking, shiftless stonemason, died bankrupt when Dwight was only four. Betsey Moody was left with nine children, including Dwight.

In Northfield, Dwight was exposed to little schooling, little Bible instruction, but lots of hard work. At the age of seventeen, Dwight had his fill of the toil of slow-paced, mundane Northfield and headed for Boston, where he took a job in an uncle's shoe store. He slept in the third floor over the shop. He described it in his almost illegible way: "I have a room up in the third story and I can open my winder and there is 3 grat buildings full of girls the handsomest there is in the city they will swar like parrets." His letter also told how he ate his meals at a hostel "where there is about twenty-five clurks and some girls we have a jolly time." Obviously, Dwight liked girls better than punctuation.

For several months he attended Sunday school at the Mount Vernon Congregational Church in Boston. The class was taught by a dry-goods salesman, thirty-year-old Edward Kimball. One day Kimball visited Moody at work in the shoe store and asked the teenager to come to Christ. Moody responded.

However, when he applied for church membership a few weeks later, he was turned down. He didn't have a clear understanding of what salvation was all about, they said.

A year later, discouraged by his church and in disagreement with his uncle who employed him, he packed his bags and hopped an immigrant train (fare $5.00) to seek his fortune in Chicago.

The prospects in Chicago excited him. In letters home, he bragged to his mother, "I can make money faster here then I can in B" (meaning Boston), and wrote to his brother George, "Hear is the place to make the money."

Although he was accepted into membership in a Congregational church in Chicago, he also attended Methodist and Baptist churches. He never worried much about denominational labels. While visiting a Baptist mission, he spotted young Emma Revell—not quite fifteen years old. Emma was teaching a class at the Wells Street Mission; Moody was impressed with both the way she taught and the way she looked. Her hair was black, her eyes dark. She was very feminine and almost quaint. There was a certain elegance about her that impressed twenty-year-old Moody, who was anything but elegant.

He was also not a Sunday school teacher. The Baptists wanted to press him into service as a teacher, but he said he couldn't teach. So instead they gave him the job of going out on the streets and "drumming up scholars," a job that DL did extremely well.

He was also quite successful in getting himself invited to the Revell home, where he met Emma's father, Fleming Revell, a shipbuilder of French Huguenot roots who had come to Chicago from London only eight years earlier because he had heard a rumor that Chicago had a future as a ship-building center.

DL liked Emma, but not her Sunday school. It was too formal; so in 1858 he began his own. At first it met in an abandoned freight car, then in an unused saloon. Within a year, with DL drumming up the scholars, attendance had grown to 600; in another year it hit 1,500.

Teaching a class of Moody's ragamuffins was no picnic, but young Emma was one of his first volunteers. There is evidence that DL enjoyed the companionship of all of his female teaching staff, but Emma became increasingly special to him. In his courtship, DL exercised unusual propriety. He normally brought two other men with him to the Revell home. This was partly because Emma had two sisters, but it was also because DL felt a bit out of place in the more formal atmosphere of the Revell home.

In 1860 they were engaged. DL made the announcement at a meeting of his Sunday school teaching staff. It went something like this: "Up until now, I have always walked all of the girls home, but I can't anymore. I'm engaged to Emma Revell."

Those were days of big decisions for DL. In 1859 at the age of twenty-two, he was making $5,000 in commissions on top of his salary as a salesman. That was in a day when mechanics were making $1.50 a day. DL's goal was to make $100,000 a year, and he doubtless would have made it. Henry Drummond later declared, "There is almost no question that he would have been one of the wealthiest men in the United States."

But DL was starting to lose interest in money. His Sunday school was taking more of his time and attention. In his spare moments he found himself working with the YMCA. Soon it became apparent that he couldn't stay in business and still do a good job with his Sunday school and the YMCA.

For three months he struggled with the decision. "It was a terrible battle," he said. It would mean delaying marriage to Emma. It would mean sleeping on a bench in the prayer room of the Y and eating cheese and crackers in the cheapest restaurants. (And Moody loved to eat.)

But he finally decided to quit his job. He took a position as visitation secretary of the YMCA. If it paid anything at all, it was a pittance. Marriage would have to wait.

At the outbreak of the Civil War, the YMCA set up an army committee, and Moody was sent to minister to the soldiers. He passed out hymnbooks—more than 125,000 of them—even though he himself had trouble carrying a tune. He went from barrack to barrack, holding as many as ten meetings a night, although he probably wouldn't have called them meetings.

"I saw the dying men—I heard the groans of the wounded," he recalls. He was criticized by Prohibitionists for giving brandy to dying men in order to revive them, so he could tell them about Jesus.

Sometimes they called him "Crazy Moody," because he was always hurrying somewhere. His uncle said, "My nephew Dwight is crazy, crazy as a March hare." His brother agreed, "Dwight is running from morning to night. He hardly gets time to eat."

In fact, he didn't have time for much of anything. "I do not get five minutes a day to study," he admitted, "so I have to talk just as it happens."

He almost didn't have time to get married. But Emma, now a nineteen-year-old schoolteacher, was still waiting for him. In his biography on Moody, J. C. Pollock writes, "Emma Revell, who had fallen in love with a prosperous shoe salesman, became engaged to a children's missioner, and was now about to marry a six-horse Jehu, wondered where it would end."

They were married Thursday, August 28, 1862. Dwight Moody was twenty-five.

His mother didn't like the idea of her son marrying a girl who had been born in England and who was also a Baptist. Really, she didn't know which was worse.

DL, had, of course, told her of the engagement: "I think, dear Mother, you would love her, if you could get acquainted with her. I do not know of anyone that knows her, but that does. She is a good Christian girl."

Since his mother had responded so negatively to the idea of his engagement to this British Baptist, he decided to take his time about informing her of the marriage. Finally, he got around to it two months later. Her reaction was what he expected.

Emma tackled the challenge with her usual calmness. She wrote her mother-in-law: "It makes very little difference to what sect we belong as long as our hearts are right in the sight of God." It took a few more letters and personal visits, but Emma and her mother-in-law, Betsey, soon became close friends.

Emma had a way of handling difficult problems. In fact, DL was sometimes unaware of all she was doing. She was practical and orderly. She made her husband eat regularly. She threw away the patent shirts that he boasted "did not need washing for weeks."

She shunned the limelight, although her gifts as a teacher were recognized. In Moody's Sunday school she taught a class of about forty middle-aged men.

Once Moody was escorting a visitor through his Sunday school, and the visitor remarked about the propriety of the situation: "Isn't that lady too young to be teacher of a class of men like that?"

Moody responded that he thought the teacher was handling the class quite well.

The visitor agreed but still insisted that it seemed improper.

Finally Moody said, and rather proudly at that, "That, sir, is my wife."

In the mid-1860s Moody's Sunday school evolved into a church. DL's closest denominational ties were with the Congregationalists, but his church was independent. At Emma's urging he included a baptistry for immersion as well as a font for infant baptism.

Moody was never ordained as a minister, so other men became the ministers of his church. Yet this didn't keep him from preaching regularly, and there was no doubt in anyone's mind that it was his church.

In his early sermons he emphasized God's wrath. Emma said that she sometimes "cringed" at his remarks.

But then the tone of his sermons changed, and it was Emma who was at least partly responsible. Also responsible was a British preacher named Harry Moorhouse, a converted pickpocket.

Moorhouse had been preaching at Moody's church in DL's absence, and when the evangelist returned, he asked Emma how Moorhouse had handled himself. She replied, "He preaches a little different from you. He preaches that God loves sinners."

Moody couldn't understand what Emma was driving at, but she insisted, "When you hear him, I think you will agree with him. He backs up everything he says with the Bible."

From then on, Moody not only preached more on the love of God than on the wrath of God, but also became more of a Bible student; and his sermons showed it.

Emma was also responsible for DL's ministry in the British Isles. After an unusually severe winter of asthma attacks, Emma, only twenty-four, was urged by her doctor to leave Chicago. He suggested that she might go to England, where her older sister lived. Always frail, she suffered from recurring headaches and a heart condition as well as asthma. On the other hand, Moody was robust and seemingly tireless. His chief musician, Ira Sankey, once prayed, "O God, tire Moody out, or give the rest of us superhuman strength."

Moody liked the idea of taking his wife to England. He needed a change of pace himself, and besides, he wanted to meet three men that he had admired from afar: George Williams, head of the YMCA; Charles Spurgeon, preacher at London's Metropolitan Tabernacle; and George Müller, who kept the Bristol Orphanage running by his prayer. Whether the trip to England did much for Emma's health is debatable, but it certainly did a lot to open up a new continent for DL's evangelistic ministry.

When he paused long enough to consider it, DL marveled at the wife God had given him. Once in a sermon Moody stated, "I think my wife would think it a very strange feeling, if I should tell how much I loved her the first year we were married and how happy I was then. It would break her heart."

Publicly, he said, "I have never ceased to wonder at two things— the use God has made of me despite my many handicaps, and the miracle of having won the love of a woman who is so completely my superior with such a different temperament and background."

By 1871, thirty-three-year-old Moody was very much a family man. Two children had been born into their Chicago home, and some of Moody's rough edges were being smoothed under Emma's gentle sandpapering. At times he was even learning to be courteous. His quick temper was usually kept under control, although occasionally he had to apologize for it in a public meeting.

He was now coming to a crossroads in his career. He had a church in Chicago, a job with the YMCA, and a growing evangelistic ministry that took him away from home for weeks at a time. He felt that God was calling him to more evangelism, but he was resisting.

The Chicago fire burned away his resistance.

On the night of October 8, 1871, the police knocked on the Moodys' door and told them to get out of the area as soon as possible. The city was aflame. Emma calmly wakened her two children and said, "If you promise not to scream or cry, I'll show you a sight you will never forget." She dressed them while they looked out the window at the inferno.

Chicago was in ashes. So was Moody's church. So was his YMCA. And no longer was there anyone in Chicago from whom he could raise money to build a new church or a new YMCA. So he went to New York and Philadelphia on a fund-raising mission. Money came reluctantly.

The problems in raising money to rebuild seemed to verify his call into full-time evangelism, and before long he was headed back to England with Emma and his two children, Willie, just four, and daughter Emma, now eight. A biographer looking at it psychologically wrote, "When problems began to pile up that were too much for him, he solved these difficulties by getting out and starting anew."

No one in England knew he was coming, except the head of the London YMCA and the doctor at a local lunatic asylum. But the Moodys stayed twenty months, and in that time the entire British Isles were set aflame for God.

In Scotland they stayed in the home of Peter Mackinnon, a partner of the British India Line. Mrs. Mackinnon, who became Emma's closest friend, enjoyed both of the Moodys. She wrote, "I liked the combination of playfulness and seriousness in Mr. Moody. . . . He is so simple, unaffected and lovable, plays so heartily with the children, and makes fun with those who can receive it. He is brimful of humor."

As for Emma, Jane Mackinnon wrote, "One day was enough to show what a source of strength and comfort she was to her husband. The more I saw of her, the more convinced I was that a great deal of his usefulness was owing to her, not only in the work she did for him, relieving him of all correspondence, but also from her character. Her independence of thought . . . her calmness, meeting so quietly his impulsiveness, her humility. . . . So patient, quiet, bright, humble; one rarely meets just so many qualities in one woman."

Moody's campaigns in the British Isles began with a whimper and ended with a bang. From the tip of Northern Ireland to Cornwall, people were talking about Moody.

When the Moodys returned to America, they made their home in Northfield, Massachusetts, where his mother, now in her seventies, still lived. Before long, DL's presence was felt in Northfield. In the staid Northfield church, he preached one Sunday and saw his own mother stand for prayer. Moody left the platform, sat down in the front pew, his face in his hands, and wept.

The family home in Massachusetts was a beautiful spot, writes James Findlay, Jr., "situated on one of the main roads into Northfield, commanding a sweeping view of the Connecticut River." It was a spacious New England farmhouse, the back portion of which was eventually converted into tiny rooms to serve as a dormitory for Moody's Northfield School.

At home DL relaxed, let his beard grow, wore shabby clothes, puttered in the vegetable garden, and played the role of a gentleman farmer. He loved horses and at one time owned fourteen of them. He cared little for sports and recreation but enjoyed going out for buggy rides and scaring his passengers out of their wits by the breakneck speeds at which he drove his horses. It was only when Emma was along that he slowed to a respectable speed.

In the homestead, Emma did the canning and made the preserves, visited the neighbors, and entertained DL's friends. She also did most of his correspondence and handled the family finances. DL once declared, "I am not going to give any man ground for saying that we're making a gain out of preaching the gospel." So he turned over the books to Emma.

Emma managed the house and, in her own quiet way, the entire family. She took responsibility for the spiritual teaching of their children, catechizing them, memorizing Scripture with them. Though she joined the Congregational Church at Northfield with her husband, she remained a Baptist in her beliefs until her death.

Unlike DL, who didn't read more than he had to, Emma enjoyed reading. As her children were growing up, she studied Latin grammar with them. Later she relearned French.

The one thing that angered Emma was people who took advantage of her husband. A son recalls, "Disloyalty to him was the unpardonable sin in her eyes, unforgivable, unforgettable and above all unmentionable. Here she was implacable."

DL and Emma often took buggy rides together into the woods and hills surrounding their home, and as their son put it, "going where fancy led them, having as it were a renewed honeymoon."

There were times when Moody turned down travel opportunities because "I could not leave my wife." But he did not turn down many opportunities to conduct evangelistic missions. These were often lengthy stays of several months, and usually Emma and the children traveled with him.

Emma wrote to Jane Mackinnon of her daily schedule in the midst of a six-month Baltimore campaign with "Mr. Moody at study and work in the meetings, the children in school, and I in all sorts of work, writing for my husband, attending to some of his calls, and helping him where I can, besides a variety of other things, that don't amount to much and yet make me tired by night."

One of the reasons Emma was getting tired in Baltimore was that she was pregnant. Their third child, Paul Dwight Moody, was born the next spring. He was ten years younger than his older brother, Will.

As the children grew up, both DL and Emma shared a deep concern for them. For instance, when Will began his college work at Yale, DL cautioned him against playing football. "It seems to me like running a great risk of being crippled for life for the sake of a half-hour's fun and exercise," but their greater concern was for the spiritual life of their children. Emma wrote, "If God will only make our children His own, it is the best that we can ask of Him for them." Moody had a special concern because his oldest son, Will, was cool to spiritual matters. Once he wrote Will a revealing letter: "I have not talked much with you for fear I would turn you more and more against Him, who

I love more than all the world and if I ever said or done anything un-becoming a Christian father I want you to forgive me. . . . I have always thought that when a mother and father are Christians and their chil-dren were not that there was something decidedly wrong with them. I still think so. . . . If I thought I had neglected to do my duty toward my three children I would rather die than live."

Later it was Emma who wrote to Will about her fear of his "being in college without reliance on the help of Christ. . . . Papa, I know, is praying and I am that God's spirit may lead you to give up yourself to Christ entirely."

The following year Will made a profession of faith. When DL heard of it, he wrote, "I do not think you will ever know until you have a son of your own how much good it did me to hear this."

The younger son, Paul, felt it was easier to confide in his mother than in his father. And Paul gave his mother credit for the success of the home: "If our home seemed so ideal, the secret was my mother." Emma also deserves some credit for the founding of Moody Bible Insti-tute in Chicago. Moody had served as president of the Chicago Evan-gelization Society, which was planning to launch a training school. But conflict developed between the board of directors and prospective staff members. Moody, who was not on the scene, felt frustrated by the con-tinual bickering. Finally he had enough. He abruptly tendered his res-ignation as president, a move which would have doomed the entire project. "I am sick and tired of it," he wrote.

When Emma heard about what DL had done, she wrote a nineteen-page letter to the people involved with the Bible Institute, and then got DL to send a wire, withdrawing his resignation.

Soon the Bible Institute of Chicago was launched.

Moody continued his busy schedule, despite his weight and his advancing age. In one three-month period, he visited ninety-nine places, often speaking three or four times a day. It is said that nothing distressed DL more than idleness.

The year 1899 was difficult for the Moodys. DL was sixty-two and had a full schedule of meetings planned. Two of his grandchildren had died rather suddenly, and the parents were suffering emotionally from it. So were the grandparents. DL had been burdened about the city of Philadelphia and had said, "If only it would please God to let me get hold of this city by a winter of meetings. I should like to do it before I die."

So, on his way to an evangelistic campaign in Kansas City, he stopped to visit John Wanamaker in Philadelphia and make final arrangements for a series of revival meetings. He was shocked to find his close friend John Wanamaker living in adultery. He continued to Kansas City, but after two weeks severe chest pains caused him to cease his preaching and he had to return home to Northfield. A month later, in December 1899, he died.

When DL's body was laid to rest, the spark in Emma's life was gone. She began to fail physically. When neuritis plagued her, she no longer could write with her right hand. So during the last two years of her life she learned to write with her left hand. It was rather typical of the way that Emma Moody handled obstacles.

D. L. Moody once told reporters, "I am the most overestimated person in America." But his wife, he would have said, was the most underestimated. Will Moody once wrote, "Moody found in his wife what he termed his balance wheel. With advice, sympathy and faith, this girl labored with him, and by her judgment, tact and sacrifice, she contributed to his every effort."

Emma supplied what Dwight lacked, and he knew it and appreciated it. She didn't like the limelight; she preferred a behind-the-scenes role. But that doesn't mean she was a nonentity. Far from it. She shaped Dwight both as a man and as a servant of God.

Bibliography

Bradford, Gamaliel. *D. L. Moody, A Worker in Souls.* New York: Doran, 1927.

Curtis, Richard K. *They Called Him Mr. Moody.* Garden City, N.Y.: Doubleday, 1962.

Findlay, James J., Jr. *D. L. Moody, American Evangelist.* Chicago: University of Chicago Press, 1969.

Moody, Paul D. *My Father.* Boston: Little, Brown, 1938.

Moody, William R. *The Life of D. L. Moody.* Old Tappan, N.J.: Fleming H. Revell, 1900.

Pollock, J. C. *Moody.* New York: Macmillan, 1963.

3

She Called Him "Tirshatha"

Charles and Susie Spurgeon

What did pretty Susie Thompson see in the short, pudgy, awkward young man?

She had culture and class; he was a country bumpkin who didn't know how to dress decently and often was too brash for polite society.

For dates, he invited her to come and hear him preach; once he forgot that she was along. That nearly broke the engagement.

It didn't.

No doubt it helped to prepare her for those times after marriage when, on a Sunday morning, he was so wrapped up in his pastoral duties that he would shake her hand and say, "Good morning, madam, how are you?" as if he had never seen her before in his life.

Charles Haddon Spurgeon, that prince of preachers, that cigar-smoking Calvinist Baptist, that delightfully colorful, cocky character who made the Bible come alive for his congregations, was certainly not regarded as a great "catch" according to London's standards. But Susie loved him and made a splendid marriage out of it.

He called her Susie, and she playfully called him "Tirshatha," the Persian word in Scripture for "the revered one." Since Charles didn't want to be called "Reverend," Susie thought "Tirshatha" would be appropriate.

"Tirshatha" became the greatest preacher of the century. He started a college, an orphanage, and an old people's home, edited a magazine, and penned 140 books and commentaries.

Susie accomplished a few things herself. She started an international Book Fund which distributed thousands of books a year, a Pastor's Aid Fund for needy ministers, and a soup kitchen to aid the poor. She also raised two boys and served as a research assistant to Charles.

Somehow the marriage between these two remarkable—and in some ways very different—individuals flourished.

What made it work?

Charles Spurgeon thought it was a mistake when London's New Park Street Church asked him to be a candidate for the pastorate there. He was only nineteen, and he had never been to seminary, while the New Park Street Church was one of London's most prestigious Nonconformist (non-Anglican) churches.

At least, it *had* been.

Things had been going downhill at the church for the past few years. The church could seat twelve hundred, but on many Sundays only eighty or one hundred attended.

A couple of deacons felt that they needed an energetic young man, someone who could make some changes at New Park Street. That is how they happened to write a letter to Charles.

The young Spurgeon had not had an auspicious beginning, though certainly there was a lifelong tie to the ministry. Born in a small rural town about seventy-five miles northeast of London, Charles was the son of a cod yard clerk who served as a Congregational minister on weekends. His mother, only nineteen when Charles was born, bore sixteen other children afterward, only seven of whom survived infancy. Because of the poverty of his parents, Charles spent the first six years of his life with his grandparents.

Since his grandfather was also a Congregational minister, the religious influence in Charles's early years was strong. His grandmother promised him a penny for every hymn by Isaac Watts he could memorize. He memorized so many that she cut the reward to a half-penny.

When Charles returned to his parents' home he was given the best education they could afford, and he made the most of it. His brother said, "Charles never did anything else but study. I kept rabbits, chickens, pigs and a horse; he kept to books."

The serious books he read—Joseph Alleine's *Admonition to Unconverted Sinners* and Richard Baxter's *Call to the Unconverted*—made him agonize internally. For nearly five years he wrestled with questions about his soul's salvation. The sermons that he heard and the prayers of his mother that he overheard only deepened his spiritual struggle.

Later he said, "Children are often very reticent to go to their parents. . . . I know it was so with me. When I was under concern of soul, the last persons I should have elected to speak to upon religion would have been my parents."

And so, he recalled, "It was my sad lot to feel the greatness of my sin without a discovery of the greatness of God's mercy."

Then on the first Sunday in January 1850, he ventured out in a blizzard to go to church. The storm prevented him from attending the church he planned to go to. Instead, he found refuge in a little Primitive Methodist Chapel and went inside.

Only twelve to fifteen people were there; even the minister didn't show up. So "a shoemaker or tailor or something of the sort went up into the pulpit to preach."

"This man was really stupid," recalled Charles. "His text was 'Look unto me, and be ye saved, all the ends of the earth.' He did not even pronounce the words right."

After ten minutes of repeating himself, the lay preacher realized that he had nothing more to say and was about to conclude when he noticed the teenage boy who had wandered in out of the snow. "Young man," he said, "you look very miserable, and you always will be miserable if you don't obey my text. But if you do obey now, this moment, you will be saved."

The unexpected shove was what Charles needed. In that moment he looked to Christ for his salvation. "There and then the cloud was gone;

the darkness was rolled away." Four months later he was baptized by immersion by a Baptist minister near the school he was attending.

A year and a half later, now seventeen, he accepted a call to be pastor of a forty-member congregation in Waterbeach, a town notorious for drunkenness and profanity. Two years after that he received his call to the church in London.

The night before his preaching debut in New Park Street, he was lodged in a boarding house in London's Bloomsbury district. His fellow boarders were incredulous when he told them where he was going to preach the next day. They told him of the outstanding preachers in all the other London pulpits, and they reminded him of the learned gentlemen who had previously occupied New Park Street's pulpit.

When they looked at Charles, they could hardly keep a straight face. He wore a great black satin stock around his neck and sported a huge blue handkerchief with white polka dots. His hair was unkempt and his manners were proof that he was from the country.

Charles tossed restlessly in his bed all night. As he put it, "I was not in an advantageous condition for pleasant dreams."

The surroundings didn't help. "Pitiless was the grind of the cabs in the street, pitiless the spare room which scarcely afforded me space to kneel, pitiless even the gas lamps which seemed to wink at me as they flickered around the December darkness. I had no friend in all that city full of human beings."

Charles wanted nothing better than to get out of London as quickly as possible. He felt he didn't belong there.

The next morning he got his first look at the church. He described it as "a large, ornate and imposing structure, suggesting an audience wealthy and critical, and far removed from the humble folk to whom my ministry had been sweetness and light."

The first morning service had only a fair attendance—about eighty—but the evening service was much better attended.

That was when Susie Thompson caught her first glimpse of Charles.

Although the rest of her family had attended the morning service, the young woman with the long chestnut curls had not gone. During the afternoon, a deacon had visited their home and lamented the fact that there had been so many vacant pews in the morning. "We must get him a better congregation tonight, or else we shall lose him." So the earnest deacon was doing everything he could to drum up a crowd.

"And little Susie must come too," he added.

Little Susie, who looked more like a teenager than a young woman nearly twenty-two, didn't like the idea of being called "little." Nor did she like some of the things she had heard about the country preacher. She preferred ministers with some decorum, and she couldn't imagine how she could respect a minister who was younger than she was. However, she reported later, "to please my dear friends, I went with them."

Her first impressions were not favorable. "I was not at all fascinated by the young orator's eloquence. . . . His countrified manner and speech excited more regret than reverence." What stuck in her mind was not the message at all, but "the huge black satin stock, the long, badly trimmed hair, and the blue pocket handkerchief with white spots." As she put it in her cultured way, "These awakened some feelings of amusement." The blue handkerchief was bad enough, but when he took it out and waved it in the middle of the sermon, it was gauche.

But the young preacher made an impression in spite of his gauche behavior. Before too long the New Park Street Church officially extended a call to Charles to be their pastor. "No lengthy reply is required," Charles responded. "I ACCEPT IT."

And about the same time, the deacons gave Charles a dozen white pocket handkerchiefs, so he would no longer have to use the dreadful blue handkerchief with white polka dots.

The handkerchiefs didn't transform Charles Haddon Spurgeon into a Beau Brummell. Charles never paid much attention to his clothing; he dressed to be comfortable, and what he wore seemed to accentuate his shape. Charles was built like a tank. His head seemed too large for his body. Until he smiled, his countenance appeared overwhelmingly heavy. Yet when he broke out into a sunny smile, which was never too far beneath the surface, everyone within a hundred yards of him melted.

A fellow minister said, "He had a remarkable face and head. The head was the very image of stubbornness: massive, broad, low, hard; the face was large, rugged, social, brightened by eyes overflowing with humor and softened by a most gracious and sympathetic smile." After a few years he grew a beard, and that improved his appearance.

It was more than physical appearance that brought Charles and Susie together. The major factor was Susie's spiritual condition. About a year before she first saw Charles, Susie had made a profession of faith, but since that time, she had become "cold and indifferent to the things of God." Yet there was a spiritual restlessness, and when the nineteen-year-old country preacher was invited back for three Sundays in January, Susie returned to hear him.

The daughter of a prosperous merchant, she was proper and reserved. Her genteel upbringing meant that she was not allowed to read the daily newspapers or discuss world events. And there were certain things that proper people didn't talk about, such as one's spiritual condition.

Yet Susie was becoming "alarmed at my backsliding state" and soon sought counsel from a cousin. It was at this time that the young minister, Charles Spurgeon, gave her a copy of *Pilgrim's Progress*. She was "greatly surprised." On the flyleaf he had written: "Miss Thompson with desires for her progress in the blessed pilgrimage." This was the beginning of a lifelong relationship.

At first, Susie was afraid to talk to Charles. Perhaps it was more reticence on her part than fear. It wasn't easy for Susie to talk to people about spiritual matters, but she was amazed at the interest that he took in her spiritual welfare. He seemed to take delight in counseling her. The counseling paid off. As she put it, "He gently led me . . . to the cross of Christ for the peace and pardon my weary soul was longing for."

Early in June 1854, only six weeks after he had given her *Pilgrim's Progress*, Charles and Susie, along with several other church members, went together to the grand opening of the Crystal Palace, London's new exhibition hall, which was a miniature World's Fair.

Everyone was joking, laughing, and talking so much that they didn't even notice that Charles was talking rather seriously to Susie. If they glanced in their direction, all that they would have noticed was that Charles was showing Susie a book he had brought with him. The book was Martin Tupper's *Proverbial Philosophy*.

"I've been reading this book recently," Charles said in a low voice.

She didn't seem to show much interest. It hardly was the appropriate place to talk about philosophy.

Charles opened the book and pointed to a passage he had previously marked. "What do you think of the writer's suggestion in those verses?"

She looked at where his finger was pointing.

The chapter was entitled "Marriage." She read the passage: "Seek a good wife of thy God, for she is the best gift of His providence. . . . Think of her and pray for her."

She feared to lift her eyes from the text. Then she heard him whispering in her ear: "Do you pray for him who is to be your husband?"

She was blushing and couldn't help it, and she was afraid to say anything for fear that it would be the wrong thing to say. The program soon started, but she didn't take "much note of the glittering pageant before her." Did he really mean what she thought he might mean? Or was she reading too much into it?

After the ceremonies, he asked her, "Would you walk around the Palace with me?"

From that time, she says, "Our friendship grew apace and quickly ripened into deepest love."

Two months later, "in a little old-fashioned garden," Charles didn't need a book to declare his love to her. "I thought I knew it already," she said, "but it was a very different matter to hear him say it."

That night she wrote in her diary, "It is impossible to write down all that occurred this morning. I can only adore in silence the mercy of my God, and praise Him for all His benefits."

In January 1855, barely a year after their first meeting, she was baptized by her fiancé. For Susie, who was still shy about sharing her spiritual feelings, it was traumatic, or as she put it, "a somewhat severe ordeal." She had to undergo public questioning about her profession of faith and also submit written testimony.

Charles was proud of how well she handled herself. Her written testimony contained some surprises; it displayed a depth that he hadn't realized before.

After that time, Charles usually spent Monday mornings at Susie's house, "bringing his sermon with him to revise for the press; and I learned to be quiet and mind my own business." His sermons were taken down in shorthand as he preached them on Sunday; then early Monday morning, they were set in type, and the proofs were returned to Charles for editing. Charles had the ability to concentrate on the subject at hand, ignoring all his surroundings, even if the surroundings included Susie. Sometimes, as Susie admitted, "I resented this." It was most obvious just before his Sunday morning service when he was preoccupied with the message or the order of service. If Susie would walk into the vestry, he might "rise and greet me with a handshake and a grave 'How are you?' as if I were a strange visitor. . . . This happened not once only, but several times." After the service was over, he joked about it. Susie learned to joke about it too.

Charles learned that sometimes it was easy for him to say he was putting God first when actually he was merely displaying poor manners and being self-centered. Susie, fortunately, had much patience.

One of the reasons for their long engagement was that Susie's father was a bit reluctant to bestow his blessing upon Charles. Charles may have been gaining a fantastic reputation as a preacher, but he was still only twenty. Another reason was that there was so much happening at New Park Street that it was difficult to fit a wedding in.

Week after week, the church was crowded, so crowded that it was stifling in the summer months. Charles was concerned that people might stay home because it was so hot in his church. So, since the windows wouldn't open and the deacons wouldn't do anything about it, he took a cane and knocked out every window in the entire sanctuary. He knew that by the following winter a building program would ensure that the church would have new windows that could be let down.

During the building enlargement, the congregation moved out of the church and rented Exeter Hall, which held 4,500 people.

London was shocked. It was unheard of for a church to rent a public hall for its worship services. Soon the newspapers were castigating the young preacher for his scandalous action.

One newspaper reported, "As his own chapel is under repair, he preaches in Exeter Hall every Sunday, and the place is jammed to suffocation. All his discourses are redolent of bad taste, are vulgar and theatrical, and yet he is so run after that, unless you go half an hour before the time, you will not be able to get in at all."

Another paper described Charles's preaching style as "that of a vulgar colloquial, varied by rant. . . . All the most solemn mysteries of our holy religion are by him rudely, roughly and impiously handled."

Charles tried to act as if the criticism didn't faze him. He wrote his father, "For myself, I will rejoice; the devil is roused, the church is awakening, and I am now counted worthy to suffer for Christ's sake." But he also admitted he had trouble sleeping.

On Sundays he preached to the large congregation without amplification. The strain on him was terrible. Susie wrote, "Sometimes his voice would almost break." His remedy for throat problems was a glass of chili vinegar which he kept on a shelf in the pulpit. (Years later, Charles said that these early challenges "macadamized" his throat.)

Renovations to the New Park Street Church didn't solve anything. By the time the building project was completed, the new sanctuary was far too small to house the rapidly growing congregation. One week they met in a field. Charles estimated the crowd at about ten thousand.

That summer Charles went to Scotland on a speaking tour. He needed the change, and he thought it might be a "working vacation." It was his first separation from Susie, and despite the adulation of the Scottish crowds, he missed her. Once he wrote her: "My Precious Love: . . . I knew I loved you very much before, but now I feel how necessary you are to me, and you will not lose much by my absence, if you find me, on my return, more attentive to your feelings, as well as equally affectionate."

Thousands had to be turned away from some of the meetings because there was no room, but Charles was not happy with what he felt inside of himself. He wrote to Susie: "Pray very earnestly for me. I fear I am not so full of love to God as I used to be. I lament my sad decline in spiritual things. You and others may not have observed it, but I am now conscious of it. . . . What is it to be popular . . . even to have love as sweet as yours if I should be left of God to fall and to depart from His ways? I tremble at the giddy height on which I stand and could wish myself unknown."

A few months later, the first volume of Charles's sermons was published. He gave a copy to Susie and on the flyleaf he scribbled, "In a few days it will be out of my power to present anything to Miss Thompson."

What he meant was that in only a few days Miss Susannah Thompson would become Mrs. Charles Spurgeon.

Charles, twenty-one, and Susie, nearly twenty-four, were married January 8, 1856. The church was packed; thousands thronged the streets to get a glimpse of the couple; police did their best to keep traffic moving around the church. The ceremony was simple, in keeping with the wishes of both bride and groom.

Afterwards, the newlyweds sailed to France for a ten-day honeymoon in Paris. Not only had Susie previously visited the city many times with her parents, but she had also lived there for several months in order to learn to speak French fluently. So on their honeymoon she served as Charles's guide as they visited Versailles, the Louvre, and the Cathedral of Notre Dame.

In his biography, Russell Conwell wrote, "With a nature like that of Mr. Spurgeon's, with many defects to repair and a lack of general education to be supplied, a cultivated and persevering wife might be considered an unquestioned necessity. . . . She could curb the uncouth eccentricities and correct his mistakes in language or history, and she hesitated not in the most affectionate manner to apply her criticisms when she saw they would do her husband good. He urged her to take the place of a public critic and notice his errors that he might the more readily correct them, and as she was a lady of excellent good sense and of quite extensive reading, she was a far safer critic than any man he could have selected."

Conwell may have slightly overstated the case, but the point is well taken. While Charles was certainly not uneducated, he lacked the refinement and polish that a London minister was expected to have. Susie was a loving guide for him, but most people never saw what went on behind the scenes.

Despite the busy schedule that Charles maintained, he and Susie found time to enjoy each other. One of those times was Sunday night after the evening service. Usually when Charles returned from the evening service, he was quite exhausted. He would flop into an easy chair by the fireside, and Susie, sitting on a low cushion by his feet, would read poetry to him. On other evenings Susie might read theological books to Charles at his request. There was certainly no shortage of reading materials, for Charles's library rapidly grew to twelve thousand volumes.

Charles seldom prepared his Sunday morning message until Saturday night. (His Sunday evening message was prepared Sunday afternoon.)

On Saturday afternoons, he and Susie would usually have friends in for tea. After tea they would have their time of family worship together. It was understood, however, that all guests would have to leave at seven. That was when Charles began preparing his sermon.

Sometimes the system didn't work too well. "I confess that I frequently sit hour after hour praying and waiting for a subject," Charles admitted. Once he had to make notes for an evening message as he was bouncing over the cobblestones in his carriage on the way to church.

But there was one Saturday evening when Charles was mulling over a text for hours. He had consulted commentaries, praying, jotting down ideas that didn't go anywhere, and becoming increasingly frustrated. "I was as much distressed as he was," Susie said, "but I could not help him. . . . At least, I thought I could not."

Finally, Susie urged him to go to bed and wake up early in the morning. He would be able to think more clearly then. And she promised that she would wake him at dawn.

Early in the morning, however, Susie heard him talking in his sleep. She listened; it wasn't gibberish; it seemed to make sense. "Soon I realized that he was going over the subject . . . and was giving a clear and distinct exposition of its meaning with much force and freshness. . . . If I could but seize and remember the salient points of the discourse, he would have no difficulty in developing and enlarging upon them."

She lay in bed, "repeating over and over again the chief points." Then she herself fell asleep about the time she was supposed to waken Charles.

When he awoke and noticed the time, he was irritated. And Susie was the focus of his irritation. "You promised to waken me very early. See the time! Why did you let me sleep? I don't know what I'm going to do this morning." Facing a large congregation without a message from the Lord was not what Charles enjoyed doing.

Then Susie told him what had happened during the night and repeated to him the main points he had made in his sleep.

"You mean I preached that in my sleep?" He could hardly believe it. "That is just what I wanted. That's the true explanation of the text."

From the explanation Susie had furnished, Charles went into the pulpit and preached a powerful sermon.

Susie the pastor's aide was also Susie the parent. Only nine and a half months after she and Charles were married, twin boys were born. They were named Charles and Thomas.

It was a difficult time for Susie. Her delivery had not been easy, and she required several weeks of bed rest.

It was also a difficult time for Charles. He couldn't find an auditorium big enough to seat his growing congregation.

Three thousand people were jammed into the 1,500-capacity sanctuary of the New Park Street Church, and hundreds more were waiting outside. According to biographer Ernest Bacon, "The conductors of the horse-drawn buses on the north side of the Thames used to entice people into their vehicles with the shout, 'Over the water to Charlie.'"

In June evening services were moved back to 4,500-seat Exeter Hall, but even it was too small. The only other possibility was the Surrey Music Hall, which held 12,000 people and was used for exhibitions, circuses, and wild beast shows as well as concerts. If the press had criticized Spurgeon for renting Exeter Hall for a church service, what would they say if he rented the Surrey Music Hall?

On the evening of October 19, 1856, a night Charles would never forget, he held his first service at Surrey Music Hall. Twelve thousand people packed the hall; another 10,000 were outside.

In the middle of the service as Charles was praying, someone yelled, "FIRE!" Someone else shouted, "The galleries are collapsing! The place is falling!"

Some of the people panicked and rushed toward the doors. Some leaped from the staircase. Seven died; twenty-eight were seriously injured; many more suffered less severe injuries.

But there was no fire; the galleries weren't collapsing. The instigators of mischief were never found, but the disruption worked only too well.

Charles tried to quiet the audience. From the pulpit he could see no problem. With considerable poise, the twenty-two-year-old was able to get many in the audience settled. He began his sermon. But then came some more shouts and another disruption. He couldn't continue.

As he turned from the pulpit, he collapsed and had to be carried into a side room.

Susie was home with her twins, not yet a month old. She had been praying for the meeting and praying specifically for Charles. Then she heard a carriage outside. She looked at the time. It was too early for Charles to be returning.

A deacon from the church appeared at the door, informing her of the catastrophe at the Music Hall. A little while later, Charles was brought home. In Susie's words, "He looked a wreck—an hour's agony of mind had changed his whole appearance and bearing."

Charles seemed on the verge of a serious breakdown. "His anguish was so deep and violent . . . that we feared he would never preach again."

The next day he was taken to a deacon's home where there was a large, restful garden, "to restore his mental equilibrium and unloose the bars which had kept his spirit in darkness." At first it didn't seem to help. He continued to be flooded with "tears by day and dreams of terror at night."

For Susie, too, it was a confusing time. Would Charles ever return to normalcy again? Even if he did, would he ever preach?

Together they walked slowly through the gardens. Then suddenly he stopped and turned to Susie. "How foolish I have been! What does it matter what becomes of me if the Lord is glorified? If He is exalted, let Him do as He pleases with me. Oh, wifey, I see it all now."

And after missing only one week from his pulpit, he returned again to resume his strenuous preaching load.

The press heaped blame upon Charles for the catastrophe. He was reviled as "a ranting charlatan" and accused of misleading gullible people.

The crowds continued to come, undaunted by the media. In fact, the tragic accident gave Spurgeon worldwide fame.

Work was progressing slowly on their new church building, to be called the Metropolitan Tabernacle. In the meantime, Charles continued to use the Music Hall for services, but to keep out mischief-makers, worshipers had to have tickets to get in. And a ticket to hear Spurgeon was a valuable possession. (The tickets were free, but they served the purpose of keeping out those who wanted to stir up trouble. They also insured that the building would not be overcrowded.) Soon all of London, including lords, earls, mayors, sheriffs, and even royalty, was coming to hear the young preacher.

Before he had turned twenty-five, a vast empire revolved around him. Besides the construction of the huge Metropolitan Tabernacle, he had started a Preachers' College that was growing each year. Most of those who came were poor and could not afford to pay tuition, and that increased the financial burden.

Susie carried the responsibility for managing the family finances. Besides Charles's salary, the sale of his sermons around the world was starting to bring in healthy royalties. With Susie as a shrewd manager, the Spurgeons were able to underwrite the college's expenses in its early years.

For the building of the new sanctuary Charles and Susie were able to contribute five thousand pounds. By sponsoring a church bazaar, Susie was able to raise an additional twelve hundred pounds. The total was about 20 percent of the building fund.

Soon an orphanage was started, housing five hundred children. Then a colportage association was launched with nearly one hundred book and Bible salesmen going door to door throughout England selling gospel literature.

Charles kept a heavy schedule of speaking engagements around London but supplemented them with other assignments throughout the British Isles. Susie enjoyed going with him as frequently as she could. She never liked to see him go without her.

In 1868, when Susie was thirty-six, "her traveling days were done." After that, as she put it, "I was a prisoner in a sick chamber."

But Charles's traveling days were not ended, and the separation was not easy for either of them. Whenever he left home, he would ask, "What can I bring you, wifey?" She would usually say, "Nothing," for as she sincerely felt, "I have all things richly to enjoy except health."

But not all things. Her health never returned. Those were difficult days for Charles and Susie. She writes, "Dark days those were for both husband and wife for a serious disease had invaded my frame, and little alleviation could be found from the constant, wearying pain it caused."

To convalesce, she went to the seaside resort of Brighton, but her condition worsened. A major operation was required, and Sir James Simpson, the discoverer of chloroform, offered his professional services without charge. Though the operation was termed a success in that some of her intense pain was relieved, Susie remained a semi-invalid.

While she remained in Brighton, some of Charles's wealthier friends suggested that they completely rebuild the Spurgeon home, and it was reconstructed from the ground up. Charles took special delight in preparing it for the return of his invalid wife. In one letter he wrote her:

> My Own Dear Sufferer:
> I have been quite a long round today—if a round can be long. First, to Fensbury, to buy a wardrobe—a beauty. . . . Next to Hewlett's, for a chandelier for the dining room. Found one quite to my taste and yours. Then to Negretti and Zambra's, to buy a barometer for my own fancy, for I have long promised to treat myself to one. On the road I obtained the Presburg biscuits, and within their box I send this note, hoping it may reach you the more quickly. They are sweetened with my love and prayers.

Though Charles remained extremely busy, he missed Susie greatly. Once he remarked that "he and the cat (old 'Dick') went up and down the stairs mewing for the mistress."

The load was heavy for Charles. The church, the preachers' college, the orphanage, the satellite churches, his magazine, his books—the pressures kept building. Once he wrote, "I feel as though I had created a great machine and it is ever grinding, grinding, and that I may yet be its victim."

Perhaps he was. A year later, when Susie was home again, the health of Charles, just thirty-five years old, was breaking. His ailment was gout, which is similar to a severe form of rheumatoid arthritis. It was an affliction from which he would never recover. While he would have temporary remissions, in the cold and dampness of the winter the disease would return in all its fury.

He wrote his congregation: "The furnace stills glows around me. Since I last preached to you, I have been brought very low, my flesh has been tortured with pain, and my spirit has been prostrate with depression. . . . With some difficulty, I write these lines in my bed, mingling them with the groans of pain and the songs of hope."

For a man who had always been so busy, inactivity brought depression, but even the depression had to give way to the intense pain. Doctors advised Charles to spend some of the winter in the warmth and sunshine of the Mediterranean. Susie knew that there was no other solution, even though, because she could no longer travel, it would mean separation for weeks, sometimes months at a time.

Susie wrote, "These separations were very painful to hearts so tenderly united as were ours."

After several weeks in southern France, Charles recovered sufficiently to resume his pastoral duties in London. These duties didn't diminish. "No one knows the toil and care I have to bear," he wrote once when he felt depressed. "I have to look after the orphanage, have charge of a church with 4,000 members, there is the weekly sermon to be revised, *The Sword and the Trowel* to be edited, and besides all that, a weekly average of five hundred letters to be answered."

Charles did find time to smoke, however.

Despite his health problems, Charles smoked heavily throughout his life. He told the newspapers that "smoking relieved his pain, soothed his brain and helped him to sleep." A London paper described him in his coach as he headed toward the Metropolitan Tabernacle:

"Wrapped in a rough blue overcoat, with a species of soft deerstalking hat on his head, a loose black necktie round his massive throat, and a cigar burning merrily in his mouth, he is surely the most unclerical of all preachers of the gospel."

This "unclerical preacher" treasured the times when he could enjoy his family, but most of the child-rearing had of necessity been handled by Susie. It was Susie who taught her sons the Scriptures. Son Thomas recalled, "I trace my early conversion directly to her earnest pleading and bright example." On Sunday nights she stayed home, conducting a service for her boys, while her husband preached to six or seven thousand people at the Metropolitan Tabernacle. Both of the boys went into the ministry later in life.

Charles had a playful sense of humor, given to puns. The top shelf of his library was filled with "dummy books" with fake titles. These included *Windows Ventilated* by Stone; *Padlock on The Understanding; Cuff on The Head; Cricket on The Green; Over the Stream* by Bridge; and *Do It Again* by Dunnett.

Charles had more serious connections with books, however. One day after Susie had read the proofs of a new book by Charles called *Lectures to My Students,* he asked her for her opinion of it. She responded, "I wish I could send a copy to every minister in England."

Charles answered, "Why not do it?"

It was a challenge that Susie took seriously. She went upstairs and searched through dresser drawers until she came up with enough money to send out one hundred copies of the book. She sent the books and thought that was the end of it, but when others heard of what she had done, they started sending her money. Soon the Book Fund was started, and Susie had her own ministry.

Charles was pleased that the Book Fund gave Susie a meaningful activity now that the boys were grown: "By this means He called her away from her personal grief, gave tone and concentration to her life, led her in continual dealings with Himself."

For several years Susie sent out about ten thousand books a year, plus an equal number of her husband's sermons.

As the work grew, Charles became worried; the Book Fund was too much work for her. "The business has overpowered her; the wagon is running over the horse."

Susie, besides her health problems, also struggled at times with fear. With Charles away in the winter and sometimes preaching at a distance in the summers as well, she had to trust the Lord, not her husband, for her safety.

On the wall of their bedroom was the Bible verse, "I have chosen thee in the furnace of affliction" (Isa. 48:10).

Both of them lived in the furnace for many years. Both of them also faced depressions. Said Charles, "There are dungeons beneath the Castle of Despair."

In 1892, Charles was once again in southern France during January. But this year was different. This year the doctor had given Susie permission to accompany him. He was fifty-seven now, although his illness made him appear older. As his physical condition worsened, Susie was at his bedside.

"Susie," he whispered.

"Yes, dear Tirshatha," she responded, bending over him and clasping his hand in hers.

Then he spoke his last words: "Oh, wifey, I have had such a blessed time with my Lord."

All of England, including the Prince of Wales and the prime minister, mourned his death. A crowd estimated at one hundred thousand came to his funeral.

For another dozen years, Susie continued her work with the Book Fund. She also assisted in preparing Charles's autobiography. She died in 1903 at the age of seventy-one.

In a sermon on marriage Charles mentioned that a model marriage is "founded on pure love and cemented in mutual esteem." He was describing his own marriage.

"Their object in life is common. There are points where their affections so intimately unite that none could tell which is first and which is second. . . . Their wishes blend, their hearts are indivisible. By degrees, they come to think very much the same thoughts. Intimate association creates conformity; I have known this to become so complete that, at the same moment, the same utterance has leaped to both their lips.

"If Heaven be found on earth, they have it."

Bibliography

Bacon, Ernest W. *Spurgeon: Heir of the Puritans.* Grand Rapids: Baker, 1967.
Conwell, Russell H. *Life of Charles H. Spurgeon.* New York: Edgewood, 1892.
Dallimore, Arnold. *Spurgeon.* Chicago: Moody, 1984.
Fullerron, W. Y. *Charles Haddon Spurgeon.* Chicago: Moody, 1966.
Ray, Charles. *Mrs. C. H. Spurgeon.* Pasadena, Tex.: Pilgrim Publications, 1979.
Spurgeon, Charles H. *Autobiography.* 2 Vols. Carlisle, Penn.: Banner of Truth, 1975, 1976.

Togetherness, Trials, and Teamwork

"Don't get me wrong. I love my wife. But after I'm with her constantly for two weeks on our vacation, I'm ready to get back to the office again." That's the husband talking.

"I don't know how I'll survive after John retires and he's at home all day long. We have a good marriage, we enjoy doing things together, we have a lot in common. But it's possible to have too much of a good thing, and togetherness can go too far." That's the wife talking.

Some couples, however, can't get enough of togetherness. They choose to work together.

Other couples—and many ministers, missionaries, and evangelists are included among them—find that togetherness has been forced upon them, and they either decide to make it work or change their calling.

The four couples in this section aren't the only ones in this book who worked through the problems of togetherness. The Luthers, for instance, had their struggles. Martin locked himself in his room to get away from the family, until Kate took the door off the hinges to penetrate his defenses. Calvin Stowe had problems with the housekeeping of his wife Harriet. Once he complained: "You have vexed me beyond endurance often by taking up my newspapers and then instead of folding them properly and putting

them in their place, either dropping them all sprawling on the floor, or wabbling them up all into one wabble, and then sprawling them on the table like an old
hen with her guts and gizzard squashed out."

But the Booths and the Sundays worked more
closely together, day by day, than most of the others.
How did they do it? How did they manage total
togetherness so successfully? Or wasn't it quite as successful as it looked on the surface?

How did marriage work for the Bryans when Mary
served as his research assistant, speech collaborator,
and political advisor? And what about the Taylors
working together in China? Hudson always restless,
Maria comfortable.

Billy and "Ma" Sunday were completely different,
and their gifts and talents complemented each other.
But the Booths were both strong-minded evangelists.

As you read the following chapters, you will get
some insights into how couples can make togetherness work, and you can also see the pitfalls that can
befall a couple when husband and wife work together
as a team on a permanent basis.

Don't Pretend Differences Don't Exist

William and Catherine Booth

William Booth reached into the dregs of London's society, preached to the down-and-outers, and organized his Salvation Army. Since then, the Army has marched around the world, ministering mercy and preaching the gospel.

His wife, Catherine Booth, is almost as famous as her general-husband. In fact, a hundred years ago, it was a moot point who was the better preacher.

How does a marriage work when both husband and wife are public figures? For that matter, when both husband and wife are strong-minded and frequently dogmatic?

At first, you may wonder how this marriage survived, but soon you will see what both William and Catherine brought to it that made it successful.

I think you'll agree that both William and Catherine are fascinating people. You'll enjoy getting to know them.

It was a big day for William, and it turned out to be much bigger than he could possibly have dreamed.

April 10, 1852, was his twenty-third birthday, and this year it coincided with Good Friday. But that wasn't what made it big.

This was the day when William Booth would become a full-time preacher. Up until this day, he had been a seventy-eight-hour-a-week pawnbroker and a Sunday preacher. Now he was saying farewell to the pawnbroker's shop in south London, where he had slept as well as worked for the past three years.

A businessman had promised him about $4.00 a week if he would go full-time into preaching. It was not an easy decision, and he had struggled with it for months. After all, he was trying to send some support to his widowed mother each week, and that would be hard to do on $4.00 a week. But now the decision was made. He had packed his suitcase and had walked out in the street looking for new lodgings.

Then, unexpectedly, he bumped into his businessman friend, who invited him to attend a church service that afternoon. Probably if anyone else had given the invitation, William would have refused it; after all, he had other things on his mind.

Instead, he decided to accept the invitation and go to the meeting. He was glad he did.

Catherine Mumford was also attending the meeting.

They had met a few times before. In some ways they seemed an unlikely couple. He was tall (about six-one), almost Lincolnesque in his appearance, gangling, a bit awkward, sporting a black beard and usually wearing a dark frock coat. She was dark, slightly built, had lustrous brown eyes, and carried herself with obvious refinement.

She had become one of his parishioners at the Walworth Road Methodist Chapel, where he frequently preached. One biographer says that "despite their brief acquaintance, a strange affinity had grown up between the tall hollow-cheeked Booth and the dark petite Catherine."

And on this Good Friday that was so significant in William Booth's life, he offered to escort her home after the meeting; she accepted.

Earlier she had admired his preaching (it had "fire" in it); now she began to admire the man. "His thought for me, although such a stranger, appeared most remarkable." She was also impressed with the "wonderful harmony of view and aim and feeling on varied matters. It seems as though we had intimately known and loved each other for years. . . . Before we reached my home we both suspected, nay we felt as though we had been made for each other, and that henceforth the current of our lives must flow together."

Catherine's mother invited William to stay at their home for the night. The next morning when he left the Mumford home, he said he was "feeling wounded." William Booth had fallen in love.

Unfortunately, it was not a good time to fall in love. If it had happened a day earlier when he still had his job, everything might have been different. But now he was a preacher, and $4.00 a week was hardly enough to meet his own bare necessities. He certainly couldn't afford to get married.

Had the decisions of this Good Friday been a mistake?

It would be easy to think so. Both William and Catherine were intense, opinionated, strong-minded, determined. Both were frequently moody and prone to depression.

How could such a marriage work out?

But it did.

Booth lived to see The Salvation Army, which he and Catherine began in the London slums, spread into fifty-five countries. The merger of social concern and aggressive evangelism among all types of people added a refreshing new dimension to Christendom. No religious movement has ever been more the product of a husband-wife team than The Salvation Army. And no family has ever disseminated the gospel farther and more effectively than William and Catherine Booth and their eight children.

Perhaps their most serious disagreement during their engagement was over women's equality. She won the argument, but a decade later it was her husband who prodded her into preaching, and a decade after that, she was in more demand as a preacher than he was.

Yes, William and Catherine were an unlikely couple, and both of them came from homes with below-par marriages.

"There is no evidence," one biographer avers, "that Mary [William Booth's mother] greatly loved Samuel Booth [his father], or indeed that she loved him at all. His cold nature and worldly ambitions and his vulgar speech and manners must have checked whatever affection she might have felt for him." His father, whom William himself describes as "a grab-a-get," was a money-minded, small-time builder in Nottingham, who tried to keep up appearances as long as possible but went bankrupt in 1842 when William was only thirteen. That ended William's schooling. His father got him a job as an apprentice to a Unitarian pawnbroker in Goose Gate, Nottingham's slums. Then within a year of his bankruptcy, William's father died, leaving a widow (who tried to eke out a living by selling toys, needles, and cotton), fourteen-year-old William (who had no take-home pay as an apprentice), and three young daughters, one of whom was an invalid.

In the next few years William saw as much of poverty as he ever wanted to see. His family was poor, but working as a pawnbroker, he saw many who were far poorer. He witnessed as poverty-stricken citizens battled soldiers and then broke into bakeries to get bread. He felt the injustice of high taxation and the inequity of the Corn Laws that protected the landowners at the expense of the poor. He even joined a political movement aimed at revolutionizing the British government.

But he also began attending a Methodist chapel in Nottingham. And one night, trudging home after a late meeting, he pondered all the deep thoughts that had been churning through his mind and decided to turn his life over to Jesus Christ. Undramatically, William Booth had become a Christian.

Six years later, having finished his appointed time as an apprentice, William tried to find a job, preferably at something unrelated to pawn-broking. But he was unsuccessful. After a year of unemployment in Nottingham, he decided to move to the big city of London. Those twelve months of unemployment were "among the most desolate of my life," William recalled later. "No one had the slightest interest in me."

London didn't seem much better than Goose Gate in Nottingham. If anything, the poverty was worse. Jobs were just as scarce. And the city, as William quickly discovered, literally stank. Smoke from three million chimneys blended in a putrid amalgam with gin, onions, dung, drying batter, and sewage. The River Thames had been appropriately nicknamed "The Great Stink."

Because he could find nothing else, he finally accepted work as a pawnbroker, a job that he was ashamed of for the rest of his life. His one joy in life came on Sundays when he often took the opportunity to preach, sometimes outdoors in a London park and sometimes in a small chapel eight miles away. It was a long walk.

He regretted he couldn't spend more time preaching, but that was impossible. "There is no way; no one wants me." After all, the Methodists had just declined to renew his church membership (he had stubbornly refused to give up his open-air preaching in Kennington Common), and his application to serve as chaplain on a convict ship bound for Australia—a job hardly any self-respecting minister wanted—had been rejected. Besides that, a doctor had warned him that he was such a bundle of nervous energy that he probably wouldn't live too long. And now he was having increasing stomach problems and was rapidly developing ulcers.

So just as he was about to give up on everything, he met this businessman "angel" who wanted to enlist him as a minister with a group which had broken with the Methodists. Shortly thereafter, he met Catherine.

Catherine's mother was rigid, narrow, and sometimes neurotic. Her father was a backslidden Methodist minister turned coachmaker, for whom both mother and daughter prayed. For a while he was active in the temperance movement, but eventually took to drink himself.

William Booth once said that Catherine's mother was "a woman of the sternest principle he had ever met. . . . To her, right was right no matter what it might entail." She refused to allow her daughter to study French because it might open the door to French novels and infidel literature. Most of Catherine's education was at home, because Mrs. Mumford was afraid of the companions with whom her daughter might have to mix at school. To avoid secular contamination, Catherine grew up without playmates. Instead she played church with her dolls and often preached to them. Table conversation was always adult and serious. The only other child in the family, a brother, left home as soon as he could (at age sixteen) to sail to America, and that left Catherine to be her mother's confidante.

Nervous and delicate, Catherine battled various health problems from childhood. When she was fourteen, curvature of the spine forced her to be bedridden for several months; when she was eighteen, tuberculosis forced her to leave home for the seaside town of Brighton for sixteen months. She returned to London from her convalescence about the time that William Booth came to London to hunt for a job.

It was said of Catherine: "Next to religion, she cared most for disputation." Strangely enough, that endeared her to William. He had never met anyone like her.

She had definite thoughts on almost everything, even as he had. She even had definite thoughts on the kind of man she wanted to marry. He would have to have religious views similar to hers; he would have to be a man of sense and character ("I could never respect a fool"); and he would have to have similar tastes. She also believed she must be physically attracted to him. Lastly, he must be a total abstainer. Besides that, she had a personal preference for a minister. William Booth met all the qualifications except for not being a total abstainer. She soon convinced him of the importance of total abstinence, and that made him her perfect match.

Within a month of their Good Friday tryst, Booth began having second thoughts about many things. People didn't seem to respond to his preaching; denominational officials were giving him the cold shoulder; congregations appeared to be so much better educated than he. Maybe he should return to pawnbroking so he and Catherine could get married. He shared his thoughts with Catherine.

In a "My dear friend" letter, she responded, "Never mind who frowns if God smiles. The words 'gloom, melancholy and despair' lacerate my heart. Don't give way to such feelings for a moment. God loves you. He will sustain you. . . . The thought that I should increase your perplexity and cause you any suffering is almost unthinkable. I am tempted to wish that we have never seen each other. Do try to forget me."

William misunderstood the letter. He thought she was rejecting him, and dashed off a frantic note in response. She wrote back: "I fear you did not fully understand my difficulty. If you are satisfied that the step is not opposed to the will of God, let us be one, come what may." A few days later they were engaged.

The engagement came easily, compared to the marriage. Their wedding would have to wait for more than three years.

On the night of their engagement Catherine wrote: "The evening is beautifully serene and tranquil, according sweetly with the feelings of

my soul. The whirlwind is past and the succeeding calm is in propor-
tion to its violence. All is well. . . . The more you lead me up to Christ
in all things, the more highly shall I esteem you; and if it be possible
to love you more than I do now, the more I shall love you."

Because William traveled a great deal in the next three years, the
correspondence of the engaged couple continued. His notes were short;
hers were frequently 2,500 to 3,000 words in length. One biographer
referred to them as "Puritan love letters." Perhaps, but there was also
plenty of emotional warmth conveyed in them.

He spoke of his problems: "I walked eight miles yesterday. I ought
to have ridden. I feel uncommonly tired and weary this morning. My
head aches and I feel altogether out of order."

In her responses, she sometimes scolded him: "Don't sit up singing
till twelve o'clock after a hard day's work. Such things are not required
by either God or man, and remember you are not your own."

Sometimes she sounded schoolmarmish: "Try and cast off the fear
of man," but soon she would sound human again: "You may justly consider me inadequate to advise you in spiritual matters, after living at
so great a distance from God myself."

She knew that she shouldn't worry about him, but she did anyway.
"The very fact of loving invests the being beloved with a thousand
causes of care and anxiety, which, if unloved, would never exist. At
least, I find it so."

Biographer William Nelson wrote, "It would never have done for a
halfhearted man to have married Catherine Mumford." Some of her
letters would have intimidated a lesser man. Once she wrote, "I ought
to restrain the tide of feeling more than I do in writing to you," but
she said that she did not want to "cool or restrain it, so that you may
know of what I am made."

She was not afraid to give him her pastoral advice: "I want you to
be a man and a Christian and then I am satisfied. . . . I have such views
of what the man must be to whom I give myself that it would be bit-
terer than gall to find myself bound to one in mind and head mani-
festly unworthy." Perhaps she was thinking of her parents' marriage,
and a father who had lost interest in spiritual matters. "God is not glo-

rified so much by preaching or teaching or anything else as by holy living."

Their marriage was delayed for financial reasons, but there were other problems as well. Booth couldn't find a congenial denomination. Before their engagement, both of them had left the Methodist Church (or were asked to leave) and had joined the Methodist Reformers. However, there was much bickering among the Reformers, and the lay leaders were vying with the clergy for power. So the young couple withdrew from the Reformers. Catherine began attending a Congregational church and encouraged William to study for the Congregational ministry. But the books they gave him to read were too Calvinistic to fit his personal theology. William and Catherine didn't know where to turn until another small Methodist splinter group invited William to take a circuit of churches about one hundred miles north of London. Though it meant parting from Catherine, it was an opportunity he could not pass up.

One of his letters to Catherine describes his feelings: "I am still whirling about the country. Tonight I go back to Spalding; Tuesday to Rinchbeck; Wednesday to Suttleton; Thursday a special sermon at Boston. . . . I wish all this writing was at an end and that you were here, mine, in my arms, and yet I cannot help having fears and doubts about the future. How I wish the Reformers would amalgamate with the New Connexion or with the Association and that all this agitation were ended. . . . But I am always running before to find doubts and fears; mine has always been a restless and dissatisfied life, and I am fearful that it will continue so until I get safe to heaven."

While William was worrying, Catherine was preparing—preparing to be a minister's wife. "I enlarged the scope of my reading, wrote notes and made comments on all the sermons and lectures that appeared at all worthy of the trouble, started to learn shorthand. . . ."

What came easier for Catherine was writing sermons and outlines for her husband-to-be. He was so busy traveling from one of his circuit churches to another that he often dashed off notes to her such as "I want a sermon on the Flood, one on Jonah, and one on the Judgment. Send me some bare thoughts; some clear, startling outline. Nothing moves people like the terrific. They must have hell-fire flashed before their faces or they will not move."

Catherine obliged, although she occasionally reminded him to "watch against mere animal excitement in your revival services. . . . I never did like noise and confusion, only so far as I believed it to be the natural expression of deep anxiety wrought by the Holy Ghost; but my love, I do think noise made by the preacher and the Christians in the church is productive of evil only. I don't believe the Gospel needs such roaring and foaming to make it effective, and to some minds it would make it appear ridiculous, and bar them against its reception forever."

Catherine developed four rules for their future married life: (1) Never to have any secrets from my husband; (2) Never to have two purses; (3) Talk out differences of opinion to secure harmony and don't pretend the differences don't exist; (4) Never to argue in front of the children.

The fact that two of the four had to do with differences of opinion underlines the fact that they were both opinionated people.

One area where they initially differed regarded women. He felt that a woman has more in the heart but a man has more in the head. Strongly disagreeing, she said that she would never marry a man who would not give to woman her proper due. She acknowledged that because of "inadequate education" most women were "inferior to man intellectually. . . . But that she is naturally so, I see no cause to believe."

William seemed to delight in the correspondence. Once he wrote: "I want you to hear me, to criticize me, to urge me on. I feel such a desperate sense of loneliness, so oppressive to my spirit. I speak and preach and act, and it is passed over; there is one with whom I can talk over my performance; to others I cannot mention it for fear of being thought egotistic or seeking for praise, and for some reasons others say little or nothing of it to me." Catherine never seemed reticent to speak out.

At times during the long engagement, Catherine seemed almost too willing to see the marriage postponed. Perhaps she enjoyed the intellectual intimacy more than she might the physical intimacy. But when he became discouraged, she talked radiantly about their future life together: "We will make home to each other the brightest spot on earth; we will be tender, thoughtful, loving and forbearing . . . yes, we will."

After a year on the Spalding Circuit, one hundred miles north of London, William joined another Methodist splinter group called the New Connexion and returned to London for six months of study. Catherine had encouraged him to make the move even though ministers had to wait four years before they were free to marry. William could hardly endure six months of schooling while thousands were dying and going to hell; and he didn't think much of the four years' probation before marriage, either.

Fortunately, his tutor was lenient and allowed William to do more preaching than classroom study; also it was fortunate that the New Connexion made a special exception in William's case and agreed to let him get married after a probation of only one year.

Early in 1855, not quite twenty-six years old, William became an evangelist with the New Connexion. Once again as he was frequently separated from Catherine, he became depressed and lonely. He wrote her: "You know me; I am fitful, very; I mourn over it, I hate myself on account of it. But there it is; a dark column in the inner life of my spirit. You know it." Despite his depression, during four months of evangelistic efforts, he saw 1,739 people profess decisions for Jesus Christ.

In June, William and Catherine, now both twenty-six, finally got married. It was a small and simple wedding with only her father, his sister, and the presiding minister present. After a one-week honeymoon, they left for his next evangelistic foray.

She wanted to accompany him everywhere—for his sake as well as hers—but her health couldn't take it. When Booth left her in London once, she wrote, "I feel as if part of myself were wanting."

A few months later she wrote her parents: "He is kinder and more tender than ever. Bless him! He is worth a bushel of the ordinary sort."

After eight months of an itinerating marriage, she wrote a letter to a friend, extolling her husband's preaching: "My precious William excelled himself and electrified the people. You would indeed have participated in my joy and pride could you have heard and seen what I did. Bless the Lord, O my soul."

The next paragraph was written with a bolder, less refined penmanship. "I have just come into the room where my dear little wife is writing this precious document and snatching the paper have read the above eulogistic sentiments. I just want to say that this very same night she gave me a curtain lecture on my blockheadism, stupidity, etc., and lo, she writes to you after this fashion. However, she is a precious, increasingly precious treasure to me, despite the occasional dressing down that I come in for."

Undaunted, Catherine resumed the letter in the next paragraph. "We have had a scuffle over the above, but I must let it go, for I have not time to write another, having an engagement at two o'clock, and it is now near one. But I must say in self-defense that it was not about the speech or anything important, that the said curtain lecture was given, but only on a point, which in no way invalidates the eulogy."

William loved his evangelistic work, but for one reason or another his fellow ministers in the New Connexion were not always as enthusiastic. So in 1858, after three extremely busy and successful years of evangelism, the Booths were assigned to a small ninety-member charge. But this small parish gave Catherine the opportunity to do some preaching herself.

Despite the fact that William was "always pestering me to begin," Catherine had personally been timid to speak in public. But in 1860, after the birth of daughter Emma, she felt "divinely compelled" to say something in a church service. She said that she heard the devil telling her, "You will look like a fool." In reply, she said, "I have never yet been a fool for Christ. Now I will be one."

The personal word that she gave at the conclusion of the morning service was so well received that she was asked to speak in the evening. That began a speaking ministry in which she often was better received than her husband.

An article in *The Gospel Guide* described Catherine's style: "In dress nothing could be neater. A plain, black straw bonnet slightly relieved by a pair of dark violet strings; a black velvet loosely-fitting jacket, with tight sleeves, which appeared exceedingly suitable to her while preaching, and a black silk dress, constituted the plain and becoming attire of this female preacher. . . . Her delivery is calm, precise, and clear without the least approach to formality or tediousness."

Each year for four successive annual conferences, William waited for the New Connexion to reassign him back to evangelistic work. He felt he had been divinely called to evangelism and that the denomination was resisting the will of God. He couldn't understand why they didn't allow him to be an evangelist.

Catherine urged him to leave the denomination; William was cautious. He had a conservative streak. Catherine explained: "I do not see any honorable course for us but to resign at once, and risk all. But William is afraid. He thinks of me and the children; and I appreciate his loving care, but I tell him God will provide."

After the denomination's 1861 conference, the Booths left. With four young children and with no visible means of support, they stepped out in faith. To help with the finances, Catherine sold the piano. For the next four years, William, sometimes with Catherine by his side, conducted evangelistic missions up and down England.

Frequently Catherine had to stop to have a baby or to restore her health or to stabilize her young family; William had his ups and downs as well.

Once when Catherine was back in London he wrote her: "I have not been in very good spirits today. I have been looking at the dark side of myself. In fact, I can find no other side. I seem to be all dark, mentally, physically, spiritually. The Lord have mercy on me! I feel I am indeed so thoroughly unworthy of the notice of either God or man."

He was a man of moods. "On bad days, he grew tense and irritable," writes one biographer, "and his children learned to make themselves scarce. Only with Catherine did Booth all his life preserve the lover's tenderness."

After bearing six children in nine years, struggling with a wandering, homeless existence, facing recurrent health problems, and trying to cheer up William, Catherine became depressed herself. During this time she wrote, "I know I ought not to be depressed. I know it dishonors the Lord. But I cannot help it. I have struggled hard, more than anyone knows, for a long time against it. Sometimes I have literally held myself head and heart and hands, and waited for the floods to pass over me. Well, at present, I am under, under, under."

Her youngest baby was suffering from convulsions; she was having trouble paying the bills; she had her hands full with an active brood of children; and her spinal problems seemed to be returning. Meanwhile, William was caught up in the emotional excitement of successful revival meetings in northern England. So he wrote her: "Cheer up. All will be well. Whatever you do, don't be anxious."

He also advised her to seek some diversion. Not long afterwards, she received an invitation to conduct revival meetings herself, entirely apart from her husband, in south London. William encouraged her to accept the invitation, and she did.

The meetings were so successful that they led to more invitations in other parts of London. Soon her husband came to London to join her.

She spoke to two to three hundred prostitutes at a meeting of the Midnight Movement for Fallen Women while William invaded the most neglected and underprivileged sections of the poverty-ridden city. Then came another turning point for the Booths.

"I remember it well," Catherine recalled. "William had come home one night tired out as usual. It was between eleven and twelve o'clock. Flinging himself in to an easy chair, he said to me, 'Oh, Kate, as I passed those gin palaces tonight I seemed to hear a voice saying, "Where can you go and find such heathen as these, and where is there so great a need for your labor?"'"

"I remember," she added, "the emotion that this produced in my soul. This meant another start in life."

It also meant more financial problems. On the plus side it meant for Catherine a permanent home at last. And more importantly, it meant the launching of the East London Mission, which gradually evolved into The Salvation Army.

The process wasn't easy.

As one author puts it, "This delicate and ill-educated man, married to a very sick woman, stood by himself on Mile End Waste and was pelted with garbage by the drunkards who reeled out of their gin palaces to deride and mock him."

William took his oldest son, Bramwell, into an East End pub and showed him the world of drunken women and violent men. Then he told his son, "These are our people. These are the people I want to live for and bring to Christ."

At home, however, William wasn't easy to live with. Perhaps he needed a place where he and Catherine could be alone without the children. His stomach problems caused him to be irritable and harsh-tempered. Undoubtedly he loved his children, but his love often came through more clearly from a distance. They got on his nerves. "His kisses," one writer says, "were more on paper than on their lips."

Biographer Begbie alleges that William was fond of his children, but was "too absorbed by his work, too distracted by anxieties, and too often tired by physical pain to give them the whole and perfect love of a father's heart."

In 1868 Catherine gave birth to her eighth child, the last of the amazing brood of Booth children. In time all of them not only made their personal confessions of faith but also became active in the ministry. When he was sixteen, Bramwell was placed in charge of five Food-for-the-Million shops where the poor could buy food cheaply; by the time he was twenty, he was appointed as his father's Chief of Staff. Their second son, Ballington, was placed in charge of a training home for men when he was only twenty. Their oldest daughter, Katie, began preaching on the streets when she was only sixteen.

Each year the work increased. By 1870, there were a dozen preaching stations, besides evening classes, Ragged Schools, reading rooms, Penny Banks, Soup Kitchens, and Relief of the Destitute and Sick Poor, not to mention a new magazine (with occasional articles from Catherine as well as William), which eventually became known as *The War Cry*.

Somehow, Catherine, besides preaching and teaching and struggling with increasing health problems, had the reputation of being a good homemaker as well. In later years, their eldest son, Bramwell, described his mother this way: "She not only patched our clothes, but made us proud of the patches." A visitor who stopped in for tea was surprised to find Catherine darning her husband's socks.

When William got gastric fever, a daughter got smallpox, and Catherine herself became ill again, depression returned: "My soul seems dumb before the Lord. A horror of great darkness comes over me at times. But, in the midst of it all, I believe He will do all things well."

It was in 1888, when the Booths were nearly sixty and The Salvation Army had become international with their children spreading the message into distant lands, that Catherine discovered a small cancerous growth on her breast. She was given about eighteen months to live.

She told her husband: "Do you know my first thought? My first thought was that I regretted that I should not be here to nurse you when you came to your last hour."

It was a blow for William. He wrote in his diary: "I am sixty years old, and for the first time during all these long years, so far as memory serves me, has God in His infinite mercy allowed me to have any sorrow that I could not cast on Him." He could not understand it.

Later he wrote: "To stand by the side of those you love and watch the ebbing tide of life, unable to stem it or to ease the anguish, while the stabs of pain make the eyes flash fire and every limb and nerve quivers, forcing cries of suffering from the courageous soul—is an experience of sorrow, which words can but poorly describe."

During the months of her illness, she said she felt as if she were "dying in a railway station." It certainly seemed like it. Urgent telegrams came at all hours, day and night. Lieutenants barged into the house reporting to General William or to Chief of Staff Bramwell. William or Bramwell was always leaving or returning on some Army business.

And Catherine herself was still deeply involved. For several months she continued preaching. When she became too weak to do more, the action came to her. Richard Collier writes in *The General Next to God*, "Her bedroom was the conference room where the finite points of the Army's expanding social policy were now argued and shaped."

Of course, William kept busy. As the months of her illness dragged by, he stayed closer to home. He was trying to keep his mind on writing a book, but it wasn't easy. Sometimes he would break down in tears, moaning, "How can it be? How can it be?" But he continued to arise daily at 6:00 A.M. for a cold bath and two hours' work before breakfast, which was often a boiled egg, buttered toast, and unsweetened hot tea.

It was amazing how rapidly The Salvation Army had grown. By 1890, there were 2,900 centers; about $50 million had been raised for the underprivileged; 10,000 Salvation Army officers were holding 50,000 meetings each week.

By 1890, Catherine had come to the end. She could no longer speak, so she pointed to a wall motto above the mantel, which said, "My grace is sufficient for thee."

After Catherine's death, the Army continued to flourish, but the close-knit Booth family started to unravel. Catherine was the one who had always held the strong-willed family members together. "I am your General first and your father afterwards," William told one daughter. Although they remained in Christian work and their zeal for God continued, six of the eight children eventually defected from The Salvation Army. With their defection, they also became estranged from their father.

One son who remained faithful to the Army and to William was Bramwell, his Chief of Staff. To him, William paid the highest compliment, "You are like her, Bramwell, your mother."

When you put together two determined people like William and Catherine, both of whom came from problem marriages, you wouldn't expect to find the love and commitment that was evidenced by the Booths. They needed each other. At times they admonished one another; at other times, they propped each other up. The fact of the matter is, they loved each other.

It's an unusual army that is founded in love, but, of course, The Salvation Army has always been an unusual army.

Bibliography

Beardsley, Frank G. *Heralds of Salvation*. New York: American Tract Society, 1939.

Begbie, Harold. *The Life of General William Booth*. New York: Macmillan, 1920.

Booth-Tucker, F. deL. *The Life of Catherine Booth*. Old Tappan, N.J.: Fleming H. Revell, 1892.

Collier, Richard. *The General Next to God*. Cleveland: Collins-World, 1976.

Nelson, William. *General William Booth*. New York: Doran, 1929.

5

He Depended on Her

Billy and Nell Sunday

Was Billy Sunday a boy who never grew up?

Why did he always refer to his wife, Nell, as "Ma"?

To what extent did Nell, who was Billy's business manager, control his life?

Billy liked the macho image. After all, it was the Teddy Roosevelt era. But he needed Nell's sure direction. Once he said that his wife "wouldn't take first prize at a beauty show, but she's got more good horse sense than any woman I ever saw in my life." And one thing that Billy respected was horse sense.

Though Billy was always up front and Nell was behind the scenes, they were a team. At first, you might think that it was Billy Sunday, the sensational evangelist, who was sure of himself. But underneath the blustery boldness was a core of insecurity. Billy was mercurial in more ways than one. Nell was hardworking and hardheaded.

Those who worked with both of them loved Billy even though he might fly off the handle once in a while. But when Nell talked, they obeyed.

Evangelism á la Billy Sunday was approached like a business, with Billy as the chairman of the board and Nell as the chief executive officer.

But marriage is more than a business relationship.

You could never be neutral about baseball-player-turned-evangelist Billy Sunday.

Some called him the greatest evangelist since the apostle Paul. Others called him a charlatan, the prototype of Elmer Gantry.

Some likened him to the Renaissance reformer Savonarola. Others said that if he had concentrated on winning souls instead of battling booze, his ministry would have been much more effective.

Some said that his meetings topped everything since Pentecost. Others said that his acrobatic style, his flair for promotion, and his insistence on making sure that finances were amply covered brought discredit upon the cause of Christ.

Sunday once said, "I'd stand on my head in a mud puddle if I thought it would help me win souls to Christ." No doubt, if he had, Nell would have been right there rounding up an audience.

When they first met, Billy was Methodist by background, but nothing by practice. Nell was a strict Scottish Presbyterian. Billy never really had a father; but Nell's father, a prominent ice-cream producer in Chicago, was very concerned, not only about his daughter, but also about the company she kept.

The year that William Ashley Sunday was born, 1862, his father enlisted as a private in the Union Army. He never returned. His widow was left with three boys under five years of age.

She remarried and had two more children. Troubles multiplied for her in the next decade. When he was six, Billy, who did not get along with his stepfather, moved into his grandfather's home a few miles away. One of his brothers was kicked in the head by a horse and had to spend the rest of his life in a home for the feeble-minded. A sister was burned to death when her clothes caught fire as she tended a bonfire. Then in the midst of the depression of 1874, Mrs. Sunday's second husband walked out on her. He apparently couldn't take any more.

When Billy was twelve, he and an older brother were shipped off to a Soldier's Orphanage, were they spent two years. At the orphanage he completed the equivalent of grammar school and learned that, while he wasn't very good in math, he was quite competent in running and fighting.

At fourteen, he returned to live with his grandfather. But both Billy and his grandfather had strong tempers, and the mix was highly inflammable. Billy soon ran away from home. In Nevada, Iowa, he collected three jobs: as a stable boy, an errand boy, and a school janitor; and he was able to earn a high school education in the process.

In 1883, when he was twenty and working as an undertaker's assistant in Marshalltown, Iowa, he played baseball for the local team. When his team won the state championship, Billy attracted the attention of "Pop" Anson, manager of the Chicago Whitestockings, owned by A. G. Spalding.

Billy went directly from the sandlots of Marshalltown to the major leagues. The small-town batboy was awestruck. In fact, he struck out his first thirteen times at bat. In time, however, he established himself as an exciting all-around player.

His lifetime average was a so-so .259 (though he did bat .359 one year), but his fielding and his speed were almost legendary. He circled the bases in fourteen seconds and stole ninety-five bases in one season, a record which, until 1962, was topped by only one other player, Ty Cobb.

One sportswriter commented: "Sunday probably caused more wide throws than any other player the game had ever known, because of his specialty of going down to first like a streak of lightning." He loved to stretch singles into doubles, though he was criticized for taking too many chances. But the fans loved him.

Every day, on his way from the hotel to the Whitestocking baseball field, Billy had to pass a Presbyterian church. It was the church that the team's batboy attended, and the batboy promised Billy that he would introduce him to his sister if he ever showed up in church.

So one Sunday evening, Billy Sunday walked into a youth service of the Jefferson Park Presbyterian Church. The first thing he noticed was Nell Thompson leading the meeting. (She also happened to be the batboy's sister.) Because she had been in charge of the youth meeting, she thought it was her responsibility to invite the newcomer to a forthcoming youth social.

That was the way it all began. The year was 1885. Nell was seventeen, Billy was twenty-two, and the road ahead was anything but smooth.

Helen "Nell" Thompson, who had made her profession of faith in Christ at the age of twelve, was now teaching a Sunday school class as well as being a leader of the youth group, and her father did not like the idea of his daughter running around with an unsaved professional ballplayer who spent his off-season as a locomotive fireman.

Of course, the biggest strike against Billy was that he wasn't a Christian; but besides that, he wasn't educated, and there were no indications that he was cut out for anything else in life except playing baseball.

Billy knew that prospects of developing a serious relationship with the dairyman's daughter were slim, but he didn't give up.

The first big development came a year later in 1886. One Sunday afternoon, after "tanking up" in a saloon in Chicago's Loop, Billy and several of his teammates sat down on the curb. Across the street, a group of musicians—trumpeters, flutists, trombonists—were playing gospel songs. Billy recognized the tunes; they were the songs his mother used to sing to him when he was a boy. Some of them were also sung in Nell's church.

A young man walked across the street and invited the ballplayers to come to the Pacific Garden Mission, where they could hear the stories of former burglars, drunks, and prostitutes who had become Christians at the mission.

None of the other players responded. But Billy accepted the invitation, walked to the mission, and went forward to receive Jesus Christ as his Savior.

Undoubtedly, Nell was a factor in his decision. As Billy put it later: "I was hot on the trail of Nell. . . . She was a Presbyterian, so I am a Presbyterian. Had she been a Catholic, I would have been a Catholic." But there is no doubt that Billy's conversion was genuine.

The change in his life was obvious to his teammates. He gave up drinking, swearing, and gambling. Soon he requested and got a contract that allowed him not to play ball on Sundays. As he traveled with the team to various cities, he frequently gave talks in YMCAs about his conversion. He even joined Nell's church.

However, Nell's father still wasn't satisfied that Billy Sunday was the man for his daughter. Nell had another suitor, a young man from a good family, who seemed to know where he was going and was destined to get there.

As Billy became more serious about Nell, he told her about his past. For the three previous winters he had been dating the daughter of the engineer on the Chicago and Northwestern Railway, where he had been working.

The news shocked Nell. Immediately she responded: "Put on your hat and coat, go out the door, take the next train for Iowa, and fix it up with Clara, before we go any further." Billy put on his hat and coat and went out the door.

A week later, Billy was at Nell's doorstep again. "What did she say when you told her?" asked Nell before she let him in.

"Well," Billy sputtered, "I didn't exactly tell her. I decided to write her a letter instead."

Billy had written the letter, but the handling of the matter didn't please Nell's father. "No daughter of mine," said Mr. Thompson, "is going to go with a fellow who kept a girl on the string for three years." It seemed to be an uphill battle for Billy.

In 1887, while Nell was attending business college, Billy felt that some higher education wouldn't hurt him a bit, especially if he wanted to impress Nell's father. He tried to get into Northwestern University, but his high school credentials weren't strong enough. So in exchange for agreeing to become baseball coach at the university, he was allowed to matriculate at Northwestern's prep school. With a little brushing up at the prep school, he would be able to pass the necessary entrance exams for the university.

But he never got to the university. He didn't need to. The following year, William Thompson, Sr., gave in. Convinced that Billy was a sincere Christian and a passable Presbyterian, Mr. Thompson reluctantly agreed that Billy might even amount to something in this world. In addition, he knew that his daughter was determined to marry no one else, and Nell's determination was something to contend with.

On Labor Day weekend in 1888, Billy and Nell were married in her Presbyterian church. She was twenty; he was twenty-five.

91

Their honeymoon was spent with the Chicago Whitestockings on the team's final road trip of the year. By now Billy was earning a substantial salary as a ballplayer. The following season, Nell frequently accompanied him on the road trips. But of course, when their first child arrived, her traveling days were over.

To complicate their married life, Billy was traded away from Chicago. Traded first to Pittsburgh and then to Philadelphia, Billy was away during much of the summer, but during the winter he was back in Chicago working for the YMCA. The more he became involved in a Christian ministry, the more he felt that this was what the Lord wanted him to do with his life.

Admittedly, he was no great speaker. He says, "When I first started out to be a Christian, I couldn't stand up in a prayer meeting and use three sentences consecutively." But in talking to men individually about their need for Jesus Christ, he was quite effective.

He and Nell talked about whether he should leave baseball and work for the YMCA. But the problem was he had just signed a lucrative three-year contract with Philadelphia. In the past he had sent some of his money to his mother and some to care for his institutionalized brother. Now he also had a wife and baby daughter to support.

Did the Lord really want him to give up baseball and work at one-sixth the salary for the YMCA, which was often six months behind in paying? He didn't know what to do.

He asked the Lord to make it very clear to him. Though it seemed unlikely, he requested the Philadelphia team to release him from his contract. His prayer was: "Lord, if I don't get my release by March 25 [when spring training was scheduled to start], I'll assume you want me to keep playing ball."

On March 17, his release came in the mail. In the same mail, however, he received an offer from the Cincinnati Reds to pick up his contract, providing an attractive salary on a one-year basis.

For Billy that clouded the issue again. Why didn't the Lord make it crystal clear?

He went to Nell and asked her what she thought. She was always good at analyzing difficult problems. And she had no doubts whatever about this one. She responded, "There is nothing for you to consider; you promised God to quit."

For the next two years, Billy and Nell lived on starvation wages at best, but more often on empty promises, while Billy passed out tracts, led prayer meetings, and aided down-and-outers to find "salvation and jobs." It was quite a comedown for a young man who had enjoyed the limelight for the previous eight years.

Then in the financial crash of 1893, the YMCA couldn't even make promises to Billy, and once again he was in a quandary about his future. Just at this time he was asked by evangelist J. Wilbur Chapman, perhaps the outstanding evangelist of the day, to become his "advance man." Eagerly he accepted the opportunity.

Prior to each of Chapman's evangelistic campaigns, Billy went into the city, organized committees, raised money to rent a hall and pay for ads, and trained the volunteer workers. It was great experience.

But in 1895, another traumatic experience engulfed the Sundays. It was during the Christmas holidays. A telegram came from Chapman. It stated simply that he was returning to the pastorate and quitting evangelism. It meant, of course, that they were once again without financial support. Billy and Nell, now with two young children, had no money saved. "We worried and prayed what to do and discussed if I should go back to play baseball," Billy recalled.

A few days later, before any other decisions were made, Billy received an invitation to conduct an evangelistic campaign himself. It was from a small town in Iowa, population one thousand. The size of the town didn't matter at all.

"We knew it was a direct answer to our prayers," said Billy.

But the meetings were scheduled to begin within ten days, and Billy had no sermons. When Billy got there, he found they had no song leader, so he led the singing himself, "though I did not know a note from a horsefly."

As a direct result of the one-week crusade, one hundred decisions for Christ were recorded, and Billy's new career had been launched.

In the next five years Billy held more than sixty revival campaigns in small Midwestern towns. Freewill offerings on the last day of the crusade provided his somewhat uncertain income.

Each year Nell seemed to become more involved. She helped him with organization and soon became regarded as his business manager. After all, she had graduated from business college. "He hated managing finances, and I love figures," she explained simply.

Two more children were born in 1901 and 1907, but Nell spent as much time as she could helping Billy. Besides being his business manager, she also led prayer meetings, conducted Bible classes, spoke at women's meetings, and occasionally even led the singing.

"The children," says William G. McLaughlin, Jr., in *Billy Sunday Was His Real Name,* "were left with their grandparents and later sent to boarding schools."

An article in the Columbus, Ohio, *Citizen* told of one example: "Sunday evening when Billy Sunday had closed an inspiring sermon in Memorial Hall and the people were halting on decision, Nell stepped into the breach, led the choir, and swung several hundred penitents to a public acknowledgment of God." And the beauty of it all was that she was not striving to establish something. No, she was just trying to show herself a real, live helpmate. Just trying to help Billy, that was all.

Sunday's official biographer, William T. Ellis, says, "Mrs. Sunday's influence upon her husband was extraordinary. He was a devoted husband . . . and had complete confidence in her judgment. She was his 'man of affairs.' He made no important decisions without consulting her. She traveled with him nearly all of the time, attending his meetings, and watching over his work and his personal needs like a mother."

After a few years, Sunday's preaching style began to change. At first, he emulated J. Wilbur Chapman's dignified style. But gradually he adopted a more popular, dramatic style, and his audiences were entertained as well as inspired when they attended his revival meetings.

Perhaps it was simply that he began to be himself on the platform. He was no dignified scholar; he was an athlete. His biographer calls him "a gymnast for Christ." The Boston *Herald* later referred to him as "a virile, agile man, sometimes a clown, sometimes a stump speaker, sometimes a minstrel monologuist, sometimes an actor, sometimes a preacher."

One of his most famous sermons was one he customarily addressed to men. It ended with Sunday's version of the poem, "Slide, Kelly, Slide."

At the climax of it, he made a running dive across the full length of the platform. Then he would leap to his feet, imitating the "Great Umpire of the Universe," and yell, "You're out, Kelly."

McLaughlin says, "It was estimated that he walked a mile back and forth across the thirty-foot platform in every sermon—one hundred and fifty miles in every campaign. But it was not merely walking; it was running, sliding, jumping, falling, staggering, whirling, and throwing himself around the platform. He did not remain in one spot or one position for thirty seconds."

His lack of formal education and his humble background frequently caused Billy to feel inferior. He had no theological training at all, so it may have been due to Nell's prompting that he sought ordination in the Presbyterian church. While his acquaintance with Scripture had been growing through the years, he still had huge gaps in his knowledge of theology and church history. Consequently, during his ordination examination, his most frequent answers were, "That's too deep for me," and, "I'll have to pass that one up."

Finally, a friend moved that the remainder of the examination be waived. After all, he said, "God has used him to win more souls to Christ than all of us combined."

Although he was ordained to the Presbyterian ministry, hardly ever was he referred to as "the Reverend Mr. Sunday."

His earliest meetings were conducted in churches; by 1898 he seemed to prefer evangelistic tents, usually erected in a vacant lot near the middle of town. Then, in the early 1900s, he had a wooden tabernacle constructed, replacing the tent. And from then on he required that a wooden tabernacle be constructed in every city he was scheduled to visit.

For several years, Nell was reluctant to have her husband hold meetings in large cities. She kept the statistics and could demonstrate that when a city was larger than thirty thousand, Billy had difficulty being as effective as he would like to be. "When they're larger than that," she said, "it is impossible to reach everybody." Their goal was to see the conversion of 20 percent of the town's population during their crusade.

Actually, in Billy's first ten years of evangelism, 90 percent of his meetings were conducted in cities under ten thousand. Gradually, how-

95

ever, despite the statistics, he and Nell accepted invitations to larger cities. By 1914 he was speaking in such cities as Denver, Pittsburgh, Philadelphia, Kansas City, Detroit, Boston, New York, Chicago, Washington, D.C., Atlanta, and Los Angeles.

Along with the size of the crusades, the size of the Sunday evangelistic team also expanded. His staff in 1917 consisted of nearly a score of workers, including Homer Rodeheaver, the well-known gospel musician. His team also included six women in addition to his wife.

Billy also had a personal masseur, a former prizefighter, on his staff, who gave him a rubdown at the close of each of his strenuous sermons.

Although their oldest son, George, was listed as business manager in 1917, Nell still made the decisions. No important moves were made without her approval. She selected the cities in which to hold campaigns and controlled his schedule. Speaking of her husband, she later said, "While supreme in his own province of preaching, he was otherwise dependent upon me. He fretted if I was not near. He seemed helpless without me."

As a crusade's opening night approached, Billy grew increasingly unpredictable. Sometimes he would lose his temper; at other times when he was slighted or when he imagined an insult, he would sulk in his room like a little boy.

It was Nell's job to be the peacemaker, or, as she put it, "My job is to be the safety valve." During his rest hours, no one was allowed to interrupt him. One biographer called Nell the buffer between Billy and the outside world. Biographer Lee Thomas says that Nell watched over Billy as "a mother hen watches over her chicks."

By 1908 Billy and Nell asked the local committees to provide a private house (or houses) for the entire crusade team. The team would eat together like a family, and each meal took on the atmosphere of a meeting of the board of directors. Billy and Nell would sit at the head of the table and hear reports from each team member. Billy was referred to as "the Boss." Nell was usually called Mrs. Sunday, although some would call her "Ma" as Billy did.

Both of them prayed informally. Nell would pray, "Father, this is Ma. You know Mr. Smith has invited us to come to Pittsburgh. What should we do about it?" Her prayers, like her husband's, were devoid of "thees" and "thous."

Billy's personality was attractive to the team members. He tended to be fun-loving, with a boyish enjoyment of practical jokes. Even though he might lose his temper in the pressure of a difficult situation, he would quickly forgive and forget all about it.

On the other hand, Nell was regarded with respect, but not especially with affection. She expected obedience, and she got it. Extremely hardworking, she called on others to work as hard as she did.

Billy was greeted as a celebrity wherever he went. At fifty-five, he invaded New York City. He was still healthy, slim, and bouncy; his platform antics hadn't changed. Five feet, eight inches tall, he dressed immaculately in a business suit. He hardly looked like a country boy from Iowa.

When opening night came, it was understandable if Billy was a bit tense and excitable. Crowds often lined up outside the tabernacle eight to ten hours before the doors opened. Sometimes police were called upon to escort Billy and Nell into the tabernacle. In his Philadelphia crusade, seventy thousand came to hear him on the first day; thirty-five thousand were turned away in the evening.

In the larger cities Billy often stayed eight to ten weeks; usually the final days of the crusade brought the greatest response. In New York City, for instance, more than seven thousand came forward on the final day.

Each evening before the service began, Billy would rehearse his sermon even though he probably had given it scores of times before in other cities.

And early in the service Billy always introduced his team to his audience. After he presented his assistants, his choir leader, his soloist, and his instrumentalist, he completed his introductions by beckoning Nell. "And this is Ma," he said. It was spoken warmly, with obvious endearment.

A controversial aspect of Billy's ministry was the freewill offering with which Billy paid the salaries of his staff as well as of Nell and himself. Never before had such financial figures been made public. But because they became public and because they were often large, the critics had a field day.

In Sunday's earliest crusades the love-offerings hardly paid to keep his children in diapers. But as he went to larger cities, the offerings increased to what in that day seemed to be astronomical sums.

But Billy had a rationale. He explained it this way: Many more denominations spend several hundred dollars to win a convert for Christ. "What I'm paid for my work makes it only about two dollars per soul, and I get less proportionately for the number I convert than any other living evangelist."

Early in his ministry, during the summer months when evangelistic meetings were not held, Billy would go on the Chautauqua circuit, speaking in small towns across the Midwest. McLaughlin says, "Preachers like Sunday were sandwiched in between performances by ventriloquists, scientific lecturers, hypnotists, opera singers, acrobats, concert violinists, returned missionaries, traveloguists, minstrels, actors, and magicians. These performers were signed up for a season by a managing agency which provided steady work throughout the summer to one town after another."

It was during one such summer circuit that he developed his famous "Booze Sermon." In that day when the Prohibition movement was building up steam, it came to be Billy's most famous sermon. As a result, Billy was in the forefront of the Prohibition movement for a number of years.

How influential he was in the passage of the Prohibition Amendment is questionable. It is also difficult to say whether his "Booze Sermon" helped or hindered his total evangelistic ministry. It is certain, however, that many who came forward to give up drink had no genuine interest in Jesus Christ as Lord and Savior.

In 1910, Billy and Nell bought a home in Winona Lake, Indiana, and moved their family there. They were in good company. Evangelist J. Wilbur Chapman had already retired there, and the Interdenominational Association of Evangelists met there every summer.

The Winona Lake home was a nine- or ten-room bungalow, overlooking the lake. It was rambling, but not pretentious. Billy said that it cost him $3,800 to build. Inside, on the walls, were portraits of various members of the Sunday family, as well as some oil paintings which Nell had painted in earlier years.

Around the house, Billy dressed casually and spent as much time as possible outdoors, doing yard work and tending plants and flowers.

In addition, the Sundays also owned a fruit farm in the Hood River district of Oregon, and they often spent part of their summers there.

A reporter for the South Bend *Tribune* interviewed the Sundays in their Winona Lake home, and some of the informal conversation is revealing.

In the middle of the interview Nell turned to Billy: "Papa," she interrupted, "I wish we could get some grass seed in before the rain."

"So do I."

"Hadn't you better put it in?"

No answer.

"There's a bucket back there. Why don't you use that?"

"All right."

A minute later a pacified Billy Sunday crossed the lawn lugging a big tin wash boiler of grass seed. Then his wife pointed out where he should sow it while she called to young Billy (their youngest son, about ten years old at the time) to go take his music lesson.

One of her children addressed a letter to her: "Dearest Mother, General Manager, General Fix-it, General All-around healer of the troubles of the world." That's the way she was regarded by those closest to her.

Billy loved Nell. There's no question about that. His personal letters are filled with warm phrases: "Lover, I can hardly wait to be with you again."

The peak years for Billy and Nell were 1914 to 1918. When World War I ended, Billy's major ministry slowed down as well. He had conducted campaigns in virtually all of America's major cities. Now his campaigns were once again in the secondary cities.

But some things were disturbing. Billy's best friend J. Wilbur Chapman ("Next to the members of my family, I loved him more than anyone else") died in 1918.

Then there were family problems, problems that "Ma," though she may have been regarded as "General Fix-it" by her family, was unable to fix. Their oldest son, George, who had assisted as business manager of the New York campaign, attempted suicide in 1923. In 1929 he was arrested for auto theft and jumping bail. In 1930 he was divorced, and in 1933 he jumped from a sixth floor window and sustained injuries from which he later died.

Their second son, Billy Jr., was divorced in 1927, remarried in 1928, and divorced again in 1929. The grounds were extreme cruelty. At the age of 37, he died in an automobile wreck near Palm Springs, California.

Their youngest son, Paul, who earlier had left for Europe after piling up debts for his parents to pay, died at the age of 33 in an airplane crash.

But it was the death of their only daughter, Helen, that was perhaps the most crushing of all. Plagued with physical problems much of her life, she succumbed to pneumonia when she was 42. Nell described her husband as "terribly broken."

That was the year Billy had his first heart attack. He was preaching in a church in Des Moines, Iowa. He staggered, and his song leader rushed to catch him. But Billy refused to halt the service. He begged his song leader to give the invitation for him, while he continued to lean against the pulpit for support. "I'd rather die on my feet than quit now," he said. The invitation was given and many responded.

Billy recovered from that attack, but two years later, at the age of seventy-three, he was stricken again and died. He had given "Ma" instructions regarding his funeral: "No sad stuff when I go."

Shortly before his death, Billy wrote, "I care not what is said about me. . . . I am and always have been plain Billy Sunday, trying to do God's will in preaching Jesus and Him crucified and arisen from the dead for our sins."

During his career he had spoken to more than 100 million people and he had seen approximately one million walk the sawdust trail.

Nell survived Billy by more than twenty years, living in Winona Lake, Indiana, until the time of her death.

Bruce Lockerbie, in his book on Billy Sunday, wrote, "Perhaps no other woman in the history of American Christianity has held such a place in the life of her husband. . . . He depended on her."

As the star on stage, Billy had his name in lights, but it was Ma who was the producer and director.

Bibliography

Ellis, William T. *Billy Sunday: The Man and His Message.* Philadelphia: John C. Winston, 1936.

Lockerbie, D. Bruce. *Billy Sunday.* Waco, Tex.: Word, 1965.

McLaughlin, W. G., Jr. *Billy Sunday Was His Real Name.* Chicago: University of Chicago Press, 1955.

I Would Not Trade You for Anything

William and Mary Bryan

On his wife's wedding ring he had inscribed "Won, 1880/One, 1884." The first year was their engagement, the second was their marriage.

But William Jennings Bryan isn't known today for winning anything. He ran for president three times on the Democratic ticket and lost each time. He served as President Wilson's secretary of state and resigned just prior to the outbreak of World War I. He argued the Scopes "Monkey Trial" against Clarence Darrow, and though court records indicate he won, the verdict of modern society is that he lost.

An orator, he is caricatured today as a pompous windbag, conceited and narrow-minded. His sharp-tongued contemporary, H. L. Mencken, called Bryan "a charlatan, a mountebank, a zany without sense or dignity . . . a peasant come home to the barnyard." Obviously, Will wasn't universally loved. But admirers called him the greatest lay preacher in American history.

And his wife Mary? What was it like to be married to a politician who lost more often than he won, and who was booed by his own party at the last convention he attended?

Like the trainer-manager of a prizefighter, Mary was always in his corner, encouraging him, advising him what to do in the next round, and dressing his wounds when he returned to his corner.

Mary accepted him as he was: a political progressive and theological conservative. He was a hard man for most people to figure out, but

Mary, of course, wasn't like most people. She had him all figured out. After all, she had helped make him. And she worked with him to preserve their storybook romance, which began in their college days.

They were both in college when they first met; he was nineteen, she was eighteen. The year was 1879 and the occasion was an open house at the Jacksonville Female Academy, which the fellows at neighboring Illinois College (now Illinois State University) dubbed "the Jail for Angels."

On one side of the room were the coeds in crinolines and upswept hairdos; on the other side were the boys. In between the two factions, which were nervously eyeing each other, were the refreshments—several plates of cookies and a giant urn of tea.

As the two sides edged toward the center, Will Bryan noticed a girl with large gray-brown eyes. Over one of the plates of cookies—and Will was often captivated by cookies—he began talking with her. He liked her sense of humor. He liked the way she looked. In fact, he liked everything about her. In a word, he was smitten.

Mary was not. She had to admit that Will was "a handsome, broadshouldered six-footer," but his nose was prominent, "too large to look well," and his black hair "was parted with distressing straightness." Yet, she had never seen such a smile. It was the broadest she had ever seen. Someone said later, "That man can whisper into his own ear."

But what bothered Mary about Will was that he seemed "too good." One biographer says he "oozed rectitude." Mary thought so too, but then decided it is better to have a man who is "too good" than one who is "not good enough," and so she decided to see him again.

Will was rooming at the home of a local physician whose wife had become an incurable matchmaker. Convinced that Mary Baird would be the ideal catch for Will Bryan, she praised each of them to the other and set up a neutral meeting place at the home of Will's Latin professor.

When Mary's mother became ill and was hospitalized in a Jacksonville sanatorium, Will had an even better excuse to be with her. From the sanatorium, they took buggy rides together, and that got them into trouble. Though they had her mother's permission, Mary's school did not allow such unchaperoned excursions. So Mary was suspended for the rest of the semester.

To make sure that Mary would not have another secret rendezvous with Will Bryan before she returned home, the principal personally escorted her to the train and waited until the train left the depot before he returned to school. What he didn't know was that Will was hiding in the baggage car. As soon as the train was in motion, he found his way to Mary's side.

The train ride was a turning point for Mary. Earlier, she had been uneasy about Will. Though he had a sense of humor, he wasn't carefree. He seemed too serious about life. He was goal-oriented. The questions he asked her were serious questions, questions about what she wanted to be in life, how important Jesus Christ was to her, and what her devotional practices were. No one had ever pinned her down on such matters before. At first, the questioning seemed almost like an invasion of privacy. But then she began to value a person who was interested in what was really important in life and was also interested in her personally.

On the train, Mary realized that she and Will were going the same direction in life.

The following fall, when Mary was allowed to return to school, Will wasted no time. With fifty dollars he won in a speaking contest, he bought a ring, and on Thanksgiving Day he traveled to Mary's home to ask her father's approval.

Her father, Mary says, was "a gentleman of the old school, tall, dignified and very reserved." He was enough to scare any twenty-year-old.

"Hope you will not be frightened," Mary wrote Will before his mission, "though I imagine it would be a rather disagreeable task." Her father could be rather stubborn, she warned, but even if he said no the first time, his mind could be changed. "There is a party concerned who can and will manage him," Mary wrote confidently.

Will guessed that the best way to approach his father-in-law would be to quote some Scripture. "Mr. Baird, I have been reading Proverbs a good deal lately, and I find that Solomon said, 'Whoso findeth a wife, findeth a good thing, and obtaineth the favor of the Lord.'"

Baird knew where the young man was headed and after a moment responded slowly, "Yes, I believe that Solomon did say that; but Paul suggests that while he that marrieth doeth well, he that marrieth not doeth better."

Bryan's college debate training had prepared him well. He cleared his throat and then responded: "Yes, Paul did say that, but we should consider whenever there is a disagreement on a subject, who is the greater authority. It seems to me, sir, that Solomon would have to be regarded as the greater authority on the subject of marriage. After all, Paul was never married, but Solomon had many wives."

Will won Mr. Baird's consent, but it took four more years before he and Mary said their vows.

Much of their courtship was done by correspondence, though Mary was less than happy about Will as a letter writer. It wasn't that he didn't write frequently; it was rather that he tended to be pontifical, didactic, and absent-minded when he wrote. Too often, he sounded like a lawyer or a minister rather than a suitor. Mary simply expressed herself honestly. If she was angry, she would say so. If she felt he was cold and stiff, she would say so. Fortunately, Will accepted her refreshing honesty, and he also had the grace to be able to laugh at himself.

Occasionally his letters show his sense of humor. Once he wrote, "How do you think I look without my mustache? As I shaved off that long-petted and delicately fondled evidence of manhood, I was deeply impressed with that awful truth that it is easier to destroy than to create. The result of weeks of patient, weary watching gone in a moment."

Will the suitor had more serious concerns than his mustache. Courtship was only one of three crucial matters on the docket during his college years. The other two were spiritual and vocational decisions.

Since his father was a Baptist and his mother a dedicated Methodist, Will as a child had decided to go to a Baptist church on Sunday mornings and to a Methodist church on Sunday evenings. But when the Presbyterians in town had revival meetings, he went to the Presbyterian church, and it was there at age fourteen that he had his conversion experience. Although it was a serious commitment to Jesus Christ, it did not greatly alter his lifestyle. "Having been brought up in a Christian home, conversion did not mean a change in my habits of life or habits of thought. I do not know of a virtue that came into my life as a result . . . because all the virtues had been taught me by my parents."

At college, however, Will was introduced to some thorny religious issues: the theory of evolution, whether the Flood really happened, whether the Scriptures were scientifically reliable, and others. Once he even wrote to Robert Ingersoll, the noted agnostic, to get input from him.

But the internal struggle didn't last long, and Will, believing there must be "a Designer back of the Design, a Creator behind the Creation," committed himself increasingly to the authority of the Bible.

Vocationally, too, Will vacillated for awhile. When he was eight, he had thought he might become a Baptist preacher. He changed his mind when he realized that he would have to be immersed first. As a ten-year-old he thought about becoming a pumpkin farmer, but pumpkins failed to keep him excited. However, when he was twelve his father ran for a seat in the House of Representatives and lost by only 240 votes. The excitement of the campaign was enough to make Will resolve to become a politician. Committing his life to Jesus Christ at age fourteen didn't change his commitment to politics; it only meant that henceforth he resolved to become a *Christian* politician.

At college Will distinguished himself as valedictorian of his class and as the best backward broad jumper in the area. He also became increasingly adept at speechmaking.

After college, Will enrolled in law school in Chicago, causing a two-year separation from Mary. He wrote her prolifically and begged her for patience regarding marriage. Before getting married he wanted to finish law school and get settled as a lawyer. He said that as soon as he made as much as five hundred dollars a year as a lawyer, he would make Mary his bride.

While at law school, he became a notary public. On his first official document, he penned: "I, W. J. Bryan, a notary public in and for the County of Cook, State of Illinois, do hereby certify that I this day appeared before myself and being duly sworn, deposed and said that I loved and do love Mary E. Baird better than I do anyone else in the world and further that I always will love her, will be good to her and contribute as largely as possible to her happiness and usefulness." Though the document was playful, Will meant the sentiment.

After law school, returning to his college town of Jacksonville, Will joined a law firm. On July 4, 1883, he hung out his shingle. (Will always enjoyed doing memorable things on special days.)

In his first month of practice he earned only nine dollars and sixty cents.

Later, he recalled those early days: "I remember with what anxious expectation I nailed up my modest sign, 'W. J. Bryan, Lawyer,' on the doorpost and awaited the rush of clients. I use the word 'awaited' advisedly, because waiting was the word. . . . The days passed wearily. There was a continuing tread upon the stairs leading up to the second floor where the firm's offices were and I would turn to the door each time I heard a hand upon the knob, only to find that the visitor had turned into the office of Mr. Brown, Mr. Kirby, or Mr. Russell."

Will briefly entertained the notion of moving to Kansas or New Mexico, where there were fewer lawyers and more opportunities to earn enough income to support a wife. But Mary was patient and hopeful, "as she would be in all dark hours," according to one biographer. "Don't be discouraged," she wrote him as their engagement was completing its third year. "You're going through the narrows now."

The following year, 1884, was a bit more rewarding for Will, and by summer they were making wedding plans. "I am practicing on 'and with all my worldly goods I thee endow' so as to make it duly impressive," Will wrote. "If you dare laugh when I say that, I won't kiss you when he tells me to salute the bride."

On October 1, 1884, four years after their engagement, they exchanged their vows. On Mary's wedding band, Will inscribed, "Won, 1880/One, 1884."

Though Will had started building a house in Jacksonville for his bride, he hadn't been able to complete it by their wedding day—even after a four-year engagement. So, after their honeymoon, they had no place to live. Will's solution? He would return to his law practice in Jacksonville, while Mary would return temporarily to her parents' home

140 miles south. Since they both prided themselves in practicality, they agreed on the arrangement.

But it didn't work.

Mary had endured a four-year long-distance engagement with patience, but she didn't want to suffer through a separation after marriage. Consequently, a couple of weeks later, she packed her suitcase and went to Jacksonville to be with her husband. Their home still wasn't completed, but they lived with friends until it was.

Mary had a mind of her own. She let Will chart the course, but if the ship seemed to be headed toward the rocks, she took over as co-pilot. Will really didn't mind. His mother had been the same kind of woman.

Mary was more than an assistant; she was a full partner. Plans were made cooperatively. For instance, one of the first matters they discussed was what to do with their leisure time. Their friends had urged them to take up tennis and join some social groups. But Will and Mary decided to devote their spare time to study. Will resolved to read books on the economy; as a romantic birthday present Mary would give him a book on railroad legislation. Mary meanwhile joined a German conversation club, took a course in early English, and began reading her husband's law books.

According to one biographer, Mary "did not take eagerly to housework." Instead, she enjoyed stretching her mind and interacting with her husband on legal issues. But life wasn't merely intellectual in the Bryan household. At least it wasn't after their first child was born, which happened one day short of their first wedding anniversary. And then Mary's parents moved in. They needed Mary's care. Her mother had been chronically ill, and her father was going blind.

To outsiders it may have looked as if Will and Mary Bryan were settling in for a long stay in Jacksonville, Illinois. Not so. Will was restless. He felt there was more for him to do than practice law and raise a family in a small midwestern town. Though he was serving as president of the local YMCA and teaching a Sunday school class, he felt confined. He wanted to become involved in politics, but the political bosses of downstate Illinois did not look kindly on young upstarts like Bryan.

So in 1887, on his return from a business trip to Lincoln, Nebraska, Will asked Mary if she would consider a move there. "You know Jacksonville," she responded. "You have seen Lincoln. If you think that a change is for the best, I am willing to go." So were the in-laws. (It was important that the in-laws also be willing to move, because Will and Mary needed a down payment for a new home in Lincoln, and Mary's father could provide one interest-free.)

On October 1, their wedding anniversary, Will went to Lincoln, leaving Mary, their two-year-old daughter, and his in-laws temporarily behind. He promised to send for them as soon as he had built a house. (Leaving his wife behind while he looked for housing developed into a habit.) In Lincoln, he slept on a folding cot in his office and lived on a diet of apples and gingersnaps.

When they were all reunited in Lincoln, the Bryans picked up where they had left off in Jacksonville. Once again he began teaching Sunday school and leading the YMCA. Mary wasn't too happy about Will's YMCA involvement. The YMCA's men's meeting was held each Sunday afternoon at 4:00, a time when Mary thought Will should be home with his family. "The men's meeting would break up the afternoon and take him from us," Mary lamented. "We laid this sacrifice on the altar, but with unwilling hands, and I doubt if the recording angel gave us any credit."

Will did find time, however, to lead his family in daily devotions, consisting of Scripture reading, prayer, and singing a hymn.

Both Mary and Will, now in their late twenties, started men's and women's discussion groups that soon involved the city's leadership. In a few months, Will became chairman of the city's Democratic committee. As he began making political speeches throughout the area, his oratory captivated the crowds.

He even astonished himself. The morning after one political speech, he told his wife, "I have had a strange experience. Last night I found that I had power over the audience. I could move them as I chose. I have more than usual power as a speaker. I know it. God grant that I may use it wisely." On their knees they prayed together, committing this talent to God.

Meanwhile, Mary continued to pore over Will's law books. After taking the necessary courses at law school, the only woman in her class of seventeen, she passed the bar examination and finished third in her class.

Why did she study law? She wanted to share as much as possible in her husband's life. "If a wife does not show an interest in her husband's work and does not go with him when he asks her, the time may come when he will cease to ask her." Studying law was simply one way to share Will's interest.

In 1890 Will, now thirty, ran for U.S. Congress. Because the area was strongly Republican, Mary thought it might be a waste of time for him to run as a Democrat. Besides, his opponents ridiculed him as "effervescent as a bottle of soda pop" and as a "calamity howler." But he waged an effective campaign and won easily.

Winning that election was only one hurdle. At times, rough political criticism bothered Mary. She knew Will better than the critics, and she knew that 99 percent of what they said of him wasn't true. He was nicknamed the "Boy Orator of the Platte." True, said an opponent, for "at its mouth the Platte is six miles wide and six inches deep." Such statements bothered Mary at first, but after a few political campaigns she understood that she couldn't take campaign oratory too seriously.

The next move was to Washington, D.C., though once again Will left Mary behind while finding a home. Then with three children and Mary's father (Mary's mother had died shortly before the election), Will and Mary went East for his two terms as a U.S. Congressman.

According to Louis Koenig, "Bryan was a latter-day Jeffersonian, jealous of liberty, confident of local government, suspicious of distant Washington, and respectful of the virtues of the small farmer." And his convictions made him bold. Despite his youth and freshman status, Will was not bashful in Congress. He quickly gained a reputation for his debating skills. And when Will spoke on the floor of Congress, Mary was often seen in the gallery, nodding, frowning, and making other signs for Will's benefit. Mary memorized Will's first major Congressional speech and, as he was delivering it on the floor, her lips were moving in the gallery in unison with his.

Mary was also his research assistant. When a major issue was scheduled to be discussed, Mary went to the Library of Congress to get as much background as she could for her husband. They worked together on answering his mail and frequently collaborated on his speeches.

As far as housework was concerned, Mary was pleased to be able to hire girls to handle it. She was a better executive assistant than she was a maid. She and Will shunned the Washington social whirl, but their youth and exuberance made them popular figures anyway.

Their oldest daughter, Ruth, a precocious child, was often asked questions by reporters. Once a reporter during a national election asked her whether she thought her father would be elected. She responded, "I don't know about the rest of the nation, but I think he will get a lot of votes on our street."

Their second child was a boy. William was described by his father as a "regular boy." His father also said, "How a boy like that ever lives through childhood is a mystery." One day Mary looked out the windows and saw young William working his way along the telephone wires, hand over hand. Frequently, when Will and Mary went visiting, they would have their conversation interrupted by a shriek when someone spotted William on top of a roof or hanging precariously from a slender limb of a tree.

Their third child, Grace, was quiet and studious, often in poor health.

Mary, busy as a mother and as a political aide to Will, adapted well to Washington. Though she enjoyed Lincoln and Jacksonville more, she liked challenges, and Washington politics was certainly a challenge. Koenig says, "A woman of intellect, she handled easily the current topics of political debate, knew the political personalities Bryan dealt with, and was shrewder than he in assessing them. Her chief indulgence was a Wednesday morning swim with the ladies. She gave little attention to dress, for which the Eastern press one day criticized her."

Apart from Mary, Will didn't make close friends. He loved people collectively, but "kept them at arm's length individually."

111

Still in his early thirties, he didn't hesitate to contradict the party bosses and even President Grover Cleveland when he felt it necessary, even though he was a member of the same political party.

After two terms in the House, he ran for the Senate in 1894 and easily won Nebraska's popular election, capturing 75 percent of the votes. But in the 1890s senators were chosen by the state legislature. The legislators snubbed Bryan and chose a man who received only 2 percent of the popular vote.

Rejection like this bothered Mary more than it did Will. After the loss, Mary came to him and said, "Will, do a favor for me."

"As long as it's not the impossible," he responded.

She asked him to give up politics and devote himself to his law practice.

"Mary," Will answered, "you have asked the impossible."

What Mary didn't realize then was that Will was almost on the verge of an even more demanding political race: the campaign for president.

The financial depression of 1893 made the economy the major issue of the day, and Will felt strongly that the answer to the nation's woes was the free coinage of silver and a graduated income tax. On behalf of these issues and others as well, Will was invited to speak throughout the West and South. He also was named editor-in-chief of the *Omaha World-Herald,* a title which required him to write editorials and shape the paper's editorial policy.

When the Democratic Party seemed to be bewildered and unable to find a candidate to succeed Grover Cleveland, Will volunteered a solution. He dashed off letters to the party chiefs declaring that he would consent to be the nominee for the nation's highest office if they couldn't find anyone else.

The thought was ridiculous. One said, "Here was a man barely thirty-six, living in a comparatively unimportant Republican state west of the Mississippi River, audaciously announcing his probable candidacy for the presidential nomination. . . . Absurdity!"

So Will was certainly the darkest of the dark horses at the national convention in Chicago in 1896. But during the meeting, he stepped to the podium and delivered his famous "Cross of Gold" address. Though he had not even been officially listed as a candidate, his dramatic oration catapulted him to the forefront. On the fifth ballot, the young nobody from Nebraska won the nomination.

Though Bryan won the nomination, he had split the party. New York's Tammany Hall politicians refused to support him and sat on the sidelines during most of the campaign.

Will had a chance to win some of them over when he opened his Eastern campaign in New York's Madison Square Garden. Only a few of the party bosses showed up, but twenty thousand New Yorkers didn't want to miss it. Knowing the importance of the occasion and fearing that he might be misquoted by the Eastern press, Will decided to read his speech rather than present it in his usual dramatic style. When Mary found out, she was horrified. She begged him not to be foolish enough to change his usual style. But Will felt it was more important to impress the reporters with a solid, substantial address.

It was a hot, sultry evening. Will's message was ninety minutes long, and many of the bored New Yorkers walked out before the speech was one hour through.

Mary had been right, and Will's chance to be president of the United States may have been lost by his refusal to heed his wife's advice.

After that, the campaign was uphill all the way. Mary campaigned at Will's side, coaching him with his speeches, helping him conserve his strength, explaining his positions to reporters, and making arrangements with reception committees at various whistle-stops.

A decided underdog, Will started climbing week by week. During the four-month campaign, he made 3,000 speeches and traveled 18,000 miles.

When the ballots were counted, he lost the election by 500,000 votes to William McKinley. A shift of only 20,000 votes in a few key states would have won him the presidency.

Whether any Democrat could have won after the economic recession of Cleveland's term in office is questionable, for the unemployed and hard-pressed had switched to the Republican side. But Bryan's vigorous campaign made it surprisingly close.

Back home in Lincoln, Will began to write a book. It was entitled *The First Battle.* For the thirty-six-year-old politician there were more battles to come.

As usual, Mary was at his side in the battles. Up at five each morning, she began to open the mail, which sometimes totaled 2,500 pieces a day. At seven, she woke the children and Will. Since Will, when he was home, liked a hearty breakfast, she usually prepared eggs, sausages, and waffles to start the day. Will especially liked waffles, but his favorite food was radishes. He could eat radishes day or night. When he traveled, he carried a package of radishes with him on the train. The way he stuffed radishes into the pockets of his suit coats ruined the shape of his clothes.

Radishes weren't the only items in his pockets, however. He frequently crumpled up telegrams and letters and stashed them into his pockets as well. It was up to Mary to unload his pockets when he returned home.

"What if he did fill his pockets with wadded-up telegrams?" Mary once said somewhat defensively. "He never lost any."

Traveling was a problem for Will in another way. His suitcases were never big enough. Biographer J. C. Long writes: "No matter how large his suitcase, he couldn't seem to make his things fit into it. Unless Mrs. Bryan was at hand to pack it for him, he would pile in the articles and then step on them until they were sufficiently mashed down to permit the closing of the lid."

Will never changed his style of clothes in forty years. He wore a black frock alpaca coat, a black string tie, and a broadbrimmed hat. His clothes were a trademark that he never changed.

His desk, disorderly in the extreme, was another trademark. Mary likened Will to a squirrel, hiding things in various places in his desk. It may have looked helter-skelter, but when he needed something "he seemed to know exactly where to dig. His eye would roam over the different piles. Then suddenly he would dig down and he very seldom failed to bring up the required document."

Mary said that as disorderly as his desk was, his mind was a neat filing cabinet. Items filed into his mind were retained for years and could be brought out again at a moment's notice during a critical debate.

But it was up to Mary to do the filing. Will seldom had time for much original research or reading. He depended on Mary. She "plodded through heavy books in order to give him the leading thoughts

114

and help form for him a background of erudition which he was too busy to acquire unaided."

During these years of intense political involvement, the Bryans gave freely and generously to needy causes. One evening, when the doorbell rang at their Lincoln home, Will and Mary were surprised to find a Japanese lad at the door. They asked what he wanted and he responded that he wanted an education. Having read one of Will's spellbinding speeches and convinced that Bryan could do anything, he came to Lincoln to enlist their aid.

Will and Mary agreed to let him stay overnight in their home until they could make other arrangements with the Japanese consul. But the young man stayed in their home for five years and finally graduated from the University of Nebraska, with Will and Mary providing room, board, and tuition.

Mary admitted that Will was often taken in by people. He was too gullible. Mary once wrote, "His universal friendliness implied a trust which was at times misplaced, and his patience and forbearance sometimes tolerated unworthy men about him."

But Mary insisted that though he was sometimes wrong about individuals, he was seldom wrong about the public as a whole. A newspaper editor once told Mary: "I watch which way people are going and run around the corner and get in front of them. Bryan takes a place in advance and the people follow him."

Will discussed most major issues with Mary. They didn't always agree. Sometimes Mary tempered Will's position; at other times, he held it in spite of Mary.

"Isn't that an extreme position?" Mary might say. "If you stand for that, people will call you a fanatic, a wild-eyed reformer."

"But I must stand there," Will would respond. "All progress comes through compromise, not a compromise of principle, but an adjustment between the more radical and the less radical. If I begin far in advance, when the compromise is made, our position will be much ahead of the place I would have secured by a less radical position."

Many of his positions were radical at the time. He pushed for an income tax, an anti-trust law, women's suffrage, a League of Nations, a minimum wage, and the popular election of senators long before these issues were enacted into law.

Quoting the Bible verse, "The common people heard him [Jesus] gladly" (Mark 12:37) he liked to think of himself as a commoner, championing the rights of the working class. One biographer says, "Bryan, the pioneer, cut down the trees of the political forest, pulled up the stumps, plowed the soil and planted the seed. Others reaped the harvest. . . . Bryan seldom won a battle, but every defeat eventually turned into a triumph." Franklin Roosevelt said that Bryan was the embodiment of the man who would rather be right than president. "He did not have to dare to do what to him seemed right," Roosevelt said. "He could not do otherwise."

When the Spanish-American War broke out, Will volunteered his services and was made a colonel, leading a regiment from Nebraska. Politically, it was a gamble, but Will didn't join the army for political reasons. He simply felt that during a time of war it was the duty of a thirty-eight-year-old man to be in uniform. As soon as the war ended, Will returned to become, for the second time, the Democratic candidate for president. This was 1900. Once again, he lost to William McKinley.

Mary's political role had been increasing. Frequently, she wrote the editorials for the Omaha newspaper. During the campaign she served as Will's press agent, handling reporters with grace and quiet humor.

In 1905, the year after Mary's father died, she and Will embarked on a round-the-world trip. Financed by the Hearst newspaper chain, the tour cost Will and Mary nothing.

In Japan, Will and Mary were warmly welcomed, partly because people had heard of the way they had "adopted" a Japanese student in their home. While there, they received letters from thirty-two other Japanese youths wishing to be "adopted."

However, the Bryans had some awkward moments in Japan. At a banquet honoring Admiral Togo for his naval victory over the Russians, Will toasted him with water instead of champagne. At first the Japanese were offended, but Will, always quick with a response, said, "Admiral Togo, you have won your great naval victory on water, so I drink to you in water. When you win a great victory on champagne, I will drink to you in champagne."

Will and Mary followed the customs of taking off their shoes whenever they entered a Japanese home. But there were no slippers in Japan big enough to accommodate Will's feet. He endured several days in his stocking feet before buying the biggest slippers he could find and then cutting away the toes to make room for his large feet.

In Russia, they met with the czar and novelist Leo Tolstoy. They struck up a friendship with Tolstoy that lasted several years.

When they returned to America, it was time for Will to plunge into yet another political campaign. After gaining his third presidential nomination, he campaigned against William Howard Taft. The year was 1908. For the third time Will lost, and this loss was the most decisive of his three attempts. "My only regret," he told his daughter Grace, "is that your mother will never be the First Lady of the Land to the nation, as she has always been to me."

Four years later, Will had another opportunity to run. This time, Mary urged him to do so, and her reasoning was sound. The Republican Party was divided, and this was an opportune time for the Democrats to win. Besides, "I wanted him to take the nomination," she said. "I wanted him to be president. I wanted him to conquer his enemies. We had worked so long and so hard."

But Will, now fifty-two, felt that someone else should be the candidate this time, and he backed Woodrow Wilson. His backing insured Wilson's nomination.

Will campaigned almost as hard for Wilson as he had previously campaigned for himself. Running against both Taft and Teddy Roosevelt, Wilson won the election, but his total popular vote was less than Bryan had received four years earlier.

Shortly after the election, Will was offered the position of secretary of state, a job he accepted with the provision that he would not have to serve intoxicating liquors at their table during official state functions. (Though Will and Mary had not before been crusading Prohibitionists, they were lifelong abstainers.)

Will's goal as secretary of state was to eliminate war, a rather tall order for anyone. Though not technically a pacifist, he vigorously opposed war as a way for nations to resolve their disputes. Once in office, he wasted no time in getting nations to sign peace treaties with one another. A major accomplishment of his term was the fact that thirty peace treaties were signed within two years.

Will opposed the notion that the way for a nation to fight militarism is to increase its own militancy. Once he said, "Those who advocate the policy of 'fighting the devil with fire' seem to overlook two important factors: (1) the devil is better acquainted with fire than his adversaries; (2) being at no expense for fuel, he has an economic advantage which tells powerfully in any prolonged contest."

Then trouble broke out in Europe. Will worked at being the mediator between Germany and England, trying to maintain neutrality. But his moves were frustrated, sometimes within the president's cabinet itself, but often by German or British diplomats. He watched as the nations drifted toward war and threatened to bring the United States into it.

It was the period of the most intense strain Will had ever faced. He stayed awake nights and then struggled to be ready to face the challenges of the next day. Night after night, Mary stayed up with him, making him tea, soothing him, and trying to get him to rest.

Then when the ship *Lusitania* was sunk by a German submarine, President Wilson drafted a letter to Germany which Will was sure would result in American involvement in the European conflict. It was Will's job to send it. Rather than do so, he offered his resignation.

Before long, America was involved in the war, just as he had feared.

Peacemaking wasn't Will's only concern. No longer officially involved in government, Will and Mary now joined to push for two constitutional amendments. Along with evangelist Billy Sunday, they campaigned for Prohibition, and just as ardently they campaigned for women's suffrage. Said Will, "I shall claim no privileges for myself that I do not ask for my wife." He said he couldn't understand how men could keep women from voting when "most of what men know about government comes from women schoolteachers."

With her children grown, without her father to take care of, and without political responsibilities, Mary seemed to have time, at age fifty-five, to do something she always wanted to do. Back home in

Nebraska, she wrote, "On the 25th of June I began my music lessons. I have always wanted to play the pipe organ and this seemed an opportunity. People can always learn the things they really wish to know. If we would only keep alive the ambitions of youth until the opportunity comes."

But physical problems soon beset both her and Will. Diabetes plagued Will, who had a gargantuan appetite and never watched his diet when he traveled. Arthritis bothered Mary. Thus in their late fifties they moved to Florida. There they found more tranquility than they had known previously. They began each day reading a few pages of a secular book; then they read a few passages of Scripture before praying together.

Once again, Will was teaching a Sunday school class. He began as a substitute teacher in a small room in the church. Soon the class grew so large that it had to move to the church auditorium. Then, when the class outgrew the church, Will took his students to a nearby ballpark. The attendance fluctuated between two and five thousand. When Florida vacationers asked to receive copies of his lessons throughout the year, Will began to syndicate them in a hundred newspapers across the nation.

Will also continued to be a popular speaker across the country. Each summer he was on the Chautauqua lecture circuit. He could speak anywhere on almost any subject at the drop of a hat. But Mary said that one of the few times she found him at a loss for words was when he was asked to speak at a rescue mission along New York City's waterfront. Will whispered to Mary, "It takes a man who has been saved from the depths to reach men like these. I cannot do it."

Through the 1920 presidential campaign Will continued to be a force in the Democratic Party. He was present at the 1924 Democratic convention, but because of her poor health, Mary was unable to attend. Will missed her advice, encouragement, and comfort. When a reporter noticed that his wife was not present and asked him about her, Will broke down in tears. Then he told of all that she had meant to him, as a wife, as a friend, and as an advisor. He feared that she would not last long, and he hoped that he would not outlive her.

New York City, the site of the 1924 Democratic convention, had always been a political disaster for Will, and in 1924 he faced humiliation there. When he rose to speak, he was booed by the galleries as well as by many of the delegates. "This is probably the last convention of my party to which I will be a delegate," Will said, and the crowd cheered and applauded. Still able to respond graciously, Will countered, "Don't applaud. I may change my mind."

His political life was finished, and he knew it. But he also was aware that his physical life was drawing to a close. His father and grandfather had both died before they were sixty. Will, at sixty-four, felt he was living on borrowed time.

He was increasingly concerned about Mary's health. At times she seemed much improved, but when her severe arthritic seizures struck, she experienced great pain and was confined to a wheelchair.

Will began cutting back on his speaking engagements. When asked to take on a speaking crusade to fight the teaching of evolution, Will responded that he did not want to leave Mary again. "I owe it to her to give her such comfort as I can by my presence."

Through the years their love had deepened. Mary wrote a note to him on his sixty-fifth birthday: "I love you better and better each year and have an increasing desire to do all I can for your comfort and happiness. I would not trade you for anything."

The final event in Bryan's declining years and perhaps the event for which he is best known today was the Scopes evolution trial. A young science teacher named John Scopes in the Dayton, Tennessee, high school was arrested for violating the state law which prohibited the teaching of evolution in public schools. Well-known lawyer Clarence Darrow was brought in for the defense, and Bryan was asked to serve as counsel for the prosecution. He was glad to do so, since he heartily opposed the teaching of evolution. He saw it as a threat to the nation's faith and ethics, and he believed the trial would help the nation see the danger.

The "Monkey Trial," as it came to be known, lasted nearly two weeks in sultry July weather. The trial, because of the two famous figures involved, received much attention from the media. It became a kind of contest between the liberalism represented by Darrow and the Christian fundamentalism represented by Bryan. Journalists at the trial helped form a lingering stereotype of fundamentalists as bigoted, ignorant, and rural.

At a crucial point, Darrow unexpectedly put Will on the stand and questioned him regarding his belief in the literal interpretation of Scripture. Confident that he could answer all of Darrow's questions, he consented to take the stand. It was a mistake. Although a very knowledgeable layman regarding Scripture, he was not a scientist. Many of Will's responses were brilliant, but Darrow was able to twist other answers for his benefit. In two hours of questioning, Darrow made Bryan look narrow-minded and foolish. Fundamentalism was not dead, but it was, for many Americans, discredited.

Ironically, some of Will's answers alienated him from the fundamentalists. For instance, he did not believe that the Creation necessarily took place in six literal days; the "days" could, he said, have been six periods of time. On the other hand, some of his answers seemed quite naive to progressives.

Scopes was found guilty and fined $100, so it can be said that Will's side won the case. But nevertheless, Will and the cause he represented came out as losers.

After the trial, Mary and Will discussed it and the broader issue of separation of church and state. Religious zeal must not encroach upon individual rights and beliefs, he said. Then he asked her if she thought his religious zeal had gone over the line.

"You are all right so far," she answered. "But will you be able to keep to the narrow path?"

"I think I can."

"But can you control your followers?" Mary asked perceptively.

Will's answer came more slowly this time. "I think I can."

It was only five days later that Will passed away as he took an afternoon nap.

The cause of death? His followers said he died because his heart was broken. Clarence Darrow retorted, "Broken heart, nothing. He died of a busted belly." But according to Dr. J. Thomas Kelly, William Jennings Bryan died of diabetes mellitus.

Confined to a wheelchair for the rest of her life, Mary returned to Florida to complete her husband's memoirs. This was a project she and Will had begun before his death. When the book was finally published, more than half had been written by Mary. Perhaps it was fitting, because probably Will would have accomplished less than 50 percent of his life's work without her.

Mary was a remarkable woman, no doubt about that. The daughter of a prosperous small-town merchant, she had been educated in one of the best finishing schools in Illinois. She earned a law degree while raising a family, taking care of her aged and ailing parents, and being separated often from her busy, politicking husband.

Though Will was loving and caring and though he genuinely wanted to see Mary fulfilled and happy, he was absent-minded and self-centered. An optimist and an enthusiast, he was something like a little toy airplane with a wind-up rubber band-powered propeller. Wind held him up and he would sputter off in surprisingly successful flights. Then he would fall abruptly and unceremoniously in Mary's lap. Undaunted and almost oblivious to his previous collapse, he would wind himself up and take off once again in another direction.

Mary understood him and appreciated his genius. At times she had to bring him down to earth.

About two years before Will's death, a noted political figure visited them in Florida and congratulated Will on his good fortune in having found such an able and understanding wife.

"Your marriage was a great romance," the visitor said.

"Still is," replied Will.

Bibliography

Bryan, Mary Baird. *The Memoirs of William Jennings Bryan.* Philadelphia: John C. Winston, 1925.

Koenig, Louis W. *Bryan: A Political Biography.* New York: Putnam's, 1971.

Macartney, Clarence Edward. *Six Kings of the American Pulpit.* Philadelphia: Westminster, 1943.

Russell, C. Allyn. *Voice of American Fundamentalism.* Philadelphia: Westminster, 1976.

Imperceptibly, She Polished Him

Hudson and Maria Taylor

Hudson Taylor was a Yorkshire lad, the son of a small-town druggist.

Half the world away, in Malaya, lived a girl named Maria Dyer. She was an orphan.

From the day Hudson was born, his father had rattled on and on about the exotic land of China. Of course, he never expected to go there, nor did he expect that his son, sickly as he was, would ever go.

When Maria was just a small girl, her father had talked about China, too; she could vaguely remember it. He went and never came back.

By the time Hudson was twenty-three, he had been engaged twice and jilted twice. About this time he wrote a letter home, saying, "There is something in my nature that seems as if it must have love and sympathy." And it was about the same time that he wrote, "Whatever I set my heart on, I lose."

Maria was under the watchful eye of an eccentric schoolmarm who was sometimes mistaken for a witch. When Hudson expressed some interest in Maria, the schoolmarm forced Maria to write a letter to him rejecting him as a suitor.

It looked as if he had lost again.

Hudson Taylor, missionary innovator, founder of the China Inland Mission, father of the faith mission movement, and a nineteenth-century stalwart who exemplified his motto of "living by faith," may seem an unlikely man to be the romantic lead in this true-life drama with Maria Dyer.

And she, the orphan who grew up in a cocoon-like atmosphere and who was expected to emerge as a moth, burst forth as a butterfly.

Yes, Hudson and Maria were both full of surprises.

Fun-loving, brash, affectionate, imaginative, with a hobby of collecting insects, he hardly seems the type to launch a pioneering mission to reach 400 million souls in China's interior.

Man of faith, yes; but he was a romantic at heart. Martin Luther's favorite book of the Bible may have been Romans; John Knox's favorite book may have been Jeremiah; but Hudson Taylor's seems to have been the Song of Solomon.

Together, Hudson and Maria made a great missionary team, although for a while, it didn't look as if they would become teammates at all.

It was Christmas 1856 when they first took a serious look at each other. He was twenty-four; she was nineteen. All the English missionaries housed in the Ningpo, China, compound were guests at a beef and plum pudding dinner given by one of the senior missionaries.

In a way, neither Hudson nor Maria fit in.

Technically, Maria was not a missionary. It was her sister who had accepted a position with the Ningpo mission school under Miss Aldersley, and Maria had tagged along. The two orphaned sisters didn't want to be separated.

As for Hudson, he did not fit in either.

The Ningpo mission compound was a pocket of Victorian propriety on the coast of China. And Hudson Taylor was anything but a symbol of Victorian propriety.

He had come to China under a maverick mission board that required him to live on empty promises. Without any other missionary philosophy, he developed his own. He thought he would be more effective as a missionary if he didn't seem to be a foreigner. So, much to the embarrassment of the rest of the missionary community, Hudson wore Chinese clothing and sported a piebald pigtail. He had a reputation, says biographer J. C. Pollock, "for meandering around China without denomination or settled purpose."

A fellow missionary referred to him as "a mystic absorbed in religious dreams. Not idle, but aimless."

You can imagine what Miss Aldersley thought of him.

Hudson had had a difficult time that year, especially in the previous few months. He had been working out of Shanghai until a fire had destroyed all his medical equipment. Shortly afterward, a servant had robbed him of almost everything he owned.

So he was a sorry, pigtailed sight as he hobbled into the Ningpo compound seeking refuge. Hobbled is the correct word, for he had been wearing the Chinese calico stockings and flat-soled black satin shoes with turned-up toes which were most uncomfortable. Earlier he had written to his sister that "average toes decidedly object to be squeezed out of shape, nor do one's heels appreciate their low position in perfectly flat-soled shoes."

That was when he could joke about it.

But between Shanghai and Ningpo, he had lost his sense of humor.

In Ningpo his discouragement increased. He was in love with a girl ten thousand miles away. He had asked her to marry him and it was taking a long time for her to respond. Whether she loved him or not is hard to tell. She certainly didn't relish the notion of spending the rest of her life in the shadow of the Great Wall of China, married to a man who wore a pigtail and a silk Chinese gown. Her father felt even more strongly than that about it.

Hudson wrote home: "At times I have felt so discouraged . . . that I have . . . even thought of giving up the missionary work, for her father said if I were living in England he would have no objections."

While Hudson was mooning over his unrequited love, a girl he had not previously noticed, Maria, thought that things might be looking up for her.

Eligible young women were not plentiful in Ningpo. In fact, since her sister Burella had just gotten engaged, that left Maria in the field by herself.

Maria, described by Hudson as "a good looking girl, despite the slightest cast of the eye," spoke Chinese fluently, and that may have been what impressed one of the members of the British Consular service so much. But when he proposed marriage to her, she turned him down. And then there was the missionary stationed in Shanghai who had also expressed keen interest in her, but she wasn't interested in him.

Hudson Taylor was another matter. There was something about that pigtailed Yorkshireman that intrigued her. She wrote: "I met a gentleman and, I cannot say I loved him at once, but I felt interested in him and could not forget him. I saw him from time to time and still this interest continued. I had no good reason to think it was reciprocated; he was very unobtrusive and never made any advances."

She decided to pray about it.

Then came Christmas. Maria and her sister were asked to play some duets on the pianoforte. Hudson seemed more impressed with the pianoforte than he was with the musicians.

But from then on, something was different.

Hudson wrote, "Ere I was aware of it, my acquaintance with Miss M. Dyer ripened into an attachment, which, as soon as I perceived, far from encouraging though unable to repress it, I strove to confine the knowledge of it to my own bosom."

He confined it quite well.

A couple of weeks later Maria confided to a friend her feelings about Hudson. The friend remarked that "she had not seen anything which would lead her to think that he was interested in me and remarked that it was a dreadful thing to love without that love being returned."

Biographer J. C. Pollock says cryptically, "Hudson was riding two mares." Gradually he was losing interest in his fiancée in England, but since he had proposed marriage to her, he felt honor-bound to "confine" his interest in Maria as long as possible.

Then he began comparing the two girls. Maria he felt was "a dear sweet creature, [who] has all the good points of Miss S and many more, too. She is a precious treasure, one of sterling worth and possessed with an untiring zeal for the good of this poor people. She is a lady, too."

In March, Hudson was temporarily in Swatow, China. He still hadn't received a reply to his proposal that he had sent several months before to England, but he couldn't wait any longer about communicating his feelings to Maria. He decided to write her a letter.

For Hudson, there was no beating around the bush.

Maria tells of the letter this way: "I had a sort of hope that it might be from Mr. Taylor, but I could not think that it was—that was not likely. . . . I then opened my letter and read of his attachment to me and how he believed that God had given him that love for me which he felt. He asked me to consent to an engagement to him. He begged me not to send him a hasty refusal which he intimated would cause him the intensest anguish."

Walking on air, Maria shared the exciting letter with her guardian and employer, Miss Aldersley, who responded curtly, "I presume you would not think of accepting him?"

Then Miss Aldersley gave several good reasons why she should immediately turn him down. First of all, she said, "He is an unconnected nobody." Besides that, he was not a gentleman, he was not educated, he had no position, he wore Chinese clothes, he was short (while she was tall), and he was associated with the Plymouth Brethren (while she belonged to the Anglican Church).

Miss Aldersley gave Maria no choice. She had to refuse him immediately. So as her guardian watched over her shoulder, Maria penned a letter to Hudson, "My dear sir: I had made the subject of your letter a matter of earnest prayer to God, and have desired I think sincerely only to know His will and to act in accordance with it. And though it does indeed give me no pleasure to cause you pain, I must answer your letter as appears to me to be according to God's direction. And it certainly appears to me to be my duty to decline your proposals. . . . I request you not to refer to the subject again as I should be obliged to return you the same answer."

And so it looked as if the unconnected nobody from Yorkshire and the orphan from Malaya would never get together.

James Hudson Taylor, born in 1832 in the Yorkshire mining town of Barnsley, was converted at the age of seventeen, after reading a gospel tract; six months later he committed himself to go to China as a missionary.

Soon there developed another interest in Hudson's life; he fell in love with a music teacher who unfortunately had no desire at all to go to China.

"I know I love her. To go without her would make the world a blank. But I cannot bring her to want," he wrote.

He felt that sooner or later the music teacher would change her tune, so in the meantime he went about preparing himself for the rigors of the Orient. "I soon found that I could live upon very much less than I thought possible."

He gave away much of his modest salary and lived mainly on oatmeal and rice. "One's spiritual muscles require strengthening," he said.

But beyond that, he learned lessons in prayer. "When I get out to China," he said, "I shall have no claim on anyone for anything; my only claim will be on God. How important, therefore, to learn before leaving England, to move man, through God, by prayer alone."

The next problem was finding a mission board to take him. His family was Methodist, but the Methodists had no work in China. He wrote to the London Missionary Society, but they didn't bother to answer his letter.

Then, in 1852, when he was just turning twenty, he heard of a newly formed mission, the Chinese Evangelization Society, composed mostly of Plymouth Brethren. Its founders, J. C. Pollock says, "were intensely sincere and impractical. They had scanty funds, one missionary, who later was dismissed for dabbling in the coolie traffic, and a journal."

Hudson loved the journal and didn't bother questioning anything else.

Within months he was training in a London hospital to be a missionary doctor under the new mission.

Convinced that he needed a wife when he went to China, he renewed his courtship of the music teacher, and within weeks they were engaged.

But the engagement was short-lived. She had second thoughts and so did Hudson. "I know I loved her, and she says she loved me, but I know she does not love me as she did. I fear it will have to be broken off."

Her father agreed. Hudson would be a suitable husband for his daughter if he were willing to reside in England and be a doctor. If he went to China, however, the marriage was out of the question.

A year later, without finishing his medical course, and without a wife, Hudson, now twenty-one, sailed for China, the only passenger on the sailing vessel. After an adventurous five-month voyage, he walked into the city of Shanghai.

He learned much in his first two weeks, including the fact that his mission board didn't know what it was doing. But Hudson wasn't going to let that stop him from being a missionary.

While learning the language, he became acutely homesick. He wrote long letters back to England: "Oh, I wish I could tell you how much I love you all. . . . I never knew how much I loved you all before."

In his room in Shanghai he grew three flowers—a violet and two forget-me-nots. "I look on them with the greatest affection and have even given them names; one I call Amelia, and another Louisa [his two sisters]—what I have called a third is no matter of yours. . . . But you know we must have something to love."

Chances are, the third was named either after the music teacher or else after Elizabeth Sissons, who had written him a consoling letter after his engagement to the music teacher was broken.

It didn't take him long to propose to Elizabeth, and it didn't take her long to respond. She wrote that she would accept his proposal of marriage although her father wanted her to wait awhile. Hudson was willing to wait, but not indefinitely.

For the first year as he was learning the language and engaging in some rather unspectacular missionary treks ("We see no fruit at present, and it needs strong faith to keep one's spirit from sinking"), Hudson took the bold step of adopting native dress. The other missionaries were appalled. The British consulate reacted with scorn. But Hudson thought it was a necessity if he was to minister effectively to the Chinese. "You wouldn't know me," he wrote home, "were you to meet me in the street."

To test his new "when in Rome, look like the Romans" approach, he established a mission base inland, at a distance from Shanghai. For a few weeks he seemed on top of the world. Then two calamities befell him: (1) the British authorities told him he couldn't establish a base there and (2) Elizabeth wrote him that she had decided she didn't love him after all.

Hudson didn't like to give up on things too readily, and that applied to such things as venturing inland and pursuing a wife.

So he continued to preach in places where few other missionaries would venture, although he did leave his forward base as the authorities had ordered him. "I do love the Chinese now," he wrote home. But he explained to his younger sister that letter writing was quite a chore. "Sometimes I stop in the middle of a sentence, kill three or four fleas and one or two cockroaches and then go on again."

But it was Elizabeth who was giving him more problems than the fleas and cockroaches. "I don't know what I shall do if I get an unfavorable letter in this mail."

It was only a few months later that he trudged desolately into Ningpo.

Five years younger than Hudson, Maria Dyer had already seen a great deal of the world. Her father, who had died when she was only six, had been one of the early British missionaries to the Chinese in Malaya. He had dreamed of evangelizing mainland China itself, but he never got there. He died off the coast of China in 1843. Four years later, his wife died.

The three orphans—Maria, Burella, and a brother Samuel, were shipped back to England to be looked after by an uncle and to be educated at a boarding school.

According to J. C. Pollock, "Maria was tall, dark-haired, dark-eyed, vivacious, and warm. She had a squint, which did not make her less attractive. She was demure, the dutiful younger sister, and no one suspected the strong currents within."

So, in 1855, when her sister responded to a missionary call to become a teacher at Ningpo, China, nobody thought it strange that Maria should want to go along with her. She knew that her parents would have been pleased to see her become a missionary to China, and so she went.

On board ship, she struggled inwardly. She couldn't understand exactly what was wrong. She was lonely, so it was understandable that she should want to stay with her sister. She was dutiful, so it was understandable that she would want to do what would have pleased her parents.

But all her life she had been reacting to shattering events. And no matter how dutiful she was, she never felt truly accepted. She even suffered pangs of guilt that maybe somehow, inexplicably, she had caused the problems of her life. No matter how dutifully she lived her life, she never had confidence that God really accepted her.

However, on her voyage to China, she gained that peace. Geraldine Taylor tells it this way: "Previously she had striven to be a Christian in her own strength. . . . Gradually it dawned upon her that she was redeemed . . . because He had suffered in her stead. God had accepted Christ as her substitute and savior, and she could do no less. . . . 'There is therefore now no condemnation to them which are in Christ Jesus.'"

No longer was she responding out of fear and duty; now she was going to China out of freedom and love. On her way to become a missionary, she had become a new creation.

Under Miss Aldersley's exacting supervision, Maria also developed into an excellent teacher of the Chinese children at the Ningpo school.

One of Miss Aldersley's other contributions to her life was to help her brush aside undesirable suitors. Probably, to Miss Aldersley, they all would have been undesirable—especially Hudson Taylor.

It was difficult for Maria to think poorly about Miss Aldersley. She wrote later to her brother, "O dear Samuel, those days were days of trial indeed. . . . It seemed to be His will that Mr. Taylor and I should love each other and yet Miss Aldersley so strongly opposed it. It seemed as if God's will and Miss Aldersley's were opposite."

She couldn't understand how such a godly woman as Miss Aldersley could possibly be wrong. "Yet it seems to me that Mr. Taylor is just the sort of person as my dear father, were he living, would approve of for me." Still she wondered: "Who was I that I should set myself up against Miss Aldersley and old established Christians?"

At first, Hudson was crushed by Maria's formal "Dear John" letter. While he didn't write home to his sister all that he was going through, he did say that he was "in much sorrow" and that he had been "tried at times almost beyond endurance."

In Shanghai for several months, he plunged into missionary efforts, aiding victims of a disastrous famine and preaching whenever he had a chance. But still he couldn't forget Maria. He had a hunch that Maria's letter could have been prompted either by a sense of duty to Miss Aldersley and the school, or that maybe Miss Aldersley had had an even more direct hand in it.

When he returned to Ningpo, his suspicions were confirmed. "Miss Aldersley got into a great stew when I came down," he wrote home. No doubt about it, he recognized that she was a formidable opponent.

But as soon as he discovered that Maria was as interested in him as he was in her, he decided to go around Miss Aldersley and write a letter to Maria's legal guardian (her uncle) in England, seeking his permission to marry Maria.

Hudson, however, wasn't the only person writing the uncle. Two weeks earlier, Miss Aldersley had already written him, informing him of the brash upstart nobody who was brazenly tampering with Maria's affections.

Maria, too, had written the uncle: "The greatest earthly pleasure that I desire is to be allowed to love the individual whom I have mentioned so prominently in this letter."

Third, but not least, Hudson wrote him his request.

No reply could be expected for at least four months.

Miss Aldersley and several others of the missionary community decreed that Hudson must not attempt to see Maria until word came back from the uncle. Most of them took Miss Aldersley's side in the matter.

One usually mild-mannered missionary said that Hudson "ought to be horse-whipped" for talking to Maria against the wishes of Miss Aldersley. Others called the relationship disgraceful. Hudson was termed "fanatical, undependable, diseased in body and mind." Besides that, he was "totally worthless." In fact, one mission leader told Hudson that he "could in no way recognize him as a Christian. He was no gentleman either."

Hudson couldn't understand what all the uproar was about. He wrote his mother: "Why? Because I don't think a maiden lady qualified to judge in love affairs?"

One other suggestion—and one that Hudson considered seriously—was that he should return immediately to England to get his medical degree. Of course, there were ulterior motives behind the suggestion. Maria responded: "If he were to leave the Lord's work for the world's honor, I would have nothing further to do with him."

Not all the attacks were flung against Hudson.

Hudson wrote his mother that "dear Maria is charged with being a maniac, being fanatical, being indecent, weak-minded, too easily swayed, too obstinate, and everything else bad."

When Maria tried to heal the breach between Miss Aldersley and herself, she only made matters worse. "I have suffered persecutions for righteousness' sake," she wrote her brother, but she still couldn't understand how a saintly woman such as Miss Aldersley could be in error. "How could she be in the wrong and I in the right?"

Separated from Maria, Hudson once again threw himself into his missionary work. He drove himself at such a pace that his health broke. Recuperating from his illness, he adopted two Hebrew words as his life mottoes: Ebenezer and Jehovah-Jireh. Ebenezer means "Hitherto the Lord has helped us." Jehovah-Jireh means "The Lord will provide." Those two words were the foundation of the mission that he would later begin.

In November, about the time that he had expected a reply from the guardian, Hudson arranged a secret meeting with Maria. According to the official biographer, "they sat side by side on the sofa." According to Pollock, "It was very naughty by contemporary standards." According to Hudson himself, he was only "trying to make up for the number of kisses I ought to have had these last few months."

When they parted, they agreed that they were engaged to be married, no matter what the response from the guardian might be. Her twenty-first birthday, after all, was only two months away.

The announcement of the engagement almost split the Ningpo mission community. Some charged Hudson with "exhibiting a total ignorance of the common amenities and proprieties of life."

Two weeks later, a letter from the guardian in England finally came. In it, he said that he saw no reason to oppose Maria's wish to marry

Hudson, but he thought it would be best if they waited until her birthday. The couple was ecstatic.

They lived in an age of Victorian propriety, but Hudson and Maria were certainly not typical Victorians. One missionary wrote: "When [Hudson] fell in love it was a headlong plunge, and by no means a slight or evanescent passion. And his fiancée, with her strong, emotional nature, was in this respect not unlike him."

The wedding was quickly arranged, and they were married four days after Maria's twenty-first birthday.

However, two weeks before the wedding, Hudson was broke. He and a fellow missionary had been providing breakfast for sixty to eighty Chinese famine victims every morning, and they were paying for it out of their own pockets. "How the Lord would care for us on Monday we knew not, but over our mantelpiece hung two scrolls in Chinese characters—Ebenezer and Jehovah-Jireh—and He kept us from doubting for a moment."

But then he thought of Maria. How would she adapt to his unusual lifestyle? Maybe it was too much to ask.

He asked her if she wished to reconsider her commitment to him: "I cannot hold you to your promise if you would rather draw back. You see how difficult our life may be at times."

She hardly paused before replying: "Don't forget that I was an orphan in a faraway land. God has been my Father all these years. Do you think I shall be afraid to trust Him now?"

Two weeks later they were married. Maria wore a silk gown and wedding veil; Hudson had only a plain cotton robe. He had sold everything else he owned in order to feed the famine victims.

Marriage pleased him. Six weeks later he wrote, "Oh, to be married to the one you do love, and love most tenderly and devotedly, that is bliss beyond the power of words to express or imagination conceive."

In the following years Maria helped Hudson mature and display more common sense. As Pollock says, "She made him take holidays. . . . He shed his moods of melancholy, he forgot to be introspective. . . . He became more assured, he was no longer on the defensive, no more a prig. Imperceptibly, she polished him."

Two years later, in 1860, they returned to England. Hudson's health had broken, and he had no choice but to take his wife and one-year-old daughter back home. In England, Hudson reverted to Western clothes and finished his course at medical school.

But more significant was his revision of the Ningpo New Testament, the recruiting of new missionaries for China, and the founding of a different kind of mission society, the China Inland Mission.

Burdened with the spiritual need of inland China, he began traveling up and down England, announcing that "a million a month were dying without God" in China. Half the heathen population of the world lived in China, and the number of missionaries there was decreasing instead of increasing.

He prayed and pleaded for twenty-four missionaries—lack of education was no barrier—to return to China with him. His new mission society would be financed—here was the revolutionary part—entirely by faith. If he made appeals for funds, it might interfere with the finances of existing denominational missions.

Within a few months, more than a score of recruits—including a blacksmith, a carpenter, a mason, a governess, a Bible woman, and a leisured daughter of a wealthy businessman—gathered at the spartan Taylor home for their missionary indoctrination. The group came not only from all walks of life but from all denominations—Baptists, Methodists, Presbyterians, and Anglicans were all represented.

Hudson Taylor had a strange kind of attraction. His illness had worn him down, but within him there was a certain magnetism. One of the recruits commented: "I half despised him at first. A sickly looking, hesitating young man, no kicking power in his makeup much."

"God chose me," Hudson Taylor said later in life, "because I was weak enough. God does not do His great works by large committees. He trains somebody to be quiet enough and little enough and then He uses him."

Hudson was certainly God's man for the hour. Six years earlier David Livingstone had ignited Great Britain with his presentation of the needs of Africa. Now Hudson Taylor was doing it regarding China. "China, China, China is now ringing in our ears," reported the great London pulpiteer Charles Haddon Spurgeon, "in that special, peculiar, musical, forcible, unique way in which Mr. Taylor utters it." Hudson normally spoke for two hours, sometimes demonstrating the use of chopsticks or Chinese ink in the course of the lecture. And though he never asked for money, the money began to roll in.

Thus, in 1866, Hudson and Maria Taylor, their four children, and fifteen missionary recruits sailed together for China. Hudson was thirty-four, Maria twenty-nine, but they were the veterans, the old China hands. One of the recruits wrote later that Hudson was "quite one with the young men of the party. Mrs. Taylor, quieter, in some ways perhaps more mature, such rare judgment; calm sweetness about her face always; most restful. She was very thoughtful and gave much time to study of the Bible and prayer. She gave a good deal of time to the children, too—used to gather them to the cabin for a little reading."

In China, Hudson had all his men immediately shave their heads, don pigtails, and dress like Chinese teachers. This jolted the established missionary community. Six years earlier when Hudson had been the only one wearing a pigtail, they had looked upon him with amusement; but now all his disciples wore pigtails, too.

Maria wasn't so sure that all the women should wear Chinese dress. She had reservations because "the Chinese despise their own females while they respect foreign ladies; will they treat us with as much respect and shall we have as much weight with them, if we change our dress?" Hudson asked her to try it for a while. She did, and soon she was convinced that his system was right.

Hudson's philosophy on missionaries wearing Chinese clothing wasn't a gimmick. "Why should a foreign aspect be given to Christianity?" he wrote. "The Word of God does not require it. It is not the denationalization but the Christianization of these people we seek. We wish to see . . . men and women truly Christian, but truly Christian in every right sense. We wish to see churches of such believers presided over by pastors and officers of their own countrymen, worshipping God in their own tongue, in edifices of a thoroughly native style."

For that day, it was a shocking missionary philosophy.

In its early years, the China Inland Mission had more than its share of problems. Hudson and Maria were severely criticized by missionaries of established societies, were attacked by the Chinese, and even faced dissension from within their own group.

Most of their young band, however, stuck with them. One of them said about Hudson, "If he were not in the habit of casting his burdens upon the Lord, I quite believe that what he has passed through he would have sunk under."

Maria was the second in command. Some members felt "she was the backbone of the mission at the time. Hudson Taylor had so learned to value her judgment and prayerfulness that he never took a step without consulting her."

She was still young, but already she had been beset by serious illness. Tuberculosis was slowly emaciating her and she didn't have the strength to withstand the diseases that struck the missionary community.

She was called "a woman of indomitable perseverance and courage, through troubles of every kind." Another commented, "She always sympathized with everyone and everybody. It showed often in little things." Another called her "humble, retiring, almost to shyness."

Hudson and Maria remained obviously in love. Once when he went inland on a preaching tour, he wrote her, "My darling one, I can now only in imagination hold your loved form in my arms. . . . For my sake and for the Lord's sake take great care of your health. . . . O if I could but give you one kiss."

A fifth child was born to Hudson and Maria not long after their return to China.

But in 1867 their oldest child, Gracie, became seriously ill. Hudson wrote home, "I am trying to pen a few lines by the couch on which my darling little Gracie lies dying. Her complaint is hydrocephalus. . . . God is the strength of our heart and our portion forever. . . . And He has not left us now."

A few weeks later he wrote his mother in England, "I know not how to write. Our dear little Gracie! How we miss her! As I take the walks I used to take with her tripping by my side, the thought comes anew like a throb of agony, Is it possible that I shall never more feel the pressure of that little hand. . . . And yet . . . she is far holier, far happier than she could ever have been here."

Gracie's death may have been a turning point in the history of the China Inland Mission. The missionaries rallied in sympathy around the Taylors, and a new unity emerged.

Hudson and Maria brought a new dignity to the role of women missionaries. For the first time single female missionaries were sent out—dressed in Chinese garb, of course—to do evangelizing without a male missionary to accompany them. For this innovation, Hudson and Maria faced criticism; but the results were outstanding. One woman wrote, "I think when I go out I often speak to more than 200 persons. Yet I am never treated in any way rudely, but with all kindness."

When Maria heard that the criticism had spread to England, she wrote in response, "I believe ten Miss Fauldings and ten Miss Bowyers could easily find work in Hangchow tomorrow."

Meanwhile Hudson pleaded for missionaries of both sexes: "Are there no servants of our common Lord rusting away at home or at least doing work that others could do if they left it, who might be out here among these numberless towns and villages?"

In June 1868 Hudson and Maria moved their headquarters to Yangchow, having lived in Shanghai and Hangchow since their arrival in China. Yangchow was their boldest incursion yet into China's hinterlands. Since the time of Marco Polo, few Westerners had spent much time there.

Yangchow was anything but cordial. First, rumors started spreading. Foreign doctors were accused of making pills out of patients' eyes; missionaries of salting down children. Then came an anti-missionary handbill campaign. Westerners were going to impoverish their country by selling opium.

The worst was yet to come. Stones began crashing through their windows, and that was just a warning.

According to an anonymous letter that Hudson received, much more would happen if the missionaries didn't leave Yangchow immediately.

Hudson went to Maria and suggested that perhaps the men should stay and the women and children go. She disagreed. "For us to go away," she said, "would only increase the danger to the men." The women and children stayed.

Then one day a mob—150 to 200 angry Chinese—filled the street in front of the mission headquarter: They threatened to batter down the door if the missionaries didn't open up. Some of the rioters were obviously drunk. Many were half-naked.

The missionaries prayed. Hudson reminded his fellow workers of the verse, "Lo, I am with you always," and bid them pray some more.

The sky darkened; thunder boomed through the heavens. One missionary was writing a letter. "As I write He is sending thunder and the threatening of rain, which will do more for us, Mr. Taylor says, than an army of soldiers. The Chinese shun the rain." The mob dispersed.

But a few nights later they returned with flaming torches. They heaved bricks at the shuttered windows.

Maria calmly put her children to bed. The other missionaries were amazed at her serenity. "She was as calm as when in the parlor in London." Hudson knew that he had to get help from the Chinese military. And it was needed as soon as possible.

He kissed Maria, slipped out a door, and ran into the darkness. "When we turned into the main street," he recalled later, "we were assaulted with stones, and a mob gathered behind us. . . . We were nearly exhausted and our legs so hurt with the stones and bricks thrown at us that we were almost fainting."

Back at the missionary house, two male missionaries along with Chinese servants tried to keep the mob out. Upstairs the women were praying. Maria was six months pregnant. Her youngest child had dysentery. Another missionary wife was eight months pregnant.

The rioters seemed to grow louder every minute. Time passed—a half hour, then an hour, then an hour and a half. Still no Hudson, and still no soldiers to come to the rescue.

Then came a voice from downstairs. "Mrs. Taylor, they are setting the house on fire." The missionaries began climbing out a back window to be lowered on knotted sheets and blankets to concealment in a wellhouse.

Before Maria could escape, a naked rioter stormed into the room. He grabbed her by the wrist and demanded money.

"I will cut off your head," he threatened. He saw her wedding ring and pulled it violently from her finger.

"Jump," hollered a missionary from the ground below. It was twelve to fifteen feet, but she had no alternative. She wrenched herself loose from her attacker and leaped downward.

A missionary half caught her, breaking her fall, but she landed on her side.

By the time soldiers arrived, the riot had subsided. Of course, the missionaries had to vacate Yangchow temporarily, but they prayed to be able to return. Maria was asked if she wanted the rioters to be punished. "The revenge I desire," she replied, "is the wider opening up of the country to our work."

When the British authorities got wind of the riot, they sent gunboats up the Yangtze River to Yangchow. "Foreigners traveling in the interior have a perfect and legal right to claim legitimate local protection," the British consul had told Hudson.

It was not the response that Hudson and Maria wanted. An international incident ensued.

Maria's only desire was to be able to return to Yangchow in time to have her baby born there. And ten days before Charles Edward Taylor was born, Hudson and Maria were able to return to Yangchow. Maria wrote, "God has given me the desire of my heart." She had wanted the baby to be born "in this city, in this house, in this very room." It seemed as if her prayer had been answered.

But it didn't take long before news of the Yangchow affair reached London. Soon the name of Hudson Taylor became a household word, but not in a favorable sense. The *Times* of London denounced him: "The Apostles and early missionaries certainly did not propagate their faith under the protection of fleets and armies." The American ambassador to China called the Yangchow affair a "high-handed action."

Even the British government itself, embarrassed by how world opinion had turned against it, wondered if there was some "efficient and stringent mode of dealing with these missionaries."

Other missionaries to China were angry with the Taylors for having placed all mission work in jeopardy.

Outwardly, Hudson seemed to bear up quite well with all the misinterpretations. Inwardly, he was "desperately hurt." Long-time friends and supporters had now believed the accusations.

But it was a time when other problems were looming large as well. Hudson was concerned about the quality of his missionary recruits. "Some persons seem really clever in doing the right thing in the worst possible way or at the most unfortunate moment," he wrote home. "Really dull or rude persons will seldom be out of hot water in China."

Besides these outward pressures were inner conflicts. One missionary called Hudson "toiling and burdened" at this time.

He wrote his mother, "I have often asked you to remember me in prayer. That need has never been greater."

Later he described the time, "I began the day with prayer, determined not to take my eye from Him for a moment, but pressure of duties, sometimes very trying, constant interruptions apt to be so wearing, often caused me to forget Him. One's nerves get so fretted in this climate that temptations to irritability, hard thoughts, and sometimes unkind words are all more difficult to control. Each day brought its register of sin and failure, or lack of power. . . . Instead of growing stronger, I seemed to be getting weaker and of having less power against sin; and no wonder, for faith and even hope were getting very low. I hated myself."

Emotionally, he was deeply depressed and he faced even "the awful temptation . . . to end his own life."

One constant that he had was Maria's love. And his love for her remained as strong as ever. "It hasn't worn off or worn out."

Biographer J. C. Pollock says that it was Maria who stood between Hudson and suicide.

When separated by travel, Hudson wrote her warmly. "I dreamed last night that I was once more by your side. . . . When I awoke . . . I was so disappointed. When shall I really see you and once more fold you in my arms?"

And Maria responded, when sending him some supplies: "My priceless treasure . . . I should like to put myself among the things that are coming."

Hudson felt that there might be a danger that they actually loved each other too much. "Oh, may He ever give us both to love Him best, most constantly and with unfailing constancy. Then we shall not love one another too much."

As Hudson traveled, he talked to his missionary crew about his own "spiritual needs." Many of them shared the same inner discomfort of which he spoke. But one of them wrote, "As for Mrs. Taylor, she wondered what we were all groping after."

A few weeks later he received a letter from one of his missionaries named McCarthy, an Irishman with a quick temper. McCarthy said that he had found the secret in "abiding, not striving or struggling." This was a breakthrough for Hudson as well. "Ah, there is rest," he wrote. "I have striven in vain to rest in Him. I'll strive no more. For has He not promised to abide with me, never to leave me, never to fail me, and . . . He never will."

It was at this time that Hudson learned the secret of the serenity that "full identification with Christ brings. . . . Can Christ be rich and I be poor?"

Maria summed it up simply, "It was just resting in Jesus and letting Him do the work."

The trials of running the mission didn't subside with his spiritual discovery, however. By 1870, when Hudson and Maria were celebrating their twelfth anniversary, the China Inland Mission had thirty-three missionaries in twelve stations in three provinces. But it was, as Hudson later wrote, "a time of great trial, a time of the greatest difficulty I have ever known in China. From Peking to Canton the people were agitated. We did not know from day to day what would take place in our inland stations. But I had unspeakable rest in my soul."

In February, their third child, five-year-old Samuel, always "exceptionally delicate," died, and Hudson and Maria felt that they needed to send their other children—Bertie, nine, Freddie, seven, and Maria, three—back to England with one of the missionaries. They would keep the baby with them in Yangchow.

It was difficult to see their children go. Hudson wrote his mother to "pray specially for Maria. When all the bustle of preparation and the excitement of departure are over, then will come the trying time of reaction. But the Lord, whose work calls for the separation, can and will support her."

Maria was pregnant again. It was her eighth pregnancy in twelve years of marriage. She continued teaching her classes as usual, despite the fact that tuberculosis had ravaged her body. She seemed happy that she had been able to complete a Chinese-English vocabulary which had now gone to the printer. Hudson was more concerned than ever about her. "My heart ached," he said, "when I saw her thin wasted frame."

The baby came in mid-July. Maria was thankful that it had been an easy delivery, perhaps her easiest. But a day or two later, she was hemorrhaging internally and was weakening perceptibly.

Within two weeks the baby died, and Maria had very little strength remaining.

Hudson went to her and asked her, "Darling, do you know that you are dying?"

"Dying? Do you think so? What makes you think that?"

"I can see it, darling. Your strength is giving way."

"Can it be? I feel no pain, only weariness."

"You are going home. Soon you will be with Jesus."

There was silence for a moment. Then Maria whispered, "I am so sorry."

Hudson looked at her gently and said, "You are not sorry to go to be with Jesus."

"Oh, no, it is not that. . . . But it does grieve me to leave you alone at such a time. Yet He will be with you and meet all your needs."

She kissed him over and over again, one kiss for each of the children.

A missionary who stood nearby said later, "I never witnessed such a scene. As dear Mrs. Taylor was breathing her last, Mr. Taylor knelt down . . . and committed her to the Lord, thanking Him for having given her to him and for the twelve and a half years of happiness they had had together."

He had to buy a coffin immediately because of the extreme heat. He looked at her in the coffin for a long while. Then he rushed upstairs to be alone.

A few days later he wrote: "I cannot describe to you my feelings. I do not understand them myself. I feel like a person stunned with a blow, or recovering from a faint, and as yet but partially conscious. . . . My Father has ordered it, so . . . therefore I know it is, it must be best, and I thank Him for so ordering it. I feel utterly crushed. . . . Oftentimes my heart is nigh to breaking, but withal I had almost said I never knew what peace and happiness were before—so much have I enjoyed in the very sorrow."

Those months were devastating to Hudson. He had lost his wife, had lost a baby, and had shipped three other children to England.

In a few days he wrote to his three in England: "How happy darling Momma must be! I am so glad for her to be with Him. I shall be so glad to go to her when Jesus thinks it best. But I hope He will help me to be equally willing to live with Him here so long as He has any work for me to do for Him and for poor China."

The Lord had more work for Hudson in poor China, much more.

A year later, he returned for a much needed furlough to England. He needed to recuperate both physically and emotionally from the twelve-month period in which he had lost his wife and two of his children. He also longed to see his other children again in England.

By coincidence, missionary Jennie Faulding was returning on the same ship. She had booked passage on another vessel, but after being unavoidably delayed, had to take the same ship that carried the head of her mission, Hudson Taylor.

The long voyage together was good for both of them. Hudson had always admired Jennie, and Jennie had always been a faithful fan of his.

The daughter of a London merchant and a convinced Baptist, Jennie was well educated, gracious, and cheerful. In fact, even when no one else found anything to rejoice about, Jennie could.

She had been among Hudson's first recruits for missionary service in 1866. On her first day aboard ship heading for China, she had written home, "Oh, I have enjoyed today! The sea is so lovely and the air is so beautiful, I never thought a voyage could be such a treat. It makes my blood tingle with pleasure."

When she arrived in China, she wrote, "It seemed like a dream to be really surrounded by pigtails and little feet."

When some of the missionaries began grumbling about adopting Chinese clothing, Jennie commented that, with the exception of Hudson Taylor, she thought everyone seemed "improved by the change."

When she traveled inland, she reported, "The canals are like beautiful rivers and if the strawberries have no taste, the wild raspberries are very nice (we have had a pie made of them) and the birds sing to one's heart's content."

Hudson characterized her with the phrase, "She never thought anything could be better."

She was only twenty-three when she ventured to China, and at the time Hudson took almost a father's concern for her. In response, she admired him as a "plaster saint."

"I have known him under all circumstances," she wrote her father, "and if you could see him daily you would indeed admire his self-abnegation, his humility and quiet never-flagging earnestness."

But there was more to Jennie than just cheerfulness. She was always loyal even when other missionaries questioned his leadership, and Hudson appreciated it. He could share concerns with her, even some of his personal struggles, as he could with his wife.

So it wasn't especially surprising that, aboard ship, the depressed Hudson Taylor and the ever-cheerful Jennie Faulding developed a romance. The following year they were married. She was twenty-nine; he was forty.

It wasn't the same kind of a marriage that he had had with Maria. With Maria, there was constant romance. With Jennie, it was different, but no less happy.

They were often separated in the following years. Jennie often stayed in London taking care of the stepchildren while Hudson traveled to China making the rounds of the mission stations.

In 1878, however, just after Hudson had returned from a sixteen-month tour of the field, he received word of an unprecedented famine in North China. Six million people were starving; tens of thousands were dying; thousands of children were orphaned and homeless.

Hudson saw the need for a woman to head the team of relief workers, invading that remote section of China with the gospel, with love, and with provisions. But who could do it?

It had to be Jennie. She was the only woman who spoke Chinese, who had the respect of the other workers, and who also had his complete confidence.

At first, she wasn't convinced. She thought she was needed just as much in London—for Hudson's sake, for the children's sake, for the mission's sake. But Hudson urged her to go, for Jesus' sake.

It wasn't that she was afraid. It was simply that she wasn't convinced it was the Lord's will. "I felt like Gideon," she wrote. "I wanted some fleeces to confirm my faith." She asked for fifty English pounds to out-fit her for the strenuous trip. It came within a few days.

Then on the day she was scheduled to depart, an anonymous check for a thousand pounds arrived. It was specified for an orphanage in North China she was to found.

No foreign woman had ever ventured into that part of China, but Jennie led the team composed of one man and two women.

When Hudson heard that her mission had been successful, he wrote her: "I do thank my God for giving me such a wife. . . . Every day I look at the little Bible marker you gave me, with the words, 'For Jesus' sake,' and I am thankful for the reminder."

After establishing an orphanage and a new mission outpost, she rejoined her husband a year later when he returned for another visit to China.

Hudson continued to use the motto: "For Jesus' sake." The true joy of life, he said, was to do all for Jesus' sake, even as Jennie had done.

As Hudson and Jennie grew older and no longer could take the frequent trips to China, they handed over the control of the mission to others. For Hudson, this was most difficult. "It's hardest of all to do nothing for Jesus' sake," he said.

Jennie died in 1904 at the age of sixty-one; Hudson died a year later when he was seventy-three. At the time of his death, the China Inland Mission, which he had founded a generation earlier, had 825 missionaries on the field.

The afternoon before he died, a group of missionaries were talking with him about bringing everything to God in prayer. One of them said that sometimes he found it difficult to bring the small things to God.

Hudson Taylor replied, "There is nothing small, and there is nothing great; only God is great, and we should trust Him fully."

Bibliography

Pollock, J. C. *Hudson Taylor and Maria.* New York: McGraw Hill, 1962.
Taylor, Dr. and Mrs. Howard. *Hudson Taylor's Spiritual Secret.* Chicago: Moody, 1950.
Taylor, Dr. and Mrs. Howard. *Hudson Taylor and the China Inland Mission.* Philadelphia: China Inland Mission, 1918.

Opening the Surprise Package

A good marriage is like a birthday party in which you keep on opening presents and each is a delightful surprise. Throughout their relationship a husband and wife keep on discovering each other's joys and abilities.

"I never knew you could paint."

"I never knew you would be so good with children."

"I never realized how good you were at carving a turkey."

No matter how much a couple shares with each other prior to marriage, there are always new discoveries—sometimes ten, twenty, or thirty years later.

The five couples in this section—the Luthers, Stowes, Lewises, Knoxes, and Müllers—all had delightfully surprising marriages.

Martin Luther never knew what he was agreeing to when he married Katie; he married more for duty than for love, but years later he said, "I would not change Katie for France or for Venice." She was more than he had bargained for—delightfully more.

The longtime bachelor C. S. Lewis was almost trapped into marriage and, like Luther, married more for expediency than for love. His attraction for Joy was more intellectual than anything else. But then the surprises came, and Lewis later wrote, "I never expected to have in my sixties the happiness that passed me by in my twenties." At the time he married Joy he would not have believed that in 1989 a play about his romance would open to rave reviews in London's West End theatre district.

The surprises that came to Harriet Beecher Stowe might have torn apart a twentieth-century marriage. But her sense of humor and her candor kept the irritations from growing into mountains.

By the time he married Marjory, John Knox had gotten to know his mother-in-law better than his bride. So Marjory was a surprise to him.

George Müller never knew what a surprise package he had until long after his marriage.

Husbands and wives change as they interact with each other and as they face the challenges of their daily vocations. But change should not disrupt a marriage. Martin Luther, Harriet Stowe, C. S. Lewis, John Knox, and George Müller might all have said, "But she (or he) is not the person I thought I married."

However, instead of allowing change to rock their marriages, they found it could delightfully enhance them.

How did they do it?

Why did these marriages turn out positively when so many today are floundering?

As you read, you will discover some of their secrets for yourself.

There's a Lot to Get Used to in Marriage

Martin and Katie Luther

You know about Martin Luther, who sparked the Protestant Reformation by nailing his Ninety-five Theses to the church door in Wittenberg, Germany. But do you know about his wife, Katie, the run-away nun?

She had a quick tongue and he had a quick temper, a combination that does not usually make for a good marriage.

So what kind of a marriage did Martin and Katie have?

A very *un*usual one.

You'll enjoy Katie's outspokenness as well as Martin's colorful outbursts. Martin and Katie seem so human and so contemporary—almost like next-door neighbors. At first you might wonder how their marriage survived. But the better you get to know them, the better you will understand their secret.

"In domestic affairs I defer to Katie. Otherwise I am led by the Holy Ghost." So said Martin Luther, a bit facetiously, about his wife.

"There's a lot to get used to in the first year of marriage," Luther once admitted. "One wakes up in the morning and finds a pair of pigtails on the pillow which were not there before." For the forty-one-year-old former monk and the twenty-six-year-old former nun, there was a lot more than that to get used to.

"I would not change Katie for France or for Venice," Luther said. Once, however, after Katie had contradicted him in front of dinner guests, he sighed and remarked, "If I should ever marry again, I should hew myself an obedient wife out of stone."

Katie was many things for Martin—a gardener, a cook, a nurse, a cattle-raiser, a bookkeeper, and a brewer. But you could never accuse Katie of being a stone. One biographer calls Katie a "quick-witted Saxon with a ready tongue," which made an interesting match for Luther, an intense debater with a short fuse. She could not be described as beautiful with "her longish head, high forehead, long nose, and powerful chin." It was her intelligence and personality that made her attractive to others.

According to one historian, "She ruled both her household and her husband, a situation which the latter accepted resignedly, since he was totally incapable of organizing the affairs of even the smallest household. She brought order into his life and not always to his satisfaction." Martin would probably change that assessment by saying, "She managed the areas that I delegated to her."

There was nothing romantic about the early days of their marriage; Martin Luther was motivated more by duty than by love in pursuing it, and Katie was marrying on the rebound. Yet undeniably a deep love grew between them. Surprisingly, the marriage of Martin and Katie Luther became a model for Protestant marriage.

Who would have thought a few years earlier that either Martin or Katie would get married? And if, by chance, either one got married, who would have thought that either one would have a happy marriage?

Born November 10, 1483, to a copper miner and his wife in Eisleben on the edge of Germany's Thuringian Forest, Martin was raised with the strictness that was characteristic of the day in both home and school. Of his parents' strictness, he later rationalized, "They meant well." Regarding the discipline measures used by his early schoolteachers, he asked, "Whoever loved a schoolmaster anyway?" Later, with his own children, he always made sure that there was an apple alongside the rod.

Throughout life he struggled against overbearing and unreasonable authority. At the same time he wanted to be loved. Sometimes shy, he delighted to be in the spotlight; sometimes crude and earthy, he was also warm and devotionally tender. From his father, he picked up a refreshing sense of humor; from his mother, a love of music. He was often moody, sometimes depressed. An indefatigable worker, he often neglected his own health.

No, Martin Luther was not a simple man.

The first major turning point in his life came when he was twenty-one. He had just received his master's degree from the University of Erfurt, and was on his way to a career in law, as his father had wanted.

He was pleasing his father, but there was a Higher Authority that he seemed incapable of pleasing. He felt the wrath of God dangling precariously over his head. *How can you become pious enough to please a holy God?* he asked himself.

One night as he was returning to law school from his parents' home, he was caught in a violent thunderstorm. A bolt of lightning rent the sky, and the twenty-one-year-old law student begged God to spare him, vowing that he would enter a monastery if He would. And two weeks later, he dismayed his parents and shocked his friends by doing just that.

The vows he took were obedience, poverty, and chastity, which of course ruled out marriage. Withdrawing from the world into the monastery, he devoted himself exclusively to prayer. But he was never satisfied that he had the answer to the question *How can you become pious enough to please a holy God?*

In a few years he was transferred to a monastery in Wittenberg, and was named lecturer in Bible studies at the new university there. As he began to teach God's Word—particularly the Epistles of Romans and Galatians—he made a new discovery. Righteousness does not come by works; it is imputed to us by faith. It does not come by what we do, but by what Christ has already done in our behalf. He termed it a "wonderful new definition of righteousness." Martin Luther had grasped the meaning of Paul's expression, "The just shall live by faith."

In 1517, when he was thirty-three, Martin Luther nailed his Ninety-five Theses to the Wittenberg door, seeking a scholarly debate. He never got the debate; he got a Reformation instead.

Four years later, he was called to appear before the Diet of Worms, where Emperor Charles V, Archduke Ferdinand, six Prince Electors, dukes, archbishops, papal nuncios, ambassadors—a total of 200 dignitaries—were gathered. Although he knew his life was at stake, Martin Luther refused to retract what he had written. His authority was not the church nor the pope; his authority was the Bible itself, the Word of God. "Here I stand. I can do no other. God help me."

A few days later, the Edict of Worms condemned both Luther and his writings and asked all citizens for their help in arresting him. If they preferred, they could kill Luther on sight.

Luther, however, had left Worms before the edict was signed. On the way back to Wittenberg, friends "kidnapped" him and secretly took him to the Castle of Wartburg, where he remained in exile for eight months, translating the Bible into German.

He was thirty-seven years old now, and still considered himself under the vows he had taken when he had entered the monastery sixteen years earlier. Later, he said, "If anyone had told me, when I was at the Diet of Worms, 'In a few years you will have a wife and be sitting at home,' I should not have believed it."

Before Worms, Luther had been a folk hero of all those who were unhappy with the status quo.

While he was in his Wartburg captivity, Luther's reformation started moving in directions that bewildered him. Monks as well as priests began to renounce their vows and get married, and this caused Luther to reexamine his own thinking about the vows of celibacy that he had taken.

Luther's first expression was: "Good heavens, they won't give me a wife."

Called back to Wittenberg to restore order to the turbulent movement he had spawned, Luther was upset by religious fanatics on one hand and political radicals on the other. Ignorant religionists were led (they said) by visions rather than the Word, and in Luther's absence they had drawn away some of those that previously had been disciples of the Wittenberg reformer. On the other hand, peasants were rising up against their feudal lords and claiming the backing of Luther's writings.

When Luther disowned their cause, he was no longer their hero. Many viewed him as a traitor.

In Saxony (east central Germany) Luther was relatively safe because the ruler of Saxony, Frederick the Wise, had promised the reformer protection. But outside of Saxony, he could travel only at his own risk.

Thus in 1525, eight years after he had penned his Ninety-five Theses in Wittenberg and four years after he had made his courageous "Here I stand" defense at Worms, Luther was hunted by the pope, hated by the peasants, and harassed by the religious fanatics. At forty-one, he had good reason to feel that the bloom was gone from the Reformation rose.

And that was the year that Martin Luther married. His bride was Katherine von Bora.

Katherine, nearly sixteen years younger than Martin, had been placed in a nunnery when she was only nine or ten years old. Her father had just remarried, and Katie's quick wit and sharp tongue did not endear her to her stepmother. So off to the nunnery. Six years later she took her vows.

In the early 1520s, tracts by Martin Luther began appearing mysteriously within the cloistered walls of Katie's nunnery. Furthermore, rumors had been circulating that elsewhere nuns and monks were leaving their monastic houses to follow this man who was teaching that salvation was a gift from God, not to be earned by religious observances.

Secretly Katie and eleven other nuns sent word to Luther in Wittenberg that they were interested in leaving the nunnery. Could he help them? Security, however, was tight and the nunnery was located in territory ruled by Duke George, an enemy of Luther. Already Duke George had executed one man for devising an escape plan for some nuns. Luther had to come up with a foolproof plan.

In the nearby town of Torgau was a respected senior citizen named Leonard Kopp. A member of the town council and a former Torgau tax collector, he had the contract to deliver barrels of smoked herring to the cloister in Nimbschen which housed the twelve unhappy nuns. Exactly how Kopp did it is unknown, but somehow when he arrived, his canvas-covered wagon seemed to be carrying twelve barrels of smoked herring, and when he left it seemed to be loaded with twelve empty barrels underneath the canvas. But the barrels were not empty.

Two days later, nine nuns (three had returned to their parents' homes) were delivered to Martin Luther's doorstep, and it was Luther's job to find either positions or husbands for them. Finding jobs for them wouldn't be easy. The nuns weren't trained in housekeeping. One historian commented, "All they could do was pray and sing." To find husbands for them would not be easy either. Since German girls usually married at age fifteen or sixteen, most of the nuns were considerably past their prime. But Martin Luther felt obligated to help them. "I feel so sorry for them; they are a wretched little bunch," he wrote to a friend.

Someone suggested that maybe Luther could help solve his problem by marrying one of them himself. He responded that he wouldn't think of it, not because he was a sexless stone or against marriage, but because he thought he might soon be killed as a heretic. Evidently by this time he no longer considered himself obligated to continue his monk's vow.

Eventually, Luther was able to find husbands for some of the nuns, but one of them remained as his biggest problem. It was Katie von Bora, who had found temporary employment in the home of Lucas Cranach, Luther's neighbor. Cranach had a large household and he seemed to need all the domestic help he could get.

It wasn't as if no one wanted her. Her personality and quick wit attracted the attention of a young man from a distinguished family in Nuremberg, and the two fell in love. But when he returned to tell his parents that he wished to marry a runaway nun, they refused him permission.

The rejection struck Katie hard, and she was heartbroken. But Luther the matchmaker didn't give up trying. Determined to find a husband for Katie, he soon had someone else in mind. Unfortunately, the next candidate didn't suit Katie, though Luther thought that she could ill afford to be fussy. Katie sent word back that while she wasn't at all against the idea of marriage, she would never marry the latest candidate; in fact, to underscore her willingness to marry, she thought she would mention a couple of possible candidates herself—even though it was obvious to friends that she was still in love with the young man from Nuremberg. Amsdorf, one of Luther's fellow professors at Wittenberg, was one candidate that she would be willing to marry; the other was Luther himself. Amsdorf, like Luther, was in his early forties.

The message from Katie got back to Luther at a very propitious time. Rumors had been circulating across Europe of the nine nuns who had been camping on Luther's doorstep. Luther's enemies—and they were legion—imagined the worst. There were jokes about Luther's harem. Katie was the only one left, and the rumors were stronger than ever. There was only one nun, but now there were nine times as many rumors.

In April 1525, shortly after he received Katie's message about the two eligible candidates for her hand, Martin visited his aged parents. His father, who had never wanted his son to become a monk, was pleased that Martin had left the monastery. Now only one thing remained before his son could say that he had made a complete break with the past. He would have to marry and father children to carry on the family name.

Luther had been preaching for several years that marriage was a divinely established institution. To elevate celibacy above marriage was unbiblical. Now it was time for him to practice what he had been preaching.

It was a big step for the forty-one-year-old monk to take. With the exception of his parents, he seemed to take counsel with no one. Even many of his closest friends were unaware of the decision he was struggling with.

Some of his friends had deserted him. His national popularity had waned and his spiritual impact was fragmenting. In some ways he felt he would have to start all over again. Perhaps at age forty-one he could begin afresh.

What better way than to get married and start a family? As he thought about it, his marriage would "please his father, rile the pope, make angels laugh and devils weep, and would seal his testimony." Perhaps it would even shut the mouths of rumor-mongers.

And hadn't Katie practically proposed to him? The closest thing to a counterproposal came when he told Katie that he might be burned at the stake, and if she was to wed him, it might mean her life as well. Apparently, the peril didn't dissuade Katie.

The courtship was anything but romantic. "I am not madly in love, but I cherish her," said Luther.

On June 10, 1525, Luther wrote, "The gifts of God must be taken on the wing." So once he made up his mind, Luther didn't waste any time.

The wedding took place June 13. Lucas Cranach and his wife were witnesses. The suddenness of it caused more rumors to fly and even some close friends like Philipp Melanchthon had second thoughts about it. But as Luther later remarked, "If I had not married quickly and secretly and taken few into my confidence, everyone would have done what he could to hinder me; for all my friends said: 'Not this one, but another.'" Many of them thought that Luther should have married a more distinguished woman than Katie, the runaway nun.

Even Luther had to pinch himself to make sure it wasn't a dream. "I can hardly believe it myself," he joked, "but the witnesses are too strong." And when he invited the herring distributor Leonard Kopp to the wedding, he wrote, "God likes to work miracles and to make a fool of the world. You must come to the wedding."

For both of them, the first year of marriage meant great adjustments. Martin had not made his bed in a year. "Before I married, no one had made up my bed for a whole year. The straw was rotting from my sweat. I wore myself out with work during the day, so that I fell into bed oblivious of everything." That was changed now. Katie even gave him a pillow.

For someone who had lived alone as long as Martin had, it wasn't easy to take someone else's views into consideration, but Katie's personality injected itself forcefully into Martin's decision-making processes. For instance, he had planned to go to a friend's wedding. When he told Katie where it was, she put up a fuss. Marauding bands of peasants were known to be in the area, and they were angry about some of Luther's writings. Katie thought it would be unwise to travel through their territory. Luther deferred to Katie's judgment.

But Martin's biggest adjustment dealt with the family's purse strings. He had never learned how to handle money. He once said, "God divided the hand into fingers so that money would slip through." He was "loath to accept anything not absolutely necessary, and he would give away anything not absolutely required."

With Katie as his business manager, fiscal planning was introduced. As one biographer puts it, Frau Luther's thrift enabled the Luthers to "accumulate a considerable property, notwithstanding her husband's unbounded liberality and hospitality." At times she had to hide money to keep Martin from giving it away. Martin would invite students to come and live with them, but Katie insisted that they pay room and board.

There is some indication that early in his marriage Martin was concerned enough about their financial situation to do something about it. He installed a lathe, perhaps thinking that he could go into business if his government stipend was cut off. There is no record that he ever used the lathe, however, and his philosophy was always "The Lord will provide." Martin's best work was done in front of books, not in front of a lathe.

He had to adjust to working with people around him. In the monastery he had been accustomed to being secluded, but Katie wouldn't stand for that. According to one story, he once locked himself in his study for three days until Katie had the door removed. Innocently, Martin asked as he saw Katie standing in the doorless doorway, "Why did you do that? I wasn't doing any harm."

Even after the children came—and they had six children—Martin, who was adjusting well to doing his work in a fishbowl atmosphere, often wanted to withdraw into himself at the time when Katie wanted to share his world. As biographer Roland Bainton points out, "The rhythm of work and rest did not coincide for Luther and his wife. After a day with children, animals and servants, she wanted to talk with an equal; and he, after preaching four times, lecturing and conversing with students at meals, wanted to drop into a chair and sink into a book." And then Katie might ask him a question about the Grand Master of Prussia or about predestination or why David in the Psalms bragged about his own righteousness when he really didn't have any.

"All my life is patience," said Luther, who must have recognized that patience wasn't his strongest virtue. "I have to be patient with the pope; I have to be patient with the heretics; I have to be patient with my family; and I even have to be patient with Katie." Katie had to be even more patient with her genius husband. He was a man of many moods; melancholy was often induced by poor health, and sometimes vice versa. "I think that my illnesses are not natural, but are mere bewitchments," he once said. Another time, he said, "I am so ill, but no one believes me." He had a shopping list of ailments, including gout, insomnia, catarrh, hemorrhoids, constipation, stone (gallstones or kidney stones), dizziness, and ringing in the ears.

Katie patiently nursed him back to health with proper diet, herbs, poultices, and massages. But once after she gave him some medicine for his migraine headaches, he responded: "My best prescription is written in the third chapter of John: 'For God so loved the world, that he gave his only begotten Son, that whosoever believeth in him should not perish, but have eternal life.'"

Katie was far more than chief cook, nurse, and bottle-washer. She had to be a remarkable woman to manage the ever-expanding Luther household. The Augustinian monastery where Luther had lived as a monk was deeded to Martin and Katie jointly by the government. On the first floor it had forty rooms with cells above for sleeping; at times every room was occupied. Besides the six Luther children, a half dozen of Martin's nieces and nephews were brought in, out of the goodness of his heart. Then when a friend lost his wife in a plague, Luther brought home the four children. To cope with the growing household, Katie in turn brought in some of her relatives, including Aunt Magdalena, who became a "nanny" for the Luther children and was nicknamed Mummie Lena.

Besides the children, there were tutors and student boarders, and of course due to Luther's fame, guests dropped in unexpectedly from England, Hungary, and elsewhere. One prince had been planning to take a room at the monastery for a few days, but changed his mind. He had received a letter, telling him the nature of the place: "An odd assortment of young people, students, young widows, old women and children lives in the Doctor's home; this makes for great disquiet."

But more and more the gregarious Luther thrived in the bustling atmosphere. The students, who got the benefit of Luther's formal lectures during the day, plied him with questions during the supper hour, and the reformer's famed *Table Talks* emerged. Katie would be at the far end of the table surrounded by the children while the students were taking notes close to her husband. No doubt she was a bit jealous that they were able to get closer to Dr. Luther than she could at the supper hour, but she knew her husband needed the attention. When she found out that the students were taking notes which they intended to publish, however, she wanted to charge them for note-taking privileges. Martin wouldn't let her do it. Later these students published 6,596 entries in their various versions of *Table Talks*. If Katie had had her way, she would have had a guilder for each entry.

At times, during these informal supper sessions, Luther's language became coarse or crude and Katie would have to rebuff him: "Oh, come now, that's too raw."

That happened often enough, for Luther was not known for delicacy of speech. But more often than that, he would spend the entire supper hour talking. When Katie, who didn't mince words, would say, "Doctor, why don't you stop talking and eat?" he would respond with something like "Women should repeat the Lord's Prayer before opening their mouths."

Katie called him "Doctor" in public conversation. Martin called her anything that came into his mind. Sometimes thinking of Eve, he called her "my rib." More often, thinking of the way she managed the manor, he called her "my lord." Sometimes, he called her "my chain," a pun on the German *Kethe.*

During the day, children played in Martin Luther's study. Once he told of his son Hans: "As I sit and write, he sings me a song, and if it gets too loud I scold him a little, but he goes on singing just the same."

Besides being a good mother and efficient housekeeper, Katie proved to be a wise manager of the farms, gardens, cattle, and livestock that the Luther family came to own, thanks to her prudent and expansive policies. She also took care of the small family brewery, and Luther frequently praised his wife's ability to make good beer.

Katie remodeled the monastery, installing a bathroom and putting in three cellars with an extra stairway. Because she had a goal to make their large household self-supporting, she grew peas, beans, turnips, melons, and lettuce in their able garden and eight different fruits in their orchard. (One year, her husband magnanimously took care of the garden.) Begrudgingly, Martin gave his consent to her to buy a second garden. The deciding factor was that a brook ran through it. Katie was able to hook quite a few fish from the brook for their supper table. Their livestock included eight pigs, five cows, nine calves, as well as chickens, pigeons, geese, and a dog named Tolpel that Luther hoped to meet in heaven. All of these were Katie's responsibility, and she even played the role of veterinary surgeon to do the job properly.

In a letter to a friend, Martin once wrote: "My lord Katie greets you. She plants our fields, pastures and sells cows et cetera. In between she has started to read the Bible. I have promised her fifty guilders if she finishes by Easter. She is hard at it and is at the end of the fifth book of Moses."

It's a wonder that she had time to read the Letter of Jude, much less the entire Bible. But Luther kept on prodding her to keep at her Bible reading, until she responded, "Would to God I lived up to it!"

Martin's appreciation of marriage deepened during his twenty years with Katie. Marriage is a school for character, and both he and Katie learned much in that school. They learned from each other, from their children, and from their mutual experiences. The father, said Luther one day, even learns from his experience of hanging out the diapers to the amusement of his neighbors. "Let them laugh," he concluded. "God and the angels smile in heaven."

He thought of the miracle at Cana in John 2 as a parable of marriage. "The first love," he once said, "is drunken. When the intoxication wears off, then comes the real married love." The best wine is saved for last. There may be times when it may appear that the wine is running out. "I will not take the vexation out of marriage. I may even increase it, but it will turn out wonderfully, as they only know who have tasted it."

Since both Martin and Katie had quick tongues, arguments were not foreign to the Luther household. "But," said Martin, "think of all the squabbles Adam and Eve must have had in the course of their nine hundred years. Eve would say, 'You ate the apple' and Adam would retort, 'You gave it to me.'"

With all the bantering, the Luthers had a good marriage. "To have peace and love in marriage is a gift which is next to the knowledge of the Gospel," he once said. And no one could deny that the Luthers had that gift.

Before his marriage, Luther sometimes spoke of matrimony as a necessity for the flesh. Afterwards, he emphasized it was an opportunity for the spirit. He came to decry the fact that many men were marrying only for physical reasons, were abusing their wives, and knew nothing about love. Marriage is no joke, he said; it must be worked on, and prayed over. "To get a wife is easy enough, but to love her with constancy is difficult . . . for the mere union of the flesh is not sufficient; there must be congeniality of tastes and character. And that congeniality does not come overnight."

"Some marriages were motivated by mere lust," Luther once said, "but mere lust is felt even by fleas and lice. Love begins when we wish to serve others."

"Of course, the Christian should love his wife," Luther declared. "He is supposed to love his neighbor, and since his wife is his nearest neighbor, she should be his deepest love. And she should also be his dearest friend."

That this friendship existed between Martin and Katie is obvious from the frequency of Luther's references to his wife. When he spoke of Paul's Epistle to the Galatians, the reading of which led to his spiritual rebirth, he called it "my Katharina von Bora." It was the epistle that was the closest to his heart.

Once when he was stressing the importance of trusting Christ in daily matters, he confessed: "I trust more in Katie and I expect more from Katie than I do Christ." Perhaps it testified more to his relationship with his wife than it did to a lack of commitment to Jesus Christ.

"Nothing is more sweet than harmony in marriage, and nothing more distressing than dissension," Luther said, and no doubt his marriage had moments of both. "Next to it is the loss of a child. I know how that hurts."

The Luthers lost their second child before she was a year old and their third, Magdalena, in her fourteenth year. "How strange it is that she is at peace and I am so sorrowful," he said at her death.

But children brought much joy to the home. Referring to his children, he said, "God has given to me greater gifts than to any bishop in a thousand years." Yet the children were certainly normal, active youngsters. To one of them, Luther cried out, "Child, what have you done that I should love you so? What with your befouling the corners and bawling through the whole house." In 1531, watching Katie fondle their youngest son, Martin, he remarked, "Surely God must talk with me even more fondly than my Katie with her little Martin."

When Luther was fifty-nine, their daughter Magdalena died. It was a severe blow to Luther at a time when he was beset with other trials as well. His health was worsening, and he was involved in several major religious disputes.

Outside the home, he was becoming increasingly bitter, cantankerous, and unbending. Some of his friends felt that he might undo all that he had accomplished in his earlier years. But the home was a refuge for him, and there is no indication that Luther's external problems soured its atmosphere.

On his deathbed, Luther admonished: "If it be God's will, accept it." Katie responded: "My dear Doctor, if it is God's will, I would rather have you with our Lord than here. Don't worry about us. God will take care of us."

In 1546 at the age of sixty-two, Martin died. Katie died four years later. Her last words were, "I will stick to Christ as a burr to a topcoat."

Martin may have been the key figure in the Protestant Reformation, but Martin and Katie together revolutionized the common concept of marriage that was held in that day.

There was a saying that Martin loved to quote: "Let the wife make her husband glad to come home and let him make her sorry to see him leave."

The success of any marriage depends on two people who aren't afraid to grow and change as Martin and Katie did.

Bibliography

Bainton, Roland. *Here I Stand.* Nashville: Abingdon, 1950.

D'Aubigne, J. H. Merle. *The Life and Times of Martin Luther.* Chicago: Moody, 1950.

Friedenthal, Richard. *Luther: His Life and Times.* New York: Harcourt, Brace, Jovanovich, 1967.

Luther, Martin. *Table Talk.* New Canaan, Conn.: Keats, 1979.

Schwiebert, E. G. *Luther and His Times.* St. Louis: Concordia, 1950.

Naturally Different

Calvin and Harriet Beecher Stowe

"Who's Calvin Stowe?" you ask.

He was the husband of Harriet Beecher Stowe, the celebrated author of *Uncle Tom's Cabin*. She was descended from the famous Beecher family in New England. According to Abraham Lincoln, she started the Civil War. She lectured in England as well as in the United States, and wrote scores of magazine articles and many books.

But you're still asking, "Who's Calvin?"

Well, I'd like to introduce him to you.

It took something for a nineteenth-century man to be married to a famous career woman. But what was that something?

What was the glue that kept these two people—who often criticized each other—from separating?

"My dear husband, I have been thinking of all your trials, and I really pity you in having such a wife. I feel as if I had been only a hindrance to you instead of a help, and most earnestly and daily do pray to God to restore my health that I may do something for you and my family. I think if I were only at home I could at least sweep and dust, and wash potatoes."

It is doubtful, however, whether Hattie Stowe would have done much sweeping and dusting even if she had been home.

In her later books, Harriet Beecher Stowe wrote of "ministering daily in holy works" and of redeeming "common toils from grossness and earthliness." But she wasn't always successful in taking her own advice.

Once when her husband was away, she wrote him, "I am already half-sick with confinement to the house." And a year later when Calvin Stowe was at a ministers' convention, she told him, "I am sick of the smell of sour milk, and sour meat, and sour everything, and then the clothes will not dry, and no wet thing does, and everything smells mouldy; and altogether I feel as if I never wanted to eat again."

At times she sounded more like a frustrated Erma Bombeck than a woman who was supposed to be able to redeem "common toils from grossness and earthliness."

Calvin Stowe was not exactly Mr. Handyman-around-the-house either. Awkward and inept, he was often overcome by his moods. A hypochondriac who sometimes slid into depression and hopelessness, he was known to go to his room and sulk for hours.

Hattie's fame as America's great novelist of the nineteenth century overshadowed Calvin's role as a seminary professor. She was acclaimed by literary and political figures on both sides of the Atlantic, from Dickens to Twain and from Queen Victoria to Lincoln. Lincoln suggested that she was the one who actually started the Civil War.

And Calvin? At times you could find him tagging along behind her on lecture tours or on the banquet circuit.

In his own field he was an erudite scholar, and Hattie was proud of him, but most people didn't see him in that setting. To tell the truth, even many of Hattie's biographers saw him as "gluttonous, neurasthenic, timid and lazy, a scatterbrain in emergencies and quite devoid of that talent for getting things done."

Maybe so, but the Stowes had a surprisingly strong marriage, glued together by love and two delightful senses of humor.

Hattie's *Uncle Tom's Cabin* became a runaway best-seller. More than 100,000 copies were sold in six months, and Hattie was catapulted overnight to the forefront of America's abolition movement. Basically, she was not a wild-eyed radical, but a mild-mannered moderate crusader, even as her minister father, Lyman, had been before her.

Lyman Beecher, a Congregational minister in Litchfield, Connecticut, had intoned against dueling, drinking, and Unitarianism, and thought that the slavery issue would best be solved by regeneration instead of by abolition. He had views on almost everything, including the birth of his sixth child in 1811. He told everyone that he wished it had been a boy. It turned out to be Harriet.

Her redeeming quality was that she was brilliant—he called her a genius when she was six—and her mind was honed by the subjects that were table conversation in the Beecher household. Her father beamed when at age twelve she wrote an essay, "Can the Immortality of the Soul be Proved by the Light of Nature?"

Hattie was small and bookish. She loved the poetry of Lord Byron and idolized the poet, but that was about the naughtiest thing in her life. In personality she was puzzling: sometimes moody and withdrawn, often witty and carefree, and introspective to an extreme. Yet she was a good listener, able to empathize deeply with others.

The Beecher family was a close-knit group of individualists. Hattie's oldest sister, Catherine, had launched a girls' school in Hartford. At thirteen, Hattie attended Catherine's school for one year, then taught Latin to younger students the next.

And that turned out to be a big year in Hattie's life. For one thing, Lord Byron died. That crushed her. She was recovering from her sorrow when she returned home the following summer to sit under her father's preaching. Throughout New England Lyman Beecher was getting a reputation as a spellbinding preacher. Normally, Hattie wasn't impressed; nor was he. "The less I have to say," he admitted, "the more I holler."

And Hattie said, "Most of my father's sermons were as unintelligible to me as if he had spoken in Choctaw."

But one Sunday was different. Perhaps because he couldn't decipher the scribbled notes which he had crumpled and stuffed into his pockets, he spoke extemporaneously. His text was the words of Christ: "Behold, I call you no longer servants, but friends." Hattie was "drawn to listen by a certain pathetic earnestness in his voice."

Hattie responded. That afternoon, she fell down on her knees in her father's study and sobbed, "Father, I have given myself to Jesus and He has taken me."

Sister Catherine, who had struggled against God for months before yielding, was dubious of the ease with which Hattie had made her decision. She was amazed, she said, that "a lamb could so easily be brought into the fold without being chased all over the lot by the shepherd."

Hattie's struggles lay ahead of her. She felt she was good for nothing, a feeling that plagued her until she wrote *Uncle Tom's Cabin*. At age fifteen, she wrote Catherine, "I don't know as if I am fit for anything, and I have thought that I could wish to die young, and let the remembrance of me and my faults perish in the grave, rather than live, as I fear I do, a trouble to everyone. You don't know how perfectly wretched I often feel: so useless, so weak, so destitute of all energy. Mama often tells me that I am a strange, inconsistent being."

Strange and inconsistent she was. At twenty-one, though she was a "handsome young woman of medium height and a slender, graceful figure," she had no suitors. She spent too much time reading and studying and daydreaming; her family thought she spent too much time "owling about." She, too, was concerned about her lack of friends. "Do you think," she asked an older brother, "that there is such a thing as so realizing the presence and character of God that He can supply the place of earthly friends?"

In her twenty-first year, she made a resolution to emerge from her shell. "Instead of shrinking into a corner I am holding out my hand and forming acquaintances with all who will be acquainted with me."

It was a good year to make such a resolution, for that was the year that her father, Lyman Beecher, was invited to become president of Lane Theological Seminary in Cincinnati, Ohio. That fall the family went west, throwing gospel tracts out the window of the stagecoach as they traveled.

Catherine was there too, and in a few months she had begun a new school for the young women of Cincinnati, called the Western Female Seminary. When Catherine saw there was a need for a geography book, she asked Hattie to write it. Within a few months, Hattie wrote her first book, but the intense pressure of meeting the deadline left her with morbid feelings again. "Thought, intense emotional thought, has been my disease. . . . My mind is exhausted and seeks to be sinking into deadness. . . . Thought is pain and emotion is pain."

Then some new friends came into her life. In August 1833, Calvin Stowe, newly appointed professor of biblical literature, came to Cincinnati with his bride, Eliza, who soon became Hattie's best friend. The three joined a literary group called the Semi-Colon Club; Hattie timidly submitted some of her stories to the Club and was thrilled with the encouragement she received.

A year later Eliza Stowe died in a cholera epidemic. Hattie was heartbroken, almost as grief-stricken as the widower Calvin Stowe. They consoled each other in their sorrows.

Like Hattie, Calvin was a New Englander. His father had died when Calvin was only six, and he was raised by "an anxious, fretful mother and two strong-minded spinster aunts." Calvin bore the psychological marks for the rest of his life. Somehow he scraped together enough money to get to college. Four years later he graduated as valedictorian. His reputation as a Hebrew scholar grew rapidly, and while still in his late twenties, he was named to the faculty of Lyman Beecher's seminary in Cincinnati.

Prince Charming for Hattie would probably have been a cross between the dashing literary Lord Byron and her virtuous preacher-father. At first glance, Calvin Stowe bore no resemblance to either; yet, he had an interest in literature and was a good preacher and an outstanding scholar. Most biographers, however, describe him as "round and rumpled, plump and balding, moon-faced and absentminded, short and stocky, timid and lazy, and a scatterbrain in emergencies as well."

Years later Mark Twain's daughter, Susy Clemens, saw him and ran home to tell her father, "Santa Claus has got loose."

Even Hattie had to laugh at some of Calvin's idiosyncrasies. She once wrote to a friend, tongue-in-cheek, that Calvin was "of Goblin origin decidedly, probably he preexisted in Germany, and certainly it was a great mistake that he was born in America."

Fortunately, Calvin had a sense of humor, too. At first he was attracted to Hattie because she enjoyed talking to him about his departed wife. But he was also attracted to the Beecher home, which, while not elegant, was adorned with taste, witty and pious conversation, and familial love. He had never known a family like that before.

Hattie, of course, was flattered that a distinguished young professor, eight years her senior, should be interested in her. One incident seemed to weld their relationship. One day only a few months after Eliza's death, Lyman Beecher, Hattie, and Calvin Stowe attended a presbytery meeting at a minister's home overlooking the Ohio River, not far from Cincinnati. They noticed that the minister lit a lantern and hung it in his window at night. When they asked the reason, he explained that any slave living across the river in Kentucky would know by the lantern in the window that he could find food and clothing in this home if he dared to escape from his master. Then the minister told stories of slaves he had helped, including a young Negro mother who had attempted to cross the Ohio River as it was beginning to thaw. Her baby was bundled to her breast. A March thaw made the crossing perilous; cracks formed in the ice. A thin film of water covered the surface, and she didn't know if the ice would support her next step. She slipped and fell, then struggled up, only to slip and fall again. Finally she reached the Ohio shore, climbed the steep bluff to the minister's home, and found food and dry clothing inside.

It was a story that neither Hattie nor Calvin would ever forget.

What cemented the relationship between the two of them was a series of evening messages preached by Calvin. Hattie took the assignment of reporting on the sermons for the Cincinnati newspaper. To make sure she had all the points of the message stated accurately, she met with Calvin both before and after each message.

About a year after Eliza's death, Calvin proposed to Hattie. A few months later—in January 1836—they were married; she was twenty-four, he was thirty-two.

On her wedding day she wrote a friend in New England, "Well, about half an hour more and your old friend, companion, schoolmate, etc., will cease to be Hattie Beecher and change to nobody knows who. . . . I have been dreading and dreading the time and lying awake all last week wondering how I should live through this overwhelming crisis, and lo, it has come and I feel nothing at all."

Three weeks later, she continued her play-by-play account of her marriage: "My dear, it is a wonder to myself. I am tranquil, quiet and happy."

Of course, she had to get used to Calvin. Since he was inept at hammering and sawing, she had to learn to do some things for herself. But his lack of physical dexterity didn't cause her to look down on him. It was obvious that she had married a brilliant man who was going places in the academic world.

Their wedding trip had been to a convention where he spoke on methods of Prussian education. Five months later he was off to Europe, thanks to a grant from the Ohio legislature (with the prodding of William Henry Harrison) to do research on education in Europe.

Before he returned, Hattie (who used her given name of Harriet more and more) bore twins named Eliza Tyler Stowe (after Calvin's first wife) and Harriet Beecher Stowe. A third child, Henry Ellis, was born a year later.

Thus, within two years of marriage, she had three children. She described her day: "Up I jump and up wakes baby. 'Now little boy, be good and let mother dress, because she is in a hurry.' I get my frock half on and baby by that time has kicked himself down off his pillow and is crying and fisting the bed clothes in great order. I stop with one sleeve off and one on to settle matters with him. Having planted him bolt upright and gone all up and down the chamber barefoot to get pillow and blankets to prop him up, I finish putting my frock on and hurry down to satisfy myself that breakfast is in progress. Then back I come into the nursery, where remembering that it is washing day and that there is a great deal of work to be done, I apply myself vigorously to sweeping, dusting and setting-to-rights so necessary where there are three little mischiefs always pulling down as fast as one can put up."

With three mischievous children and one absent-minded husband, Harriet had enough on her mind, but other problems were closing in. Economic problems were threatening the seminary, and the slavery question was embroiling the city of Cincinnati in civil unrest.

Calvin fretted. Harriet seemed almost oblivious to the outside problems: "I am but a mere drudge with few ideas beyond babies and housekeeping."

The longer they were married, the more they realized how different they were. Calvin put it this way: "I am naturally anxious, to the extent of needlessly taking much thought beforehand. You are hopeful to the extent of being heedless of the future, thinking only of the present." Calvin moped while Harriet hoped.

Calvin's mother came to help with the children, but she didn't help the marriage. She criticized Harriet for being extravagant with expenses and for wanting to be waited on. According to Harriet, her mother-in-law kept up "a perpetual state of complaint," until Calvin began to view his wife in "a wrong light."

As Calvin's salary checks became slimmer and slimmer, Harriet decided to write some magazine articles and submit them to Eastern publications. Her success was immediate. "I have realized enough by writing one way and another to enable me to add to my establishment a stout German girl who does my housework, leaving Anna full time to attend to the children, so I have about three hours per day in writing and if you see my name coming out everywhere, you may be sure of one thing—that I do it for pay."

Harriet's writing style was conversation on paper. She didn't have time to polish her phrases, so she just talked in ink. And people loved it.

So did Calvin. He was grateful for the checks received from the Eastern magazine editors, and he was thankful that his wife had an opportunity to develop her talents. Once when she was in New York talking to editors, he wrote her, "My dear, you must be a literary woman. It is so written in the book of fate."

Calvin's income had been sliced in half because of the seminary's plight. During these days she wrote, "I suffer with sensible distress of the brain, as I have done more or less since my illness last winter, a distress which some days takes from me all power of planning or executing anything. . . . When one cannot think or remember anything, then what can be done?"

173

Then when her brother George, only one year older, was found shot to death outside his home in Rochester, New York, everything caved in. Depressed, she stopped writing entirely. About the only thing she could laugh about was the way her husband tried to take charge: "My husband has developed wonderfully as a housefather and nurse. You would laugh to see him in his spectacles, gravely marching the little troop in their nightgowns up to bed, tagging after them, as he says, like an old hen after a flock of ducks."

When her health failed to improve, she eventually went to a sanatorium in Vermont to see if a special water treatment would help.

Those days were more difficult for Calvin than they were for her. Their letters frequently disclosed their love for each other. He loved her, he said, "as much as I am capable of loving a fellow creature."

But the letters also showed Calvin's self-doubts. He wondered if he should give up the ministry, not because of the seminary's dire financial situation but because of his own lack of spirituality. "I try to be spiritually minded," he wrote her, "and I find in myself a most exquisite relish and deadly longing for all kinds of sensual gratification."

She replied devotionally, "My love, you must know the wonderful knowledge of Jesus which so subdues and transforms. You seek knowledge with a burning thirst. Even so you must seek Christ, that you may know him. . . . If you had studied Christ with half the energy that you have studied Luther—if you were as eager for daily intercourse with him as to devour the daily newspaper—then would he be formed in you, the hope of glory. . . . You do not sufficiently control your own mind on this subject—all your carefulness, prudence, caution and honesty I admire and commend—but when you become nervous, anxious, fretful and apprehensive of poverty, then you have taken matters out of Christ's hand into your own."

But the admonition wasn't one-sided. When her letters got gloomy, he wrote back: "Is the high state of spirituality which you seemed to enjoy all gone? It was my chief hope—the darkness and despondency of my own mind—that you could be continually a guide and support to my feeble and tottering steps in the way of life."

174

When her letters sounded as if she was in "a high state of spirituality," he took "great comfort amid the terrible sorrow" of his life that his wife was growing in grace.

In 1850, Calvin and Harriet finally left Cincinnati when he received an opportunity to teach at his alma mater, Bowdoin College, in Maine. During the long winter, Harriet once again had time to write.

But what should she write about? Her sister Catherine urged her to write a story about slavery: "Hattie, if I could use a pen as you can, I would write something that will make this whole nation feel what an accursed thing slavery is."

She asked her brother, Henry Ward Beecher, and he replied, "Do it, Hattie, do it. Write something and I myself will scatter it thick as the leaves of Vallombrosa."

Hattie didn't feel inspired, but she scribbled a few pages on the subject. Calvin picked it up, read the pages slowly, and then responded in tears: "Hattie, this is it. Begin at the beginning, work up to this and you'll have your book."

So she plunged in and soon *Uncle Tom's Cabin* was written. Her first subtitle was "The Man Who Was a Thing," but later she changed it to "Life Among the Lowly."

It appeared first in serial form in the magazine *The National Era*, and Hattie could barely meet the magazine's deadlines. To get out of the house, she used her husband's office at Bowdoin where she could write in tranquility.

Though the story was an instant success in the magazine, the book publisher wasn't sure he wanted to take a risk on it. He asked Calvin Stowe to put up half the money for the cost of publishing it, but Calvin had no money.

Eventually, he agreed to give the Stowes a 10 percent royalty and printed 5,000 copies. In two days the first edition sold out. The publisher went back to press and three months later had sold out the next edition of 20,000 copies. Then he went back to press again.

Overnight Harriet became a celebrity. The publisher hadn't paid her the first royalty check yet, but he said she could expect a check in the thousands. For several years Calvin's annual salary had only been a thousand dollars.

She traveled to New York City where she was greeted as a star. She wrote back to her husband: "It is not fame nor praise that contents me. I seem never to have needed love so much as now. I long to hear you say that you love me."

When someone suggested that this sudden fame might lead her to pride and vanity, she replied, "You do not have to be afraid of that. You see, I did not write the book."

"What do you mean?" she was asked.

"I was only the instrument. The Lord wrote the book."

Soon *Uncle Tom's Cabin* was printed in England, France, Germany, Italy, and Portugal, and her fame became international. Within a year, she and Calvin had been invited to visit England, all expenses paid.

To a British writer she identified herself with her usual sense of humor, as "a little bit of a woman, somewhat more than forty, about as thin and dry as a pinch of snuff, never very much to look at in my best days and looking like a used up article now."

And her husband? Harriet described him this way: "a man rich in Greek and Hebrew, Latin and Arabic, and also, rich in nothing else."

The tour of England was more fun for Harriet than it was for Calvin. He reported to friends in the States: "Wife bears it all very well. She is meek, humble, pious and loving, the same that she ever was. As for me, I am tired to death of the life I lead here. From the lowest peasant to the highest noble, wife is constantly beset, and I for her sake, so that we have not a moment's quiet."

Everyone from Charles Dickens to the Archbishop of Canterbury seemed enraptured at the thought of shaking hands with Harriet Beecher Stowe. Calvin could hardly believe it.

Back in America, Harriet found herself thrust into the role of leader in the anti-slavery movement. What riled her upon her return was that northern clergymen were not unanimous in their condemnation of slavery. So with the help of her brother Edward and her husband, Calvin, she drafted an anti-slavery petition, got 3,000 ministers to sign it, and traveled to Washington to present it to Congress.

Not many years later, Harriet was Lincoln's guest in the White House. The President put out his great hand and took Harriet's small hand in his. "So this is the little lady who made this big war?" he said.

On January 1 she was sitting quietly in the balcony of the Boston Music Hall, enjoying a concert, when a telegram came from Washington, announcing that Abraham Lincoln had signed the Emancipation Proclamation. Cheers erupted throughout the large auditorium, hats were thrown into the air, and people hugged and kissed each other. Then someone spotted Harriet in the balcony and shouted, "Mrs. Stowe! Mrs. Stowe!" Soon the entire Music Hall was ringing with shouts, "Mrs. Stowe! Mrs. Stowe!" She was the little lady who had done the most to rouse the North to the plight of the slave. Perhaps as much as Lincoln himself, she had caused that Proclamation to be written.

But life at home with Calvin was quite mundane compared to the plaudits of the crowds.

Occasionally he chronicled her shortcomings for her. She wasn't the easiest person to live with, he told her: "I am naturally very methodical. Anything out of place is excessively annoying. This is a feeling to which you are a stranger. You have no idea of either time or place. Permanency is my delight; yours everlasting change."

That wasn't all. He continued his criticism: "I am naturally particular, you are naturally slack—and you often give me inexpressible torment without knowing it. You have vexed me beyond endurance often by taking up my newspapers and then instead of folding them properly and putting them in their place, either dropping them all sprawling on the floor, or wabbling them all up into one wabble, and then sprawling them on the table like an old hen with her guts and gizzard squashed out."

His next complaint was: "I am naturally very irritable, take offense easily, utter my vexation in a moment, and then it is gone; you are naturally more forebearing, take offense less easily and are silent and retain the wound."

All of these criticisms of Harriet were contained in a letter Calvin wrote to her while she was traveling. But five days later, he had second thoughts. He apologized for spelling out their differences so sharply, before tacking on a few fresh complaints: "You seldom hesitate to make a promise, whether you have ability to perform it or not, like your father and Kate—only not quite as bad—and promises so easily made are very easily broken."

Harriet's response was a mixture of an apology and a defense. Her main complaint against him was: "If when you have said things hastily and unjustly you would only be willing to retract them in calmer moments. This is what you almost never do. You leave the poisoned arrow in the wound."

But then in a calmer mood she wrote, "With such a foundation for mutual respect and affection as there is in us—with such true and real and deep love, it is good that we can exercise a correcting power over each other—that I might help you to be kind and considerate, and you me to be systematic and regular."

Throughout life, Calvin tended to be the pessimist; she the optimist. He was the penny-pincher, who felt every luxury would be a step toward the poorhouse; she was the visionary who always had a fresh dream to replace an old one that had gone sour.

In 1863 Calvin, now sixty, retired from teaching, and Harriet, eight years younger, was planning a dream home for them to live in. Calvin, of course, was not much help, either in dreaming or in building. He was sure that he would be able to say "I told you so" this time.

But she wrote cheerily: "My house with eight gables is growing wonderfully. I go every day to see it. I am busy with drains, sewers, sinks, digging, trenching and above all with manure. You should see the joy with which I gaze on manure heaps, in which the eye of faith sees Delaware grapes and d'Angouleme peas and all sorts of roses and posies."

After they had moved in, Harriet had to admit, albeit reluctantly, that Calvin was probably right this time. Once, Calvin was taking an afternoon snooze in his bedroom when the plumbing in the ceiling erupted and he was ingloriously drenched. One biographer lists the problems: "Pipes were forever bursting, windows jamming, cellars flooding, and other wholly undreamed-of difficulties were always arising. When bills for repairs were added to the high cost of simply maintaining the house, the lawn and the greenhouse, the result was staggering."

It was about that time that Harriet is said to have prayed, "Lord, don't take me until my dear husband is gone, for nobody else can do for him what I can."

One thing she did for him was to get a manuscript of his published. For years he had been working on a manuscript, a theological work on the origin of the books of the Bible. Though he was one of the foremost theologians of the day, he had a psychological block about putting his thoughts in print. With little success, Harriet had been urging him to complete the manuscript. Finally, she privately contacted a publisher: "In regard to Mr. Stowe, you must not scare him off by grimly declaring that you must have the whole manuscript complete before you set the printer to work. You must take the three quarters he brings you and at least make believe to begin printing; and he will immediately go to work and finish the whole; otherwise, what with lectures and the original sin of laziness, it will all be indefinitely postponed. I want you to make a crisis, that he shall feel that now is the accepted time, and that this must be finished first and foremost."

Harriet's plan succeeded. And much to the surprise of the publisher and Calvin, but not to Calvin's optimistic wife, so did the book. It sold extremely well and stopped Calvin's thinking about the poorhouse for a while.

The Stowes had seven children: the twins, Eliza and Harriet, neither of whom ever married; Henry Ellis; Frederick William; Georgiana May; Samuel Charles, who died of cholera in infancy; and Charles Edward, born when his mother was thirty-nine.

Henry drowned in the Connecticut River near the campus of Dartmouth College, where he had been studying. Both Calvin and Harriet were crushed by the tragedy, but it was Harriet who bounced back more quickly. Several times a day for weeks, Calvin visited his son's grave. "I am submissive, but not reconciled," he said. Finally Harriet, pretending that she needed a vacation, coaxed him to take the family to Maine for a few weeks.

But their problem child was Fred, who returned from the Civil War as a captain wounded in action at Gettysburg. More of a trial was the fact that Fred had become an alcoholic.

For a long time Harriet the optimist refused to admit that her son had a serious problem. Calvin knew better. She buried herself in writing prodigiously and in other projects such as building her new house, so she wouldn't have to think about Fred so much. Between 1863 and 1870 she wrote ten books, a volume of short stories, another of religious poetry, as well as dozens of magazine articles.

Finally, however, unable to ignore Fred's alcoholism any longer, she thought of a way to keep him busy.

What a grandiose scheme it was. She rented an old cotton plantation near Jacksonville, Florida, and installed Fred as manager (even though his knowledge of growing and marketing cotton was nil). She was sure that outdoor work would be good for him. One hundred former slaves would be employed on the project.

Fred's problems with alcohol continued. After two years of failure—both in the cotton business and with staying sober—Fred was switched by his mother to a 200-acre orange grove nearby. Once again the results were disastrous.

A few years later, Fred Stowe disappeared. He was last seen in San Francisco, then was heard of no more.

The loss of this son in whom she had invested so much made an old woman out of Hattie. In a short time her hair turned white.

For several more years she continued writing and even did some lecturing, but when Calvin died in 1886, Harriet's public life stopped. She lived ten more years and then was buried at his side in Andover, Massachusetts.

It was an unusual marriage, especially for the nineteenth century. Though Calvin's fame as a scholar was far eclipsed by his wife's achievements as a popular writer, he seemed sincerely happy with his wife's prestige. In a book she once wrote about Bible characters, her description of Abraham and Sarah may give a clue to her own relationship with Calvin: "While Sarah called Abraham 'lord,' it is quite apparent from certain little dramatic incidents that she expected him to use his authority in the line of her wishes."

In pursuing their separate careers, Calvin and Harriet spent considerable time away from each other. Though they frequently criticized each other, their deep love for one another was obvious.

It was Calvin who had encouraged her to launch her writing career, and it was Calvin who had served as her literary agent both in America and in England in the early stages of her writing.

Calvin had streaks of instability, stemming, no doubt, from his background. During these periods Harriet's strength undergirded the family. When he became moody and pessimistic, she maneuvered him out of his despair. When he was King Saul in a fit of depression, she had to be his King David playing a harp to bring him out of his moods.

Like many modern marriages, the union of Calvin and Harriet Beecher Stowe was a relationship that can't be put in a box. Each strengthened the other, and probably neither would have achieved fame without the other's support.

Bibliography

Bradford, Gamaliel, ed. *Portraits of American Women*. Boston: Houghton Mifflin, 1919.

Gerson, Noel B. *Harriet Beecher Stowe: A Biography*. New York: Praeger, 1976.

Johnston, Johanna. *Runaway to Heaven*. Garden City, N.Y.: Doubleday, 1963.

Stowe, Charles Edward. *The Life of Harriet Beecher Stowe*. Boston: Houghton Mifflin, 1889.

Wilson, Robert F. *Crusader in Crinoline: The Life of Harriet Beecher Stowe*. Philadelphia: J. B. Lippincott, n.d.

A Matter of Friendship and Expediency

C. S. and Joy Lewis

What made a nice Jewish girl like Joy Davidman marry an Oxford professor like C. S. Lewis?

Why would a confirmed bachelor in his late fifties marry a divorcée when he was so vehemently opposed to divorce? Or was he, to put it bluntly, trapped into marriage?

If you count the months that they lived together as man and wife, it was a short marriage indeed. But it was a surprisingly good one, one that endured suffering and pain, miracles and joy.

It taught both of them how good marriage could be, and both of them were caught by surprise. In fact, you might even say that they were "surprised by Joy."

You have to admit, however, that the first announcement of the marriage was hardly romantic: "You may as well know (but don't talk of it, for all is still uncertain) that I may soon be, in rapid succession, a bridegroom and a widower. There may, in fact, be a deathbed marriage." That was the way the marriage of Jack and Joy Lewis began.

In 1925, Helen Joy Davidman (her friends called her Joy) was a little ten-year-old Jewish girl attending grade school in the Bronx.

In 1925, Clive Staples Lewis (his friends called him Jack) was a young don teaching English literature at Oxford University. He was a "determined atheist."

By 1937, Joy Davidman had graduated from college, had become a card-carrying Communist, and had ventured to Hollywood to write movie scripts for MGM.

By 1937, Jack Lewis had become a convert to Christianity, had become a recognized classical scholar, and was beginning to think about writing a book about the devil, to be called *The Screwtape Letters*.

By 1943, Joy Davidman—now associate editor of the Communist *New Masses* and a "confirmed atheist"—was married to a fellow Communist, an alcoholic who was a free-lance writer.

By 1943, Jack Lewis was broadcasting a series of talks called *Mere Christianity* for the British Broadcasting Corporation.

Jack Lewis, the dignified Oxford don, and Joy Davidman, the feisty Jewish Communist from the Bronx, seemed farther apart than ever.

The story of how they got together—and their brief but unusual marriage—is just as unlikely as any of the science fiction that C. S. Lewis penned.

C. S. Lewis, of course, became famous in many areas. He earned a scholarly reputation in language and letters. His *Chronicles of Narnia* are beloved by children (as well as their parents). His science fiction is read and admired by many. His apologetics (*Mere Christianity, The Pilgrim's Regress, Miracles*) have helped woo many (including Charles Colson) to Christ. Other books (*The Screwtape Letters, The Problem of Pain, The Great Divorce*) have become Christian classics. He is regarded by many as the premier Christian writer of the twentieth century.

But who was Joy Davidman? For C. S. Lewis-watchers (and his fan club was growing rapidly in the 1950s), she seemed to erupt into his life suddenly and then was wrenched away from him in death almost before they knew her.

But Joy Davidman was more than a shadowy figure, a mysterious woman in black, a blip on the screen of C. S. Lewis's life.

A poet who had her efforts published in the prestigious Yale Younger Poets series when she was only twenty-three, and a novelist whose first work, *Anya* (published when she was twenty-five), was acclaimed by

183

The New York Times and *Saturday Review of Literature*, Joy Davidman exuded writing talent.

She was born in 1915. Her parents, both educators in the New York City school system, saw that she was raised a good atheist. "[We] sucked in atheism with [our] canned milk," she said later. By the time she was eight years old, she delighted her father by announcing that, following in his footsteps, she had become an atheist. By the time she was twenty, she had a master's degree from Columbia University.

In her early twenties she drifted into Communism. "My motives were a mixed lot. Youthful rebelliousness, youthful vanity, youthful contempt of the stupid people who seemed to be running society, all these played a part."

Having gotten her Communist card, she joined the staff of the semi-official party magazine, *New Masses*. Her excursion to Hollywood as a film writer was brief. MGM apparently didn't like her scripts, and she responded by calling the movie moguls a bunch of buffoons.

Back in New York she plunged into Communist party concerns. "She worked very hard to convert her friends," one of them reported. An associate editor of *New Masses*, she concentrated on book and movie reviews and also served as poetry editor.

One acquaintance described her as "unattractive physically, not particularly ugly or interesting, but rather dumpy and though obviously female, rather unfeminine. Her manner and mannerisms were almost a stereotype of the 1930s radical. She was aggressive, impatient, and intolerant." At twenty-seven, she was charmed by fellow Communist Bill Gresham, a folk singer, storyteller, and writer who had fought in the Spanish Civil War. He had been married before, but the marriage had been ruined by his alcoholism and his inability to settle down. He was a wanderer.

Joy overlooked his problems and married him in the summer of 1942.

In the next three years, Joy and Bill had two boys, several cats—Joy loved cats—and three residences, from Manhattan to Queens to Ossining. Joy always had the notion that a change of residence would solve the problems of her marriage, but it never did. Bill kept on drinking, kept playing around with other women, and could never provide a suitable income for a family to live on.

Joy, who always prided herself on being in control of things, was at her wits' end. It all came to a climax when "one day he telephoned me . . . to tell me he was having a nervous breakdown. He felt his mind going, he couldn't stay where he was and he couldn't bring himself to come home." Frantically, she phoned every haunt and den which she thought he might frequent, but without success. "There was nothing left to do," she said, "but wait and see if he turned up alive or dead. I put the babies to sleep and waited. For the first time in my life I felt helpless."

"My pride was forced to admit," she says, "that I was not, after all, the 'master of my fate' and 'the captain of my soul.' All my defenses—the walls of arrogance and cocksureness and self-love, behind which I had hid from God—went down momentarily, and God came in."

To her own amazement she found herself on her knees praying. "I must say, I was the world's most surprised atheist."

Joy didn't arise from her knees with a full-blown theology, but from then on she had no doubt in her mind that there was a living God.

She began reading literature from a fresh viewpoint. Francis Thompson's poem "The Hound of Heaven" ("I fled Him down the night and down the days; I fled Him down the arches of the years") caused her to break into tears. C. S. Lewis's works were now devoured ("I snatched at books I had despised before"). But most of all, she began reading the Bible, and there she met the Redeemer. "When I read the New Testament, I recognized Him. He was Jesus."

When Bill came back home, he was so impressed with the change he saw in his wife that he began attending church with her. Soon he made a profession of faith as well.

Joy became as ardent a Christian as she had been a Communist. One friend wrote that Joy "was sure of what she believed, and she loved to take people on in debates. She was argumentative, and she spoke with contempt for those she felt were superficial thinkers."

One Christian writer whose thinking she admired was C. S. Lewis, and because she admired his thinking, she wrote a letter to him early in 1950. She took exception to a point he made in one of his books;

Lewis responded quickly and decimated her arguments. She was amazed. "Lord, he knocked my props out from under me unerringly, one shot to a pigeon. . . . Being disposed of so neatly by a master of debate, all fair and square—it seems to be one of the great pleasures in life. . . . What I feel is a craftsman's joy at the sight of a superior performance."

Though her husband had made a Christian profession, he soon began dabbling in cults and other religions. Then he returned to his alcoholic patterns.

But as Lyle Dorsett says in *And God Came In,* "The most devastating blow to the marriage came with Bill Gresham's continuing infidelity. . . . The hard-drinking novelist, trying to fill the empty space inside himself with liquor . . . sought satisfaction in a string of extramarital liaisons—short-lived affairs and one-night stands. Bill never tried to hide these indiscretions, and he could not understand why Joy was hurt by them."

Early in 1952 Joy's cousin Renee Pierce came to live with the Greshams. Separated from her husband, Renee needed lodging for herself and her two children. In the arrangement, Joy got a good housekeeper. Joy loved writing and gardening, not cleaning the house, as anyone who set foot in her house could immediately recognize.

Throughout the first half of 1952 she became more and more confused about her relationship with Bill. As a Christian she wanted to preserve her marriage, but she had lost all respect for him. Preserving the marriage seemed to be a losing battle. Because of his infidelity, she no longer wanted to sleep with him. And yet she felt sorry for him. He was psychologically troubled and insecure. She didn't know what to do, where to turn.

Finally she decided she needed to get away, "to run away from him physically" in order to clarify her thinking. She needed to talk with someone, someone she could respect, so she turned to the man whom she regarded as "one of the clearest thinkers of our time," C. S. Lewis.

Joy had other reasons for going to England. As a student of English literature, she could enjoy the visit for educational reasons. And because she was recovering from a recent flare-up of jaundice, she would profit physically from the time abroad. She also had a book manuscript to complete. But her main reason for going was to meet the man she idolized, C. S. Lewis, and to see if he could give her some spiritual understanding regarding her muddled matrimony.

So in early September 1952, Joy left her children in the care of her cousin Renee and sailed to England to meet the confirmed bachelor, C. S. Lewis.

Born near Belfast, Ireland, in November 1898, C. S. Lewis grew up, he says, with "good parents, good food and a garden . . . to play in." His only brother Warren ("Warnie"), three years older, was what Lewis termed "a confederate from the first." A nurse enthralled him with tales of leprechauns and buried treasures, and his parents surrounded him with books.

Before he was ten, however, his mother died of cancer, and in reaction his father's behavior became alternately depressed and erratic. "All that was tranquil and reliable," C. S. Lewis wrote, "disappeared from my life." Warren and Jack grew closer; "two frightened urchins huddled for warmth in a bleak world," is the way Lewis puts it in *Surprised by Joy*. For the next eight years Warren and Jack were enrolled in a variety of educational experiences (Jack attended five schools in eight years) before World War I.

In 1917 he joined the army, and late that year he was ordered to the military front in France. He wired his father to come and see him off. His father responded, "Don't understand telegram. Please write." Jack Lewis shot back another wire, but his father still didn't come.

In April 1918, the Germans launched their second putsch. It was a time Lewis never forgot: "the cold, the frights . . . the horribly smashed men still moving like half-crushed beetles, the sitting or standing corpses, the landscape of sheer earth without a blade of grass, the boots warn day and night until they seemed to grow to your feet."

On April 15, Jack Lewis was wounded. Shrapnel from an exploding shell lodged in his chest. "The one under my arm," he wrote a month later, "is worse than a flesh wound, as the bit of metal which went in there is now in my chest."

As Jack Lewis returned to civilian life and to Oxford University, there is a mysterious gap in his autobiography, *Surprised by Joy*. He writes: "One huge and complex episode will be omitted. I have no choice about this reticence. All I can or need say is that my earlier hostility to the emotions was very fully and variously avenged."

Green and Hooper in *C. S. Lewis: A Biography* suggest that "the only really overwhelming 'love affair' of his early life" took place in this mysterious gap.

The situation seems to have begun when Jack was recuperating from his war injuries in a London hospital. He begged his father in Ireland to visit him: "Come and see me. I am homesick," he wrote. His father didn't respond.

A month later Jack was moved to a convalescent center in Bristol, near the home of an army buddy and former school friend, Paddy Moore. Previously Jack had visited in Paddy's home and had enjoyed his brief stays. Now Jack, motherless since ten and feeling psychologically fatherless, turned to Paddy's mother, Janie Moore.

Paddy had asked Jack to look after his mother in case he didn't return from France, and about the time that Jack arrived in Bristol, Janie Moore received official word that her son had been killed in action.

The developing relationship between Jack Lewis and Janie Moore is hard to describe because Jack did not want to talk to anyone else about it and also because he hinted that Janie had been more to him than a foster mother. Janie was attracted to him, not only because she had lost a husband and a son, but also because, as she wrote, "he possesses such a wonderful power of understanding and sympathy."

The following year, when Jack was enrolled in Oxford, his father started showing some concern that his son was spending his vacations in Bristol with Janie Moore rather than in Belfast with him. He wrote to his other son, Warren, "I confess I do not know what to do about Jack's affair. It worries and depresses me greatly. All I know about the lady is that she is old enough to be his mother, and that she is in poor circumstances." He was also concerned because Jack was "an impetuous, kindhearted creature who could be cajoled by any woman who had been through the mill."

188

In 1920, Janie Moore and her daughter Maureen moved from Bristol to Oxford, renting a small house there. Jack helped with the rent, though he himself was continuing to receive financial aid from his father. A few months later Jack, still an undergraduate himself, found larger accommodations, rented them, and invited the Moores to move in with him.

He was twenty-two at the time; Janie Moore was forty-eight. He wrote to a friend: "I combine the life of an Oxford undergraduate with that of a country householder—a feat which I imagine is seldom performed."

His father didn't like it at all; he described himself as "estranged from his son."

Even his brother Warren couldn't understand it. "What actually happened," he wrote, "was that Jack had set up a joint establishment with Mrs. Moore, an arrangement which bound him to her service for the next thirty years and ended only with her death in January 1951. How the arrangement came into being no one will ever know, for it was perhaps the only subject which Jack never mentioned to me, more than never mentioned, for on the only occasion when I hinted at my curiosity he silenced me with an abruptness which was sufficient warning never to re-open the subject."

Between 1930 and 1950, Warren lived with Jack Lewis and Janie Moore. During that period the relationship seemed to be that of an overly possessive and selfish mother to her son. "I do not think I ever saw Jack at his desk for more than half an hour without Mrs. Moore calling for him. 'Coming,' Jack would roar, down would go his pen, and he would be away perhaps five minutes, perhaps half an hour, and then return and calmly resume work on a half-finished sentence."

Jack Lewis and Janie Moore lived together not as man and wife, but as son and mother. Yet the relationship was shrouded in mystery and suspicion. Granted, Jack had vowed to Paddy Moore that he would look after his mother, but he wasn't obligated to live with her. A psychological dependency obviously had developed.

Later in life, Jack referred to her as "Mother," and there was a sense in which they had adopted each other after Paddy Moore died on the battlefield in France.

Jack Lewis, of course, went on to become an Oxford don and literary scholar. In those early years he was also a convinced atheist. Janie
Moore, bitter about her lot in life, no doubt fed his atheism.

Little in Christianity attracted him. "Christianity," he writes in *Surprised by Joy,* "was mainly associated for me with ugly architecture,
ugly music, and bad poetry." But what bothered him most was "my
deep-seated hatred of authority. No word in my vocabulary expressed
deeper hatred than the word 'interference.' But Christianity placed at
the center what then seemed to me a transcendental Interferer."

Gradually, Jack's atheism crumbled, no thanks to Janie Moore, who
remained an atheist till death. At first Jack began to realize that atheism didn't make good sense philosophically. He thought he could accept
a universal Absolute, an impersonal, uncaring, abstract Principle. "We
could talk religiously about the Absolute; there was no danger of Its
doing anything about us. . . . There was nothing to fear; better still,
nothing to obey."

It was, however, one step closer to truth. "And so," he says, "the
great Angler played His fish, and I never dreamed that the hook was
in my tongue."

Reading George Herbert, George Macdonald, and G. K. Chesterton
unnerved him. They were unabashed Christians who were good writers—and their Christianity made surprisingly good sense. "A young
atheist," Lewis says coyly, "cannot guard his faith too carefully. Dangers lie in wait for him on every side."

Lewis liked to engage in philosophical argument, and he was ready
to discuss whether the Infinite could be a personal being. But soon he
realized that if he lost the argument and had to believe in God as a personal being, it was a new ball game. "I was to be allowed to play at philosophy no longer. . . . My Adversary . . . would not argue about it. He
only said, 'I am the Lord.'"

Later he said that his conversion did not result from his search for
God. For him it was more like "the mouse's search for a cat."

And then he tells of that night in Oxford in 1929 when "I gave in,
and admitted that God was God, and knelt and prayed; perhaps, that
night, the most dejected and reluctant convert in all England." He

described himself as "a prodigal who is brought in kicking, struggling, resentful, and darting his eyes in every direction for a chance to escape."

Once he was in the fold, however, his writings brought many other prodigals, also struggling and resentful, into the kingdom of God.

As a scholar, Lewis specialized in medieval and Renaissance English literature. But as a Christian he soon branched out into other areas, including science fiction, with *Out of the Silent Planet* in 1938, various types of theological and apologetic works (*The Great Divorce, The Screwtape Letters, The Problem of Pain, Miracles*) and children's works (the Narnia series).

Perhaps his best known and most quoted work is *The Screwtape Letters,* fictional correspondence from an experienced devil named Screwtape, who was high in the Infernal Civil Service, to a junior colleague, who happened to be his nephew, named Wormwood. Wormwood had been sent on assignment to earth to secure the damnation of a young man who lived with a very trying mother. (Some Lewis buffs have thought the "very trying mother" resembles Janie Moore.)

During World War II he was asked to give a restatement of Christian doctrine in lay language over the British Broadcasting Corporation. The talks were later brought together in one volume called *Mere Christianity.* Along with his restatement of orthodox Christian doctrine, Lewis took a strong position for Christian marriage. "The Christian rule is: Either marriage, with complete faithfulness to your partner, or else total abstinence." Marriage between Christians is for life, he taught.

In 1948, Janie Moore, having lost the use of her legs, and with her mind slipping away as well, had to be placed in a nursing home. Jack continued to visit her every day. When she died in 1951, it seemed a great weight had been lifted from Jack's shoulders.

He never thought of himself as much of a letter writer, but his output of correspondence multiplied after 1950. The first letter in his *Letters to an American Lady* (an anonymous woman) is dated only shortly before Janie's death, about the same time Joy Davidman began her correspondence with Jack Lewis.

He couldn't reply to all the letters he received, but Joy's letters to him "stood out from the ruck" because they were "amusing and well-written."

Two years later, Joy Davidman came to England. Accompanied by a friend from London, she visited Oxford and asked Jack Lewis to have lunch with them. (Curiously, when Joy walked into his life, he was working on his autobiography, entitled *Surprised by Joy*.) Evidently Jack, now fifty-four and still shy among women, enjoyed the luncheon, for shortly afterward he reciprocated, inviting Joy and her friend along with a fellow professor to lunch at his place.

A few weeks later, Jack's brother, Warren, was included in another luncheon engagement. In his diary, Warren described Joy as of "medium height, good figure, horn-rimmed specs, quite extraordinarily uninhibited."

While in England, Joy completed her manuscript on the Ten Commandments, *Smoke on the Mountain,* dedicating it to C. S. Lewis. He agreed to write the introduction. In it, he said, "Joy Davidman is one who comes to us from the second generation of unbelief; her parents, Jewish by blood, rationalists by conviction. This makes her approach extremely interesting to the reclaimed apostates of my own generation; the daring paradoxes of our youth were the stale platitudes of hers."

For Joy, England was delightful. "I've never felt at home anywhere as I do in London or Oxford," she wrote during her stay.

But back in the States there was trouble awaiting her. Instead of diminishing in her absence, her marital problems were becoming more complicated. Shortly after Christmas and only a few days before her scheduled return, Joy received a letter from her husband, Bill. "I didn't want to cloud your holiday with things that would upset you," he told her, but "Renee and I are in love."

He said that he appreciated "what resolutions you have made about coming home and trying to make a go of our marriage." But it wasn't worth it, he said, to sacrifice human life "on the altar of will power." His four-page, single-spaced letter concluded by suggesting that the "optimum solution would be for you to be married to some really swell guy, Renee and I to be married, and both families to live in easy calling distance so that the Gresham kids could have Mommy and Daddy on hand." Obviously, Bill Gresham had it all worked out.

Only with Jack Lewis did Joy share the letter. He expressed his strong feelings against divorce; but he admitted that he saw no way that the marriage could be saved.

Joy didn't know what to expect when she arrived back in the States. But as soon as she arrived in New York, she found out. "Bill greeted me by knocking me about a bit and half choking me." He had been drinking again.

Before long, she resigned herself to the divorce. She wrote to a friend, "I always took it that divorce was only the last possible resort, and felt I ought to put up with anything I could bear for the children's sake. And I hoped that Bill's adulteries, irresponsibilities, etc., would end, if he ever recovered from his various neuroses; also that his becoming a Christian would make a difference."

But Bill's previous Christian profession had been forgotten; he had renounced Christianity.

So Joy despaired of seeing any change in him, and she didn't fight it when Bill followed Renee to Florida. In Florida he filed for divorce on the grounds of desertion and incompatibility.

It didn't take Joy very long to decide what to do next. There was nothing to keep her in America any longer. And in November 1953, eleven months after she had left, she was back in England, this time with her two boys. David was nine; Douglas was eight.

With little money but with confidence that she was in God's will, she found a two-room apartment in a section of London where several other writers lived. From intermittent alimony checks and equally intermittent royalty checks for free-lance writing, she struggled to pay the rent. Nevertheless, she faced her challenges positively. "The Lord really is my Shepherd, by gum," she wrote in a letter back to the States.

Occasionally, she took her boys to visit Jack Lewis in Oxford. Warren and Jack taught the boys how to play chess; they also took frequent walks in the woods together.

Joy's first eighteen months back in England were difficult. Not only were finances tight, but her brash personality didn't win any friends for her. As Lyle Dorsett says, "Joy's aggressive attitude and facial expressions, her sharp language and love of argument for the challenge of it . . . were viewed as rudeness and vulgarity. . . . Joy's status as a divorced . . . woman made things worse. . . . Her obviously brilliant mind, the breadth of her reading, and her nearly photographic memory intimidated still others."

The one friend she could count on was Jack Lewis, though she hesitated to presume on his friendship. She restrained herself from visiting Oxford as often as she wanted to, because she felt her two active sons might be too much of a strain on the two bachelor professors.

But when Lewis became aware of her financial needs, he volunteered to help. One of the ways he did this was by paying the tuition for the boys' schooling.

In 1955 Joy moved to Oxford to a duplex apartment about a mile from the residence of the Lewis brothers. It was Jack himself who had encouraged Joy's move and had found the house for her.

In the beginning, Jack was undeniably the pursued, not the pursuer. According to the Hooper and Green biography, he was even known to hide when he saw Joy coming to visit him. No doubt this was due to several factors: his shyness, his fear of developing a relationship with a divorced woman, and his desire to preserve his lifelong independence.

But that changed. Though Jack continued to hold that he could not marry a divorced woman (the Church of England contended that remarriage after divorce constituted adultery), he soon was walking to her house every day to see her. And Joy wrote that "the most wonderful ecstasy came from just holding hands and walking on the heather."

Brother Warren wrote in his diary that Jack and Joy "began to see each other every day. It was obvious what was going to happen." For Joy, at the beginning, it was hero-worship. Quickly it moved toward genuine love. For Jack it started as intellectual stimulation, then a compatible friendship. Love may not have blossomed for him until after marriage.

It all happened after the British Home Office decided not to renew Joy's permit to remain in England. After all, she had been a card-carrying Communist a dozen years earlier. Lewis, who did not cherish any fondness for the United States, could not bear to think of Joy being forced to return "to that dreadful place."

The only way to keep her in England was to marry her. Yet his church opposed marriage to a divorced woman, and Jack was a loyal churchman.

To get around the problem, he decided to marry Joy in a civil ceremony, but not to seek permission for a religious ceremony from the Church of England. In addition, they would not live together as man and wife.

Jack told his brother Warren that nothing would change. Joy would continue to live in her house with her two boys, and he would continue to live in The Kilns with Warren. "The marriage," he told Warren, "was a pure formality designed to give Joy the right to go on living in England."

The fact that Joy consented to such an arrangement is even more amazing than the fact that Jack had proposed it. Moreover, both of them agreed to keep the civil marriage as secret as possible.

Jack told biographer Roger Green that it was "a pure matter of friendship and expediency."

But a few months later there was a complication. Joy complained of pain, especially in her left hip. At first it was diagnosed as acute rheumatism; but it was much worse.

Meanwhile, Jack was increasingly uncomfortable about the marriage arrangement. He visited her every evening, and with each visit his love for Joy seemed to be strengthened.

Eventually he decided to ask permission for a religious ceremony. He thought that the church might grant permission because Joy's first husband had been divorced prior to his marriage to Joy. Jack argued that this would invalidate Joy's first marriage, and so she should be declared free to marry again. The church authorities did not buy his reasoning.

In October, Joy was taken to a hospital "in excruciating pain." The diagnosis was now changed to cancer in an advanced stage. It had already eroded her left femur.

There seemed to be little hope. In November three operations were performed, but they seemed merely to delay the inevitable.

By now, Jack was conscience-stricken about hiding the fact of his civil marriage to Joy. In December, with Joy in the hospital, he brought her boys to live in his home and told Joy to write her friends in America and announce the marriage. On Christmas Eve, Jack placed an announcement in *The Times*, London's prestigious paper: "A marriage has taken place between Professor C. S. Lewis . . . and Mrs. Joy Gresham, now a patient in the Churchill Hospital, Oxford. It is requested that no letters be sent."

Joy's case seemed terminal. She could live a few weeks, perhaps a few months.

She handled her plight surprisingly well. Warren wrote, "Her pluck and cheerfulness are beyond praise."

She spoke of her physical agony being "combined with a strange spiritual ecstasy. I think I know now how the martyrs felt. All of this has strengthened my faith and brought me very close to God."

But as the pain continued, day in and day out, Joy became discouraged. She was not getting better; she was only lingering. The radiation therapy merely seemed to be prolonging her misery. In one letter she confessed, "I am trying very hard to hold on to my faith, but I find it very difficult; there seems such a gratuitous and merciless cruelty in this." A week later, however, she seemed more positive. "I feel now that I can bear, not too unhappily, whatever is to come."

While she prayed for "grace to accept her condition," many were praying for her recovery. Her husband was actually praying that God might allow him to bear her pain so that she might have relief from it.

The following March, Jack called in a minister to come and pray for her. He had been successful in other cases in which he had laid hands on the sick.

When he arrived and saw Joy's desperate physical condition—she was far worse than he had imagined—he laid his hands on her and prayed for her. But unexpectedly, he also consented to perform an ecclesiastical ceremony so that Jack and Joy could have their union solemnized by the church. It was, in Warren's words, "a notable act of charity" for the Anglican cleric to perform the wedding.

After the ceremony, Joy was signed out of the hospital, placed in an ambulance, and driven to The Kilns, where Jack and Warren lived.

There they expected she would soon die; doctors had given her only a limited time to live.

But she didn't die. Instead, she began to improve. Pain in her hip gradually disappeared. Her health steadily improved. As Chad Walsh wrote, "The expert on miracles [C. S. Lewis had written a book on the subject] began to witness one before his very eyes."

Just as surprisingly, Jack Lewis was beginning to notice a problem in his own bones. He had asked the Lord to allow him to take Joy's pain; now it seemed that was literally happening. While Joy was gaining calcium in her bones, he was losing it in his. His disease was diagnosed as osteoporosis.

In September, Lewis wrote, "My wife's condition . . . has improved, if not miraculously (but who knows?) at any rate wonderfully."

In October, Joy wrote, "I am slowly learning to walk again." The following month she was riding in a car and even going up and down steps. By January, doctors had to acknowledge it: Joy's cancer had been amazingly arrested.

Six months later, Joy was still exuberant: "Jack and I are managing to be surprisingly happy, considering the circumstances; you'd think we were a honeymoon couple in our early twenties, rather than our middle-aged selves."

As more strength returned, she directed the redecorating of The Kilns. It hadn't been decorated for thirty years. "The walls and carpets are full of holes," Joy wrote; "the carpets are tattered rags." She also said facetiously that she was afraid to move the bookcases lest the walls should fall down.

She also began to manage Jack's finances. Money had always been a nuisance to him. Until Joy took over, he never even had a savings account.

In August they vacationed in Ireland. Jack called it a "belated honeymoon." Four months earlier when he and Joy had stayed at a country hotel he wrote, "I'm such a confirmed old bachelor that I couldn't help feeling I was being rather naughty staying with a woman at a hotel. Just like people in the newspapers."

It was a joyful year. "I never expected to have in my sixties the happiness that passed me by in my twenties," he told a friend.

Joy resumed work again, assisting both Jack and Warren with their manuscripts. In spare time, they did crossword puzzles and played Scrabble together.

Joy liked walking, though she now had one thigh three inches shorter than the other and had gained weight since the radiation therapy had begun.

And Jack knew very well that cancer's sword of Damocles still hung over them.

Then in October 1959, the grim news came. Jack wrote, "We are in retreat. The tide has turned. Apparently, the wonderful recovery Joy made in 1957 was only a reprieve, not a pardon."

This time, however, they faced the outlook differently. At Christmas 1959 he wrote, "We hobble along wonderfully well. I am ashamed . . . to tell you that it is Joy who supports me, rather than I her."

In March, Joy wrote, "I've got so many cancers at work on me that I expect them to start organizing a union."

Joy still had one unfulfilled dream. She had always wanted to visit Greece. Though a classical scholar, Jack had never been there. In fact, he had never been out of the British Isles except for his World War I experience in France. He hesitated to visit Greece because he feared that the reality might disillusion him; the mental images that he had inflated through the decades might be punctured.

For Joy's sake, he consented to take the trip. It was admittedly risky, because Joy's pain was increasing steadily. But she was insistent. "I'd rather go out with a bang than a whimper," Joy said, "particularly on the steps of the Parthenon."

So they went. Joy exerted all her strength to limp to the top of the Acropolis and through the Lion Gate of Mycenae.

"From one point of view," Jack wrote a month later, "it was madness, but neither of us regrets it."

He also wrote, "Joy knew she was dying. I knew she was dying, and she knew I knew she was dying—but when we heard the shepherds playing their flutes in the hills it seemed to make no difference."

Shortly after their return to England, Joy was taken again to the hospital. This time there was no reprieve.

By July she was on her deathbed and knew it. "Don't get me a posh coffin," she said to her husband. "Posh coffins are rot."

"It is incredible how much happiness, even how much gaiety, we sometimes had together after all hope was gone," Jack wrote. "How long, how tranquilly, how nourishingly, we talked together that last night."

Two of her last remarks to Jack were "You have made me so happy" and "I am at peace with God."

Though Joy's passing was calm, Jack was crushed by the loss. His two years of married life had been his happiest and most relaxed. Now he had lost the catalyst. He had written books on pain and had counseled people on suffering and bereavement, but now he himself was the victim.

His book *A Grief Observed* grew out of this period of despair. In the book he grappled with the doubt and depression into which his bereavement had plunged him. He spoke of "the agonies, the mad midnight moments." He complained, "I have no photograph of her that's any good. I cannot even see her face distinctly in my imagination." God seemed far away. He asked for divine comfort and all he got was "A door slammed in your face, and a sound of bolting and double bolting on the inside. After that, silence."

He couldn't understand what God was doing. God seemed cruel; could God at the same time be good? Was God only a Cosmic Sadist? He wrote his true feelings; he hid nothing.

Then gradually he saw his grief from a better perspective. "What sort of a lover am I to think so much about my affliction and so much less about hers? Even the insane call 'Come back' is all for my sake. I never even raised the question whether such a return, if it were possible, would be good for her. . . . Could I have wished her anything worse? Having got once through death to come back and then, at some later date, have all her dying to do over again? They call Stephen the first martyr. Hadn't Lazarus the rawer deal?"

Then suddenly after his long bout with depression he records: "Something quite unexpected has happened. It came early this morning. For various reasons, not in themselves at all mysterious, my heart was lighter than it had been for many weeks. For one thing I suppose I am recovering physically from a good deal of mere exhaustion."

But Jack Lewis never completely recovered from the passing of Joy. He plunged himself into his work, no longer teaching at Oxford, but now at Cambridge. Then his own body began to fail. It was a combination of physical ailments.

He continued writing, finishing his book on prayer, *Letters to Malcolm,* and an article, a few months before his death, on the right to happiness. He told his brother Warren, "I have done all I wanted to do and am ready to go."

On November 22, 1963, the day that President John F. Kennedy was assassinated, C. S. Lewis died. It was only a few days before his sixty-fifth birthday.

Though his brief marriage to Joy was not a long segment of those sixty-five years, it was an extremely significant time.

Between the time of the civil ceremony and the religious ceremony, C. S. Lewis was working on a manuscript which later evolved into his book *The Four Loves.* The book traces the meaning of the four Greek words for love—translated as affection, friendship, eros, and charity.

In *A Grief Observed,* Lewis tells how Joy and he "feasted on love; every mode of it—solemn and merry, romantic and realistic, sometimes as dramatic as a thunderstorm, sometimes as comfortable and unemphatic as putting on your soft slippers. No cranny of heart or body remained unsatisfied."

He spoke of her as "my daughter, and my mother, my pupil and my teacher, my subject and my sovereign . . . my trusty comrade, friend, shipmate, fellow-soldier. My mistress, but at the same time all that any man friend has ever been to me."

His views of women were incomplete until he married Joy. After all, his mother had died when he was only a lad. From the time he was ten to the time he was twenty-two, he was in male company almost constantly. Janie Moore was the first woman who showed him compassion, but her love was so needy that it was apparently warped psychologically.

In his early books Lewis concentrated on "the legalities of sexual love," but in *The Four Loves* he did not depreciate eros, as long as it is not "honored without reservation and obeyed unconditionally."

Despite the backgrounds that both Joy and Jack brought into their marriage, and despite the cultural differences that could have driven a gulf between them, their marriage did what any good marriage should do—it made each of them into stronger, more complete human beings.

It may have begun as a friendship, but as it grew it eventually explored all of the "four loves." For Professor Lewis, theory became reality. For ex-Communist Joy Davidman, she discovered a true comrade in arms.

Bibliography

Dorsett, Lyle. *And God Came In*. New York: Macmillan, 1983.

Green, Roger Lancelyn, and Walter Hooper. *C. S. Lewis: A Biography*. New York: Harcourt, Brace, Jovanovich, 1974.

Kilby, Clyde S., ed. *Letters to an American Lady*. Grand Rapids: Eerdmans, 1961.

———, and Marjorie Lamp Mead, eds. *Brothers and Friends*. San Francisco: Harper and Row, 1982.

Lewis, C. S. *A Grief Observed*. New York: Seabury, 1961.

———. *Letters*. New York: Harcourt, Brace, 1966.

———. *Surprised by Joy*. New York: Harcourt, Brace, 1956.

Soper, David Wesley, ed. *These Found the Way*. Philadelphia: Westminster, 1951.

Vanauken, Sheldon. *A Severe Mercy*. San Francisco: Harper and Row, 1977.

11

Evidently, Heart Triumphed over Head

John and Marjory Knox

What John Knox, the tell-it-like-it-is Scottish Reformer, really needed was a good press agent.

How could an old curmudgeon like John battle a young romantic like Mary Queen of Scots and hope to win?

Why did he take his mother-in-law on his honeymoon?

How could he virulently blast the rule of women when the reign of Queen Elizabeth was about to start?

Yes, John Knox could use a good press agent, even today.

But what about his wife Marjory Bowes? Was she only a toy that John played with while he waited to talk with her mother? Was she a real person? For that matter, was the marriage of John Knox and Marjory Bowes a real marriage?

And was John Knox really the woman-hater he is alleged to have been?

Granted, John Knox was more of a Howard Cosell than a Walter Cronkite. Things always seemed to happen around John Knox. He was a lightning rod, no doubt about that. But he was also the spark plug, the energizer, not only of the Scottish Reformation, but also of the Scottish Revolution. Yet the question remains: what about his marriage?

In Scotland, the memories of Robert Burns, Walter Scott, and John Knox can still be felt across the bonnie braes and heathered hills. While

Burns and Scott are more beloved, it was Knox who shaped the country. His influence on Scotland was more pronounced than Luther's was on Germany or Calvin's on Switzerland.

It was John Knox who challenged his nation to struggle for freedom and to fight against unjust rulers. In doing so, he laid the groundwork for modern democracy. Modern Presbyterianism owes as much to John Knox as it does to John Calvin.

But few men in history have been so castigated and vilified—unless you count Nero and Attila the Hun—as John Knox.

And what about his mother-in-law? Historian Will Durant writes, "Rarely in history has a mother-in-law been so loving and so loved." He claims that John Knox married Marjory Bowes "because he loved her mother."

Let's take a closer look at John and Marjory Knox, a most unusual couple in a most unusual time in history.

First, let's admit that John Knox didn't seem to have a very good sense of timing. For years he had looked for a close friend. Finally, at the age of thirty-one, he found one, a man named George Wishart. Two months later, Wishart was strangled and burned as a heretic.

For years Knox had been a priest without a parish, a minister without a congregation. Finally, at the age of thirty-three, he received his call and preached his first sermon. Three months later the town was invaded by the French; he was captured and forced to become a slave on a galley ship.

At the age of thirty-eight, he asked a young woman to marry him. She was willing, her mother was willing, and her father finally gave his reluctant approval. Seven months later, "Bloody Mary" came to power in England, and John had to flee the country, leaving his fiancée behind.

Poor timing? Maybe. But timing wasn't the only thing that seemed awry in the relationship between John Knox and Marjory Bowes.

Consider the picture when they first met. John was thirty-five, and an old thirty-five at that. He had spent nineteen months as a galley slave, had served as a chaplain to a gang of assassins, and had lost his best friend who was burned at the stake. Marjory, only fourte, was the daughter of a country gentleman and had been reared in a rather genteel style in Norham Castle.

He was a Scotsman from a town repeatedly ravaged by the British, and as one contemporary wrote, he was "descended but of lineage small." She was from one of the most influential families of northern England, a section of the country whose citizens made a point of belittling the Scots.

Though Marjory was flattered by John Knox's interest in her, her father was understandably irate. The age difference wasn't a problem to him; that was commonplace in those days. But he didn't approve of any daughter of his (and he and his wife, Elizabeth, had ten daughters) marrying a low-class Englishman. A low-class Scotsman was a hundred times worse, and a low-class Scottish refugee priest was unimaginable. Priests had no business getting married to anyone.

That was the way Richard Bowes viewed the relationship. His wife, Elizabeth, had another view. For that matter, she always seemed to look at things differently, and that was getting to be politically embarrassing to Richard Bowes.

When Henry VIII repudiated the authority of the pope in 1534, the Bowes family, as a leading family in northern England, was expected to follow their political leader. It wasn't easy for Richard, but he did it; yet at heart he remained a nominal Catholic. However, his wife, Elizabeth, took the change seriously. She started reading her Bible and began asking questions about what she read.

"Why do you always have to ask so many questions?" Richard Bowes must have queried his wife many times. He knew that people kept their heads on their shoulders a lot longer when they didn't ask questions. Besides, it wasn't normal for a woman to ask questions.

So when John Knox arrived on the scene in 1549, Elizabeth had fifteen years of unanswered questions bottled up within her. And for the first time in her life she found someone who took her questions seriously.

Now that you've met the principal characters, let's take a closer look at the enigma known as John Knox.

John Knox was born in Haddington, Scotland, near Edinburgh in about 1514, twenty-two years after Columbus discovered America and four years before Luther nailed his famous theses to the door in Wittenberg, Germany.

Scotland was at the rim of the civilized world in those days; one of Knox's contemporaries said it was "almost beyond the limits of the human race." Another said it was separated from the society of man. To Europeans it was the land where the devil lived; to the British it was infested with barbarians.

Whenever the British invaded Scotland, they seemed to march through Haddington, massacring a few men, women, and children along the way. If the British weren't invading, the clans were marauding and feuding. When John Knox was six, the Hamiltons battled the Douglases, leaving eighty-seven men dead in the streets of Edinburgh.

For a hundred years, every Scottish monarch had met a violent death. None had lived beyond the age of forty-two.

While violence wracked the nation, corruption riddled the church, which possessed half of the country's wealth. The feudal lords who ruled the countryside were a law unto themselves and intimidated even the king. The common people were caught in the middle.

The Knox family was among those caught in the middle. John's mother probably died when he was only an infant, perhaps even in giving birth to John; but his father was able to get him an education in the local schools. Because John was quite bright, it was decided that he should study for the priesthood; that was the only way a poor boy could better his station in life.

In those days priests were more plentiful than churches, so John, after his studies at the University of St. Andrews and after his ordination as a priest, became a lawyer and a grammar tutor back in his hometown of Haddington.

John had read the Bible occasionally while at university, but it wasn't until he was back in Haddington that the seventeenth chapter of John's Gospel grabbed him. He called it his "anchor" and it formed the basis of his future theology. Verses such as, "This is life eternal that they may know You, the only true God and Jesus Christ whom You have sent" not only gave him an assurance of salvation which he had never had before, but also transformed his life.

However, it wasn't until he met George Wishart that his newfound Protestantism was really activated.

Wishart, tall, young, and possessing a strange habit of washing himself in a bathtub every night, was taking Scotland by storm. But Knox's section of the country was leery of strangers and made it a habit to duck unannounced visitors in the village pond, or worse. So Wishart needed a bodyguard, and the feudal lord whom Knox was serving as a tutor volunteered John's services. As a result, John, though still a priest in good standing, carried a two-handed sword as he accompanied Wishart for the next five weeks.

John was certainly not an activist or a revolutionary at this point. Life as a tutor to wealthy students was fairly comfortable; and he wasn't thinking of a career change. He might have carried a sword to protect Wishart, but he wasn't eager to use it.

As biographer W. Stanford Reid puts it, "He enjoyed the relative obscurity of a member of a laird's household, where he could study and expound the Bible, teach grammar, and encourage intellectually two or three teenagers without having to face the hurly-burly of the violent world around him."

When his five weeks of service with Wishart were ended, Knox had mixed emotions. He idolized Wishart; the man had become the closest friend he had ever had. Yet at the same time he was ready to return to his teenage charges. "Return to your bairns [pupils]," Wishart told him and then added prophetically, "One is enough for the sacrifice." A few hours later Wishart was arrested for Protestant heresy; within a few weeks he was executed.

Knox was shaken. As a priest who had betrayed his position by serving as a bodyguard for a Protestant heretic, he was a marked man. Sooner or later, they would track him down; sooner or later he would face the same destiny as Wishart.

He thought of fleeing to Luther's Germany, where he could study in tranquility, but first he consulted with the lairds whose sons he was tutoring. What did they think he should do?

Not wanting to lose an able tutor, they suggested that John take their sons to St. Andrews, the Protestant stronghold university city in which Knox had been educated.

St. Andrews could hardly be confused with a haven of rest. Scotland's Roman Catholic archbishop had just been assassinated and the perpetrators of the crime were holed up in St. Andrews Castle. So it was not exactly an ideal spot for a young teacher trying to stay out of trouble.

At first he was simply a tutor at St. Andrews. But when some of the men overheard him teaching, they asked him to become chaplain of the castle. When he refused, saying, "I will not run where God has not called me," they held a public meeting and voted him in unanimously.

John burst into tears. There was no turning back now. He was in the middle of the fray and there was no way out.

The following week he preached his first sermon. His congregation was a strange mix of assassins and saints, peasants and professors.

In the sermon he stressed the importance of reliance on Scripture and the necessity of the doctrine of justification by faith alone. While criticizing the Roman Catholic church, he also called upon his Protestant congregation to repent. He censured them for their conduct and told them that unless they humbled themselves, God would send the French to capture them.

"Our walls will protect us," they shouted back.

"Your walls are like eggshells," John retorted.

Less than three months later, the French took the castle. Along with the others, John was condemned to the galleys as a common criminal to spend the rest of his life rowing for the king of France.

It might have been worse. If he had been released to the Scottish authorities, he would have suffered the same fate as Wishart.

Chained in irons, at times dangerously close to death, he spent nineteen months on the high seas. Then early in 1549, when he was thirty-five, John was released, thanks to the negotiating efforts of the British government.

Returning to Scotland was out of the question; instead he took up residence in Protestant England and before long he was given a church in Berwick in northern England, near the Scottish border. It was as W. Stanford Reid says, "a typical rough, tough border town." The mix of this congregation was not much better than his previous one. It was composed mostly of British soldiers who hated Scotsmen and Scottish refugees who hated the British. Having developed stomach ulcers and kidney problems while on the galleys, John didn't find Berwick the place to recuperate—except at Norham Castle.

Norham Castle was a retreat from the storms of the parish. But more than that, at Norham Castle, perhaps for the first time in his life, he was able to interact with women who were not afraid to use their minds. It fascinated him.

Elizabeth Bowes became a mother-figure for John Knox. She had two sides to her. As Reid says, "She was a person with strong convictions who at times strengthened even him when he was faint. . . . On the other hand she had continual doubts and fears about her own spiritual condition: whether she had true faith, whether she was of the elect, whether she had committed the unpardonable sin."

At times John found her endless questions "a cross to bear," yet he delighted to teach her. Her questions challenged him to go back to the Scriptures and examine them for answers. By eliciting his warmth and devotional practicality, Elizabeth helped John as much as he helped her.

When she told him that the devil was tempting her so much that she doubted if she could really be a Christian, he responded, "The devil is a roaring lion, seeking whom he may devour; whom he has devoured already, he seeks no more." The fact that Satan was troubling her was a good sign, not a bad one.

When she felt she had committed the unpardonable sin, he wrote her, "Despair not, mother, your sins (albeit ye had committed thousands more) are remissible. . . . I am just as certain of your election in Christ as I am that I preach Christ to be the only Savior."

It was because of her urging that he wrote a very practical tract on prayer. In it he defined prayer as "an earnest and familiar talking with God," to whom we declare our miseries, from whom we ask help, and to whom we give prayer and thanks.

Because most of his letters to Elizabeth discussed biblical and doctrinal issues, they were deemed valuable and were kept for posterity. Letters written to her daughter Marjory were more personal and probably didn't deal with such weighty matters. Regardless of the possible reasons, we have many letters addressed to Elizabeth but only one letter addressed to Marjory.

One letter to Elizabeth is admittedly controversial. "Call to your mind," John wrote to her, "what I did standing at the cupboard in Alnwick; in very deed I thought that no creature had been tempted as I was. And when that I heard proceed from your mouth the very same words that he troubles me with, I did wonder, and from my heart lament your sore trouble, knowing in myself the dolour thereof, and no other thing, dear sister, meant I; and therefore think not that I either flatter you, or yet that I conceal anything from you; no, for if I had been so minded, I had not been so plain in other cases."

As biographer Jasper Ridley says, "It would be interesting to know what Knox had done at the cupboard in Alnwick." Our minds immediately read sexual innuendoes into such a letter. But Ridley concludes, "The more we read Knox's letters to Mrs. Bowes, the more obvious it becomes not only that there was nothing physical and sexual in their relationship, but that there was nothing strange or abnormal about it."

It was to Elizabeth that John revealed most candidly his innermost self. Sometimes he did so in the process of assuring her that he was tempted just as much as she was. "Externally, I commit no idolatry, but my wicked heart loveth the self, and cannot be refrained from vain imaginations. . . . I am no mankiller with my hands; but I help not my needy brother so liberally as I may and ought." And again, "There is a spiritual pride which is not hastily suppressed. . . . I write to you by my own experience."

Years later, Knox explained that Mrs. Bowes had a "troubled conscience . . . which never suffered her to rest." He went on to add that "her temptation was not in the flesh . . . but in spirit; for Satan did continually buffet her. . . . I have seen her . . . pour forth tears and send to God dolorous complaints, ofter than ever I heard man or woman in my life. Her company to me was comfortable (yea, honorable and profitable, for she was to me and mine a mother); and yet it was not without some cross; for . . . my mind was seldom quiet, for doing somewhat for the comfort of her troubled conscience." In other words, as much as he appreciated her, even admired her, she sometimes got on his nerves.

Even before his engagement John depended on Marjory to keep her mother on an even emotional keel. Once he wrote to her, "The Spirit of God shall instruct your heart what is most comfortable to the troubled conscience of your mother."

The biggest spiritual problem that Marjory seemed to have was how to live a Christian life as the daughter of the captain of Norham Castle. She had been reading in the Epistle of James that Christians should not give the seat of honor to the wealthy guest while ordering the poor to stand in a corner; she wondered how that applied to her when, in Norham Castle, guests were seated according to rank.

John answered her that in Jesus Christ, all who profess Him are equal before Him, and that riches and worldly honors are regarded as nothing in His sight. "True Christians," John wrote to Marjory, "should have more respect to the spiritual gifts" that God gives His servants.

Meanwhile, Marjory's mother asked questions, the answers to which could fill an encyclopedia. Some of her questions were philosophical ("Why do some philosophers teach that the world has always existed?"); some were biblical ("Did Jacob's sons act properly when they killed the Shechemites shortly after the Shechemites agreed to be circumcised?"); but more often they dealt with her personal doubts and her feelings of sinfulness ("I think I have committed the sins of Sodom and Gomorrah").

In the two years after John Knox had begun his ministry in Berwick, his clerical stock rose rapidly, and as it rose Richard Bowes started thinking that maybe the outspoken Scotsman might not be such a bad catch for his daughter after all. By the fall of 1551 he was touted as the most famous preacher in northern England and he was being talked about in the halls of Westminster and Canterbury. In 1552 John was preaching before the king of England himself and had been named as one of the royal chaplains.

John was not a tall man; in fact, he was slightly shorter than average, but he was broad-shouldered, and his black hair and beard added dignity as well as authority to his bearing. With deep-set gray-blue eyes, he seemed as if he could see straight through you.

Richard Bowes was still not overjoyed about having John Knox as his son-in-law, but finally, in December 1552, he consented to a prenuptial contract between his daughter and the Scotsman. Marjory was about seventeen; John about thirty-eight.

John had just come from London where he had preached to the king, and rumors were flying that he might be the next bishop of Rochester. How could a prospective father-in-law refuse him?

But in the next couple of months Richard Bowes got word from his brother in London that the king's health was failing, and if he died there was a better than fifty-fifty chance that Catholic Mary Tudor would become England's next ruler.

On hearing this, Richard Bowes thought that maybe he had been a bit hasty in agreeing to the engagement. Maybe he had let his wife talk him into it. There had to be something he could do to nullify it; the most important thing he could do now would be to delay it as long as possible.

By the following July the king had died, Mary Tudor was on the throne, and John Knox was a hunted man. His friends, one by one, were being imprisoned in the Tower of London. Burning at the stake awaited most of them.

It was amazing how rapidly his fortunes had turned. By now, not only was Richard Bowes dead set against the wedding, but John wasn't so sure he wanted to push for it either. With Mary Tudor on the throne, what future could a Protestant preacher offer a seventeen-year-old bride?

But Elizabeth Bowes wasn't giving up. Her husband could switch religions at the drop of a monarch, but she knew what she believed in and nothing could change her. She also believed that John Knox was the man for her daughter and nothing would change that, either.

She urged John to contact her brother-in-law, Robert Bowes, in London. If Robert could be convinced, then he might be willing to try to convince Richard.

It wasn't a good idea, but John tried it anyway. Robert was even more opposed to the wedding than Richard was. In fact, he blamed all the problems of the Bowes family on Elizabeth and John. They were trying to arrange the wedding apart from Richard's better judgment, he said, and he was probably right.

"I am not a good orator in my own cause," John wrote back apologetically to Elizabeth.

Emotionally, John was hurt. Insults had always been hard for him to swallow. Depressed, he wrote, "My life is bitter unto me." He despaired that the marriage would ever happen; and having talked to Robert Bowes in London, he despaired of his own life. Robert Bowes would sooner see him handed over to the authorities than married to his niece Marjory.

There was no way he could think of marriage now. Already his own life was in jeopardy; but if he married Marjory he would jeopardize the lives of two others: Marjory and Elizabeth. John was certain now; the marriage would have to be postponed.

But there was another problem. Richard Bowes was already thinking of other suitors for Marjory. The prenuptial contract could easily be nullified, for John was a Catholic priest, wasn't he? And under Mary Tudor it would be once again illegal for priests to marry.

Before long, the handsomest prospective bachelors in all of northern England would be parading to Norham Castle, and there would be little that John could do to stop it. How long could he expect a seventeen-year-old to remain faithful under such circumstances?

John struggled with the decision. Should he stay in England and suffer a martyr's death? Or was it wiser to flee to Europe? It seemed wiser to flee; but, of course, that would mean deserting Marjory.

Then he got another letter from Elizabeth. Could he come to Norham Castle and talk to her husband? To her, it seemed to be the only hope.

John didn't think it would work any better than the visit to Richard's brother. On the other hand, he wanted to see Marjory again, so he decided to give it a try. He wrote ahead to Elizabeth to tell her that he planned to come. "If I escape sickness and imprisonment, you will see me soon. Yet, mother, depend not upon me too much, for what am I but a wretched sinner? Whatever becomes of me, remember, mother, the gifts of God are not bound to any one man."

Frankly, John was scared. Going to Berwick would be dangerous because he was so well known there. John couldn't even trust what Richard Bowes might do. In a neighboring town he stayed with some fellow Protestants who begged him not to go on to Berwick and Norham Castle. "Partly by admonition, partly by tears, they compelled me to obey, somewhat contrary to my own mind."

So without seeing either Marjory or her mother, John turned around. He had to flee the country, but he didn't like the prospect of doing that either. "Some will ask then, 'Why did I flee?' Assuredly I cannot tell, but of one thing I am sure, the fear of death was not the chief cause of my fleeing." Soon afterward, he crossed the English Channel to France.

In Dieppe, France, he sat in a small room, considering himself to be a failure. He had deserted his fellow Protestants in England; he had forsaken his fiancée, and he had left behind a future mother-in-law whom he had urged to be strong and courageous. He asked himself how strong he had been. His heart, as he puts it, was "sore trubillit." He admits that "in the beginning of this battle I appeared the faint-hearted and feeble soldier, yet my prayer is that I may be restored to the battle again." He was also praying that he would be restored to Marjory.

For the next eighteen months, Knox traveled between Dieppe, France (the message center that kept him in contact with both England and Scotland), Frankfurt, Germany (the publishing center of Europe and a haven for many English Protestant refugees), and Geneva, Switzerland (where John Calvin was transforming the city into what Knox later called "the most perfect school of Christ").

During those months, the news from England did not get any better. Mary Tudor was earning her nickname "Bloody Mary"; and the news from Norham Castle indicated problems there as well. John wrote to Elizabeth Bowes, "Be not moved with any wind, but stick to Jesus Christ." He confessed that he doubted that they would ever meet again on earth.

Elizabeth's closest friends were returning to Roman Catholicism. Richard, of course, was one of the first to do so, and now he was demanding that Elizabeth and Marjory follow his lead.

The pressure on Elizabeth and Marjory was intensifying week by week; by her letters Elizabeth made sure that John was kept up to date on all the developments. And along with the news, she kept inserting subtle (and some not-so-subtle) reminders that his presence was needed in both England and Scotland. England needed him, Scotland needed him, and above all, Marjory needed him.

John wasn't easily convinced. All the other reports that he was getting indicated that it definitely was not safe to return to England. The traffic was all going the other way. English Protestants were flocking into Frankfurt with their horror stories of what life was like under Mary Tudor.

And from what he could tell, Scotland didn't look any better. John hadn't seen his native Scotland for eight years, and the idea of returning now and facing immediate arrest was, as he put it, "most contrarious" to him.

But Elizabeth kept prodding. Biographer Geddes MacGregor says, "Evidently heart triumphed over head." More likely, it was Elizabeth who triumphed and finally Knox decided to venture back into his native Scotland for a brief visit. He had two items on his agenda: first, to marry Marjory at long last; and second, to access the spiritual climate of his homeland. Later he acknowledged that he wouldn't have returned at this time at all if it hadn't been for Elizabeth's prodding.

So it was that in September 1555 John Knox slipped as quietly as possible into Scotland. First, he met Marjory and married her, although historians do not agree on exactly when and where it took place.

Some say that John went across the border to Norham Castle in England and married Marjory there. But that's unlikely. Richard Bowes had become increasingly embarrassed (perhaps angered would be a better term) by the two staunch Protestants in his home. By refusing to go to Mass, they faced arrest. To have his wife and daughter arrested would be politically embarrassing for a man of Richard Bowes's standing in northern England. For the past two years he had been trying to cajole them into some religious compromises, but he knew how stubborn his wife was; now he was convinced that his daughter Marjory was equally stubborn. They refused to cut their loyalties to their Protestant faith and, even more reprehensible to Richard, they refused to cut their ties with that blustery Scots preacher.

Finally, Richard Bowes gave his ultimatum. They had to choose: attend the Mass or else. The "or else" meant "get out." They would have to leave Norham Castle and all its rights and privileges.

They chose to leave Norham Castle.

It must have taken considerable courage for those two women, one twenty years old, the other about fifty, to leave the comfort of upper-class life in a British castle, sneak across the border into Scotland, and wait for John Knox to come, hoping that he would risk his life as they had risked theirs to enter Scotland.

But he came. And it was probably in Edinburgh, Scotland, shortly after his arrival, that John at last married Marjory after a thirty-month engagement.

Now that he was in Scotland, he had to check out the religious climate for himself. There were both similarities to and differences from England. Like England, Scotland was ruled by a queen named Mary. Like Mary Tudor of England, Scotland's Mary of Guise had forced the Protestant Christians underground. But in the crags and crannies of sparsely settled and still clannish Scotland, she was finding it more difficult to round up the heretics than Mary Tudor was in England. So house churches were sprouting up all over. During his visit John took the opportunity to visit as many house churches as he could.

Everywhere he went, he was greeted enthusiastically. He writes of the "fervent thirst of our brethren, night and day, sobbing and groaning for the bread of life." To his mother-in-law, waiting for him to return to Edinburgh, he writes, "If I had not seen it with my eyes in my own country, I could not have believed it." His speaking tour was extended longer than he had originally planned; he apologized to Elizabeth and Marjory for the delay and he asked them to "patiently bear . . . for depart I cannot, until such time as God quench their thirst a little."

By the following spring, the authorities, alarmed by the way that John Knox was crisscrossing the land, decided to put a halt to his unauthorized preaching. When he was summoned to a trial, he decided it was time to think of leaving. He put Elizabeth and his bride, Marjory, on a boat to Dieppe, France, while he wrapped up his business. He stayed a few more months, teaching the Scots how to conduct their worship services and urging them to read the Bible every day, even if it might seem monotonous. "Every day you eat bread, don't you?" he asked them.

215

Hardly had he fled the country when another summons was issued for his arrest; he was hanged in effigy. Once again, he had gotten out just in the nick of time.

He took his wife and mother-in-law to Geneva, Switzerland, where he had been called to the pastorate of a thriving English congregation. It was as much of a honeymoon as John and Marjory would ever enjoy. John joked about Geneva being his "den of ease," and certainly in comparison to what was going on elsewhere, it was.

It was an adjustment for John at the age of forty-two to settle down to married life. In one letter he requested prayer because he was "now burdenit with dowbill cairis." Not only did the congregation impose demands on him, but so did his family, which included, no doubt, more questions from his mother-in-law. In addition, he felt he was also pastor-at-large to Protestants in both England and Scotland.

The following May a delegation arrived in Geneva from Scotland urging him to return. They said that they thought the situation might be improving. John wasn't convinced. He had other reasons why he didn't want to leave Geneva too quickly. First, Marjory was pregnant, and he didn't think he should leave her now. Second, he felt his presence in Scotland would do more to incite a political revolution than a religious reformation; and third, his congregation in Geneva was just starting to show some spiritual progress. But he replied to the messengers that he would come with "reasonable expedition," which apparently meant that he would come as soon as he felt he could.

Five months later, he said good-bye to his congregation and family and ventured four hundred miles north to Dieppe, France, en route to Scotland. Shortly after arriving in Dieppe, however, a letter arrived from Scotland indicating that it might be better if he didn't come now.

John was irked, and he didn't hide his feelings. "To some it may appear a small and light matter that I have cast off and as it were abandoned . . . my house and poor family destitute of all head, save God only, and committing my small flock to the charge of another."

For two months he waited in Dieppe, corresponding with his Scottish brethren and writing religious tracts, but it wasn't a happy two months. What was God's purpose in uprooting him from Geneva to come on this wild goose chase? He finally returned, still disgruntled, to Geneva.

Back in Geneva, he spent a busy year, writing letters and tracts prolifically. Marjory assisted him with the correspondence, as well as in the transcription of his manuscripts, because she "wrote with a good hand." Jasper Ridley remarks that "not many married women would have been sufficiently literate and well-educated to render such assistance." One letter written to John Foxe (author of *Foxe's Book of Martyrs*) shows a flare for style and a graciousness of expression which could have been learned only through her upbringing at Norham Castle. In the letter Marjory thanked Foxe for the gifts sent to her and her mother. Because of her able assistance, John referred to her as his "left hand."

John didn't speak openly of his affection for her; it was not easy for a Scotsman in that era to do so. But he did refer to her as "of earthly creatures most dear to me." John Calvin spoke of Marjory as "the most delightful of wives," and called her "suavissima." Geddes MacGregor adds, "Only such gentle sweetness as was hers could have been powerful enough to hold as it did the enduring affection of so stormy and dominating a personality as John Knox." Undoubtedly, the next few years revealed John Knox at his stormiest.

It had been during those two disgruntled months in Dieppe that he began penning his most famous work, "The First Blast of the Trumpet against the Monstrous Regiment of Women." John Knox was, to put it mildly, against women rulers.

Everywhere John turned he saw nations ruled by women. His native Scotland was ruled by the Queen Regent Mary of Guise. John hadn't minded the fact that she had permitted him to be hanged in effigy, but what he didn't appreciate was the fact that she had considered one of his writings a joke. France's influence was rising in Scotland, and if Mary had her way, Scotland would follow France in religion as well. John feared that.

In France, John witnessed the ruthless power of Catherine de Medici, who later ordered the St. Bartholomew's Day Massacre of the Protestant Huguenots. And in England Mary Tudor ("Bloody Mary") had burned many of John's friends at the stake and sent many others to rot in the Tower of London.

Admittedly, it was surprising in that day to have women monarchs. After all, women generally had few rights; they could hold no political office (except the office of queen); they had no legal authority even over their own children. To John, it didn't make sense.

Unlike many of his contemporaries, both Protestant and Catholic, John was not a woman-hater. Far from it. More than half his letters (of which we have record) were addressed to women. When he refers to women, it is usually with dignity and consideration. As far as friendships go, his closest, most intimate confidences were with women—not only his wife and mother-in-law, but also Anne Locke, Mrs. Hickman, and Janet Adamson. He may have consulted with a man such as John Calvin, but it was to Elizabeth Bowes that he unburdened his soul.

However, when he saw women as leaders of the most powerful nations of the world, he judged it to be completely unnatural and against God's plan. Jezebel was his prime example. Of course, he had to acknowledge that some women—such as Deborah in the Book of Judges—might be exceptions, but you can't use an exception to change a rule.

The main thrust of John's argument was directed against Queen Mary Tudor of England and "the cruelties and tyrannies" that characterized her reign.

In fact (and here is where John made everyone sit up and take notice), John urged that nobles and clergy had the responsibility "to remove from honor and to punish with death such as God has condemned by His own mouth."

That was treason. John Calvin himself was scandalized by the book (he banned it in Geneva) and was chagrined that such a report could be printed in his fair city. Other Reformers were also shocked. No Protestant leader had ever gone as far as John Knox had gone. Previously, Protestants had held, "We must obey our kings whether they are good or evil." John Knox was arguing that if you went along with unjust rulers, you yourself were incurring the wrath of God. In fact, people who failed to seek to overthrow wicked regimes by revolution should be punished.

Once again, John's timing got him into trouble.

Less than six months after he had published his literary blast, Mary Tudor died, and Queen Elizabeth, a Protestant, took the throne. Since John's condemnation applied to all women rulers (though admittedly Mary in particular), Elizabeth never forgave him, and John could never again think of returning to live in England.

But, fortunately, it wasn't the English church that called him to return; it was the Scottish church. A letter was sent to him and another letter to John Calvin, who was urged to apply pressure to John Knox and make him want to return to Scotland.

Once again, John dallied. Marjory was expecting their second child, and John didn't want to leave until he was sure that Marjory had delivered the child safely.

Then a few more months passed before he finally left Marjory, their two children, Nathaniel and Eleazar, and his mother-in-law, Elizabeth Bowes. He asked a colleague to take care of them until he felt it safe for them to join him in Scotland; he didn't know how long that would be.

It was in May 1559 that forty-five-year-old John Knox set foot once again in Scotland. And he was made to feel "at home" immediately. Five days after he arrived he was officially proclaimed an outlaw. A reward was offered to anyone who would either seize or kill him; bounty hunters lurked everywhere. One of his first letters from Scotland asked for money so he could buy a faster horse.

But John was not going to be stopped now. Everywhere he went, he roused the citizenry. He had little time to write letters. He complained, "In twenty-four hours I have not four free to natural rest and ease of this wicked carcass."

Outwardly, the growing Protestant force seemed ineffective. As Knox says, "We do nothing but go around Jericho, blowing with trumpets as God giveth strength, hoping victory by his power alone."

After only a month in Scotland, despite the turbulent atmosphere, John asked Marjory to come. He was eager (he said "thirsty") to have her join him. So Marjory, her mother, and their two sons, along with

Christopher Goodman, Knox's ministerial colleague, left Geneva, went to Paris, and there applied for permission to pass through England. Unlike John, who was refused permission by Queen Elizabeth herself, Marjory and Mrs. Bowes had no trouble at all getting a visa. In fact, they stopped at Norham Castle.

But things weren't the same there. Elizabeth's husband, Richard, had passed away nine months earlier, only a few weeks before Mary Tudor had died and Queen Elizabeth had come to the throne. It was also about the time that Knox's seditious "First Blast" had begun circulating in England.

Neither Elizabeth nor Marjory were mentioned in Richard's will. He bequeathed his estate to his other children, including four unmarried daughters; but the daughters could receive the inheritance only if their uncles approved their marriages.

Obviously, Marjory had married John against Richard's will, and thus had forfeited her right to an inheritance. As far as Elizabeth was concerned, how could he leave anything to her when she chose to be associated with the man who had written the "First Blast," advocating revolution against his queen?

Temporarily Mrs. Bowes stayed in England with relatives until the fighting in Scotland cooled down. Intrepidly, Marjory and the two boys, Nathaniel, two, and Eleazar, ten months, entered Scotland at its most perilous time. They joined John in Dundee in northern Scotland.

Marjory must have been concerned that John was working himself to death. A month before she arrived he had been ill. Immediately she pitched in. Besides managing the children, she did a considerable share of John's correspondence. Knox wrote, "The rest of my wife hath been so unrestful since her arriving here that scarcely could she tell upon the morrow what she wrote at night."

Those were some of the most eventful days in Scottish history. About a month after Marjory and the boys arrived in Scotland, the Queen Regent of Scotland, Mary of Guise, was deposed. Fighting continued, however, between Mary's allies, the French, and the motley band of Scottish Protestants for another eight months.

John was only the cheerleader for that band, but what an effective cheerleader he was! The English ambassador reported that Knox's voice could "put life into them more than 500 trumpets."

While the fighting continued, John and Marjory lived in St. Andrews where he had served as chaplain twelve years before. Then in mid-April 1560 the Knoxes moved to Edinburgh where John became minister of St. Giles Church. Two months later Mary of Guise died, and a treaty ending the civil war was signed in July.

In Edinburgh, John and Marjory lived in a house on the west side of Trunk Close, north of High Street. It had a garden and some extra land attached. The Edinburgh council paid the rent as well as the cost of furnishing the house. They also paid for a lock on the door. Apparently, not everyone in Edinburgh loved John.

At last he and Marjory could settle down. Geneva was pleasant, but he was a pilgrim there. Edinburgh was home; finally he could begin life as a parish preacher and enjoy his family again.

However, it was only a half year after they had moved into their new home on Trunk Close in Edinburgh that Marjory suddenly died. She was only twenty-five.

No one knows the cause of her death. Some have suggested that she wore herself out during the previous year and was not able to resist one of the epidemics that ravaged Edinburgh periodically. Or perhaps she died in childbirth.

We do not know. What we do know is that John was devastated by her death. Although he had known her for the previous ten or eleven years, they had been married for only five years, and during those years John had been absent from her for months at a time.

Years later, in the writing of his will, he still referred to Marjory as "darrest spouse" of "blessit memorie." His friend Goodman commented on the severe blow it had been to Knox to lose his wife so suddenly.

In his *History of the Reformation in Scotland,* John made it a point to omit most personal matters, and certainly emotional reactions to personal matters; but he could not refrain from commenting on Marjory's death by saying that he "was in no small heaviness by reason of the later death of his dear bedfellow."

From Geneva, John Calvin wrote to console him, "As you have rightly learned where to seek consolation in sorrow, I am sure that you are bearing this calamity with patience."

John, now forty-six, was left with two small boys under four years old, the leadership of a brand new national church, and a national government in tumultuous transition.

Elizabeth Bowes returned to help John raise the two lively boys. But by this time, she was nearly sixty years of age and was no match for the youngsters.

Two years later, John Knox took a second wife, Margaret Stewart. A few eyebrows were raised that John, who was now fifty, was marrying a girl of only seventeen. But the shocking thing in Edinburgh was that John, a man of humble birth, should marry into the Stewart family, a family with royal connections.

Margaret was descended from James II. She was the daughter of one of John's strongest Protestant backers, Lord Ochiltre. Jasper Ridley comments, "It is evidence either of Lord Ochiltre's Protestant zeal or of Margaret's affection for Knox." It may also be evidence of John's need of a vigorous young woman to be mother to his two young children.

It, too, was a good marriage, and in the coming years John and Margaret had three children of their own.

John had no problem with his wives, his first mother-in-law, or his second father-in-law, Lord Ochiltre. But he did have continuing problems with queens—Mary Tudor and Elizabeth of England, Mary of Guise, and ultimately Mary Queen of Scots. Mary Queen of Scots was the latest female monarch to plague John, or vice versa. She was beautiful, young, charming, clever, and full of intrigue. She was also Roman Catholic and deathly afraid of John Knox. John had fought too long and hard to get Protestantism recognized in Scotland to let a charming young queen take it away. Her tactics reminded him too much of Mary Tudor's to allow him to rest easily.

The English ambassador wrote back to London about the reception that Mary Queen of Scots had received in Edinburgh. Everyone had been favorably impressed by Mary, he said—everyone "saving John Knox, that thundereth out of the pulpit. . . . One day he will mar all. He ruleth the roost, and of him all men stand in fear."

For six years the battle raged between the pretty, young queen and the man "that thundereth from the pulpit." Though politically he was much less active, yet as a pulpiteer he remained as vigorous as ever. His home life also became more precious to him. MacGregor writes, "For years he had known scarcely any privacy. He had seen too little of his children, and he had enjoyed too few of the pleasures of friendship. . . . Now in the company of his young wife he felt he could enjoy what he had missed. After striving with royal courts he could appreciate her ingenuousness. Her artless laughter soothed him. Her simple, girlish earnestness in the regular family devotions filled with peace the heart of the man who had thirsted after righteousness."

After John married Margaret, Elizabeth Bowes returned to England. Interestingly, a few years later the two boys were sent to England for their education, where they spent considerable time with their grandmother Bowes. At least once, John came to visit them there.

When Mary Queen of Scots was forced to abdicate in 1567, her infant son, James, was crowned king, and John Knox preached the coronation sermon. To John that was a great victory. But his ultimate triumph came in December of that year when the Protestant Church of Scotland was recognized as the official church of the nation.

Five years later, at the age of fifty-eight, John Knox lay dying. He asked his young wife, Margaret, to come and read the fifteenth chapter of 1 Corinthians (the resurrection chapter) to him. Then late in the afternoon he asked Margaret to read another passage of Scripture. "Go read where I cast my first anchor," he asked.

She knew the passage well. Automatically she turned to the Gospel of John and read the seventeenth chapter, which had been so instrumental in his conversion. He passed away shortly thereafter.

During the past 400 years biographers as well as psychologists have puzzled over John Knox and his attitudes about women. They often conclude their studies with more questions than answers.

However, this much is certain. What could have been a disastrous triangle of John, Marjory, and her mother, Elizabeth, worked out surprisingly well. Each had strengths and each had weaknesses. John and Marjory developed a strong love for each other that Elizabeth not only respected but also sought to strengthen.

John appreciated Elizabeth's strength of character, her sensitive spirit, and her inquiring mind. She was teachable and John liked that in a woman. But even more admirable in John's estimation was her strength in standing for what she believed in, in spite of the loss of all her physical possessions and earthly friendships. Early in his life, John was ashamed of how often it seemed that he had run away from conflict; Elizabeth faced conflict head on.

Of course, having Elizabeth in the home was, as John put it, "not without some cross; for . . . my mind was seldom quiet, for doing something for the comfort of her troubled conscience."

Marjory, despite her youth, was the steadying influence in the family. She kept her mother from groveling in introspection and gave John a "left hand" of constancy, stability, and love that he needed.

Bibliography

McCrie, Thomas. *The Life of John Knox*. London: Thomas Nelson, 1847.
Ridley, Jasper. *John Knox*. New York: Oxford University Press, 1968.
MacGregor, Geddes. *The Thundering Scot*. Philadelphia: Westminster, 1957.
Reid, W. Stanford. *Trumpeter of God*. New York: Scribner's, 1974.
Brown, Hume. *John Knox*. London: A. and C. Black, 1895.
Perry, Eustace. *John Knox*. London: Hodder and Stoughton, 1937.

12

A Mother for His Orphans

George and Mary Müller

You remember George, I'm sure. He was the man who started those orphanages in Bristol, England. A year and a half before Charles Dickens alerted the world to the plight of nineteenth-century orphans in his novel *Oliver Twist,* George Müller was doing something about the problem. He started orphanages and then got down on his knees and asked God to feed the orphans.

You might remember the story of how the orphans were seated around the long dining room table one day, and there was nothing on the table but empty dishes. No food anywhere, and no money to buy food.

Then George asked the blessing on the nonexistent meal: "Dear Father, we thank Thee for what Thou are going to give us to eat."

A knock on the door interrupted George's prayer. It was the baker. "Mr. Müller," said he, "I couldn't sleep last night. Somehow I felt you didn't have bread for breakfast, and the Lord wanted me to send you some. So I got up at two o'clock and baked some bread for you."

George thanked him and brought the loaves of bread inside for the orphans.

Hardly had the children got their hands on the bread when a second knock was heard at the door. This time it was the milkman. He said that he was sorry to disturb Mr. Müller, but his milk cart had broken down in front of the orphanage. Since it would take a while to fix the milk cart—and by that time the milk might start to turn sour—he wondered if Mr. Müller would do him a favor and take the cans of milk for his orphans.

Now you remember George Müller, don't you?

But what about Mary Müller?

What was she doing when George was praying?

What was it like to be married to this Prussian immigrant to England?

And what strains does it place on a marriage to be parents to two thousand children with no visible means of support?

Like most young couples, neither of them knew what they were getting into when they got married.

George was twenty-three when he stepped onto British soil for the first time.

He had come to be a missionary to Jews in London, but he had two minor problems. He didn't know Hebrew and he spoke English with such a thick German accent that he could hardly be understood. So he spent twelve hours a day trying to correct both problems.

Shortly after his arrival he heard of a dentist from Devonshire in southwestern England who was forsaking his practice to go to Persia as a missionary. What made it more remarkable was that the dentist had said he was going to depend on God alone for his needs.

That was something that George would never forget.

Nor would he ever forget the dentist's name: Anthony Norris Groves.

Twelve hours a day of study was more than George could take; soon he became ill. His doctors advised him to get away from London.

Where should this Prussian immigrant go to recuperate?

Why not go to Devonshire? He might even have a chance to talk to the dentist, Anthony Groves.

Unfortunately, Groves had left for Baghdad before George arrived. George did meet a Scotsman, Henry Craik, who, like George, was twenty-three years old and had been converted during his university days. Even more interesting to George was the fact that Henry had been the private tutor in the Groves home until only a short time before.

George began associating with the Christians who were praying for Groves. Though these Christians later became known as Plymouth Brethren, at this time they had no special name. Some of them were in the established Church of England, but most were associated with Baptist or Methodist chapels.

After three months of recuperation in Devonshire, George returned to London to resume his studies. But now he was impatient to get into action as a missionary. The mission leaders wanted him to resume his studies, to attain more proficiency in Hebrew as well as English. George felt that more studying would be a waste of time and health.

George was usually better at giving orders than at taking them, and this time was no exception. The mission charged that he "was unwilling to submit to their guidance with respect to missionary operations." But George's position was that "as a servant of Christ he ought to be guided by the Holy Spirit in his missionary endeavors and not by men."

So he left his studies and London to return to Devonshire. Though he had little money and spoke broken English, he was able to make a sparse living by preaching to the Plymouth Brethren groups of the area. One assembly with eighteen members asked him to become their minister. The vote was by no means unanimous. "Some of them left and never returned," George recalled.

While preaching in one small assembly, he was invited to lodge overnight at a nearby boarding school. After accepting the invitation, he discovered that the boarding school had been the home of dentist Anthony Groves. In fact, Anthony's sister Mary was still living there, assisting the couple who were managing the school.

Obviously, Mary was a woman to whom George wanted to talk. And he did. And he came back to talk some more.

At first he seemed interested in finding out more about the dentist. But gradually he became interested in finding out more about the dentist's sister.

George had intended to remain a bachelor. He looked upon marriage as a restriction on his Christian ministry. As he put it, he wanted to "remain free for traveling about in the service of the gospel."

Then, after a few months in his ministry, he began to think that "for many reasons it was better for me as a young pastor to be married. The question now is 'To whom?'"

Every time he asked the question, the face of Mary Groves loomed in his mind. He prayed long hours about it, and as he prayed, everything kept pointing to Mary. Why had God brought the name of Mary's brother to his attention shortly after he had arrived in London? Why was Henry Craik, who had lived with the Groves family, one of the first people he met when he had come to Devonshire to recuperate? Why was Mary here now? And why did he enjoy talking to her so much?

George thought he knew the answer. God had intended that Mary would become a permanent part of his life.

He admired her brother; he admired Henry Craik; and the more he talked with Mary Groves, the more he admired her.

Granted, she was seven years older than he was and she didn't know German yet. But she seemed to have everything else that he could possibly desire. She knew French, Latin, and even Hebrew, George had to admit, but she didn't know German. However, she was also artistic and intellectual, and she could keep house. Most important to George was the fact that she was a deeply devoted and disciplined Christian.

Undoubtedly, the Groves family was exceptional. The father of Anthony and Mary was a prosperous businessman; an uncle was a noted dentist in London; a cousin was a surgeon. After practicing dentistry for a decade, Anthony had gone to Trinity College, Dublin, to get theological training prior to going to the mission field. Then he withdrew, saying that he now felt neither academic credentials nor ordination were necessary for missionary service.

Anthony Groves also had strong views on what discipleship meant. He stated, "It is the duty of everyone to give up all for Christ, absolutely and unreservedly." He wrapped up his views in a strong and unwavering faith, trusting God for everything. And with that faith, he took his family and became a missionary in Persia.

In the process of living with her brother and sister-in-law, Mary had absorbed much of his thinking. She had enjoyed the stimulating times in the family devotions. But now they were gone. And she was lonely.

Then standing in front of her was this tall, thin young man from Prussia. He was eager, energetic, and deeply spiritual.

Word had gotten around about George. She knew he wasn't a polished speaker. She knew he was still learning his theology. But she was also aware that when George Müller began preaching, things started happening. Things were never dull when George was around. He and Henry Craik and her brother Anthony were three of a kind.

George was a bit afraid of romance. Back in Germany he had had a romantic relationship with a girl and had allowed it to steer him away from God's will for his life. So he didn't want his relationship with Mary to be clouded by romance.

But since she seemed to be God's choice for him, he saw no reason to delay going ahead with proposing to her. To make sure that romance didn't interfere with the decision and also to insure that he was communicating properly (he still was not confident of his spoken English in such delicate matters as a marriage proposal), he wrote his proposal in a letter and said he would call on her as soon as possible to get her response. A few days later, when he called on her, Mary had her answer ready. She accepted. "The first thing we did was to fall on our knees and to ask the blessing of God on our intended union."

Mary, who had met him only a few weeks before, was soon to learn that things happened quickly when George was around.

Things had always been happening quickly for him.

Born in 1805, he was the son of a Prussian tax collector who left his money in places that were too accessible for a curious youngster. Before he was ten, George started pilfering. Soon it became a habit. When his father caught him, he was severely punished, but young George treated it like a game. He resolved that next time he stole from his father he wouldn't get caught. And he became increasingly clever as a thief and as a con artist.

He was only fourteen when his mother died. While she lay dying, young George was half-drunk, carousing at a tavern. Even her death was no serious blow to him. "This bereavement made no lasting impression on my mind. I grew worse and worse."

He certainly didn't turn over a new leaf during the following year. Only a few days prior to his confirmation he confessed, "I was guilty of gross immorality," and on the day of his confirmation he defrauded the parish minister out of some money.

His behavior continued to go downhill. At age sixteen he stole some money from his father in order to spend some time with a girlfriend in a certain town. He vacationed at two expensive hotels, running up high charges, and then walked off without paying. Shortly afterwards, he was caught and thrown in prison. Three weeks later his father bailed him out.

One biographer comments, "This boy of sixteen was already a liar and thief, a swindler and a drunkard." Once he drank ten pints of beer in a single afternoon.

Biographer Roger Steer is a bit kinder: "One of his great failings was still an inability to make ends meet; he had contracted debts that he had no means of repaying."

But George was beset with other problems, too. He admits to having lived a "profligate and vicious life. . . . I did not care in the least about God, but lived secretly in much sin."

At nineteen, he entered the famed University of Halle and resolved to change his life for the better. He decided to study theology and thought of entering the ministry. That pleased his father, who felt that as a clergyman George would be insured of a comfortable living.

But becoming a theology student didn't help George reform. Once he organized a vacation trip to Switzerland for his classmates. To get passports, he taught them how to forge letters. Then the students pawned their books to get spending money. As treasurer of the group, George found it quite easy to appropriate some of the other students' money. "I managed so that the journey cost me but two thirds of what it cost my friends."

Not a very noble character!

George didn't like himself very much, either.

In his second year at the university, he was invited to a Bible study group. He was profoundly stirred by it. As he walked home, he told a friend, "All we have seen on our journey to Switzerland and all our former pleasures are as nothing compared with this evening."

"That evening," George wrote later, "was the turning point in my life. . . . I have not the least doubt that on that evening he [God] began a work of grace with me."

Soon George was considering mission service. At least he considered it until he fell in love with a girl that he had met at the Bible study group. He and his girlfriend were both thinking about becoming missionaries, but when her parents disapproved of her going to the missionary field, George decided that he would put missions out of his mind as well. He would continue studying for the ministry but forget about missionary service.

But as he forgot about missions, the joy seemed to fade from his spiritual life. Prayer became routine. He felt that he, like Esau, had bartered his birthright. Esau had done it for the pottage; he was doing it for a girl.

Convicted by God, he gave up the girl he loved and decided to pursue his missionary calling again.

At first he thought of becoming a missionary to Bucharest, but a war between the Russians and the Turks put a damper on that idea. Then he considered going to Poland as a missionary to the Jews in Warsaw. But in the end he headed for London to serve under the London Society for Promoting Christianity among the Jews. A year after he had graduated from Halle, he was crossing the English Channel to London.

Only a year and a half later, he and Mary Groves were wed. He was twenty-five, she was thirty-two. After walking together to the church for the wedding, they went through a very simple ceremony. "In the afternoon," George recalled later, "we had a meeting of Christian friends . . . and commemorated the Lord's death, and then I drove off in the stagecoach with my beloved bride . . . and the next day we went to work for the Lord."

Years later he wrote, "I have never regretted either the step itself or the choice."

George the newlywed was still forming his theology. Denominationally, he wasn't sure what he was. The strongest influence upon him was a man he had never met, his brother-in-law, Anthony Norris Groves. Groves' views were reinforced not only by George's friend Henry Craik but also by George's bride.

231

Like Groves, George began to celebrate the Lord's Supper every Sunday. When challenged by three women to study the Scriptures on the subject of baptism, George adopted Baptist views regarding believers' baptism by immersion.

While his views on the sacraments were being shaped, he was also thinking deeply about the matter of salary. George was bothered by the fact that his salary as a minister came from pew rents. Because the better pews were more expensive, he felt the practice discriminated against the poor. So he abolished pew rents, making all seats in the church free, but in the process of abolishing pew rents, he also eliminated the basis of his salary.

Within three weeks of his marriage, and with encouragement from Mary, George announced to his congregation that he would no longer accept a set salary. It was a step of faith that emulated what Anthony Norris Groves had done before going to Persia.

For anyone who wished to contribute to the support of the minister and his wife, he put a box in the chapel for freewill offerings. Furthermore, and this was the biggest decision, he and Mary resolved never to ask anyone—except God—for money.

In Germany in his teenage years, the love of money had been the root of much of his evil. He had pilfered it from his father and had gotten it fraudulently from others. Now he and Mary resolved to "go to the Lord alone" for their financial needs.

For Mary, who had been accustomed to hearing her brother talk in a similar way, it was not a difficult adjustment.

But this doesn't mean that there weren't difficult moments.

In only a few weeks George and Mary were down to their last shillings. As they prayed together in the morning, George rehearsed the problem to God. Four hours later, a woman approached him and said, "The Lord has told me to give you some money."

George kept a journal, which tells how his faith was stretched. "On the 6th, 7th and 8th of Jan., 1831," he wrote, "I had repeatedly asked the Lord for money, but received none." He confessed that he started to doubt. "I began to say to myself, that I had perhaps gone too far in living this way."

A few minutes later, a woman came into their home and brought them two pounds and four shillings. "So the Lord triumphed," George rejoiced, "and our faith was strengthened."

One of the problems that George and Mary faced was in getting the men of the chapel to open the little box in the church that contained the gifts for the pastor. It was supposed to be opened every week and the contents given to the Müllers on a regular basis, but sometimes the church trustees forgot. In fact, sometimes they forgot about it for three or four weeks. As a matter of principle, George would not remind them of their responsibility.

"Once," he wrote in his journal, "I asked the Lord repeatedly for money. . . . Yesterday passed away and no money came. We had nine pence left. This morning we were still waiting upon the Lord and looking for deliverance. We had only a little butter left for breakfast, sufficient for Brother E. and a relative living with us, to whom we did not mention our circumstances, that they might not be uncomfortable."

George, of course, was very much aware that the box in the chapel had not been opened recently. So he prayed "that the Lord would be pleased to impress it on Brother Y. that we wanted money, so that he might open the box."

And that is what happened. Brother Y. did indeed come with the money. He explained that "he and his wife could not sleep last night on account of thinking that we might want money."

After fifteen months of following the practice of living by faith, even George and Mary were amazed at the results. "We are never losers from acting according to the mind of the Lord," he wrote. "For had I had my regular salary, I should not have had nearly as much."

Living by faith was such an exciting experience for George that he almost forgot about the fact that he was soon to become a father. The truth of the matter was that he didn't want to think about it. Mary's pregnancy disturbed him. Just as he had previously feared that marriage would be a hindrance in the Lord's work, so now he feared a child in the family would keep him from fully serving the Lord.

The baby was stillborn and Mary became seriously ill immediately afterward. Because of the fears he had had about being a father, George felt personally responsible. For several days George didn't know whether Mary would survive. "The life of my dear wife was hanging, as it were, on a thread, and in the midst of it, my conscience told me, that my state of heart made such a chastisement needful." As Mary regained strength, George praised God for his mercy.

With this crisis behind, George set his sights on new employment. After spending about two years as minister of the little Teignmouth church and watching it grow from eighteen to fifty members, George wrote in his diary, "I have again felt very much this day that Teignmouth is no longer my place, and that I shall leave it."

Only a week later, he accompanied his friend Henry Craik to Bristol on a preaching mission. There they spoke to crowds of a thousand, with hundreds more being turned away.

The crowds continued to come to hear the unlikely team of a Scotsman and a German. Craik with his Scottish burr was a better preacher and theologian, but George's "strong accent and pronunciation" attracted many who came simply for the novelty. (He never lost his German accent. It remained a trademark. When he spoke, either in conversation or in the pulpit, he "spoke with slow and measured articulation.")

Before long, George, now twenty-six, and Mary, thirty-three, moved what few belongings they had to Bristol, which became their center of operations for the rest of their lives.

Mary was pregnant again. This time there was no doubt about George's concern for her. It was not only because she had experienced difficulty during and after her first pregnancy, but also because Bristol was riddled with a cholera epidemic. In her weakened condition, how could Mary fight the disease?

Henry Craik wrote in his diary, "The funeral bell is incessantly tolling; it is an awful time."

People swarmed to church, even for the 6:00 A.M. prayer meeting, to pray for relief from the epidemic. George and Henry visited those who were suffering. They were available for counseling night and day. Continually exposed to the disease, George thought that it was inevitable that he would catch it. "Into thy hands, O Lord, I commend myself," he wrote one night. And another time he said, "If this night

I should be taken in the cholera, my only hope and trust is in the blood of Jesus Christ shed for the remission of all my many sins."

As Mary went into labor, George spent the entire night in prayer, not only for Mary but also for the baby to be born. The next day, little Lydia Müller was born, the only child of the Müllers to survive infancy.

Eighteen months later, another child, Elijah, was born, but Elijah lived only a little more than a year before succumbing to pneumonia.

During the hours that little Elijah was struggling for life, George spent more time praying for Mary than he did for his infant son. He prayed for Mary "that God would be pleased to support my dear wife, under trial." The day before Elijah's death, George wrote in his journal, "The Lord's holy will be done concerning the dear little one."

Some have questioned why George, the man of such great faith, didn't pray more fervently for the life of his son. But he distinguished between what he called the gift of faith and the grace of faith. Biographer Steer comments, "It would need the gift of faith to believe that a seriously ill person would be restored, for there is no promise [in God's Word] that he should be; but it simply needs the grace of faith to believe that God will give us the necessities of life . . . for this is promised in Matthew 6."

Appropriating the grace of faith was exciting for George, and in his journal he recorded answers to prayer for small matters as well as for large matters.

"This is now the fourth hat," he wrote in 1833, "which the Lord has sent me, whenever or even before I needed it. How very kind of the Lord."

Other matters were more significant. George suffered frequently from physical problems, especially a stomach disorder. Nervous ailments also plagued him.

But he at times was even more concerned with the struggle he had with impatience. One biographer called it "constitutional irritability" and commented that he didn't always "suffer fools gladly." In his journal George sometimes refers to this tendency: "These last three days I have had very little communion with God, and have therefore been very weak spiritually and have several times felt irritability of temper."

Another struggle for George and Mary was whether or not they should go out as foreign missionaries. Ever since his conversion, George had wanted to be a missionary. And unlike the girlfriend he had in Germany during his teenage years, Mary was willing, almost eager, to go overseas.

Then a letter arrived from Mary's brother, Anthony, begging them to come and join him in his missionary labors in Baghdad. So convinced was Anthony that they should come to Persia that he enclosed two hundred British pounds to finance their journey. He had lost his wife and child during his brief missionary labors, and he desperately needed help.

Both Mary and George were moved by the appeal. They practically idolized Anthony; he had shaped their biblical and theological thinking and had given the motivation to their life of faith. Could they turn him down now when he had such need? It became a matter of intense family prayer. "I do not know what may be the Lord's mind," George wrote in his journal.

George also shared the matter with Henry Craik, and the two prayed about it for two weeks.

But the timing of Anthony's appeal didn't seem right. Mary was slowly recovering from a difficult pregnancy. Little Lydia was only a few months old. And besides, God was doing some exciting things for them in Bristol. In their first two years of ministry there, two hundred people professed faith in Christ, and even greater blessings seemed to lay just around the corner.

How close those blessings were George and Mary didn't realize!

About this time George began to read the biography of a German theology professor, August H. Francke. He had heard of Francke before, because George had attended university in Halle, where Francke had started schools for poor children and established homes for orphans. In fact, while he was at the university, George had even stayed in one of Francke's orphanages for two months.

But George had never read Francke's life story before. As he read, he was deeply stirred. "The Lord graciously help me to follow him," he prayed.

The needs were obvious in Bristol. He wrote, "Most of the Lord's people whom we know in Bristol are poor, and if the Lord was to give us grace to live more as this dear man of God [Francke] did, we might draw much more than we have as yet done out of our heavenly Father's bank for our poor brethren and sisters."

George and Mary had always been concerned for the poor. Every morning they dispensed bread to between sixty to eighty poor people (from young children to the elderly) who lined up in front of their house. George even began telling Bible stories to the boys and girls from his front steps, and later in the day he taught the adult beggars. His neighbors didn't like the kind of people that George and Mary were attracting to the community, and they complained. Reluctantly, the Müllers halted the practice but felt somewhat guilty about their decision.

When George and Mary first arrived in Bristol, they had been astonished by the large number of poor children begging in the streets. It was unforgettable.

Later he wrote in his journal of a "poor little orphan boy, who for some time attended one of our schools," but then was taken away to a poorhouse. "May this," he prayed, "lead me to do something also for the supply of the temporal wants of poor children."

In England during the 1830s, many orphans were sent to workhouses, along with the insane, the mentally handicapped, and the senile. Few private orphanages existed, although one or two had been established for "children who are respectably descended." Not many of the Bristol children were "respectably descended."

Though George had been temporarily stymied by his neighbors in teaching and feeding orphans from his front steps, he and Henry Craik devised another plan. Concerned about the spiritual as well as material needs of the poor, the two men launched an organization known as the Scriptural Knowledge Institution for Home and Abroad. In the first seven months of its existence, it had established a Sunday school in which 120 children were enrolled, adult classes that included forty adult men and women, and four day schools with 200 children. In addition, it distributed more than a thousand Bibles and New Testaments and sent large sums of money to missions overseas.

That helped to provide for some of the poor children spiritually, but it did little to help them physically. George kept thinking back to what Francke had done both physically and spiritually.

At first he was depressed. One entry in his journal says, "Today I am thirty years of age. I feel myself an unprofitable servant." He felt he needed to do something worthwhile in life for the glory of God.

Shortly after his birthday he wrote, "Today I had it very much impressed on my heart, no longer merely to think about the establishment of an orphan house, but actually to set about it."

It was about the same time that he read Psalm 81:10: "Open thy mouth wide, and I will fill it." To George it was God's promise that if he would start an orphanage, God would feed the hungry mouths.

Always quite analytical about what he did, George listed his motives: "(1) To benefit the bodies of poor children, bereaved of both parents; (2) To be used by God in getting the dear orphans trained up in the fear of God; and (3) The primary object . . . that God might be magnified by the fact, that the orphans under my care are provided, with all they need, only by prayer and faith, without anyone being asked by me or my fellow laborers."

About five months later, George's first orphan house was opened.

Ever since their marriage in 1830, George and Mary had been living by faith, without a salary and without asking anyone for money. God had provided. Sometimes their faith was stretched. But God had always brought what they needed.

But running an orphanage by faith was a big step beyond providing for a small family by faith. If it failed, if the orphans were left to starve, George would be denounced by every decent citizen in Bristol.

However, five years of experience of living by faith had convinced George and Mary that God could be relied upon to provide for orphans, too.

While George never asked for funds, he did not launch anything without public announcements. An expert businessman, he concerned himself with the minutest details of the planning. When plans were drafted, he called a special meeting to set forth the program. A public announcement was made in the city newspaper; handbills were circulated. The whole area became aware of the orphanage that George Müller was beginning.

But though the work was well-publicized, George never asked for funds either publicly or privately.

Money, supplies, and volunteer helpers began to pour in, and four months later, on April 11, 1836, the first orphanage was opened. For George Müller, it was the beginning of a new era.

A second house opened in October. Soon a third home was opened, and in time another and another. Finally, more than two thousand orphans were housed in George and Mary's homes. "Those two thousand orphans are not only to be fed, but clothed. . . . Hundreds of fresh orphans are received each year, and the newcomers are to be fitted out."

A year after the first orphanage was established, George wrote the first volume of his *Narrative of Some of the Lord's Dealings with George Müller,* a work that made Müller a household word among Christians in many parts of the world. He added four additional volumes to his *Narrative* and published widely read annual reports of the orphanages.

George Müller the man of faith was also the epitome of a Prussian entrepreneur. While he depended on God to keep the orphanages operating, he felt it his duty to manage them with as much business savvy as he could muster. George once described himself this way: "I am not a fanatic or enthusiast, but, as all who know me are well aware, a calm, cool, quiet, calculating businessman."

This calculating businessman had, according to one biographer, "a certain indescribable air of authority and majesty" about him, yet at the same time there was "a simplicity so childlike that even children felt themselves at home with him." He seemed to be the right man to run an orphanage.

At a distance people talked about the orphanages as George Müller's orphanages, but anyone who lived near Bristol knew that the orphanages were a team effort.

Mary served in a variety of roles. She was purchasing agent, business manager, quartermaster, and auditor. Pierson states, "Month by month she examined all the account books, and the hundreds of bills of the matrons of the orphan houses, and with the eye of an expert detected the least mistake."

She also directed the cooking and serving and managed the sickrooms, schools, and dormitories connected with the orphanages. Because she possessed such a "thorough knowledge of every kind of needlework and of the quality of material for clothes, linen, etc. . . . it was her duty to order hundreds of thousands of yards of all kinds of material. She would approve or reject the material which was delivered."

Their daily schedules revolved around the orphanages. George usually woke up around 5:00 A.M. after seven hours of sleep. (He claimed that men needed only seven hours of sleep, while women needed eight.) He got dressed quickly, stuck his head in some cold water to wake himself thoroughly, and began to read his Bible. Early in his Christian life, he began his day with prayer, but after ten years of following that routine, he realized "that the most important thing I had to do was to give myself to the reading of the word of God and that thus, by means of the word of God, . . . my heart might be brought into experimental communion with God."

In good weather he took a large-print New Testament outdoors, "walking about in the fields," while reading a verse, meditating upon it, and talking to the Lord about it. Then he would read the next verse, meditate on it, and pray about it. After an hour of "field-walking," he would return for breakfast with Mary around six.

At breakfast the Müllers had their family prayer and Bible reading. Mary and daughter Lydia, as well as anyone else living in their household, were part of this time. For a while this included Mary's brother, whose health had deteriorated in Asia and forced him to return to England after only a few years of missionary service.

They read verse by verse through the Bible, taking about fourteen months to finish the whole Bible.

After the family prayer time, George and Mary withdrew to have "a short time of prayer together when the most important points for prayer with regard to the day were brought before God." George records in his journal that Mary "heartily joined me in prayer for help from God, and, with me, looked out for help and help came; and then we rejoiced together and often wept for joy together."

At about eight in the morning he began going through his correspondence, and at ten, nine assistants came to him to report on their various areas of responsibility and receive instructions for their work during the day.

But his most trusted assistant was Mary. He seldom knew where she was during the day, but sometimes he would turn a corner in Bristol or walk into a room at the orphanage and bump into her unexpectedly.

George found these serendipitous meetings delightful. "Every year our happiness increased more and more. I never saw my beloved wife at any time, when I met her unexpectedly anywhere in Bristol, without being delighted to do so. I never met her even in the orphan houses, without my heart being delighted so to do."

They usually ate their evening meal together at the orphan houses. Afterwards they went to her room and sat together on the couch. "I knew that it was good for her, that her dear active mind and hands should have rest, and I knew well that this would not be except her husband was by her side. Moreover, I also needed a little rest after dinner, on account of my weak digestive powers, and therefore I spent these precious moments with my darling wife. There we sat, side by side, her hand in mind, . . . having a few words of loving intercourse, or being silent, but most happy in the Lord, and in each other, whether we spoke or were silent. . . ."

But their day wasn't completed yet. There were other things to check and oversee, and George, a stickler for detail, made sure that everything was operating smoothly. The last hour of the day at the orphanages was for prayer. "My beloved wife came then to my room, and now our prayer, and supplication, and intercessions mingled with thanksgiving." Sometimes these prayer times lasted a whole hour. "At these seasons we brought perhaps fifty or more different points, or persons, or circumstances before God."

It is understandable that they had fifty or more points to bring before God. After all, they had up to two thousand orphans to feed and clothe and salaries to pay to matrons, cooks, and workmen. During the first two years, when the work was growing, finances were seldom a problem, but then the contributions dwindled. For the next eight years the Müllers scraped the bottom of the barrel.

His journal reads thus:

> Aug. 18, 1838: I have not one penny in hand for the orphans. . . . My eyes are on the Lord.
>
> Sept. 1: This is the most trying hour that as yet I have had in the work. . . . But I know that I shall yet praise the Lord for his help.
>
> Sept. 5: Our hour of trial continues still. The Lord mercifully has given enough to supply our daily necessities, but he gives by the day now, and almost by the hour, as we need it.
>
> Sept. 8: It has not pleased my gracious Lord to send me help as yet. Yesterday and today I have been pleading with God eleven arguments why he would be graciously pleased to send help.
>
> Sept. 17: The trial still continues. It is now more and more trying, even to faith, as each day comes. But I am sure God will send help, if we can but wait.

During this period God answered the prayers of George and Mary each day—but only for that day. Surprisingly, the orphans themselves didn't realize there were any financial problems. As George put it: "These dear little ones know nothing about it, because their tables are as well supplied as when there was eight hundred pounds in the bank, and they have lack of nothing."

One day that November, George wrote, "Lower we have never been, and perhaps never so low." In two of the three orphan houses, bread and milk were lacking. They needed them for the next meal.

"All seemed dark," George recalled. He and Mary joined other staff members in prayer. As they prayed, a knock was heard at the door. Mary went to answer it, while George and the others continued praying. As the prayer time was finished, George arose from his knees saying, "God will surely send help." Then he noticed a letter that Mary had brought in to him. In the letter was a gift of ten pounds, more than enough to buy the bread and milk for the next meal.

But during this time, finances were not the only challenge that the Müllers faced. George was struggling with recurring physical problems.

Doctors said he had an inactive liver. George knew his digestive system was not right, and at this time in his life he also had violent headaches. In his journal, he complained of having a "weak head."

Doctors advised him to get away from the orphanages and to take a vacation. George wasn't sure if he could; he didn't have money for a vacation and the orphanages needed him for daily management.

But when a gift arrived, earmarked for George's personal use, he felt it was a sign from the Lord that he should take the vacation he needed.

So he did. However, the vacation by the ocean didn't seem to help. His headaches worsened. He feared he was going insane, but his doctors assured him that it was only frazzled nerves.

Recovery didn't come quickly. In fact, for a few weeks he felt so weak and exhausted that he feared he was going to die. He wrote his father in Germany that it might be the last letter he would write.

Gradually, however, as his health came back, he returned to his responsibilities at Bristol. Perhaps he returned too soon. Pressures of the church as well as the orphanages were weighing heavily upon him, and at times he was ashamed of the way he was responding. In his journal he wrote, "This morning I greatly dishonored the Lord by irritability, manifested towards my dear wife, and that almost immediately after I had been on my knees before God, praising him for having given me such a wife."

Then, only four months after his previous time of recuperation, his doctor advised him to go on a second vacation. This time he was away from Bristol for five months. Mary accompanied him for a while. Then she returned to Bristol with daughter Lydia to keep an eye on the orphanages. Mary was pregnant again; because her previous pregnancies had been difficult, they both felt it would be better for her to be home in Bristol.

Meanwhile George went from Trowbridge to Oxford to Leamington Spa seeking a cure for his maladies. At Leamington his health seemed to improve, but without Mary his spirits plummeted; in addition, without Mary he experienced inner drives and temptations that he didn't like to admit. In his journal he wrote, "Grace fought against evil suggestions of one kind and another. . . . It was a very trying season. . . ." He prayed that Mary would come and join him in Leamington, "as I feel that by being alone, and afflicted as I am in my head, and thus fit for little mental employment, Satan gets advantage over me."

God answered his prayer the next day. Mary arrived, and the two of them began to take long walks together in the countryside.

Before George returned to Bristol, however, he went to visit his native Germany again. Because she was pregnant, Mary could not accompany him.

George was still only thirty-two when he came back to Bristol, but from that time on his health improved. Two years later he commented, "I ascribe this to God's blessing through the instrumentality of early rising and plunging my head into cold water when I rise." Many years later he said that he felt better in his seventies than he had in his early thirties.

George's concern now focused on Mary, forty years old, with a history of difficult pregnancies.

She went into labor at nine in the evening, and after ten hours she delivered a stillborn child. George wrote in his diary, "The whole of the night I was in prayer, as far as my strength allowed me."

Whether Mary herself would survive or not was uncertain. The following day George wrote, "My dearest wife is alive, but I am depending upon God for her life every moment." Then three weeks later, he penned the words, "She seems likely to recover."

Soon she was back at work again. As she grew older, rheumatism caused severe pains in her arms. George said it was caused by overwork. "My dearest wife worked so hard . . . with the opening of the new orphan house . . . that her health has been brought into a very low state, and her strength has been greatly reduced. I begged her not to work so much, but it was in vain. She loved work; she could never bear to be idle."

She found relief by taking warm sea baths, and George, who had been urging her to take a rest, found himself praying for her quick recovery. Her absence from the orphanages presented more of a problem than his absence did. Things didn't run as smoothly when Mary wasn't around.

George and Mary loved the ocean; perhaps their favorite vacation was climbing along the ocean cliffs with their daughter Lydia. Biographer A. T. Pierson tells how George once "walked a little in advance, seated himself until Mary and Lydia caught up with him, and then, when they were barely seated, rose and quietly said, 'Well now, we have had a good rest; now let us go.'" It was George's attempt at being playful.

When Lydia was eleven, she was sent away for special schooling, and this gave Mary a chance to travel more with her husband. They traveled twice to George's homeland of Germany. Mary, with her aptitude for language, was able to add German to the list of languages in which she was fluent.

It had grown to become an excellent marriage. At first, George sometimes took Mary for granted, almost as a necessary encumbrance. But their love grew strong as they prayed and worked together.

Repeatedly, George says of Mary that she was "exquisitely suited" to him. At least once he told her, "My darling, God himself singled you out for me, as the most suitable wife I could possibly wish to have had." A practical woman, Mary possessed "useful knowledge." She "never hindered me in the ways of God," George wrote, but "sought to strengthen my hands in God."

Were they a happy married couple? George answers it, "Verily we were. With every year our happiness increased more and more."

What was the secret of their marital happiness? George had an answer to this question as well. Of course, Mary was a devoted Christian and "exquisitely suited" to him, but "this was not enough for the continuation of real conjugal happiness . . . had there not been more."

As usual, George organized his answer and listed his points:

1. Both of us, by God's grace, had one object of life, and only one, to live for Christ.
2. We had the blessing of having an abundance of work to do. . . . By God's grace we gave ourselves to it; and this abundance of work greatly tended to the increase of our happiness. . . . Our mornings never began with the uncertainty of how to spend the day, and what to do.
3. [As busy as we were, we] never allowed this to interfere with the care of our souls. Before we went to work, we had, as an habitual practice, our seasons for prayer and reading the Holy Scriptures.

4. Lastly, and most of all to be noticed, is this: we had for many years, whether twenty or thirty years or more I do not know, besides our seasons for private prayer and family prayer, also habitually our seasons for praying together.

Evidently, the Müllers did not pray together at the beginning of their marriage—except for family prayers. But it was this addition that strengthened their marriage most of all.

"I judge that it was the great secret for the continuation, not only of conjugal happiness, but of the love to each other, which was even more abundantly fresh and warm than it had been during the first year, though we were then exceedingly fond of each other."

But the marriage bond that began when they were "exceedingly fond" of each other became stronger each year.

Mary's health during her sixties remained remarkably strong, except for the aches and pains of rheumatism. In fact, she wasn't bedridden a day during the entire decade.

But at the beginning of 1870, Mary, now seventy-two, caught a bad cold. The fifth and final orphanage building had just been completed, and as usual Mary had overworked in the preparation. So she tried to dismiss her cold as just a minor problem and continued to bustle about at the orphanage. After weeks went by and she didn't shake her cold, a doctor was called in. He diagnosed it as rheumatic fever and ordered her to bed.

Before another week had passed, the doctors told George that "all hope of recovery was gone." And on February 6, 1870, in the fortieth year of their marriage, Mary died. George preached the funeral sermon. Prior to the service, he paced back and forth groaning, "Oh, Mary, my Mary." Thousands came to the funeral. Among them were twelve hundred orphans and hundreds of believers from miles away. It was one of the most difficult sermons George ever preached. But when the service began, he asked God for strength to preach on Psalm 119:68: "Thou art good, and doest good." And God gave him the strength he needed. He says that he "was sustained by the Lord to the utmost."

"Every day I miss her more and more," he said. "I feel the void in my heart." Though he felt that he needed her more than ever, "That lovely one is no more with me, to share my joys and sorrows."

In the following months the loss ate away at George. He wrote in his journal, "My earthly joy is all but gone." He especially missed her during the evening, which had always been a time of togetherness for them.

Two years later George remarried. This, too, was a happy marriage. Susannah, his second wife, enjoyed travel, and since George was now an international figure and received invitations to speak from all around the world, they spent many of their years together traveling. They traveled more than 200,000 miles together.

George died in 1898 at the age of ninety. His second wife had died four years earlier, after nearly twenty-six years of marriage.

As a young man in his twenties, George had not been convinced that the institution of marriage was for him. He was afraid it would interfere with a true work for God. How could any man who was single-mindedly following the Lord get tangled up in marriage? It would certainly divide his loyalties. But he had found that, far from being a hindrance to the work, Mary had been a partner in it, and his life had been enriched as a result.

In later years, he enjoyed giving advice about marriage because he had found marriage a delight. Not all marriages, he knew, were as successful as his had been. Marriage, he cautioned, "cannot be too prayerfully treated. Our happiness, our usefulness, our living for God or for ourselves afterwards, are often most intimately connected with our choice."

How does one make a good choice? According to George, "Neither beauty nor age nor money nor mental powers should be that which prompts the decision."

Then George began his list of criteria for making the right choice: "(1) Much waiting upon God; (2) A hearty purpose to be willing to be guided by him; (3) True godliness without a shadow of doubt . . . should be the first and absolutely needful qualification; and (4) Suitableness. An educated man should not marry an uneducated woman or vice versa."

George knew that those criteria worked because they had worked for him. After all, by following those guidelines, he married a woman who was "exquisitely suited" to him.

Bibliography

Harding, William Henry. *The Life of George Müller.* Glasglow: Pickering and Inglis, 1914.

Müller, George. *The Life of Trust.* Boston: Gould and Lincoln, 1873.

Pierson, A. T. *George Müller of Bristol.* London: Pickering and Inglis, 1899.

Steer, Roger. *George Müller: Delighted in God.* Wheaton, Ill.: Harold Shaw, 1981.

What Went Wrong?

Good Christians don't have bad marriages . . . do they?

Of course they do.

But what about Christian leaders?

They do too.

But what about great Christians, those Christians who really made a difference in church history, those Christians whom God used to change the lives of thousands of their fellow men and influenced generations that followed? Did they have poor marriages too?

Yes, unfortunately they did.

But why? If they were so godly, if they were Spirit-filled, if God was using them so powerfully, how could it be that their home life was a disaster?

You can probably guess some of the reasons, and you will learn a few others as you read this section. We will be looking at four outstanding men and women of God whose marriages were extremely difficult. In other sections of this book you will note other couples who struggled with their marriages as well. The Livingstones, the Marshalls, and the Stowes were three couples who went through difficult times and would have been prime candidates for the "Can This Marriage Be Saved?" section of the *Ladies Home Journal.*

But the Wesleys, the Smiths, the Careys, and the Hills had marriages that seemed to be beyond redemption. Hannah Whitall Smith, author of *The Christian's Secret of a Happy Life,* was anything but happy when she wrote, "It is hard for me to believe that any husband and wife are really happy together."

Of course, they lived in days before marriage counselors and family psychologists were prevalent and before Christian bookstores promoted dozens of bestsellers dealing with every aspect of married life.

Could the marriage have been saved if both husband and wife had recognized the problems earlier? What mistakes loomed early? What were the harbingers of future conflicts? What similarities do you see with the problems that couples are facing today?

Christians are certainly not immune to marital problems. In fact, sometimes their marriages are held together only by church activity and propriety. At other times single-mindedness for their divine mission may stretch their earthly ties to the breaking point.

When you read of these floundering marriages, you will recognize some of the same problems that you have struggled with in your marriage. As you identify the problems, perhaps you will also be able to work toward solutions that seemed to evade these great Christians of the past.

13

Love Is Rot

John and Molly Wesley

Most of you don't need to be introduced to John Wesley, the father of the worldwide Methodist movement. You sing the hymns written by John and his brother Charles. You are aware of his Aldersgate experience, and the entire world has been affected by John's concerns for evangelism and personal holiness.

But you have probably never encountered Molly Goldhawk Vazeille Wesley, John's wife.

Maybe after I've introduced you, you will wish you never met her.

I can guarantee, however, as you interact with John and Molly, that you will have much cause for thought.

What were the factors that made it such a miserable marriage?

How could it have been otherwise?

What can you learn from it to avoid in your own marriage?

One of the early Wesley biographers stated that, along with Xanthippe and Job's wife, Mrs. John Wesley had to be rated as one of the worst wives in all history.

A later biographer responded by saying that if that was so, then surely John Wesley must be regarded as one of the worst husbands in history.

Both allegations seem quite extreme.

But what are you to do with the story that Molly Wesley was seen dragging her husband around the room by his hair?

And what about the correspondence that John Wesley continued to maintain, despite his wife's objections, with his female admirers?

John Wesley is well-known as the intrepid evangelist of Methodism who traveled a quarter of a million miles on horseback, who claimed the world as his parish, and who rose at four each morning for his devotional time. But his home was a shambles. Four years after his marriage, he wrote to his brother Charles, "Love is rot."

He preached 42,000 sermons, often preaching four or five times a day during his fifty-three-year ministry. Crowds of up to 30,000 came to hear him preach. When he died at the age of eighty-eight, Methodism had 153,000 adherents, and the movement had spread to America as well as to Holland, Ireland, and Scotland.

He was a remarkable man, and God used him mightily. Yet his marriage was a miserable failure.

He waited for marriage until he was forty-seven; he probably waited too long. (Some would say he didn't wait long enough.) He had serious romances when he was twenty-five, thirty-five, and forty-five. He retreated from each one at the last minute. Perhaps any one of the three would have provided him a happier marriage than he had with Molly. But had Wesley had a happier marriage, we might not have had the outgrowth of the formidable Methodist movement.

In order to understand John Wesley and his problems in marriage, you have to take a glimpse of the fascinating home in which he was reared.

John Wesley was the fifteenth of nineteen children born to Samuel and Susanna Wesley. Samuel was a stern, argumentative Anglican cleric who spent most of his ministry in an out-of-the-way parish, trying to exhort a bunch of uneducated ruffians. His biggest joy in life seemed to be when he could get away from Epworth to go to Convocation in London. It had been an honor for him to be named to this top-ranking study commission; it was a joy as well because during the sessions he got to argue theology with eminent theologians.

At home, he argued with his wife, Susanna, a well-educated, well-bred woman who wanted the best for her husband and for her children, and who had a reason for everything she did.

Both Susanna and Samuel were stubborn, and Samuel had a quick temper besides. Once during family prayers, after Samuel had properly prayed for the reigning English monarch, King William of Orange, he noted that his wife had not said her traditional "amen." In fact, come to think of it, she had not said the appropriate "amen" for several days. The reason was obvious. Susanna did not favor King William of Orange; she thought he was a usurper of the throne. She favored the Stuart line. So, in Susanna's words, her husband "immediately knelt down and imprecated the divine vengeance upon himself and all his posterity if ever he touched me more or came into bed with me before I had begged God's pardon and his."

Whereupon Samuel left for a timely Convocation in London. King William soon died, which was an answer to prayer for Susanna and maybe even for the equally stubborn Samuel, because upon William's death Queen Anne, a Stuart, came to the throne. Thereafter Susanna could say "amen" when her husband prayed for the reigning monarch.

The story is typical of the marriage. Here are some quotes from Susanna's writings: "Since I'm willing to let him quietly enjoy his opinions, he ought not to deprive me of my little liberty of conscience." And "I think we are not likely to live happily together." And another, "It is a misfortune peculiar to our family that he and I seldom think alike."

A little more than nine months after the coronation of Queen Anne, John Wesley, the fifteenth of the Wesleys' nineteen children, was born. Nine of the children died at birth or in infancy, and that left ten to be raised on the modest income derived from the remote parish of Epworth. When John—or "Jackie," as his mother called him—was only two years old, his father was imprisoned for three months for his inability to pay a thirty-pound debt. During his prison term, his biggest concern was his family, but he wrote, "My wife bears it with the courage which becomes her and which I expected from her."

Later when Samuel was in London attending another of the lengthy Convocations, an interim minister preached in his pulpit and made repeated aspersions about the regular minister's chronic indebtedness and about other foibles that Samuel undeniably had.

When the congregation dwindled, Susanna began holding evening services in her kitchen. Soon her evening flock outnumbered those in the morning congregation at the Epworth church. The interim rector didn't like it. He wrote to Samuel in London urging him to take immediate action and stop this outrage. Simultaneously, Susanna wrote, justifying her actions. Something needed to be done, she said, and no man in the congregation had as strong a voice as she had; furthermore no one else could read well enough to lead the congregation in the prayer book and the reading of the sermon. She said that although she knew that God approved of what she was doing, she would submit to her husband if he would definitely put his foot down. But he had to say so definitely. Then she asked her husband if he wanted to put his foot down or not. The way she wrote it was like this: "Do not tell me that you desire me not to do it, for that will not satisfy my conscience; but send me your positive command in such full and express terms as may absolve me from all guilt and punishment for neglecting this opportunity of doing good, when you and I shall appear before the great and awful tribunal of our Lord Jesus Christ."

Samuel Wesley decided that since the problem would go away as soon as he returned home in a few weeks, he would take no immediate action.

As if the Wesleys didn't have enough troubles, the old parsonage caught fire one night in 1709. Nearly everything was lost, but fortunately the children had all escaped to the garden. All except one. Five-year-old John was missing. The father tried to reenter the house, but the smoke and flames made the stairway impassable. Finally a ladder was brought and was raised to little John's window. The boy was saved, just before the roof collapsed.

Susanna called it divine intervention and spoke of John as "a brand plucked from the burning." After the dramatic rescue, while she was mindful of the spiritual welfare of all her children, she was especially concerned about young John. She had made a resolution to be "particularly careful of the soul of this child, which God had so mercifully provided for."

Susanna raised her children strictly. At the age of one year, they were instructed to cry softly when they had to cry. She took responsibility for their early education, and her daughters were treated as the educational equals of her sons. She regimented her spiritual activities and expected her children to do accordingly. She assigned a day of the week when she would take time to provide personalized scriptural and moral instruction to her children. Each child was assigned a day; John's day was Thursday.

Growing up, John was tended by seven sisters. Later most of the sisters, like John himself, experienced unhappy marriages. Where the blame lies for the string of mismatches is hard to tell. Some blame the father, who had a knack for crushing his daughters' promising love affairs, until in rebellion they ran off with totally unsuitable mates. One of the daughters openly spoke of the father's "unaccountable love of discord." His paternal concern made him censorious and overly protective.

Samuel Wesley was a man who had never come to terms with himself. His parish was too small and remote. He wasn't properly appreciated in the community. At home he was frustrated by his inability to cope with Susanna and his children. And at times this frustration erupted irrationally.

Susanna herself was such a dominant force that her influence was indelibly imprinted on her children's personalities—especially on John's. She was John's spiritual advisor until her death when John was thirty-nine. One biographer says, "Hers was the decisive voice that sent her two sons on their ill-starred mission to Georgia; it was to her steadfastness that John looked for reassurance when he returned to England with his faith shaken and his future in jeopardy. As soon as he had a settled home, his mother became its permanent inmate. He himself admitted that in his early youth he put aside all thoughts of marriage through despair of finding any woman her equal."

John Wesley grew up with his mother's logical mind. His brother Charles was heir to their father's poetic flair. But John became a skilled debater with a love for wit and humor. His wit and humor made him quite popular during his youth. One of his sisters said that no one could be sad when John was around.

At seventeen, John went to Oxford University, where he studied the classics and had his first serious romance. One of the earliest entries in his diary, which he kept for more than sixty years, asks, "Have I loved a woman or company more than God?" It was a question that plagued him through the years.

There were four young women in a circle of friends, and John had an interest in each of them. He wrote to his mother about Betty Kirkham, describing her as a "religious friend," but it is obvious from his diary that she was a special kind of religious friend. However, after waiting several years for John's expressions of affection to materialize in a proposal of marriage, Betty Kirkham accepted the hand of another suitor. His diary indicates that he had thought of marriage, but something had kept him from it.

He kept his friendship with Betty alive for several years—even though her husband was jealous of Wesley's attention to his wife. John at the same time was beginning his solicitations of another young woman in the circle. When the only way the relationship could progress any further was by a proposal of marriage, John backed away again.

John was twenty-nine now, had his master's degree from Oxford, had been appointed a teaching fellow and had, with his brother Charles, started the "Holy Club," a group that because of its methodical way of attaining spirituality became known as the Methodists.

His seventy-year-old father wanted him to take over his parish at Epworth, but John refused the offer, wanting to stay at Oxford, where he could promote his own holiness. He told his father that only where he himself could be holy could he effectively promote the holiness of others.

At this point in his life, John preferred the role of tutor to that of professor. He wanted to disciple those who were earnestly seeking the path of salvation. But he had two problems: (1) he was not sure of his own salvation and (2) he was very naive about those who pretended to be spiritually minded, especially young spiritually minded women. To be blunt, John was much more attractive to women than he realized.

This was clearly seen in 1735 when he was appointed as a chaplain to accompany James Oglethorpe to the new colony of Georgia in America. John's job in America would be to assist the motley band of set-

tlers—ex-convicts, Jews, German exiles, and debtors—and to preach
to the heathen Indians whom he considered to be "little children, humble, willing to learn." But Wesley's main reason for going to America
was simply in his own words: "My chief motive, to which all the rest
are subordinate, is the hope of saving my own soul." He was also quite
certain that in Georgia he would no longer be tempted by the lusts of
the flesh for he would "no longer see any woman, but those which are
almost of a different species from me."

He didn't realize how wrong he was.

On board ship, John was "in jeopardy every hour," as he wrote in
his diary. He thought of asking his brother Charles to pray for him,
because of the many young women aboard, some of whom were feign-
ing spiritual interest. He felt he needed prayer that he should "know
none of them after the flesh."

When a storm arose on the Atlantic, he realized he was in jeopardy
another way. The German Moravians on board seemed to be the only
passengers who were calm in the face of what seemed to John to be a
possible grave in the angry deep. When John asked the reason for their
serenity, he in return was asked a few questions: "Do you know Jesus
Christ?" "Do you know you are a child of God?" "Do you know you
are saved?"

John was perplexed. He was a minister and a son of a minister. He
was even a missionary, and he was rigorously practicing holiness, elu-
sive though it was, and he was intent on pursuing it even if his chase
took him around the world. But he had to admit that he did not pos-
sess the calm assurance of salvation that the Moravians had.

After arriving on terra firma in America, things did not improve.
Though he attended to his disciplines faithfully—arising at four, services at five, etc.—he was ineffective both as a minister to the settlers
and as a missionary to the Indians.

But he was not ineffective in reaching the heart of Sophy Hopkey,
the eighteen-year-old niece of Savannah's chief magistrate. John, now
thirty-three, found in Sophy everything he wanted in a woman. She
was "all stillness and attention" when he read books of sermons to her.
She was quick to learn when he instructed her in French grammar.

257

She was also quite ready for marriage, since she was unhappy at home with her aunt and uncle.

John didn't know what to do. When he was with her, he confessed that he was under the weight of "an unholy desire." He admitted to her that he would like to spend the rest of his life with her. Half the colony, it seemed, was urging him to marry the girl, but John pulled away from the flame. "I find, Miss Sophy, I cannot take fire into my bosom and not be burnt. I am therefore returning for a while to desire the direction of God."

Getting away from Sophy didn't solve the problem. So for his definitive answer on whether to get married or not, he decided to draw lots. One slip of "Marry"; another, "Not this year"; a third, "Think of it no more." The third slip of paper was drawn.

Though John found it difficult, he broke up with Sophy. By the end of the year, John had returned to England. In his journal, he described his break with Sophy as an escape, and that once again he was "a brand snatched from the burning." On his way back to England, he had several weeks to think about his missionary term in America. It had lasted less than two years, and John was realistic enough to assess it as a failure.

But six months later, Wesley's new life began. Depressed, he attended a meeting near Aldersgate Street in London and listened to the reading of Luther's *Commentary on Romans*. Wesley felt his heart "strangely warmed." He had been converted. He had discovered "salvation by faith only." Now he knew Jesus as the German Moravians did.

A year later in 1739 Wesley began his preaching in the fields. The crowds were huge. Wesley estimated twenty thousand at some of the preaching services. Quickly the work expanded. A school for poor children was started at Kingswood; a new meeting house was built in Bristol. An old cannon foundry near Moorfields was transformed into a 1,500-seat chapel.

During the next fifty years, he crisscrossed England on horseback over rough country roads, preaching the gospel nine months a year, starting Methodist societies all across the British Isles. Wesley became one of the dominant figures of the eighteenth century.

It was during the early years of this itinerant ministry that he met Grace Murray and entered into his most serious love affair. Grace Murray was in her late twenties, the widow of a sailor. Converted by Wesley's preaching, she soon became the leading woman Methodist, addressing the women's classes.

In 1745, Wesley, now forty-two, became ill and was tended by the "amiable, pious, and efficient" Mrs. Murray. John didn't exactly propose to her on the spot, but he did say, "If ever I marry, I think you will be the person." The widow Murray was flattered by his attention.

When Wesley was well enough to resume his preaching schedule, Grace was asked to join the troupe. A few months later John conducted evangelistic missions in Ireland, and Grace was once again a part of his team. In fact, she rode on the same horse behind Wesley. Wesley reported on her ministry, "She examined all the women in the smaller societies, and the believers in every place. She settled all the women bands, visited the sick, prayed with the mourners." She was, as one report has stated, the only co-worker with whom John was able to work closely for a long period time.

John was deeply in love with Grace, and he debated the pros and cons of matrimony. As usual, he kept a scorecard. In all seven marriage areas (housekeeper, nurse, companion, friend, fellow laborer in the gospel of Christ, spiritual gifts, and spiritual fruit from her labors), he rated Grace as excellent. He concluded, "Therefore all my seven arguments against marriage are totally set aside. Nay some of them seem to prove, both that I ought to marry and that G. M. is the Person." G. M. was his business-efficient way of referring to Grace Murray.

John realized that there might be some problems. For instance, what about children? His solution would be to place the children in the Methodist school at Kingswood while he and his wife continued their evangelistic ministry. One writer commented: "He was incapable of real domesticity; he wanted a coadjutor, not a wife."

But John faced some other obstacles too, the biggest of which was his own procrastination. And then there was the promise that he had made to the Holy Club not to marry without their permission. That meant that he needed to get the approval of his brother Charles, among others.

Grace was not happy with John's dillydallying. One of John's helpers, John Bennett, was waiting in the wings for Grace, and he was ready to step in whenever John Wesley's ardor cooled. Prior to Wesley's coming on the scene, it was Bennett who had been Grace Murray's suitor. During a lull in the action, Wesley had entered, center-stage. Bennett was still available.

Some Methodist leaders thought it wouldn't look right for Wesley to marry Grace Murray. It would look as if she had been his mistress during the past several years of evangelistic forays. Others felt for John to marry someone not of his social class would be a horrible mistake. They thought it would split the movement.

That's when his brother Charles Wesley stepped in. "Jumped in" would be a more accurate phrase.

In his opinion, the entire Methodist movement would go down the drain if John married. Any other minister in the movement could marry, but John was a special case. Besides, if John married Grace, Charles thought that half of the leadership would pack their bags. John's diary records his brother's feelings this way: "The thought of marrying at all, but especially of my marrying a servant and one so low-born, appeared above measure shocking to him." Charles didn't have a moment to spare. Hurriedly, he jumped on his horse and galloped to see Grace. He convinced her that if she went ahead with marriage to John, it "would destroy himself and the whole work of God." Two hours later, he took Grace away, brought her to Bennett, convinced both of them that for the good of Methodism they should marry each other, and in a few days the marriage took place.

One biographer doubts that Wesley would ever have married Grace Murray, despite what he had told her: "There can be no doubt that John Wesley delighted to dream of Grace Murray as his promised wife, but in view of his past history, the question arises whether even without Charles's intervention, that promise would ever have become performance."

But fifteen months later, John Wesley did get married, and he was determined that no one would ride off with his bride this time.

One of the few Methodist stalwarts who took John Wesley's side in his disagreement with his brother was Vincent Perronet. Perronet felt that John needed to be married; in fact, he urged it upon him as a duty. At this point, John probably didn't need much urging. Perronet consulted with banker Ebenezer Blackwell and came up with a candidate, Molly Vazeille, the widow of a London merchant who had left her an inheritance of ten thousand pounds.

With Grace, John Wesley had a checklist to see if his bride-to-be measured up. With Molly, there was no checklist. With Grace, John consulted his brother in advance, and that proved to be a mistake. With Molly, John didn't consult his brother, and that also proved to be a mistake.

He didn't consult with Charles; rather, he told Charles what he intended to do, and he didn't mention the name of his bride-to-be. Charles wrote in his diary, "I was thunderstruck." A few days later when he learned who the woman was, Charles "retired to mourn." He "groaned all the day, and several following ones, under my own and for the people's burden. I could eat no pleasant food, nor preach, nor rest either by night or by day."

Despite his inner turmoil, he dared not intervene this time. John wasn't going to let a courtship interfere with his preaching schedule, and it didn't slow him down one bit until a fortuitous accident. Crossing London Bridge in mid-February 1751, he slipped and badly sprained his ankle. Despite the pain, he preached on schedule in the afternoon and then hobbled to the home of Widow Vazeille. His fiancée Molly acted as his nurse for the rest of the week. At her home he spent the time "partly in prayer, reading and conversation, partly in writing a *Hebrew Grammar* and *Lessons for Children.*"

The conversation with Molly must have settled some things about their marriage. Wesley wanted to make sure that Molly knew he would never touch a penny of her fortune. At least one of her four children was strongly opposed to the marriage, and John probably wanted to remove any suspicion that he was marrying her for her money. No doubt, he also informed her about his evangelistic missions, which kept him away from home 75 percent of the time. She would have her choice of accompanying him on his arduous trips or staying home with her family.

John probably told her, as he had told others, that no Methodist preacher, least of all himself, should "preach one sermon or travel one day less in a married than in a single state." What this meant, of course, was that John would not be making any adjustments to married life; Molly would have to make the adjustments.

The following Monday, his sprained ankle notwithstanding, John and Molly were married. The previous day, Sunday, he had preached on his knees, because he was not able to stand on his sprained ankle. On Tuesday, he was preaching again, once again on his knees. In between he sandwiched in the wedding, and presumably he was married on his knees. We don't know much about his wedding, because he neglected to mention it in his journal.

It was a short courtship, perhaps only sixteen days. And undeniably, it was marriage on the rebound, for John was still smarting from the loss of Grace.

Yet at forty-seven, John had a need to be married. He had always enjoyed feminine companionship, and being attractive to women, he usually had it. But as the Methodist movement grew, he had become more and more isolated in his tower of leadership. Even his brother Charles was now separated from him, separated by the happy marriage that Charles had with Sally Gwynne and separated by Charles's rash action in breaking up John's relationship with Grace. So although he met thousands of people a year and knew hundreds as friends, John was a lonely man at times, and when illness or accident confined him to bed, he was at his loneliest. It was while recuperating that he had fallen in love with Grace. This time he had been confined with a sprained ankle in Molly Vazeille's home on Threadneedle Street in London. The conversation which he enjoyed with Molly in those days of convalescence was delightful. In his words, she gave him "all the assurances which words could give, of the most intense and inviolable affection."

Molly Goldhawk Vazeille Wesley, forty-one, had been a servant girl before marrying a London merchant "who had pampered and indulged her." She had become accustomed to a settled middle-class family life. She had four children, the youngest under five years old. John spoke of her having a "middling understanding," and one biographer speaks of her as being "no more than conventionally religious." Wesley's early biographers denigrated Molly and exonerated John, so some of the early comments on Molly's character may be biased.

Some of these early biographers think that by marrying John, Molly was climbing the social ladder of middle-class respectability and that she inveigled him into marriage, something that Grace Murray and Sophy Hopkey had been unable to do. That is too crass an assessment. Two of her late husband's friends had recommended John Wesley to her. She was flattered by his attention, just as he was pleased with hers. Both of them were ripe for marriage.

The marriage started poorly and went downhill from there. The Sunday after the wedding, John felt he had to explain to his fellow Methodists why he had married so suddenly and had not consulted with his brethren in advance. The explanation confused his brethren and incensed Molly. He spoke of marriage as "a cross that he had taken up" for their sakes and that he had married to "break down the prejudice about the world and him."

Molly was dumbfounded. Was this the man that she had married?

A week later John was off to a conference, then home for a week and then off again on a long road trip in the north. His first day out he scribbled in his diary, "In respect of traveling abroad, the Methodist preacher who has a wife should be as though he had none." But at night he wrote a warm letter home to Molly, "You have surely a right to every proof of love I can give, and to all the little help which is in my power. For you have given me even your own self. O how can we praise God enough for making us help meet for each other."

John even wrote to his friend Blackwell the banker and asked him to look out for Molly in his absence: "She has many trials; but not one more than God knows and knows to be profitable to her."

Among her trials was John himself. Molly had already gone to Blackwell and complained about her husband's lack of sensitivity to her needs. Then she went to Charles Wesley, only four months after the wedding. It took courage for her to approach Charles because she knew how strongly he had disapproved of the wedding. He agreed to talk to John privately about the problems and then have a meeting among the three of them to engineer a reconciliation. The meeting accomplished little. Molly listed all of the faults, not only of John but also of Charles; John insisted that he couldn't halt his God-given ministry in order to coddle Molly; and Charles felt called upon to recite Latin poetry to calm the waters.

Charles never got along with his sister-in-law. "I must pray or sink into a spirit of revenge," he said after enduring one of Molly's seasons of complaint and insult. Charles's negative feelings were contagious and infected other Methodist leaders. Molly was starting to feel paranoid; she was the wife of the leader of Methodism, and yet everyone was against her.

Molly had tried one alternative—staying home while John was on the road—and it hadn't worked. Now she was ready to try the other. If she traveled with her husband, maybe the marriage bond would be strengthened and the negative vibes that she was feeling would disappear.

But it didn't work. Grace Murray had been an ideal traveling companion for John; Molly was not. He didn't want to make the comparison, but he couldn't help it. England's roads were not easy to travel, especially the way John Wesley traveled them. And for one who had a penchant for complaining, Molly found she had plenty to bemoan.

Besides the grueling travel schedule, Molly had to face pouring rain, driving winds, winter cold, stones thrown by angry mobs, and taunts of jeering antagonists. Once, when she arrived at the site of the next meeting, she and John were met by a bevy of adoring women all arrayed in "remarkable neatness." She was conscious of two things: first, that she looked her worst after a fifty-mile ride on horseback and second, that the women were gathered around her husband and didn't care a bit about her. After the meeting, while John was exulting about spiritual blessings, she was complaining about the hard beds, the itchy bedcovers that were too small, and the crawly little bugs.

It was no doubt after circumstances like that that Molly's hair-pulling story took place, if indeed it did take place. According to one of Methodism's traveling preachers: "Once when I was in the north of Ireland, I went into a room and found Mrs. Wesley foaming with fury. Her husband was on the floor, where she had been trailing him by the hair of his head. She herself was still holding in her hand venerable locks which she had plucked up by the roots." Allegedly, this took place about a year and a half after their marriage.

Later biographies partially discredit the story, though they don't discredit it completely. Molly's temper was legendary, and when she lost it, she became quite irrational. John once wrote, in the impersonal way by which he sometimes referred to his wife, "It is a pity. I should be glad if I had to do with reasonable people."

There were occasional respites, and at first, John's letters show love and affection. He appreciated her assistance with business and financial matters. He even naively encouraged her to open any letters that came to their home while he was traveling. And when Molly opened some of his mail, it started her off on another tantrum.

The problem was that John's intimate counseling of women did not change after his marriage. He was as warm, loving, and solicitous as ever. So after John and Molly mutually agreed that Methodism's best interests weren't served by her traveling with her husband across the British Isles, she stayed at home, read John's mail, and imagined the worst.

Sarah Ryan, a recent convert and only thirty-three years old, had been appointed by John to be matron of the Kingswood School. She had been married three times without benefit of divorce, and was certainly not the people's choice for the coveted post.

Wesley gave her his pastoral counsel. In his letters to her, he told her his problems with Molly, and the language he used to speak of his spiritual interest in her could easily have been misunderstood. And it was.

In return, Sarah's letters to John said things like: "I do not know how to steer between extremes, of regarding you too little or too much." When Molly ripped open one of these letters, she obviously thought it was too much. What John viewed as *agape* love seemed suspiciously like *eros* love to Molly. She demanded that John stop the correspondence.

"I afterwards found her in such a temper," John writes, "as I have not seen her in several years." And then Molly walked out on him, "vowing she would see me no more."

The temper tantrum and Molly's departure didn't stop John from writing to his female lieutenant at Kingswood. A month later, however, at a meeting that Wesley had with more than sixty of his Methodist ministers and with Sarah Ryan presiding, Molly burst into the room, waving her finger at Sarah and shouting, "The whore now serving you has three husbands living."

After that explosion, Molly returned to John, but as you can imagine, life wasn't any easier. At times, the relationship resembled a pitched battle. Molly was the violent one, John the self-righteous. She accused him of having his brother's wife as a mistress. He accused her of poisoning the minds of the servants against him.

In one letter to Molly, John listed ten major complaints, including Molly's stealing from his bureau, his inability to invite friends in for tea, her making him feel like a prisoner in his own house, his having to give an account to Molly of everywhere he went, Molly showing his private papers and letters without his permission, her use of fishwife's language against the servants, and her continual malicious slander.

He vowed that he would be willing to do anything to keep her "in good humor," as long as it didn't hurt his soul or hers or the cause of God. Writing his warm letters to Sarah Ryan and other women was necessary to the "cause of God."

Naturally, John had a problem appearing in public with Molly because he was never quite sure what she would say. He writes that she "could not refrain from throwing squibs" at him and would speak to him as "no wife ought to speak to a husband."

She knew she had an acid tongue. However, not all the blame for their unhappy marriage was hers, and she wanted the world to know it.

She resented the pastoral letters she received from her husband, as if she were no nearer and dearer to him than Sarah Ryan. John would write her: "How do you look back on your past sins?" And "If you were buried just now, or if you had never lived, what loss would it be to the cause of God?" She didn't like to be preached at by her husband.

Besides that, her health was poor. She suffered painfully from gout and had a difficult time going through menopause. She had been defrauded of much of her inheritance, and her children had been a concern to her. One had died, another was sickly, and two of her sons proved to be "grievous crosses." John wrote her about these personal problems, suggesting that perhaps these afflictions had come from God "to break the impetuosity and soften the hardness" of her heart. She admitted to herself that this might be so, but she wished that her husband didn't have to keep reminding her.

John Wesley pleaded with her, lectured her and, when that didn't work, he ignored her. John could persuade most women, but he was unable to budge Molly. "One might as well try to convince the north wind," he said.

For more than twenty years, the Wesleys' "marital history pursued its thorny course," writes Stanley Ayling. "A marriage largely nominal and often almost irrelevant; separation frequent, but never final until 1776; perennial mutual resentment."

Sometimes there was a short period of togetherness, as in 1766 when Wesley, now sixty-three, wrote, "My wife continues in an amazing temper. Miracles are not ceased. Not one jarring string. O let us live now."

But four years later, on what was almost their twentieth anniversary, Molly walked out again; Wesley's journal records it: "January 23. For what cause I know not, my wife set out for Newcastle, purposing never to return. 'Non eam reliqui; non dimisi; non revocabo [I have not left her; I have not sent her away; I shall not ask her to come back].'"

A year later she came back on her own. Not only did she come back, but she also traveled with him on one of his speaking tours. She was sixty-two at the time.

As they traveled, she felt the strong antagonism of Methodist leadership against her. She felt that they were placing John on a pedestal and her in the gutter. In 1774 she wrote her husband, "For God's sake, for your sake, put a stop to this torrent of evil that is poured out against me."

The torrent did not stop. In 1776 (when he was seventy-three and she sixty-seven) they separated for the last time. "The water is spilt," John wrote. "And it cannot be gathered up again."

Two years later, he wrote her his last letter. It was bitter. "If you were to live a thousand years, you could not undo the mischief you have done."

In 1751, at the age of seventy-two, Molly Vazeille Wesley died. She bequeathed nothing to John except her ring. According to the will, the ring was left as a "token that I die in love and friendship towards him."

John Wesley continued his almost herculean labors. He crossed the Irish Sea forty-two times. When he was eighty he conducted a mission tour in Holland. His bitterness against Molly passed away in his final years, and he viewed those stormy years of marriage with the idea that if "Mrs. Wesley had been a better wife," he might have been unfaithful to the great work to which God had called him.

John Wesley was married to his work, and he felt it would have been a grievous sin to be unfaithful to that divine marriage. But sometimes a servant of God fails to distinguish between loving God and loving God's work.

Bibliography

Ayling, Stanley. *John Wesley.* Cleveland: Collins-World, 1979.

Brailsford, Mabel. *A Tale of Two Brothers.* New York: Oxford University Press, 1954.

Flint, Charles. *Charles Wesley and His Colleagues.* Washington, D.C.: Public Affairs Press, 1957.

Lee, Umphrey. *The Lord's Horseman, John Wesley the Man.* Nashville: Abingdon, 1954.

Wesley, John. *The Heart of Wesley's Journal.* New Canaan, Conn.: Keats, 1979.

14

Thee Is a Dry Old Stick

Hannah Whitall and Robert Pearsall Smith

One of the hottest best-sellers of the past 125 years has been *The Christian's Secret of a Happy Life,* written in 1874 by a forty-three-year-old housewife, Hannah Whitall Smith.

It was published in the year that Hannah's husband, Robert, had to leave the ministry because of hanky-panky in the bedroom of a female admirer.

Hannah also wrote a book on raising children. That book was published in 1894, the year that Hannah's younger daughter married the noted atheist Bertrand Russell. Three years before, her older daughter had left her husband and two daughters to shock society by a fling across Europe with her art teacher.

Over the last one hundred years, millions of readers have benefited from Hannah's *The Christian's Secret of a Happy Life.* There's no doubt about that. But neither is there any doubt that Hannah didn't have a secret for a happy marriage.

But then, it might have been impossible for anyone to have had a happy marriage with a man as unstable as Robert.

Frustrated by her inability to make marriage with Robert work, Hannah soured on marriage altogether. In her seventies she wrote, "It is hard for me to believe that any husband and wife are really happy together."

The questions you might ask are, "When did Hannah's marriage turn sour?" and "Could anything have been done to change the situation?" and, as her biographer suggests, "Was Hannah a part of the problem instead of the solution?"

The year was 1850; the city was Philadelphia, the City of Brotherly Love, founded by the noted Quaker, William Penn.

Two young people, both born into Quaker families, had just met. Hannah Whitall, age eighteen, was the daughter of a prosperous glass manufacturer. Robert Pearsall Smith, twenty-four, from a highly educated family, was beginning a career in publishing.

To all onlookers, it seemed like a perfect match. Hannah's parents thought so, too.

Though Hannah usually displayed proper Quaker piety, sometimes she seemed too fun-loving, too ambitious, or too materialistic. She liked pretty clothes, treasured a gold watch that her father had given her, and wrote in her diary of becoming a woman preacher. "I would be so magnificently eloquent, so grandly sublime. And then I would go on a religious visit to England, where the whole nation, even the queen herself, would crowd to hear the young, eloquent Quaker girl." After that, she dreamed of going to Paris and then making a "religious visit to the moon."

At other times the unpredictable teenager lamented, "I have been so rebellious. I have so entirely neglected prayer. . . . My mind entirely acknowledges my own worthlessness."

So when Robert Pearsall Smith came courting Hannah in proper Quaker style, her parents were certainly pleased to see a young man of such apparent propriety and stability enter her life. After all, Robert was a descendant of James Logan, William Penn's secretary, and his family tree blossomed with publishers, printers, and librarians.

Robert was pious, handsome, and gifted. What more could Hannah's parents desire in a son-in-law?

And he was romantic, too. For Hannah, that was frosting on the cake.

By the time he had courted her for five months, he had rented a cottage just outside of Philadelphia which would become their first home after marriage.

From the garden in back of the cottage, Robert plucked a bouquet of flowers and sent them to Hannah with the note (in proper Quaker idiom), "Mayest thou live to enjoy many beautiful flowers and happy hours there as my bride, my friend, my congenial companion, and ardently loved (may I say it?) wife."

Robert combined spirituality and romanticism. Once he told Hannah that he never let five minutes go by without considering what was right. Their formal, supervised "dates" were spent discussing spiritual matters.

Two months after sending the flowers from his garden, Robert wrote her, "Having come thus far on our way, do not let us, my dearest friend, be discouraged but press on for the mark of the prize of our high calling in Christ."

A spiritual young man indeed.

In November 1851, after a year of courtship, Hannah Whitall became Hannah Whitall Smith and moved into the Germantown cottage that Robert had rented.

The first six years of married life seemed normal enough. Two children were born into the family, while Robert was working hard trying to build up his publishing business.

But underneath the surface, there was unrest. Among them was spiritual struggle. Hannah's journal tells it like this: "I felt myself cast off from God entirely. I felt like a sinking boat. . . . I no longer trusted God." She couldn't understand how evil could be allowed to exist in God's world.

Robert wasn't much help in her struggle; neither were the Quaker meetings that she and Robert attended faithfully. Her mind demanded answers; her spirit was restless.

She talked with Robert about her going to college. Robert liked the idea and hired a tutor so that at the age of twenty-five she could brush up on her high school subjects. At first elated, Hannah soon changed her mind about college because she feared she might have to neglect her children.

271

But what happened in the next couple of years taught her more than any college curriculum could ever have done.

That Christmas, their five-year-old Nellie contracted a severe bronchial infection, ran a high fever, and then, after struggling for life for five days, died.

"My heart is ready to burst," Hannah wrote in her journal. Death had never come so close to her before.

In her sorrow she wandered into a noonday prayer meeting in downtown Philadelphia. There she had a new spiritual experience. "God was making himself manifest. . . . My soul leaped up in an irresistible cry to know Him."

That summer, after Nellie's death and her experience in the noonday prayer meeting, she took her Bible with her on a summer vacation in Atlantic City and resolved to read it until she found something to satisfy her soul.

When she reached Romans 5:8, "While we were yet sinners, Christ died for us," she discovered all she needed. "I know now that I don't have to wear a sugar-scoop bonnet to please God. Christ has done it all for me on the cross. His sacrifice is all I need to be restored to right relationship with God."

Effervescent Hannah bubbled her new discovery to everyone she met, including her husband. Soon Robert shared her enthusiasm. Together they visited other churches, much to the dismay of Hannah's parents. Though some of Hannah's first spiritual influences were Christians associated with Plymouth Brethren assemblies, she was baptized about a year later in a Baptist church by a German Reformed minister and frequently studied the Bible with Methodists. To round out the Smiths' interdenominationalism, Robert became a Presbyterian.

Hannah's withdrawal from the Society of Friends shocked her family, and for a few years she and Robert were ostracized by the Whitalls. It was a blow to Hannah, but she and her husband did not remain friendless. Robert invited a wide variety of religious figures to their home, and Hannah was always delighted for the opportunity to converse.

During these years, Hannah latched onto the doctrine of universalism, the belief that God will eventually save everyone and that no one will really go to hell. Despite strong opposition, she persisted in this view throughout her life.

Not all the struggles of this period of their lives were spiritual; some were financial. In 1861, Robert's publishing business went bankrupt. Hannah felt that Robert had made impulsive decisions which had ruined the business. She felt that if he had asked her advice, or the advice of a veteran businessman like her father, he might have been spared financial disaster.

In general, though, Hannah felt she and Robert were a good match. She was pleased at how much Robert shared with her in areas apart from his business. He was not like many husbands she knew. But sometimes, on important matters, Robert did not confide in Hannah. He operated intuitively; she operated more rationally. She did not trust his approach to decision making, and he feared that if he consulted her on every decision, she would control him.

Robert's business was not the only business in trouble in those years. Publishing enterprises had been especially hard hit. The nation's economy, after the financial crash of 1857 and under the threat of a war that would split the nation, was very shaky.

Yet Hannah's father weathered the national disasters quite well. In fact, his prosperity along with Robert's bankruptcy brought the two families back together again.

Conscientiously, Robert tried to pay back his creditors, but couldn't. He also wanted to provide for his family without going to his father-in-law for help, but that too seemed impossible. The strain eventually began to tear him apart.

Hannah believed that his disorientation had been caused by a recent fall from a horse. More likely, however, Robert was a manic-depressive, and his depressions were often triggered by the trauma from excessive stress and a feeling of failure.

During the Civil War, Robert volunteered to serve in a hospital in Harrisburg, Pennsylvania, and while there he seemed to recover his emotional equilibrium.

After returning home, he was appointed by his father-in-law to manage the family glassworks in Millville, New Jersey, forty miles south of Philadelphia.

Once again, Hannah was disturbed at being left out of the family's decision making. In true Quaker idiom, she told him, "Thee and father have doubtless worked out a good plan, but I had not five words conversation in this decision that is to affect my future as well as yours. Of all the husbands I know, thee is the only one who treats thy wife as an equal. And now this. I am sorely disappointed."

Hannah was bothered not only because she wasn't consulted, but also because she didn't enjoy the prospect of moving to Millville, a blue-collar town.

Robert apologized, but they moved to Millville anyway, and it was in Millville that Hannah entered into a new phase of her life.

After a hiatus of ten years, Hannah began bearing children again. Four children—two boys and two girls—were born to them in Millville during the next four years. Hannah had to care for five children, two doves, two parrots, two cats, and two monkeys. "It makes a lively scene when they all express their feelings at once," she wrote.

But that wasn't all that occupied Hannah in Millville. Though she had a difficult time adjusting to the town, she gradually began associating with the townspeople after a dressmaker invited her to a Methodist Saturday night meeting. Hannah went "with my importance and superiority," aware that most of those attending would be factory workers. In fact, it was a factory woman with a shawl over her head who led the meeting. However, as Hannah listened, her attitude began to change. "When I got sight of Jesus as my Savior, this great big Me melted down to nothing."

The Methodist doctrine of holiness captivated her. The following summer she persuaded Robert to go with her to a Methodist camp meeting to seek the "second blessing" or "the baptism of the Spirit."

Though nothing unusual happened to Hannah, it was different for Robert. "Suddenly from head to foot, Robert was shaken with what seemed like a magnetic thrill of heavenly delight and floods of glory seemed to pour through him."

Disappointed that she couldn't have such an experience, she wrestled with God for another year. But the experience never came. At times she became disappointed, but eventually she concluded, as biographer

Marie Henry says, "What was called 'the blessing' was simply the emotional response of emotional natures such as Robert's."

Although she never experienced the spiritual "highs" she sought, she was amazingly adept at escaping spiritual lows. "As to ups and downs," she once wrote, "don't thee know that I am one of the kind who never have any? My path seems to lie along a sort of dead level arrangement that is very comfortable, but not at all glorious."

To emotional, intuitive Robert, it was aggravating to have a wife who seemed always in control of every situation and who never appeared to lose her equilibrium.

The next few years, however, would certainly test anyone's equilibrium.

In the fall of 1872, their oldest son, Frank, a sophomore at Princeton, was stricken with typhoid fever.

In the previous three years when her husband was traveling a great deal during each winter and her four young children—all under eight years old—were difficult to manage, she had appreciated the growing maturity and spirituality of her teenaged son. At school he was not only a spiritual leader, but also a scholar and an athlete. He seemed to be everything a parent could want in a son.

But then the Lord took him home. Hannah kept telling herself that he was happier now in heaven than he could ever be on earth, and so she should be content with his happiness. But deep inside her was a grief that she didn't want to explore. "I dare not go into the depths of this sorrow," she wrote a friend. "After a while . . . I shall be able . . . to speak of it."

That was only the beginning of her testing.

Hardly had she written those words when Robert suffered another nervous breakdown. He was no longer managing his father-in-law's Millville plant; that hadn't worked out too well. Perhaps it was the stress of constant travel, made worse by his grief at Frank's death. Perhaps it was the feeling of inadequacy or failure again.

Whatever it was, Robert, along with Hannah and the four young children, journeyed to Clifton Springs, New York, that fall so that he could be treated at a sanatorium rest home.

The head of the sanatorium had some novel ideas for curing emotional and mental problems. Sometimes he was successful, sometimes not. Meanwhile, the rest home was no rest for Hannah; she was miserable. Separated from parents and friends who meant much to her, she had her hands full with her four young children, one of whom had a persistent fever.

For her own sanity, Hannah tried to get privacy. While her children were sleeping or attending classes, she began writing a book chronicling the life of her "noble and glorious" son Frank. Somehow she managed to finish a book-length manuscript in a month and send it off to a publisher. (The following year it was published under the title *The Record of a Happy Life.*)

It took her only a month to write the book, but it took Robert longer to recover. In fact, after two months at the sanatorium he seemed worse instead of better. She described him in a letter, "All the color had drained from his face and he was wild-eyed. . . . He paced up and down like a caged beast."

Her calm demeanor aggravated him further. He lashed out at her, blaming her for his problems. She was not sexually responsive, he charged. She was too unfeeling. "I need love from a wife. I need warmth and touching and tenderness. Thee is like a dry old stick. . . . I could get well if only thee could get thy dead emotions kindled."

"I cannot help being the sort of person I am," she countered. "Try and bear with me."

The problem from Robert's perspective was that Hannah, by her calm approach and rational handling of problems, always seemed to be in control. Though she was always loyal to him, she sometimes treated him condescendingly.

The doctor in charge of the sanatorium counseled Robert that he shouldn't feel guilty or ashamed about his sexual feelings. According to the doctor, they were given by God.

However, the doctor went further than that in his therapy. Along with some cults in the nineteenth century, the doctor taught that heightened sexual feelings could be a sign of the Holy Spirit's presence. According to him, the baptism of the Holy Spirit was a physical thing "with delightful thrills from head to toe." And Robert, who was not only frustrated by his wife's coldness but also eager for any new manifestation of the Holy Spirit, was a ripe candidate for the novel teaching.

When Robert shared the teaching with Hannah, she was shocked—and puzzled. After all, the head of the sanatorium was a saintly man, but Hannah was bothered by what was happening to Robert. "Things which he once considered as fleshly he now considered spiritual."

Accordingly to the doctor, what Robert needed most was total rest—away from the pressures of the family and away from the pressures of his father-in-law's business. (Hannah's father would have to find another salesman.) What the doctor ordered was a stay at a sanatorium in the Swiss Alps.

And that's where he headed in March 1873.

He started in the right direction by boarding a steamer across the Atlantic. But when he stopped in England, he met a Bible teacher, William E. Boardman, who talked much about the "Higher Life" and whose views on holiness were similar to his own.

Boardman asked Robert to speak at a Bible conference. Robert's enthusiastic style and experience in salesmanship, coupled with his knowledge of Scripture, made him an engaging speaker. After only a few weeks he was asked to address a larger meeting and then a national conference. Boardman felt that Robert didn't need a rest in Switzerland as much as he needed some active involvement in the Lord's work.

On the surface, that seemed to be the case. Maybe, he reasoned, the problem wasn't having too much work; maybe it was not having the right kind of work.

But to Hannah it came as a shock when he finally wrote to her and told her what he was doing. How was it possible? When she had said good-bye to him in March, he seemed far from being cured. Now he was preaching day after day in England.

Moreover, he vowed that he would never go back into secular business again, and Hannah, practical as always, wondered how they would live on the uncertain income of a traveling Bible teacher.

Hannah was dismayed, but she was helpless to do anything about the situation. Not only was she an ocean away from her husband, but she was also burdened with the care of four children—aged nine, seven, six, and four—and also pregnant again at the age of forty-one. It was her seventh pregnancy.

Robert's comments about her didn't help matters any, either. Though he was enjoying a spiritual "high," he continued to carp at Hannah's lack of love for him. Finally, she could take it no longer. Six months pregnant, she fired a letter back at him, "Thee says it is only friendship that I feel for thee. . . . But I do not understand it. . . . I cannot comprehend any love different from that which I feel, and I do not think I want to. . . . If it is only friendship, darling, it is at least pure and true . . . and finds its happiness in thy happiness. I suppose I am a pragmatic sort of person, incapable of the heights and depths of love. Well, darling, I did not make myself; and if thee tries very hard, I think thee might perhaps put up with me as I am, for the few remaining years of our life."

They had been married for twenty-two years.

It was a difficult summer for Hannah, and it became even more difficult when she lost her baby. "I had looked forward to this baby more longingly than ever before," she wrote.

She felt herself a failure. She couldn't satisfy her husband. She couldn't bear another child. She didn't fit the conventional image of a nineteenth-century woman in the church or in society. "Life with its failure has pressed upon me of late with the most unspeakable sadness," she wrote to a friend. For Hannah the optimist, it was an unusually low period.

But about that time her own public ministry started to soar. She was surprised when her book about her son Frank became a best-seller and was translated into several foreign languages. And she began to accept speaking engagements as a Bible teacher. She acquired a reputation for her "command of easily flowing language, a not incongruous wit, and a simplicity of manner."

Finally, after an absence of an entire year, Robert wrote suggesting that Hannah bring the children and join him in England. She wasted little time in complying with her husband's suggestion.

As soon as she arrived, she was thrust into the spotlight. In some ways she seemed so prim and proper with her "thees" and "thous" and dressed in black with a small lace cap on her head, but in other ways she tended to shock Victorian England. Her views on universal salvation were certainly unorthodox, and her candor on other subjects also kept her audiences agape.

The entire family returned to the United States for the winter of 1874, but as soon as the following spring began to break through, Robert had his bags packed and was on his way back to England, leaving Hannah with the four children.

Robert went on to Berlin, Germany, and, using an interpreter, preached to thousands. The newspapers carried the account: "Immense crowds attend the meetings and members of the nobility occupy seats on the platform. The Empress Augusta has given a private audience to Mr. Smith."

In exhilaration, Robert exclaimed, "All Europe is at my feet."

As soon as school was out, Hannah and the children planned to join Robert again. She was being asked to speak alongside her husband at numerous summer conferences and retreats. Whether she would be allowed to speak at the prestigious Brighton Convention, however, was up in the air. Robert wrote her that a distinguished committee would decide.

By the time the committee had given its approval, Hannah wasn't sure she wanted to start traveling the circuit as a conference speaker: "I feel as if I were a sort of traveling Barnum's Hippodrome [circus] with a 'woman preacher' on show instead of a tightrope dancer."

But regardless of her reservations, Hannah got her children ready and they boarded a steamship for their second trip across the Atlantic.

Between bouts of seasickness she finished the final chapter of a manuscript she had been writing for her husband. The manuscript was entitled *The Christian's Secret of a Happy Life.*

Two years earlier, while he was still recovering from his nervous breakdown at the New York sanatorium, Robert had launched a small publication called *The Christian's Pathway to Power.* Hannah had opposed the idea from the start. He was not well enough to do it; it would only put added stress on him; and it would probably end again in failure because there were too many other Christian papers being published already. But if he went ahead and published it anyway, she vowed that she would never write a line of copy for it.

Nonetheless, he launched it, paying no heed to Hannah's protests.

When he went to England, however, and got busy preaching every night, he begged Hannah to reconsider. He needed her help. Hannah wasn't eager for the writing assignment. She thought that he should know that she was busy enough raising four children with no husband available. She had no time to deal with magazine deadlines and an article on the victorious Christian life. But she didn't want the stress of overwork to trigger another breakdown for her husband, so she countered by agreeing to write an article if he would quit taking his daily glass of wine. Hannah was getting interested in the temperance movement and was increasingly concerned about Robert's wine-drinking. The daily glass had been prescribed by the doctor, but Hannah didn't trust Robert's doctor regarding anything. When Robert agreed to her counteroffer, Hannah agreed to write his article, but as she says, "It was dragged from me at the point of the bayonet without one ray of enthusiasm and hating to do it all the time."

To Hannah's surprise and Robert's chagrin, her article drew more favorable response than anything else Robert published in his paper. So Robert asked her to do another, and then another. This continued for nearly two years. Finally a book publisher noticed Hannah's series of articles and asked for the privilege of publishing them in a book.

As she sailed across the Atlantic to England, Hannah had one last article to write before the ship docked in England. Though she said she felt "most uninspired," she wrote anyway. "I was seasick at the time," she recalled later, "and as near to cursing as a person who had experienced 'the blessings of holiness' could dare to be."

The last chapter—which became chapter 20 of her book—is entitled "The Life on Wings." In it she tells the story of how three Christians might cope when they came to a spiritual mountain that had to be crossed. "The first one would tunnel through it with hard and wearisome labor; the second would meander around it in an indefinite fashion, hardly knowing where she was going, and yet, because her aim was right, getting around it at last; but the third . . . would just flap her wings and fly right over it."

That's what Hannah usually did. She flapped her wings and flew over her problems.

But not always.

Certainly the problems of the next few months were ultimate tests for her flying ability.

Her first challenge in England was speaking to crowds of two to three thousand people. There were no microphones in those days, and she became, she said, "as hoarse as a crow."

Since there was a two-week gap between the first conference and subsequent meetings of the summer, Hannah took a quick trip to Switzerland to see the Alps. Robert would continue his preaching schedule, and Hannah would rejoin him at England's famous Keswick conference. By that time Hannah's voice would be restored.

However, not long after Hannah left, Robert got himself enmeshed in a situation that marred his reputation for life.

A young woman asked to talk with him after a meeting. In a state of spiritual anguish, she said she needed a counselor to talk to. She invited Robert to her room. "I thought at the time that that was not quite proper," Robert confessed later, "but her spiritual distress seemed so great."

Nearly hysterical, the young woman was sobbing uncontrollably. As she sat on her bed, Robert recalled, "she looked so forlorn there, so lonely and sad. I went over and sat beside her on the bed and put my arm around her to soothe her."

Robert may have thought he was giving her pastoral counseling or fatherly advice. Maybe. He recalled the teachings of the head of the sanatorium and shared them with her. "As the two of us sat together on the bed, I explained to her the precious doctrine. I told her how Christ wanted us to feel thrills up and down our bodies."

According to Robert, that was all that happened.

According to the woman, Robert had tried to make love to her. She said that he had told her of physical thrills that a man and a woman can enjoy together while holding one another closely and while praying.

The head of the conference took immediate action. Robert was summoned into his office the next morning and was told that all his meetings in England were being canceled.

Robert Pearsall Smith was indeed finished. The local newspaper ran this headline: "Famous Evangelist Found in Bedroom of Adoring Female Follower."

281

Devastated, Robert fled England and tried to make his way to Hannah. He got as far as Paris. There he checked in at the Hotel Louvre and collapsed.

A telegram found its way to Hannah: "Mr. Smith ill in Paris at the Hotel Louvre."

On arrival, she took one look at him and recognized the wild, tormented look in his eyes. She had seen it thirty months earlier at the sanatorium in New York. To a friend she wrote, "Robert has had a complete breakdown. He has lost twenty pounds already and is suffering very much from almost constant nausea."

As soon as he was able to travel, Hannah got her husband aboard ship and back to America.

Had Robert been trapped by his own naïveté? Hannah thought that this was the case. At least she did for a while. And the Brighton Convention Committee thought so too. In its official release, it stated that Robert's conduct was "free of all evil intention." The committee seemed more concerned about the fact that he "on some occasions, in personal conversations, inculcated doctrines which were most unscriptural and dangerous." From that, it may be assumed that he had at other times also imparted his teaching of "physical thrills" that accompany the infilling of the Spirit.

Back in Philadelphia, Robert, now forty-nine, returned to sales work for his father-in-law's plant, the Whitall-Tatum Glassworks, but as Marie Henry points out, "the heart had gone out of him."

Hannah thought so too. Nearly a year after his breakdown in the Paris hotel, Hannah described his status to a friend: "His life is blasted. . . . a more sensitive, tender-hearted, generous man never lived, and this blow has sorely crushed him in every tender spot." What had happened to him, Hannah wrote, "utterly crushed from his nature all power of trusting anyone."

Though Robert was coaxed to preach one more time the following summer, and though Hannah, ever the optimist, felt that her husband was preaching better than ever, Robert demurred. "No more meetings. I am done." From that point, Robert began a spiritual slide from which he would never recover.

Hannah meanwhile struggled with God about the meaning of all of it. Romans 8:28 ("All things work together for good") didn't make sense in the light of Robert's circumstances. Why was God allowing it all to happen? At times she felt that she too was losing her faith in God. Though she wanted to trust, she feared that any little thing might give her faith an irreversible setback. She wrote, "It is a ticklish seat on top of a greased pole, and the least push one way or other might upset me."

As a salesman, Robert spent a great deal of time away from home. Concerned about him, Hannah urged him to spend time with Christians when he traveled. "I think it is a very critical time with thee and if thee wants to get back to the old place, thee must put thyself under the right sort of influences."

Apparently Robert didn't want to "get back to the old place," but Hannah did. And about three years later, she found a place of spiritual rest. Writing to a friend, she said, "Like a poor little child who has lost its way, I creep into the dear arms of my Father and just ask Him to carry me, since I cannot understand His directions. He doeth all things well, and I can leave myself with Him."

If Hannah thought that the worst of her trials were over, she was certainly mistaken. Their silver anniversary in the fall of 1876 was certainly mired in doubt and confusion, but after that, things got even worse.

In 1877, Hannah's father died. Though she accepted his homegoing graciously as she did the death of all elderly people, the loss of the one male bulwark in her life was a blow.

Three years later, in January 1880, her mother died, and then only one month after that, her youngest child, Ray (short for Rachel), succumbed to scarlet fever at the age of eleven.

Ray was the fourth child to be taken from them. "For her loss," Hannah wrote in the last entry to appear in her thirty-two-year journal, "there was no comfort, but simply and only the sweet will of God."

Now forty-eight and going through menopause, Hannah felt very much alone. Her husband was spending more time on the road, her beloved parents who had been next-door neighbors for several years were now deceased, and her three surviving children were all away at school.

Uncharacteristically depressed, Hannah wrote her sister, "Somehow it did not seem worthwhile to go on living any longer."

Robert, of course, was having troubles of his own. Hannah, frankly, was too much for him. He was a salesman, she was a manager. He could wax eloquent, and his natural enthusiasm made him a success either as a salesman or as an evangelist, but even-keeled Hannah always had the right answer and the last word. A grandson later wrote, "He had married a pretty young woman, but found out later that she was a giantess. He never thought he measured up."

When he was on the road, it was different. There, he was his own man. He could make his own mistakes, think his own thoughts, make his own friends, both male and female. And he did.

It wasn't that he didn't care about Hannah and the children. He did, very much. If he didn't, he wouldn't have returned from those long trips to California, and he wouldn't have gone on those family vacations to Maine or the Adirondacks or Yellowstone.

Once he even took his family to California, where they saw Yosemite. He wanted Hannah to meet some of his friends in California, but she refused to meet them. She didn't want to enter that part of his world.

That bothered Robert. But most of all he was still bothered that Hannah didn't show more affection or tenderness. She admonished him frequently to "bow thy neck submissively to the yoke the Lord has put upon thee and not question His dealings." But why could she talk so much about being submissive unto God and so little about being submissive to her own husband? Whenever he found a woman who showed tenderness and affection or who came to him in need, he responded to her. He believed Hannah didn't have enough needs. She seemed to be too perfect. She was able to manage quite well without him.

That was it. It was her omni-competence that got to him the most. He was the one who started the paper, but it was Hannah whose articles were turned into a best-selling book. He was the one who established a preaching reputation in England, but it was Hannah who picked up the pieces when he fell apart.

And so it was that Hannah and Robert led increasingly separate lives. Biographer Marie Henry thinks that Hannah must have discovered a love note from one of Robert's lady friends. But whether she did or didn't, she eventually realized that Robert's longstanding complaint that she was a "dry old stick" had prompted him to seek female companionship elsewhere.

But Hannah was hardly a "dry old stick" when it came to romping with her kids. Though she had rheumatism and though she detested camping, she still went camping with the family every summer (and sometimes with a niece and nephew as well). Often, but not always, Robert went along too.

Her children loved her deeply, but they tended to follow their father's growing skepticism in regard to religion.

Mary, the older daughter, caused particular heartache to her parents. She renounced a belief in a personal God at age nineteen and then two years later married an Irish lawyer against the wishes of both Hannah and Robert. But before too long, Mary became bored with her marriage. Infatuated with her art teacher, she left her husband and two children to travel around Europe and settle in Florence, Italy. Eventually, when her husband died, she married the art teacher, but even her second marriage was marred by numerous infidelities.

After their first granddaughter was born, Hannah and Robert began spending more time in England and soon became permanent residents in London, four doors from their daughter and her first husband.

Alys, the younger daughter, fell in love with and married the brilliant British philosopher and atheist Bertrand Russell. According to Marie Henry, Alys's faith "did not last more than a month after their marriage." The marriage survived a bit longer than her faith, but not much longer. After about eight years, Bertrand told her that he didn't love her any more. The legal separation and then the divorce came a few years later.

The middle surviving child, Logan, claimed that he had lost his faith while sitting in a cherry tree when he was only eleven years old. He never married.

"Alas for motherhood," Hannah once wrote, "how it hurts."

But heaviest upon her were her dealings with Robert. In England he seemed to be more open about his immorality. Regularly he would sneak out of the house to see a "lady friend," but Hannah and the children knew what was going on. Though Hannah and Robert continued to live in the same house, they had separate bedrooms and lived separate lives.

When Robert died in 1898 at the age of seventy-two, it was a relief for Hannah. "His long time of darkness is over, and God's light has shone upon him at last."

In her sixties, Hannah returned to writing again, and two of her most famous books were written while she lived in England. *Everyday Religion* was written when she was sixty-one, *God of All Comfort* when she was seventy-four.

Somehow, Hannah made her retirement years enjoyable. The woes of her marriage and her family couldn't rob her of enjoying life. Income from the glass factory and from her books enabled her to live comfortably.

Her other involvement in her later years was her grandchildren. One of them wrote that she studied the business of being a grandmother "as thoroughly as she studied the temperance question, and brought to it the same vehement partisanship."

Regarding grandchildren, she said, "There is no fun for old people like it." She described herself as a "perfectly idiotic grandmother."

In 1910, Hannah wrote to one of her children and told them how to behave when she died. "I have forbidden you to mourn for me. You are not to wear mourning, nor shed any tears, or I will haunt you in the shape of a waterspout."

Just before Hannah died, her daughter Alys came into her bedroom. Hannah could tell that Alys had been crying and assumed that the doctor had told her something, so she asked what the doctor had said.

Alys responded, "He says thee is losing thy hold on life, Mother."

"Oh, good," said Hannah.

Shortly afterward, she died.

Hannah's views on marriage were once outlined to a suitor of one of her daughters. "My ideal of marriage is an equal partnership, neither one assuming control over the other. . . . Any marriage other than this is to my mind tyranny on the one hand and slavery on the other. . . . I believe there ought to be an equal partnership in all property of

286

incomes that accrue to them jointly after marriage and that each partner should have equal authority in disposing it."

Only a year before her death, she wrote to a daughter, "It is hard for me to believe that any husband and wife are really happy together."

Five years earlier she had written: "My experience of life has taught me to look upon the vagaries of the male portion of the race as one looks upon avalanches or earthquakes—things that cannot be stopped or altered, but must simply have way made for them, with as little personal inconvenience to one's self as possible. And just as one would always be glad to know when avalanches or earthquakes are coming, so I always like to know what the men of my acquaintance feel about things or what they want, in order that I may get out of the way."

Someone once said about Hannah, "She liked men, but she didn't like husbands."

Hannah may have been somewhat bitter about husbands, but few other things in life soured her. And considering all the travail she passed through, that is remarkable.

In her book, *Every-day Religion,* Hannah wrote, "Trouble and sorrow, therefore, are not our curse, but one of our most cherished rights. We are like statues, which can only be perfectly shaped by the chisel's blows, and these blows are surely the statue's rights. Why should we allow ourselves to be so needlessly unhappy with thinking that our trouble is one in which God has no part?"

She wrote those lines as her seventy-year-old husband was sneaking off to visit a paramour, as one daughter was cavorting in Italy with her art teacher, and as a second daughter was beginning to date the atheist Bertrand Russell.

Hannah was a remarkable woman.

Bibliography

Henry, Marie. *The Secret Life of Hannah Whitall Smith.* Grand Rapids: Chosen, 1984.

Smith, Hannah Whitall. *The Christian's Secret of a Happy Life.* Waco, Tex.: Word, 1985.

———. *The Common Sense Teaching of the Bible*. Old Tappan, N.J.: Fleming H. Revell, 1985.

———. *Philadelphia Quaker: The Letters of Hannah Whitall Smith*. New York: Harcourt Brace, 1950.

———. *The Record of a Happy Life*. New York: Fleming H. Revell, 1873.

———. *Religious Fanaticism*. London: Faber and Gwynn, 1928.

———. *The Unselfishness of God and How I Discovered It*. New York: Fleming H. Revell, 1903.

15

He Could Be Impossible

Grace Livingston Hill and Her Two Husbands

Millions of people around the world have read Grace Livingston Hill's novels, but few know anything about her personal life. Fewer still know her first husband, Frank—or for that matter have ever heard of him.

All her novels (and she wrote more than eighty of them) end with happiness. Most of them are love stories with the girl marrying the fellow in the final chapter.

But her readers never found out what characterized Grace Livingston Hill's own marriage. Did it have a happy ending?

Grace didn't like to write of unpleasantness. "I feel that there is enough sadness and sorrow in the world, so I try to end all my books as beautifully as possible," she once said. And that was one reason why she seldom talked about her second marriage, to a music teacher named Flavius Josephus Lutz.

Few American writers, either secular or religious, have sold more books than Grace Livingston Hill. More of her books have been reprinted than books by Dickens, Scott, or even Zane Grey. Yet the facts of her own life, her marriages, and her family are largely unknown.

What was she really like? Who was the woman behind the novels that continue to sell hundreds of thousands of copies a generation after her death? And who was Frank Hill?

Perhaps if Frank Hill had lived, Grace might never have written a novel. Perhaps she would have settled down to be the kind of minister's wife that she envisioned in some of her novels.

But Frank and Grace did not live happily ever after. He died suddenly at the age of thirty-four, leaving Grace with two small children.

And that's where Grace's life had a second beginning, as she picked up the shattered pieces. A bereavement that brought her close to a nervous breakdown turned into a new life.

As 1899 began, life seemed idyllic for the Rev. and Mrs. Frank Hill. The Wakefield Presbyterian Church in the Germantown section of Philadelphia had been under their care for the previous six years. A brilliant student, Frank had developed into a powerful preacher. Grace was coming up with creative ideas for use in the Christian education outreaches of the church.

Less than twenty-five years old, the church already had more than six hundred members in its Sunday school. Its Christian Endeavor groups enrolled nearly one hundred young people, and Frank's messages kept the congregation coming to both morning and evening services.

Their two children, though still young, were both showing signs of the same mental quickness that characterized their parents.

It was the life that Grace Livingston Hill had dreamed of.

Though she wrote occasionally for Sunday school and Christian Endeavor publications, she seemed to be finding her contentment and fulfillment as a pastor's wife, not as a writer.

It was not really surprising. After all, in her immediate family were seven ministers. In her mind there could be no higher calling for a woman than to become the wife of a minister.

Then a few days before Thanksgiving, after only seven years of marriage, Frank Hill was stricken with acute appendicitis. He never recovered.

For a while, friends wondered if Grace would ever recover from it either.

Grace was born in 1865, two days after Abraham Lincoln was assassinated. She died in 1947, two years after Hiroshima. In those fourscore years she was no stranger to unpleasantness.

Her father, Charles Livingston, a Presbyterian minister from a good New York family, was strict, determined, and frequently stubborn. He was also a good father, a wise counselor, and a dedicated family man. Family is something that meant a lot to the Livingstons.

In Grace's novels, Charles is sometimes seen as an older minister or father-figure. In *Beauty for Ashes,* Grace writes of the main character, "It seemed to Gloria that her father was the wisest man living." That's how Grace thought of her father.

He never sacrificed his principles; some of his parishioners called him bullheaded. His strong stands frequently precipitated church conflicts; in fact, the Livingstons seldom stayed very long in any one parsonage.

Little Grace, the only child in the Livingston home, dreamed of a permanent home, a large stone house with a big backyard. Jean Karr, in her biography, writes, "Grumbling and complaining about their lot in life was not a part of the Livingston family tradition, so the child's dream world grew and gave her whatever was lacking in her material existence."

In the sixteen years between 1876 and 1892, Grace and her parents lived in at least nine different parsonages in six different states—New York, Ohio, Florida, New Jersey, Maryland, and Pennsylvania.

Instead of breeding insecurity, this bouncing from one parsonage to another every two years knit the Livingston family together.

It was because of her family that Grace put her trust in Jesus Christ. "I listened as my family talked with God, and I became inevitably acquainted with the Lord Jesus. . . . My family lived the faith they preached. I saw Jesus Christ in their daily lives."

Grace often accompanied her father when he spoke at small rural churches. She liked being his assistant, playing the organ, teaching a Sunday school class for the children, and sometimes singing a solo.

Growing up, she was probably closer to her father than to her mother. She learned to play tennis on a homemade court that he had built behind one of their parsonages. She rode horseback with him. And it was a great achievement when she could beat him in chess.

As they drove by horse and buggy through the Ohio and New York countrysides, she was flattered when he discussed politics and theology with her. "My father taught me to think," she said later.

It was from her mother's side, however, that her literary interests developed. Her mother wrote romantic love stories of the Civil War period and occasional Christmas pieces for weekly magazines during the 1860s and 1870s.

Her mother was not only Grace's severest critic—always correcting her diction, grammar, and spelling—but also her mind-expander to the beauties of nature and to the possibilities of the imagination.

No one, however, exerted a stronger literary influence on her than her Aunt Isabella, whom she called Auntie Belle. Auntie Belle was known to hundreds of thousands of young readers across the country as Pansy, the popular author of a series of best-selling novels for youth.

At the peak of her popularity she and her husband stayed with Grace and her parents. Youthful, imaginative, and lively, Auntie Belle was a "combination of fairy godmother, heroine, and saint" to Grace. "I thought her the most beautiful, wise, and wonderful person in my world, outside of my home. I treasured her smiles, copied her ways, and listened breathlessly to all she had to say. . . .

"I measured other people by her principles and opinions, and always felt that her word was final. . . . I even corrected my beloved parents sometimes when they failed to state some principle or opinion as she had done."

Besides being a minister's wife and writing one "Pansy" book after another, Auntie Belle also edited a magazine for children called *The Pansy* and answered fan mail from boys and girls who belonged to the Pansy Society. Grace was enthralled by it all.

The Livingston family read books together every night. In their various parsonages, they went through the novels of George Macdonald, William Dean Howells, Charles Dickens, and Walter Scott. But a special treat came when Auntie Belle had completed writing another of her Pansy novels. Then they would interrupt their reading of Dickens or Scott and enjoy the latest "Pansy," fresh from the typewriter.

Occasionally, Auntie Belle allowed Grace to peck away on her type-writer and try to write her own stories. And one Christmas Auntie Belle gave her niece a thousand sheets of typing paper and suggested that she turn the thousand sheets "into as many dollars."

In a few weeks Grace turned out a nine-chapter, 4,000-word book called *The Esselstynes; or, Alphonso and Marguerite*. The story describes what happens when two street urchins (Alphonso and Marguerite) are taken into the home of a wealthy and childless couple (the Esselstynes).

Auntie Belle was so impressed by Grace's efforts that she took the manuscript and inveigled her publisher to print a limited edition of it. It was a surprise for her twelve-year-old niece, and it became the first big step in Grace's writing career.

Grace was always a better storyteller than a student. She disliked writing themes, but if she could write a story instead, she excelled. Her education had begun in the home with her mother tutoring her in the early grades. Once she had been sent away to a boarding school, but Grace became so homesick for her parents that she begged to return home.

She also had a flair for art. As a teenager she sometimes accompanied Auntie Belle on speaking tours. While her favorite aunt told one of her "Pansy" stories, Grace would illustrate the talk with a blackboard sketch.

Aware of her talent, her family convinced her to go to art school. So she studied at Cincinnati Art School and later at Elmira College in New York, where a famous artist was teaching.

Despite her abilities in writing and art, she ended up working as a physical education instructor at Rollins College in Florida. Her father was serving a church in Winter Park at the time.

The following year, when Grace was twenty-six, she accompanied her parents to their next church. It was in Hyattsville, Maryland. The church membership was barely at the one-hundred mark.

Though Grace had written a couple of stories for the Christian Endeavor World and had done a longer piece for the Chautauqua Assembly where her family vacationed almost every summer, she didn't think of writing as a career. In Florida, when she wasn't teaching at Rollins College, she had spent a great deal of time assisting her father in his home missionary activities. But she realized that this was his work and not her own. So at the age of twenty-six, she was still living under her parents' umbrella and had not found her niche in life.

That summer at a Bible conference, however, as she was going out to play tennis, she met the man of her dreams. It was almost as though he had walked out of the pages of a novel.

In her own novels Grace often borrowed from real life, and it is quite possible that her first meeting with Frank Hill is described in *Beauty for Ashes:*

> She heard whistling. . . . It wasn't like any whistling she had ever heard before. . . . It was like a bird in the early morning, and sweet quaint tunes that she had never heard before, though occasionally there was a melody she recognized. . . . The whistler was familiar with fine music, that was evident. Sometimes there was a bit of Scotch melody, and then hymn tunes, whistled with such perfect rhythm that one could almost hear words with the melody.

Then she looked up and "saw a very good-looking young man with a tennis racket under his arm, coming toward her."

In the book he is Murray MacRae, "tall and straight and fine."

In real life he was the Rev. Thomas Guthrie Franklin Hill, tall and straight and fine.

By the time Grace met him, Frank had already graduated from Washington and Jefferson College, south of Pittsburgh, had received his divinity degree from Western Theological Seminary, and had done post-graduate work in Edinburgh, Scotland.

Like Grace, he had grown up in a manse, and also like Grace, his father was a Scotch Presbyterian. His first two names had been bestowed on him in honor of a Scottish cleric who had launched "Ragged Schools" to reclaim juvenile delinquents.

He seemed a perfect match for Grace. Though she was never a serious scholar herself, she admired others such as her father (and Frank) who delighted in poring over books. His enjoyment of athletics, his concern for underprivileged young people, his sense of humor—these were things in which Grace shared as well. But underlying all of that was his spiritual commitment.

A few weeks before Christmas 1892, when both Grace and Frank were twenty-seven, they were married in her father's small church in Hyattsville. Charles Livingston conducted the ceremony.

At the time, Frank was the minister of a small church in western Pennsylvania; but four months after the marriage, he received a call to the Wakefield Presbyterian Church in the Germantown section of Philadelphia. It had a new church building, but was not large in numbers (about two hundred members). The Sunday school, however, had over four hundred on its rolls. Both Frank and Grace were excited by the chance to work with so many boys and girls.

They wasted no time in making changes. Frank began a men's club, the Vicar of Wakefield Club. The first action was to prepare a baseball field and tennis court for church young people (as well as young adults the age of Grace and Frank). The name, "The Vicar of Wakefield," was a reference to the title of Goldsmith's eighteenth-century novel. Apparently, however, some of the Presbyterians thought that the word "vicar" sounded too Episcopalian. After a year Frank consented to have the name changed. The group renamed itself the Wakefield Men's Club.

Besides providing athletics, the men's group held discussions on current political topics as well as theological issues; Frank even offered to teach a course in Latin to any man who wanted to learn. The official church records do not indicate, however, whether anyone signed up.

Frank also started a Boys' Club; and then to promote attendance at the Sunday evening Christian Endeavor meetings, he changed the time of the church's evening service.

But it was in the pulpit where Frank showed his greatest strength. Word was spreading that the young minister at Wakefield was developing into a powerful preacher.

In their first year of ministry, the church grew from 200 to 266 members, and the Sunday school expanded to a membership of nearly 600. The Christian Endeavor groups were also mushrooming. In the following years, growth continued.

While Grace played a creative role in the Sunday school and kept a hand in Christian Endeavor, her major concern during those years was her children. Her first daughter, Margaret, was born late in 1893, and the second, Ruth, was born in 1898. In any spare moments, she sat down at her typewriter and wrote short stories for the Christian Endeavor weekly publication. She also did some oil painting.

Then came November 1899. Frank and Grace were attending a church social one Friday evening. Complaining of stomach pains, he went home early. That night the pain became worse, and he was taken to the hospital. The next day he underwent an appendectomy. The operation appeared to be successful, but afterward an infection set in. Without antibiotics, Frank fought a losing battle; three days later he died.

Grace knew very well the comfort of the Scriptures in those days, but the loss of her husband devastated her, nonetheless. Church friends and relatives rallied to her support.

But nothing could bring Frank back to her.

It was a time of insecurity for the entire family. "I remember many tears," her daughter Ruth recalls. Ruth also remembers crying in her crib because she was in terror of the dark. Grace came in, took her in her arms, and told her of the Shepherd Jesus who held her in His arms like a little lamb.

"I never forgot that," said Ruth. In those difficult days of bereavement, Grace was trying hard not to forget it either.

With her two little girls, Grace tried to pick up the pieces. Frank had left $5,000 in life insurance, but Grace knew that they could not live on that for very long. As soon as the church called another minister, she and her daughters would have to vacate the parsonage.

Her first thought was to return temporarily to live with her parents. That would give her time to think of other options. Then came the second shock. Her father died.

Within a few months the two men in her life whom she had idolized and upon whom she had depended had been snatched from her. Nothing had meant more to her than her family, but now God had chosen to disrupt both the family in which she had been raised and the new family she and Frank had been building.

How could she possibly manage? She would have to care for her widowed mother as well as her children. Though depressed by the twin losses, she couldn't allow herself to become paralyzed. She had to go on.

With an uncle and a church elder providing advice, she moved to the suburban town of Swarthmore. It was a college town, and that seemed to be the main reason it was chosen. Though her daughters were young, Grace was concerned that they be given the best education possible. When they grew up, they could live at home while attending college.

Temporarily, the family rented a small house, but Grace had other plans for the future. Throughout her early years she had persistently dreamed of owning her own home. She had grown up in a succession of small parsonages; since her marriage, she had lived in another one. Her daydreams envisioned a spacious stone house with a large lawn, big trees, a huge porch, and a winding staircase. The house had to be made of stone because stone spoke to her of permanence.

But if she used Frank's life insurance to build a house, she wouldn't have enough money to live on month by month. She needed additional income.

Of course, she had continued to write her short stories for Christian Endeavor. She had even begun to write weekly Sunday school lessons which were syndicated to several small suburban newspapers in the area. But none of that brought in a great deal of income for the family. Either the Lord would have to bring a second husband into her life who could help support the family, or else He would have to provide income some other way.

With her small children she knew she couldn't go out and get a job; she also knew that she couldn't make money as an artist. But she remembered how Auntie Belle had succeeded quite well by writing novels at home. Perhaps if she wrote a full-length novel and had it published, it might ease some of the money pressures.

So she sat down at her typewriter and wrote a novel, calling it *The Story of a Whim*. The setting was a college in Florida. From her experience at Rollins College, Grace could picture it well. In the plot, a new church is started amid the orange groves. That was the kind of home missionary work she and her father had been doing fifteen years earlier. Grace began the story, however, with another image in mind. The scene opens in a stone house on a hill. A stone house for her family is what Grace hoped would be the outcome of selling her book.

297

The Story of a Whim was not extremely successful. Though it did not bring in much income, Grace was sufficiently encouraged to move ahead with plans for her stone house. More than anything else, however, the publication of the book opened Grace's eyes to a new ministry.

From the start, Grace's real motive in writing was more spiritual than financial. "Ever since I was a little girl," she said later, "I wanted to make other people feel the same way about God that I did. I think He knew that and made it possible for me to have my wish."

The two men Grace had most admired had their pulpits, and now the Lord had provided a pulpit for Grace through writing.

It was in 1903, shortly after *The Story of a Whim* had been published, and while the builders were constructing her new stone house in Swarthmore, that she met Flavius Josephus Lutz.

Grace was thirty-eight; Flavius was several years younger. Like Grace, he was a newcomer in the suburb of Swarthmore. Like Grace, he had recently moved from Philadelphia and now attended the Swarthmore Presbyterian Church. Flavius enjoyed the arts—music especially, but also art and literature—as did Grace. In fact, he was a music teacher and played the organ at the church.

The previous two men in her life—her father and her first husband—had been scholars, not artists. Flavius was different.

In addition, he was a charmer. Although he didn't charm Grace's mother and other relatives, he did sweep Grace off her feet. And she was flattered that a younger man would show such interest in her.

Grace was vulnerable. She liked to have a man to talk with, and Flavius was a great conversationalist. Perhaps financial pressures also prompted her to move quickly into marriage.

Family members warned her not to get serious about Flavius; they said it would be a tragic mistake. But of course, she thought they didn't know Flavius as well as she did. And in 1904, Grace married him.

Flavius was accustomed to getting his own way. He had grown up in a household that had catered to him, probably because of his musical talent. In Grace's family, however, emotional outbursts were thought of as childish; people gained respect for their logical arguments, not for their emotional tantrums.

When Flavius didn't get his way, "he could be impossible," reported one family member.

He tried to dominate his house by tirades, but Grace would not be bullied. He only lost her respect when he displayed his irrationality.

As the children grew up, they were embarrassed to have their friends come inside the house, for their stepfather's behavior was totally unpredictable and frequently unspeakably rude. He wanted to rule his house, but he didn't know how.

For Grace, her family was vital, primary, essential. For Flavius, it seemed a bothersome appendage. He found, of course, that he had not married only Grace, but her family as well. It was an adjustment he could not make.

Before long, Grace saw that the marriage was not working out, but she didn't know what to do. She had always opposed divorce, so that was not an option for her. Meanwhile, the tension in the home continued to mount.

For a while Grace and her mother had tutored her daughters in the home; but then, after Grace's marriage to Flavius, as Margaret was ready for sixth grade and Ruth for second, she sent them to public school.

This gave Grace more time to write, and her family was urging her to write another novel. No doubt they felt that with her second marriage in a shambles she needed something to occupy her mind.

Her publisher suggested that she try her hand at a historical novel. Grace wasn't so sure. She wouldn't enjoy the research that would be necessary to produce it.

But then she received unexpected help. A great-aunt over a hundred years old told her about a Livingston who had become a substitute bride in the 1830s. As Grace heard the fantastic true story, she recognized that it had the makings of a strong plot. A cousin, who was an artist specializing in drawings of the 1830s, took time to tell her about the costumes and traditions of the period. It was enough to get Grace going again.

Out of those ingredients came Grace's first truly successful novel, *Marcia Schuyler,* published in 1908.

Literary magazines, however, did not treat it kindly. One commented: "Little new, brilliant, or finished in the way of narrative writing can be discovered."

A year later, she wrote a sequel called *Phoebe Deane.* Commented *The New York Times:* "A pretty wholesome story of the most artificial kind."

Perhaps the most blistering review came from the *Saturday Review of Literature:* "Mrs. Hill's latest story is a singularly sentimental and pious tract, clumsily written, fatuous, and illogical. To be candid, the book is awful."

Her growing audience of readers disagreed. They loved her wholesome approach.

Grace herself had no illusions about her literary ability. She jokingly remarked that it was her quantity, not her quality that she would be known for.

And once she got started writing, she couldn't stop. The publisher was always asking for another novel from Grace Livingston Hill, because readers across the country had started going into the bookstores to ask if the next Grace Livingston Hill novel had been published.

To Flavius Lutz, it was the last straw. Why was she known as Grace Livingston *Hill?* Why wasn't his wife known to the world as Grace Livingston *Lutz?*

Grace said that since she had begun her career as Grace Livingston Hill that was the way her readers knew her. Flavius was vehement that since she was Mrs. Lutz, she shouldn't be ashamed to put it on her books.

Finally, Grace gave in to please her husband. After eight years of marriage and several books, she became known as Grace Livingston Hill Lutz. The name of Lutz appeared on most of her books between 1913 and 1918.

Grace tried to cover up the unpleasant home situation, but it wasn't always possible. When Flavius unexpectedly missed Sunday morning services at church, Grace sent her daughter Margaret to pinch-hit for him on the organ. Eventually, however, when Grace was wondering how much more of Flavius's irrational behavior she could take, he walked out of their stone house and never returned.

Grace never made much of an effort to look for him.

Raising her two girls was easier when Flavius wasn't around.

"Mother screened our friends very carefully," her daughter Ruth recalled. "I mildly resented it at the time, but since then I have been very grateful."

As soon as she could, Grace laid out a tennis court in her backyard, and soon all the Christian Endeavor young people from the church were finding their way to the Hill house.

Grace enjoyed young people, and young people enjoyed her. For years she took an active leadership role in the church's Christian Endeavor Society. She could always be counted on to develop a special game or contest.

What impressed people was her indefatigable energy. She made the children's clothes, did housework, worked with the church's Christian Endeavor, taught a Sunday school class; and then after the children were put to bed, she went to her room to write—sometimes until three or four in the morning. "She never knew when to go to bed," a neighbor reported.

Grace wrote some lines about her Auntie Belle that might just as well have applied to herself: "All these things she did—and yet wrote books. . . . Perhaps she wrote more and better because she was doing so eagerly in every direction: her public, her church, her family, her home."

Grace was a doer. When she felt that the biblical instruction she was receiving from her church's pulpit was inadequate, she rented a meeting hall and invited outstanding Bible teachers to come to Swarthmore and speak. This developed into a community Bible class which she continued to sponsor for fifteen years.

Outside Swarthmore near an old stone quarry was an Italian settlement about which Grace was concerned. In her novel *The Witness,* the hero of the novel purchases and renovates an abandoned old church. This is just about what happened when Grace started a mission Sunday school among the Italian immigrants and then renovated the Leiper Presbyterian Church which had been abandoned for several years.

"All these things she did—and yet wrote books."

After a few historical books and mystery novels, she found herself more at home with the genre of romantic fiction, and between age sixty-five and eighty she wrote forty-three novels, nearly three per year.

A few of her earlier books also display her strong social concern for the underprivileged. But in all her books, her Christian commitment is obvious. At one point her publisher, J. B. Lippincott of Philadelphia, asked her to eliminate some of the religious passages which they thought might offend some of their reading audience. Grace flatly refused. She did what her father would have done: she left the publisher and sought another. Harper and Brothers was glad to have her on any terms.

Before long, Lippincott asked her to come back. She consented, and J. B. Lippincott never blue-penciled a line of her manuscripts after that.

"I am not writing just for the sake of writing. I have attempted to convey in my own way, and through my novels, a message which God has given and to convey that message with whatever abilities were given to me. . . . Whatever I've been able to accomplish has been God's doing."

Her writing style was unorthodox. In an article in *The Writer,* she explained: "It often amuses me to have eager young writers ask me to give them the inside story about my methods of work. For the truth is I never did conscientiously prepare for my literary career, and furthermore I have no method at all. . . . I just sit down at my typewriter and go ahead. Sometimes a sentence just pops into my head and that starts me off. . . . Until the book is finished, I have no idea how the story is going to be worked out myself. I almost never rewrite a story."

At another time, she said, "My working hours? I work whenever I can find the time. . . . I can't say that I shut myself up in a room. My door is open at all times. The telephone constantly interrupts, and then I go back to my writing. Friends drop in on me or members of the family hold a conclave in the next room. If I'm busy, I simply disconnect my mind and keep working."

She shunned the realism of modern writers and was criticized for it, but she never lived her life in a garret. "I've refused to consider my career separate from my daily life," she once said.

To her, teaching a Sunday school class among Italian immigrants was every bit as important as grinding out another manuscript for her publisher.

Her first true success as a novelist came with the publication of *Marcia Schuyler* when she was forty-three years old. She died at the age of eighty-two, leaving a half-finished novel on her desk.

During her lifetime 4 million copies of her books were sold. Since her death in 1947, another 4 million have been sold.

She has been criticized for her idealistic novels, yet she saw two marriages end in different kinds of tragedy. She valued family ties deeply, yet she had to pick up the pieces and hold her family together without a man in the house.

Could Grace have made her second marriage work? The fact is that Flavius Lutz was unable to cope with Grace's strength. He was too weak a man. When he flailed out in his frustration, she appeared stronger than ever.

In the process, she lost a husband, but kept her daughters. Her two daughters grew up, had happy marriages, and both became deeply involved in Christian ministries.

What would have happened if Frank Hill had lived a long life? And what would have happened if Flavius Lutz had not walked out on her? Would Grace have been a best-selling novelist? Would she have gone on to be described as "America's most beloved author"? Probably not.

Out of the dual crucibles of bereavement and marital disappointment came the works of a writer known for romance and idealism, a novelist who has directed millions of impressionable lives toward wholesome family relationships and solid Christian values.

Bibliography

Kart, Jean. *Grace Livingston Hill*. New York: Greenburg, 1948.

Poor Mrs. Carey Was like Lot's Wife

William and Dorothy Carey

When William Carey sailed to India in 1793, he launched the modern missionary movement. David Livingstone, Hudson Taylor, Adoniram Judson, and thousands of others followed his example, taking the gospel message to those who had never heard it.

William Carey was the pioneer among missionary pioneers and the Bible translator *par excellence*. So you will certainly want to meet William Carey. He was a most remarkable man.

But don't forget Dorothy Carey. She may be over in the corner or she may be trying to manage the children or she may have gone home early.

I may as well tell you openly: Dorothy had emotional problems.

William and Dorothy lived in a day before psychologists and counselors, so they didn't have the benefit of scores of books that may have given them some understanding.

Would you like to play the role of amateur psychologist for Dorothy? What counsel would you give to help William and Dorothy understand themselves and each other? Could anything have been done to help Dorothy be a productive servant of the Lord?

In the process of answering these questions, you might find some clues that will help you preserve the mental health of your own marriage.

What drove Dorothy Carey insane?

If it is proper to call William Carey the father of the modern missionary movement, what would you call Dorothy?

If William was somewhat of a self-made man, was Dorothy a self-destructive woman? Or was it something in the mix of the two that made them what they came to be?

As you can guess, the marriage of William and Dorothy Carey was not exactly idyllic.

For more than forty years, William Carey pioneered—he would say *plodded*—as a missionary to India. Dorothy lasted fourteen years, reluctantly and pitifully.

The story of William Carey, the humble shoemaker who became a brilliant missionary linguist, is one of those spiritual Horatio Alger stories of how God plucked an unlikely candidate to be the leader of a multitude. But what about poor Dorothy?

Let's begin with William:

Hometown: Paulerspury, an obscure village about eighty miles north of London.

Year of Birth: 1761, fifteen years before the American Revolution.

Father: Edmund Carey, a journeyman weaver who worked with woolen cloth on a loom in their small cottage.

Family Income: About ten shillings a week.

Family Members: Sharing the cottage with Edmund and his rather large loom were his wife, Elizabeth, their five children, and Edmund's mother. William was the oldest child.

Not content with being a journeyman weaver, Edmund was named parish clerk and schoolmaster when William was six. In communities like Paulerspury which happened to have a charity school, poor children between seven and twelve years of age could learn the three R's and religion up to the level of the schoolmaster's understanding—which often wasn't very high.

Thus, William not only had the privilege of a few years of education, but also had access to books because of his father's position, and he became an insatiable reader. Books like *Robinson Crusoe* and *Gulliver's Travels* telling of imagined travels around the world had been published fifty years earlier. William read them and dreamed.

At the age of twelve, when his schooling ended, he began to work in the fields. But two years later a skin rash developed whenever he worked in the hot sun, so he had to shift careers. A shoemaker took him on as an apprentice.

William slid to the level of the boys that hung around the blacksmith's shop. He later spoke of his addiction to "swearing, lying and unchaste conversation," and of being led "into the depths of that gross conduct which prevails among the lower classes in the most neglected villages." He also liked a good argument. He called his teenage years "restless." "I wanted something," he wrote later, "but had no idea that nothing but an entire change of heart could do me good."

Then one Christmas, while making deliveries for his employer, he was given a couple of tips. Among the tips was a counterfeit shilling. He decided to tell his boss that it had been given as payment for some shoes. Thus, his boss had the counterfeit coin and William kept as his tip a genuine shilling from an actual payment. When his boss somehow discovered the deceitful exchange, William was both shamed and frightened. The lie had been bad enough, but British law was extremely strict about thievery. The theft of more than a shilling was grand larceny and that was a capital offense.

In his shame, Carey refused to go to church for a while. But that didn't stop him from arguing about religion with a fellow apprentice who went to a Dissenter church. Eventually, Carey agreed to attend church with his friend. Hearing a sermon on Hebrews 13:13: "Let us therefore go out unto him without the camp, bearing his reproach," Carey, now seventeen, made his commitment to Christ. At the same time, he left the established Anglican church where his father and mother worshiped, and joined the Dissenters' Congregational Church.

When Carey's employer died, another cobbler hired him as an apprentice, and within two years Carey married his new employer's sister-in-law, Dorothy (Dolly) Plackett. Nothing is known of their courtship.

Carey was nineteen; she was twenty-five. He was short and slight, a cobbler's apprentice, making five or six shillings a week. She was illiterate, the daughter of the lay leader of the Congregational church in Piddington which Carey now attended. There was no charity school in Piddington. Even if there had been one, Dorothy wouldn't have been able to attend because, for one thing, her parents were Dissenters and for another, she was a girl. So at the time of her marriage to William, she signed the church's register with a "large, wobbly cross."

They were extremely poor, but they didn't seem to notice. Within a year they had another mouth to feed, a daughter named Ann. Behind the shanty which they called home, William planted a garden. When he wasn't cobbling or gardening, William was reading or studying Greek. Or preaching. The church at which he preached regularly was eight miles away. He walked both ways. The tiny congregation was so poor that "he did not receive enough for the clothes he wore out in their service."

Once a month he also preached in the Dissenters' church in his home town of Paulerspury, much to the embarrassment of his father, who was serving as a parish clerk of the Anglican church. His sister recalled: "We should rather have wished him to go *from* home, rather than come home to preach."

His sister also recalled his zealousness: "Like Gideon, he seemed for throwing down all the altars of Baal in one night." She also resented a certain self-righteousness in his youthful enthusiasm: "Nothing but my love for my brother would have kept me from showing my resentment."

Yes, that first year of marriage was exciting for William. The birth of a daughter made it exciting for Dorothy, too. But obviously, she couldn't walk with William to the church at which he preached, and with the baby she couldn't attend her parents' church very often either. And of course, she couldn't share in William's study of Greek. It was enough of a struggle for her to learn the English alphabet.

Year two of the marriage was more traumatic than exciting. Daughter Ann died, and Dorothy was crushed by the loss. Then the same disease struck William. With him bedridden, the poverty-stricken family was destitute. Unable to cope with the calamities, Dorothy started to retreat from reality. Everything she loved was being taken away from her, and she was helpless. When William's mother came to visit, she was appalled at the living conditions of the home. William's teenaged brother gave him what he could to help the family. His home town of

Paulerspury took up a special offering to enable William and Dorothy to buy a small cottage in a better part of Piddington.

The high fever left William bald at twenty-one. And the daughter's death left Dorothy despondent and fearful. William bought a wig; Dorothy found nothing to cover her emotional hurts.

Economically, the following years weren't much easier. When twenty-two, William officially became a Baptist by being immersed in the River Nene. The records of John Ryland, who baptized him, say, "This day baptized a poor journeyman shoemaker."

Two months later, when William's master died, the "poor journeyman shoemaker" took over the business. He also took over the care of the master's widow and her four children. Unfortunately, it was not the best of years for business in Great Britain. The country was licking its wounds after its humiliating defeat in America's Revolutionary War. Some customers were cutting back on their orders, others had canceled their orders completely, and William was faced with many customers refusing to pay for shoes that had previously been ordered.

It was a mercy when William, now twenty-three, got a call from a Baptist church in nearby Moulton. Moulton had been without a pastor for ten years, and the salary was on a par with what William had been getting as a cobbler—about fifteen pounds a year. But at least he wouldn't have to worry about canceled orders, and now he could do what he enjoyed doing. He never thought he was a good shoemaker anyway.

To supplement his income, he taught school. He didn't do very well at that either, because he couldn't discipline the children. "When I kept school," he said candidly, "the boys kept me." He occasionally had to return to some part-time shoemaking to make ends meet. For William, Dorothy, and their infant son Felix, it continued to be a meager existence. One observer wrote, "He and his family have lived for a great while together without tasting animal food and with but a scanty pittance for other provisions." One of the provisions that Carey spent money on was secondhand books. To him they were more important than meat; Dorothy would rather have had the meat.

After four years of preaching, Carey decided that it was time for him to be ordained. But he was turned down. His preaching was criticized as colorless; he was asked to try again in two years. Nevertheless he continued pastoring the church at Moulton that no one else wanted. In his spare time he learned foreign languages—Greek, Latin, Hebrew, French, Dutch, and Italian—all of which were relatively easy for him. Dorothy, meanwhile, was still struggling with English.

Besides languages, Carey was fascinated with geography. A neighboring pastor who visited Carey when he was cobbling again wrote, "I remember that on going into the room where he employed himself at his business, I saw hanging up against the wall a very large map consisting of several sheets of paper pasted together by himself on which he had drawn with a pen a place for every nation in the known world and had entered into it whatever he met with in reading, relative to its population, religion, etc. These researches, on which his mind was naturally bent, hindered him, of course, from doing much at his business . . . and he was at this time exposed to great hardships."

Nobody knew the hardships better than Dorothy. The family was growing. Between 1785 and 1790, four children were born, and William wasn't much help in changing diapers. Biographer Mary Drewery writes: "The strain must have been particularly great for Dorothy with her young husband so completely absorbed in his preaching and studying—interests which it would be difficult for an unlettered girl to share. She must have felt at times very much alone. Carey drove himself relentlessly, disciplined himself and used every minute of every day."

Somewhere in the course of the marriage, William apparently taught Dorothy how to read and write, though it doesn't seem as if she used these newly acquired skills any more than necessary.

Dorothy may have been fearful and insecure, but she was also stubborn. She had a mind of her own. And William apparently was so concerned about disciplining his mind that he was not concerned if his children were undisciplined in behavior.

In 1787 Dorothy decided to be baptized by immersion. William had been immersed in 1783 and had been a Baptist minister since 1785. But not until two years later did Dorothy submit to immersion. William must have taken great delight in performing the baptism.

Quite possibly she felt neglected, even abandoned, by her husband. He seemed always to have important things to do. William's parents had the same problem with him; they wondered why they seldom saw him or heard from him despite his living only fifteen miles away. In response to his father's irritation, William spelled out his busy weekly schedule and said, "You will see that you must not expect frequent letters."

As William moved into his world of dreaming the impossible, Dorothy gradually drifted into her dream world, too. William's world was growing; Dorothy's was shrinking. Besides the big homemade map on his wall, Carey enjoyed the stimulation of regular ministers' meetings and the rather radical Philosophical Institute which met in Leicester. Coming from a lower class, Carey supported both the American and the French Revolutions, and as a religious dissenter, he hoped and prayed for a revolution of sorts in England.

From the time of his ordination, Carey had been pushing his fellow ministers for involvement in foreign missions. At first his fellow pastors looked at him as an uneducated young upstart and humored him. Then finally a senior minister put him in his place by calling him a "miserable enthusiast" and by informing him that if God wanted to save the heathen, He was sovereign and would do it in His own way, "without your aid or mine, young man."

Carey went home, looked at the huge map on the wall, read the Great Commission, and decided he would write out his reasons why foreign missionary efforts should be launched. When he presented his reasons, his paper got no farther than his oral pleas. His fellow ministers thought it "was a wild and impracticable scheme that he had got in his mind, and therefore gave him no encouragement."

But he didn't give up. At this point in his life, it would have been easy for him to quit, but he didn't. He may not have been a natural leader, but he was a natural plodder. He may have failed as a cobbler, as a teacher, and even as a husband. But he wasn't going to quit in his burden for a missionary outreach.

Nearly five years later, Carey published his treatise, now a bit more polished, with a forty-one-word title beginning *An Enquiry into the Obligations of Christians. . . .* It was a masterpiece, chopping all opposing arguments into shreds.

Three weeks after its publication, Carey was invited to speak at the ministers' meeting, and his fellow clergymen knew what he would be talking about. He was thirty-one now and had matured in many ways, but when it came to the ministers' meeting, Carey had a one-track mind. His text was Isaiah 54:2, 3 ("Enlarge the place of thy tent"), and the motto that he hammered home was this: "Expect great things from God; attempt great things for God."

Despite Carey's emotional cry for the establishment of a missionary society, the ministers did not respond. Most of them represented congregations almost as poor as Carey's. Then, as the meeting was about to adjourn, an exasperated William Carey asked the chairman, "Is nothing *again* going to be done?"

That extra shove got the ball rolling. At the next meeting, the Particular Baptist Society for the Propagation of the Gospel among the Heathen—the first British missions society—was officially formed.

Carey thought that Tahiti or Africa would be good places to start, but when a medical doctor, John Thomas, showed up, it made more sense to start with India. Thomas, who had formerly worked with the East India Company in Calcutta, was eager to go back as a missionary, and Carey was eager to go with him.

Carey had waited several years for his fellow ministers, but now things were happening so quickly he was hardly prepared for them. Without question, however, he was more prepared than Dorothy.

Carey was still thirty-one, Dorothy thirty-seven. They had three boys: Felix, eight; William, five; and Peter, three. Lucy, their youngest, had died during the past year while William was preparing the final version of his *Enquiry*. Dorothy couldn't help but resent the ugly map with all the scribbling on it, tacked upon the wall. She couldn't understand why William wouldn't be content to stay where he was. With Lucy's death, she had become depressed again. And now in February 1793, she was five months pregnant, expecting to bear a sixth child before summer. More than ever, she needed security, love, and attention.

But William couldn't stop now. At the January meeting, one of the pastors had said, "There's a gold mine in India, as deep as the center of the earth."

"I'll go down," Carey was reported to have said, "but remember you must hold the ropes."

No, William Carey couldn't stop. He had gone too far for that. So it must have come as a severe jolt to him when Dorothy said bluntly, "I'm not going." He was hoping that she would change her mind before their scheduled sailing date in April.

Dorothy wasn't the only one who couldn't understand William's eagerness to go to India. His church didn't want him to leave either. They had had a hard time finding a pastor before he had come, and they had grown rather fond of him.

Of course, William's father couldn't understand it either. "Is he mad?" he asked, thinking of the lad who twenty years earlier had left farming because he couldn't stand the heat. Now William was heading for India, of all places.

But William was determined to go to India. He wrote his father: "I have many sacrifices to make. I must part with a beloved family and a number of most affectionate friends. Never did I see such sorrow manifested as reigned through our place of worship last Lord's Day. But I have set my hand to the plow."

William knew that he would have to leave his church behind, and he knew he would have to leave his father with the knowledge that he would probably never see him again. But he hoped he would not have to leave his wife behind. Yet he felt he must do what God was calling him to do.

No doubt many were shocked by Dorothy's decision. It was accepted that a wife would blindly follow her husband wherever he would lead. It was unthinkable for her to refuse to go with him.

But consider Dorothy. Here she was "unlettered, unimaginative," as Mary Drewery puts it, and was "expected to venture halfway around the world to a country with a strange people, strange languages, strange climate and customs, with no settled home to go to."

Dorothy needed security. She needed a "settled home." She probably had good reason to question her husband's judgment. They had been married twelve years now, and they had made several moves already, none of which seemed to make life easier for her. They had lived in Hackleton, Piddington, Moulton, and Leicester; William had tried his hand at shoemaking—as an apprentice, as a manager, as a journeyman; he had tried teaching school twice, and had served as pastor of three churches. It would be understandable why Dorothy would not have a deep sense of security in following her husband to India.

Her children must have also concerned her. She had already seen two of them die in her arms; now her husband was asking her to board ship knowing that she was five months pregnant and that she, at thirty-seven, would be having her child before landing in India. There would be scores of men on board, mostly roughhewn sailors, but only one other woman. Yes, Dorothy had plenty to fear.

No doubt, she had also heard that France had just declared war on England, so all British vessels were in danger of attack on the high seas. Voyages under normal conditions were hazardous; in wartime, civilian travel was foolhardy.

William finally accepted Dorothy's decision. The agreement was this: eight-year-old Felix would accompany him to India, but Dorothy and the two younger boys would move back to Piddington where she would share a cottage with her younger sister, Kitty. After a three-year term in India, during which time he would prepare a suitable home for his family, he would return and fetch Dorothy from Piddington.

So in April 1793, Dr. Thomas, his wife, and their daughter, along with William Carey and Felix, set sail for India, down the Thames into the English Channel, then westward along the southern coast of England to the Isle of Wight. And there they stopped. Contrary winds and the hazards of French military action caused the ship's captain to delay sailing any farther.

The delay brought good news and bad news to Carey. The good news was that a delay in departure might give Dorothy a chance to change her mind. The bad news concerned Dr. John Thomas, the medical missionary. Thomas was motivated to sail to India not only by the Great Commission but also by some "great omissions." He had a bad habit of not paying his bills. Consequently, he had a dire need to get out of the country. In Carey's words, "Thomas's creditors were hunting him like a partridge." Thomas was affable enough but always getting deeper in debt.

While Thomas was eagerly trying to book passage on another ship to India, Carey wrote to Dorothy. Word soon came back that his wife had given birth to a fourth son. William responded immediately: "This is pleasant news indeed to me. Surely goodness and mercy follow me all my days, but now I see the goodness of God in it." Then he got to the point. "If I had all the world, I would freely give it all to have you and my dear children with me; but the sense of duty is so strong as to overpower all other considerations. I could not turn back without guilt on my soul. . . . You want to know what Mrs. Thomas thinks, and how she likes the voyage. . . . She would rather stay in England than go to India, but thinks it right to go with her husband." William was surely hoping that Dorothy would take the hint.

His letter continues: "Tell my dear children I love them dearly and pray for them constantly. Felix sends his love. . . . Trust in God. Love to Kitty, brothers, sisters, etc. Be assured I love you most affectionately. Let me know my dear little child's name."

Then William added as a postscript, "My health was never so well. I believe the sea makes Felix and me both as hungry as hunters. Farewell."

The letter, though warm and affectionate, did not budge Dorothy. She was resolute in her decision to stay in Piddington. As Drewery writes, "She must have been a woman of exceptional stubbornness or else Carey must have been more than usually tender and considerate, for, at that period, women were completely subject to the dictates of their husbands."

William joined Dr. Thomas in London, seeking a ship to India. When they finally found a Danish ship that would be departing in five days, William decided he would try one more time to change Dorothy's mind. William, along with son Felix and Dr. Thomas, traveled overnight to get to Piddington at breakfast. Dorothy was overjoyed to see her husband, but she wasn't persuaded by his arguments. Her baby was only a few weeks old. "I had better stay here with Kitty," she said.

Discouraged, they left to visit their mission leaders at the nearby headquarters. Then Dr. Thomas suggested they return to Piddington to try again. Carey said it was useless and besides, "We are losing time." But on this visit to Piddington, Thomas did most of the talking; he told Dorothy that if she didn't come with them, "she would repent it as long as she lived."

Reluctantly, she gave in with the proviso that her sister Kitty be allowed to accompany them. William gladly agreed.

Thanks to the goodness of the ship's captain, the Carey family got the best cabin on the craft even though they were sailing at half price. The voyage was relatively uneventful but it lasted five months, and they didn't stop at any port en route. Of all the passengers it was Dorothy who suffered the most from seasickness. But she suffered in other ways, too.

"Poor Mrs. Carey," Thomas wrote back to England. "She has had many fears and troubles, so that she was like Lot's wife, until we passed the Cape; but ever since, it seems too far to look back to Piddington that she turns her hopes and wishes to our safe arrival in Bengal."

Five months aboard ship with an infant and three boys aged four to eight would pose a challenge for any mother, but it was especially trying to Dorothy. Carey called his sons "complete sailors," but since he spent a good deal of time studying Bengali with Thomas, he may have had a tendency to overlook their behavior problems.

Dorothy must have sensed that she would probably never see England and loved ones again. She no doubt realized that people didn't last too long in India. Not sharing her husband's missionary commitment, she felt as if she were sailing toward a slow death.

The first year that the Careys spent in India did nothing to alleviate such fears. For both William and Dorothy it was a nightmare that they would never want to relive. If Dorothy had felt insecure due to William's frequent starts and stops around Piddington, think of how she must have felt around Calcutta.

First stop, Calcutta, November 1793: Upon arrival the Careys moved into the large home occupied by the Thomases. The expenses of the large home didn't seem to faze Thomas, but worried Carey, who wrote, they "filled my mind with anxiety and wretchedness." The lifestyle of the European community in which they found themselves was fast-paced and hedonistic. The Careys felt out of place.

Second stop, Bandel, December 1793: Both the Careys and the Thomases moved to a smaller village, thirty miles north of Calcutta; financial problems continued to plague them. Creditors from Calcutta hounded Thomas, and Carey, now thoroughly disillusioned with his companion, wrote, "He is a very good man, but only fit to live at sea." Carey was hoping that both families could be self-sufficient by farming, but with debts piling up, he wasn't so sure. Thomas decided to move back to Calcutta and resume his medical practice; when Carey heard of a position available at Calcutta's Botanical Garden, he decided to move back there too.

Third stop, back in Calcutta, January 1794: The job at the Botanical Garden had been filled by the time Carey arrived. Unable to afford anything better, the Careys were forced to live in a marshy malarial area, where gangs of robbers roamed. They were now eating curry and rice, day in and day out—a far cry from what those in the European quarter were enjoying, and probably a far cry from what the Thomases themselves were eating. Carey scribbled in his diary: "My wife and sister too who do not see the importance of the mission as I do, are continuing exclaiming against me, and as for Mr. T., they think it very hard indeed that he should live in a city, in an affluent manner, and they be forced to go into a wilderness and live without many of what they call the necessaries of life, bread in particular." The haranguing of both Kitty and Dorothy seemed to be getting him down.

Soon Dorothy and the two oldest boys had dysentery; William, deeply concerned for his family's health but also frustrated by his inability to do any meaningful missionary work, was depressed. How could he learn Bengali when there were so many problems plaguing him? "If my family were but hearty in the work," he wrote, "I should find a great burden removed, but the carnal discourse of the passage and the pomp and grandeur of the Europeans here have intoxicated their minds, so as to make them unhappy in one of the finest countries in the world and lonely in the midst of a hundred thousand people."

Well, India is certainly a fine country, but the Careys were living in a malarial swamp. And while there may have been hundreds of thousands of people in Calcutta, they all spoke Bengali, a language that Dorothy would never be able to master.

Stop four, Debhatta, forty miles east of Calcutta, February 1794: William was offered some land rent-free, if he would clear it and build a house on it. All he needed were a few tools, some money to pay for transportation, and some seeds for a garden. Carey went to Thomas.

Surely there must be some mission money remaining. There was none, and, of course, Thomas had plenty of financial troubles of his own. Seldom did Carey get discouraged, but this was an exception. "I am in a strange land," he wrote, "alone, no Christian friend, a large family and nothing to supply their needs."

William's discouragement did nothing to buoy Dorothy's spirits. Her depression deepened into neurosis. Carey wrote that she had "relapsed into her affliction and is much worse than she was before," indicating that it was not the first time for Dorothy to have such a relapse. Her sister naturally blamed William for everything. And William didn't know whom to blame. Sometimes he blamed Thomas. At other times he blamed himself. "I blame Thomas," he wrote, "for leading me into such expense at first, and I blame myself for being led."

He felt Job-like: "My temporal troubles remain just as they were. I have a place, but cannot remove my family to it, for want of money. Now all my friends are but One. I rejoice, however, that He is all-sufficient, and can supply all my wants spiritual and temporal. But why is my soul disquieted within me? Everything is known to God."

At times he wrote like David in the Psalms. He lamented that he didn't feel as close to God as he should. He described himself as "spiritually barren," "full of perplexity," and "at an awful distance from God." "Oh, what a shame," he wrote, "that I am not always satisfied with Him."

Finally, Carey received the money he needed, not from Dr. Thomas but from an Indian moneylender who charged him an exorbitant interest rate. Carey wasted no time getting his family on a boat upriver to Debhatta. For three days they traveled through an area teeming "with tigers, leopards, rhinoceros, deer, buffalo. No one dares to go on shore." Neither Dorothy nor Kitty had any confidence that Debhatta would be an improvement over Calcutta.

But near their destination, they found a hospitable Englishman— an answer to prayer—and while Carey cleared the land and started to build a house for his family, Dorothy, Kitty, and the children stayed with the Englishman. Actually, Kitty stayed there longer; she fell in love with her host and remained in Debhatta, thus reducing the Carey household by one. But in Carey's words, Dorothy was still "so ill."

317

Stop five, Malda, 250 miles north, March 1794: Carey hadn't made much progress in building his family a house in Debhatta when he got word from Thomas that in Malda, an indigo factory needed a manager for three months a year. The job paid well and the rest of the year would be his own for missionary activity. It sounded like another answer to prayer, or as Carey put it, "a remarkable opening in divine providence for our comfortable support."

Dorothy would have preferred staying in Debhatta near Kitty. It must have been an emotional farewell when the two sisters parted. This time the Carey family spent three weeks on the water as they plied their way up the river. It was the hottest time of the year, with mosquitoes everywhere, and Dorothy was in "a very weak state." Carey navigated the boat himself, which probably accounts for the three weeks it took to travel 250 miles. "Travelling," wrote Carey, "I have always found unfriendly to the progress of the divine life in my soul, but travelling with a family more particularly so."

Sixth stop, Dinadjpur, July 1794: The stop at Malda was brief. In Malda he learned a little about the indigo business; his salary would be about twenty-five pounds a month, and he and his family would have a large two-story house in which to live. Thomas would be managing a factory not far from Malda; the Careys would be located thirty-two miles north in the Dinadjpur district.

The Careys had made six moves in their first nine months on the mission field.

At last, Carey could devote a large part of his time to spreading the gospel.

But not quite yet.

In September he was stricken with malaria while Dorothy and their oldest son, Felix, were still suffering from dysentery. Then Peter, their five-year-old, also came down with dysentery. Within a few days he died.

William and Dorothy tried to find someone to dig Peter's grave, but the Hindus of the area refused. Finally, they contacted four Moslems who agreed to dig the grave but were unwilling to carry the body to it. Although they were too weak to do much, William and Dorothy were ready to do it themselves, when finally two servants consented to assist with the burial.

Peter was the third child that the Careys had lost. But Dorothy thought she had lost everything. Kitty was left behind; Dorothy would never see her again. Once again Dorothy slipped into a depressed state. From this time on, William seldom referred to her in his writings. He spoke rather of his "domestic affliction."

Eight months later Carey wrote in his diary, "I have had very sore trials in my own family, from a quarter which I forebear to mention. Have greater need for faith and patience than ever I had."

No doubt he was referring to the fact that Dorothy had just written a secret letter to Dr. Thomas, telling him how William had been abusing her. Knowing Dorothy's mental state, Dr. Thomas didn't believe a word of it. Instead he replied to William, "You must endeavor to consider it a disease. . . . Were I in your case, I should be violent, but blessed be God, who suits our burdens to our backs. Think of Job; think of Jesus."

There were occasional glimmers of light for Dorothy. Baby Jonathan was born in 1796, when Dorothy was forty. It was their fifth son, along with two daughters, both of whom had died in infancy.

After the birth of Jonathan, William reported back to England, "We are well in health, except that my poor wife is in a very distressing state of mind; not maniacal, it is true, but afflicted . . . with 'ideal insanity.'" Probably Dorothy was retreating from her neurotic depression into flights of fantasy. Her heart was still in Piddington; probably her mind had a tendency to return there as well.

Later that year Carey wrote home regarding qualifications for future missionaries. One thing was that "it is absolutely necessary for the wives of missionaries to be as hearty in the work as their husbands." Previously, it hadn't dawned on William that this was so important. After all, merchants would go to the Orient with their wives, and no one asked how dedicated the wife might be to the rubber, cocoa, or tea business. But Carey was learning that it was different for missionaries.

As Dorothy became more and more isolated from society because of her mental illness, Carey grew in social grace and acceptance. In

England he had been a cobbler and a village preacher. In India he was hobnobbing with the ruling and the merchant classes. At the same time, his missionary work was expanding; though not a single Indian had as yet accepted Jesus Christ as Savior and Lord, Carey had made some European converts.

A new day dawned for the missionary venture in 1799 when a fresh batch of eight missionaries arrived in Serampore, fourteen miles north of Calcutta. They wanted to join Carey but were refused permission. So Carey, now thirty-eight, and Dorothy, forty-four, joined them. It meant leaving the indigo business which had treated Carey well, but William knew of the advantages of a team of missionaries working together. Since one of the new missionaries was a printer and another a schoolteacher, it sounded like a good combination. It would also be helpful in dealing with the children and the problems of Dorothy.

When the Careys arrived at the new mission headquarters at Serampore, "Dorothy was so deranged that she was quite incapable of sharing in any of the domestic responsibilities." Hannah Marshman, one of the new workers, took the Carey boys under her wing, and not a year too soon. Dorothy had been unable to handle them, and William, even in his schoolteaching days, was not known as a disciplinarian. Mrs. Marshman wrote home to England about the situation: "Owing to Brother Carey's domestic affliction [meaning Dorothy], his perpetual avocations [probably gardening, or perhaps referring to Bible translation work] or perhaps an easiness of the temperament not wholly free from blame, his two oldest sons were left in great measure without control; hence obstinacy and self-will took a very deep root in their minds." Felix was fifteen; his brother, William, twelve.

Felix was the biggest problem, and Carey couldn't handle his own son. "The good man saw and lamented the evil but was too mild to apply an effectual remedy," wrote Mrs. Marshman candidly. "I could not see this without trembling for the consequences. . . . I thought that to refrain longer would be criminal." And Hannah Marshman waded in.

Hannah Marshman gets credit for providing the discipline, but the new missionary printer William Ward provided a combination big

brother and surrogate father for Felix. At thirty, Ward was a little closer
to Felix in age than was Felix's own father.

The transformation in the oldest Carey boy was amazing: "From
being a tiger, he was transformed into a lamb." Within a year, young
Felix was preaching his first sermon. Soon he became a valued member
of the missionary team. In time, three of the four Carey boys became
missionaries. The fourth, Jonathan, became an attorney of the Calcutta
Supreme Court, serving also as treasurer of the Serampore mission.
Apparently Mrs. Marshman and Mr. Ward arrived on the scene at
exactly the right time.

It was partly through the witnessing of young Felix Carey that the
first Indian was converted after William had been preaching and teaching for seven years. Carey was ecstatic: "Yesterday I had the happiness
to desecrate the Ganges by baptizing the first Hindu and my son Felix."

Meanwhile, Dorothy grew worse. In 1801 Carey wrote: "Mrs. Carey
is obliged to be constantly confined. She had long gotten worse and
worse. But both fear of my own life and hers and the desire of the police
of the place, obliged me to agree to her confinement." Because she was
sometimes violent, she had to be confined to her room.

In 1804 Carey wrote home to England: "Poor Mrs. C. is rather worse
than better. A very distressing object indeed. This affliction is heavy.
Oh, may I bear it like a Christian, and may it be of benefit to me." Later,
Carey wrote of her condition as being "maniacal."

Despite Carey's domestic distress, those early years in Serampore
brought a string of successes. The New Testament was translated into
Bengali, a church was formed, and Carey was appointed teacher and
later professor of Oriental languages at the newly founded Fort William
College in Calcutta. Carey could hardly believe it. Since he had only
a sixth-grade education, he had to write back to England to find out
how a college class should be conducted. But he was also amazed that
he, a Dissenter, should be officially appointed by the governor-general.
Carey's specialties in Oriental language were Sanskrit and Marathi,
besides Bengali. Within ten years of his arrival in India, he had mas-
tered all of them.

Then, late in 1807, at the age of fifty-one, Dorothy Carey passed
away. She had been in India for fourteen years and had been somewhat

deranged for nearly twelve of them. John Marshman wrote that he was amazed that William Carey could have accomplished so much in his "arduous biblical and literary labors . . . while an insane wife, frequently wrought up to a state of most distressing excitement, was in the next room, but one, to his study."

What caused Dorothy's mental illness? It may have been a hereditary weakness or problems caused by her early upbringing in the home of her parents in Piddington. Yet, undoubtedly the insecurity of living conditions both in England and in India accelerated Dorothy's decline. Perhaps even poor nutrition played a part. Though he disciplined himself like a hard taskmaster, William seems to have been easygoing and indecisive in his dealings with his family. He didn't provide the security and stability that Dorothy needed, so she lost confidence in him and her psychological fears were intensified. She needed a security which William couldn't provide physically and wouldn't provide emotionally.

Yet despite these apparent weaknesses as a husband, William Carey saw his sons grow up—though undisciplined at first—to love him and follow in his footsteps.

Six months after Dorothy died, William remarried. His bride was a Danish countess, Charlotte Rumohr. She was somewhat crippled and had come to Calcutta, of all places, for her health. Emotionally, culturally, and intellectually, she was the exact opposite of Dorothy. She had been introduced to Jesus Christ by Carey. The governor-general described the marriage as that of a learned and pious man and a Danish countess "whom he had converted from a Christian to a Baptist by very near drowning her in the ceremony of baptism."

It is difficult to know whether there had ever been any tenderness of emotion between Dorothy and William in the early years of their marriage. But there is no question about Charlotte's emotion toward William. "My dearest love," Charlotte wrote him, "I feel very much in parting with thee and feel very much in being so far from thee. . . . I cannot help longing for thee."

To Carey, Charlotte was everything a missionary's wife should be. After she died in 1821, Carey wrote a friend: "We had been married thirteen years and three weeks, during all which season, I believe, we had as great a share of conjugal happiness as ever was enjoyed by mortals. . . . My loss is irreparable."

Whatever else their marriage showed, it demonstrated that Carey could enjoy a successful marital relationship. In fact, Carey was so elated with the joys of his second marriage that he married a third time. Once again it was a happy marriage, ending with his own death eleven years later, in 1834.

By the time of his death he had translated the Bible into forty-four languages and dialects, had opened mission stations in India, Burma, and Bhutan, had established several schools, and had become an authority on horticulture and agriculture in India. Not bad for a plodder.

Yes, a plodder. Toward the end of his life, he said that if anyone should ever write his life story, he should "give me credit for being a plodder" and that "will describe me justly. I can plod. . . . To this I owe everything."

He would probably evaluate himself as a failure in business, in teaching, in the ministry, as a parent, and as a husband. But he succeeded because he continued plodding . . . and perhaps also because of his motto: "Expect great things from God; attempt great things for God."

It's very hard to evaluate Dorothy. In fact, no one really knows what went on inside her head during those twenty-six difficult years of marriage to William Carey. She probably had no estimation of his greatness nor his genius. Probably she was more concerned about the frequent moves—at least four in their thirteen years in England and seven in their thirteen years in India, not counting the boats and ships of various kinds on which they spent half a year. No doubt she would have been much happier at Piddington, where she had been born and reared by protective parents. Her health and her children's health were perpetual concerns; so was the scarcity of food. She didn't like the vegetable diet on which their poverty forced her to live in England, and she didn't appreciate the curry and rice diet in India.

Perhaps one of the rare clues to Dorothy's thinking comes in the names of two of her children. Most of their seven offspring were named after William's relatives. Two children, however, had unusual biblical names. One of these was certainly bestowed by Dorothy; probably the other one was also.

Felix had been born in 1785. *Felix* means "happy," and despite other uncertainties in her life, Dorothy was certainly glad to have had a son born to her. Ann, her first child, had died two years before, so the birth of Felix brought happiness.

The biblical Felix (Acts 26) was an indecisive man; Paul the missionary was trying to convince him of the Christian message, but Felix's unwillingness to antagonize the Jews delayed his response for two years. Dorothy, too, had a problem in making up her mind when Felix was born. Should she follow her husband and become a Baptist and break with her parents? She waited two years before allowing her husband to baptize her.

The next son that Dorothy probably named was Jabez. Jabez was born while William and Dr. Thomas were on a boat heading for India. Pressure was being placed on Dorothy to join her husband and do what a dutiful wife should do. But she couldn't do it. According to 1 Chronicles 4:9, Jabez's mother gave him that name, "because I bare him with sorrow." Dorothy's heart was also heavy.

In the next verse Jabez as an adult prayed to God to "enlarge my coast, and that thine hand might be with me, and that thou wouldest keep me from evil." For Dorothy to pray the prayer of Jabez meant that she, too, may have wanted God to "enlarge her coast." But she had inner struggles that were bigger than she could handle.

Bibliography

Drewery, Mary. *William Carey*. Grand Rapids: Zondervan, 1979.

Marshman, John. *Life and Labours of Carey, Marshman, and Ward*. London: Ward Publishers, 1867.

Smith, George. *The Life of William Carey*. London: J.N. Dent and Sons, 1885.

Stevenson, P.M. Grand Rapids: Zondervan, 1953.

Does Absence Make the Heart Grow Fonder?

Sometimes.

And sometimes absence makes the heart go *yonder.*

During courtship, a fellow and his sweetheart sometimes agree not to see each other for a while to determine their true feelings for each other. Theoretically, at least, a trial separation during courtship days can help the couple assay the lasting value of their love for each other.

But after the marriage, extended separations are often a strain—sometimes an intolerable strain.

In earlier centuries it was usually the husband who had to leave home for weeks or months at a time. In this generation it may be either the wife or the husband who travels on business or to visit friends. Today a man or a woman may travel across the country or even to another part of the world and still return in a week. A century ago, such travel would have required months of separation.

But the strain on the marriage relationship was and is the same.

The three couples in this section all were separated for long periods of time during their marriages, and the results of the separation were quite different in each case.

However, you could examine a half dozen other marriages in this book and find lengthy separations as well. The Newtons fell more deeply in love; the Luthers grew to appreciate each other more; the Stowes recognized their need for each other; the Wesleys were wracked by jealousy and incompatibility; the Smiths ran into other problems.

But the Livingstones, the Grahams, and the Bunyans capsulize the challenges of separation.

What made it possible for Ruth Graham to survive and thrive as a person when her evangelist-husband was off on extended crusades in Europe, Africa, or Asia? And why did Mary Livingstone fall apart when her explorer-husband was working his way through the African hinterlands? And then there was young Elizabeth Bunyan, with four young stepchildren and one of her own on the way, while her husband was hauled off for an extended prison term. What kept her going, and how did it happen that by the time John finally got out of prison Elizabeth had grown to be a tower of strength to him?

What makes the difference? And what did the husbands do to help their wives handle the separation? You'll find some interesting answers in the following three chapters.

Does absence make the heart grow fonder?

Sometimes.

But it usually tests the marriage. And some marriages are strengthened by the testing, while others are threatened by it.

Devoid of Family Cares

David and Mary Livingstone

It would not have been easy for anyone to have been married to David Livingstone. He was a loner, he was intensely driven, and he found it difficult to work closely with people.

In fact, some of his biographers say that he should never have married.

Fortunately, Mary was not hard to get along with—at least at first. David himself described her as "amiable and good-tempered." He also described her as "a matter-of-fact lady, a little, thick, black-haired girl, sturdy and all I want."

It was not what you would call a romantic marriage, but it certainly was not without love. It was a marriage full of frustration for both of them, especially for Mary. It was also a marriage that provided plenty of ammunition for gossips, second-guessers, and various critics, including Mary's parents as well as David's.

There were so many questions the critics wanted answered. Why did David take Mary and the children on dangerous African expeditions? What drove Mary to drink? Is it possible to be unhappy when you're married to the most popular man in the world? What fascinating questions! What a fascinating couple! After all, they were involved in a lover's triangle, and the third party was named Africa.

David Livingstone was a confirmed bachelor when he first volunteered for missionary service. In answer to the simple question "Are you married?" he wrote on his application form: "Unmarried; under no engagement relating to marriage, never made proposals of marriage, nor conducted myself to any woman as to cause her to suspect that I intended anything relating to marriage."

But during the next couple of years he was frequently reminded that he would be sorry if he didn't get married soon. People told him that a missionary's life is a lonely one.

Missionary life can be wretched without a partner. Livingstone feared that missionary life might be even more wretched with the wrong partner.

But after he had spent three years on lonely missionary service in Africa, Livingstone reluctantly admitted that maybe his advisers had been right after all. By this time he was begging parents and friends to write him more often, but because letters sometimes took half a year to arrive, it was difficult to carry on a meaningful dialogue. He was lonely, and he needed a close companion.

But where would he find a wife in the middle of Bechuanaland in the 1840s? The only eligible candidates in all of South Africa were daughters of missionaries and daughters of government servants. And according to Livingstone, who usually expressed his opinions bluntly, "Daughters of missionaries have miserably contracted minds; colonial ladies worse and worse." Prospects didn't look good.

But then, after some hand-to-paw combat with a lion, he was convalescing at the Kuruman mission station where Robert and Mary Moffat had been serving as missionaries for a score of years. Strolling under the syringa trees with Mary, the eldest daughter of the Moffats, David experienced some emotions that he had thought were deeply buried.

"In love!" he wrote to his old bachelor friends in London. "Words, yea thoughts fail, so I leave it to your imagination."

She was twenty-three, and he was thirty. One biographer states, "She happened to be the first young woman that he had met since he had left England." Three months later, they were engaged.

He wrote a friend, "After nearly four years of African life as a bachelor, I screwed up my courage to put a question beneath one of the fruit trees."

From his standpoint, she would make an ideal wife for him. The daughter of pioneer missionaries six hundred miles inland from Cape Town, South Africa, Mary had been raised in a mud hut. She knew how to make her own clothes, bread, candles, and soap. She was hardy, knew what missionary life was all about, and was "good-tempered." She wouldn't win any beauty contests, but David didn't care about that.

Her parents were both strong-minded and strong-willed. Her mother—outspoken, pious, and often domineering—bore ten children and raised three native children in addition. Her father had risen from Scottish poverty to dominate South Africa's missionary landscape. He had what one writer called "a smothering effect on his colleagues."

And except for his wife, who was the power behind the throne, his family was smothered too. The children grew up with inferiority feelings—especially Mary, who was neither attractive physically nor brilliant mentally.

Standards in the Moffat home were high, and anyone who didn't meet those standards could expect criticism. Younger missionaries were made to feel like teenagers who weren't allowed to grow up. That's the way Mary felt too.

But David didn't respond to her father as other missionaries did. Though he was new on the field and was nearly twenty years younger than her father, he talked to him as an equal.

What Mary saw in Livingstone was a man with the same strength of character that her father possessed, but a man who, unlike her father, had a basic modesty, a sense of humor, and a deep regard for honesty. Not only was he unlike her father, but his background was very different from hers.

While Mary was living in a mud hut in Africa, David had been growing up in a one-room tenement in a factory town outside Glasgow, Scotland. The Livingstone parents and their five children were squeezed into a ten-by-fourteen-foot room, which was their kitchen, bedroom, and living room combined. Biographer Tim Jeal writes, "Truckle beds were pulled out at night to cover the whole floor space. Cooking, eating, reading, washing and mending all went on in the one room."

When he was ten, David went to work in the mill that controlled life in Blantyre. He became a "piecer," piecing together threads on the spinning frames. Like everyone else, he worked six days a week from eight in the morning until eight at night, with a half hour for breakfast and an hour for lunch.

Somehow David forced himself to go to the company school from eight to ten every evening. There he not only managed to keep his eyes open, but he also got his education. Often he returned home and read until midnight, when his mother made him blow out the candle. His sister recalled that he was "determined to learn."

David's father abhorred alcohol and "trashy novels," which were how he classified all books that weren't religious. David refused to read the religious books that his father set in front of him. He preferred scientific works and travel books. It "reached the point of open rebellion on my part," David admitted later, "and his last application of the rod was on my refusal to peruse Wilberforce's *Practical Christianity.*" David said he hated "dry doctrinal books."

The Independent church in Hamilton to which he applied for membership "dooted if Dauvit was soun'" and gave him personal instruction for the next five months.

The following year, after reading a tract by a missionary to China calling for missionary doctors, David had a direction in life. And when David started moving in a direction, nothing deterred him. Two years later, he left the mill at which he had worked for the previous twelve years and entered medical school in Glasgow.

Then he applied to the London Missionary Society for overseas service with China in mind. The society did not seem too impressed with his credentials but accepted him on probation.

Because he was "hardly ready" for theological college, he was given private tutoring. The society's directors spoke negatively about his rusticity (meaning he was a country bumpkin from Scotland) and his heaviness of manner (meaning that he took himself too seriously).

They tried him out as a preacher in a church, but he failed at that. As he stood before the congregation, his mind went blank. He read his text, repeated it slowly, swallowed deeply, and then said, "Friends, I have forgotten all I had to say." He left the church as quickly as he could.

Another problem for the directors was David's praying. When he led in prayer, he seemed to pause interminably while thinking what he should pray for next.

Instead of rejecting him, however, the directors decided to extend his probation. After a few more months they approved him as a missionary candidate because of his good sense and quiet vigor. While awaiting the decision of the directors, he began courting a girl from a middle-class family. It was apparently his first serious courtship. Feeling awkward in her presence, he confessed to her that he was "not very well acquainted with the feelings of those who had been ladies all their lives."

He was twenty-six now, but David Livingstone was considered no great catch for a young woman. A friend said, "I have to admit he was no bonny. His face wore at all times the strongly marked lines of potent will." Another friend remarked that "by no means did he have a winning face," though he did have "an indescribable charm."

When his first love rejected him, David—with a bit of a sour grapes reaction—commented that she was probably too much of a lady to become a good wife for a missionary.

In 1839 the Opium War between China and England broke out, and that changed the thinking of the London Missionary Society about sending more missionaries to China. The directors then suggested that Livingstone think of the West Indies. David didn't like the idea. The West Indies were too civilized. The dark continent of Africa would be more of a challenge.

Then he happened to bump into Robert Moffat, home in England after a score of years in the interior of South Africa. Said Moffat to David, "At dawn I can look out and see the smoke of a thousand villages where the gospel has not been preached." From then on David aimed at Africa, regardless of what the board of directors said.

His fellow missionary candidates liked David. He had a "certain roughness or bluntness of manner," and there was a "great persistence in holding to his own ideas," but there was also a "great kindliness" about him.

David's persistence in holding to his own ideas frequently got him into trouble. With the mission directors, he seemed to wage a continuing debate. He did not like the idea of taking orders from anyone.

Just before going to Africa, he took his finals with the Glasgow medical facility, and he almost had to forfeit his degree because of his outspoken disagreement with them regarding the value of a stethoscope. He didn't think it had the potential that they said it had.

On board ship to Africa, David, one of the few passengers who didn't get seasick, tended medically to those that did. Arriving in Africa, he was assigned to work out of Moffat's mission station at Kuruman, six hundred miles inland from Cape Town. The Moffats were still on furlough in England, and the station needed the services of a doctor. David was told to think about establishing a station farther inland, but any action would have to wait until the Moffats returned to the field.

That opened the door a crack for David. Though Kuruman was the farthest inland of any mission station, it was still too civilized for him. He wrote letters to the directors in London, requesting that they allow him to do more than just think about a new station. David had been in Africa only five months, and already he was convinced that missionary strategy was either too conservative or simply misguided.

He explored the interior; that was the necessary research for a later decision. When he returned to Kuruman, he wrote, "I did not come to Africa to be suspended on the tail of anyone. What is of infinitely more importance [is that] souls are perishing while I have no power to point them to the Cross. I could not settle down at Kuruman."

His research took him farther inland than any white man had ever been before, although he had been in Africa for less than a year and was still struggling to pick up the African languages.

Then in 1843, when Roger Edwards and his wife left Kuruman to begin a new station, David eagerly accompanied them. The spot they selected was Mabotsa, about 220 miles from Kuruman. "A lovelier spot you never saw," David wrote. It was here where David felt his loneliness more than ever before.

And it was in Mabotsa where David had his wrestling match with a lion. Lions had been marauding the cattle pens of the Africans, and the villagers were reluctant to do anything about it.

David told them that if they would kill one lion, the other lions would get the idea that they weren't welcome and would leave the area. The Africans weren't so sure that this newcomer knew what he was talking about.

David accompanied the Africans as they stalked the lions. Spotting several of them, he took aim and fired both barrels of his rifle; then he stopped to reload. Suddenly he heard a shout. "Looking half round, I saw the lion just in the act of springing upon me. . . . He caught my shoulder as he sprang, and we both came to the ground together. Growling horribly close to my ear, he shook me as a terrier dog does a rat."

An African, coming to David's rescue, fired at the lion. He missed, but the lion turned his attention to his new assailant. Another African then speared the lion, and soon the beast, wounded previously by David's bullets and then by the spear, fell down dead.

David's upper arm was splintered, and the lion's teeth made a series of gashes. Never again was he able to lift his left arm above his shoulder.

Later David was asked what his thoughts were as he lay on the ground wrestling with a lion. He responded, "I was wondering which part of me he would eat first."

For weeks he was extremely ill, but then he recovered enough to be taken to Kuruman where he could receive better assistance. The Moffats had just returned to the station after four years on furlough. And the Moffats' daughter Mary became his nurse.

Before long, Mary the nurse became Mary the fiancée.

After he sufficiently recovered from his lion wounds and received Mary's consent to become his wife, he headed back to Mabotsa to build a house.

On his way he stopped to write Mary a letter. In it he reminded her to get a marriage license and to order some household goods for their Mabotsa home. He closed the letter with the words, "Let your affection be towards Him much more than towards me."

His letter to the mission board, informing them of his proposed marriage, appears as if he had simply made a cold business decision: "Various considerations connected with this new sphere of labor, and which to you need not be specified in detail, having led me to the conclusion that it was my duty to enter into the marriage relation, I have made the necessary arrangements for union with Mary, the eldest daughter of Mr. Moffat, in the beginning of January 1845. . . . And if I have not deceived myself I was in some measure guided by a desire that the divine glory might be promoted in my increased usefulness."

But that was the kind of King's English that he normally used when he wrote to his directors. Only to some personal friends and to Mary did his letters convey warmth, humor, and informality.

The home he built for Mary in Mabotsa was fifty-two feet by twenty feet, with walls a foot thick: "It is pretty hard work," he wrote Mary, "and almost enough to drive love out of my head, but it is not situated there; it is in my heart, and won't come out unless you behave so as to quench it."

He also put in a couple of lines for Mary's mother, who had her opinions on everything and was seldom bashful about expressing them. She had apparently told Livingstone (whom she always called by his last name) not to put too many windows in the house. David wrote to Mary that if her mother "thinks there are too many she can just let me know. I can build them all up in two days and let the light come down the chimney if that would please."

In David's mind was the notion that he could build Mabotsa into a mission station similar to the one that Mary's parents had built at Kuruman. At the same time he wanted to incorporate some new ideas, like using African evangelists and starting a seminary to train African pastors. But there was a hitch in that plan: David already had had a taste of exploration, and he was on the verge of becoming addicted.

For now, he wanted to get something started at Mabotsa, "whence the rays of divine light might radiate far and wide." When he wasn't constructing his house, he was trying to get a school started for African children. It was rather frustrating because on some days he might have fifty youngsters, but on other days he would have only five.

334

Wedding day was January 2, 1845, in Kuruman, with Robert and Mary Moffat looking on. David and Mary honeymooned in Mabotsa, which name, incidentally, means "wedding feast." If David hoped that it would prove to be one for Mary and himself, he soon had to face reality.

The problem was his colleague in Mabotsa, Roger Edwards. "We parted in apparent harmony when I went to get married," said David, "and when I returned, a storm burst on my head such as I had never had before." David spoke of him as being "a fiery old gent."

Livingstone was too much of a go-getter for Edwards, and the older missionary couldn't handle it. Edwards felt that he had been a "lackey" for Moffat in his first ten years of missionary service, and now for the first time he had a chance to do something on his own without Patriarch Moffat looking over his shoulder. But when he set up his new base at Mabotsa, Livingstone was with him. It was Livingstone who came up with new ideas and pushed them through. The junior partner in the operation was taking over, and Edwards strongly resented being "a mere appendix to this young man."

To top it off, Livingstone married Moffat's daughter. Edwards must have felt that even in Mabotsa, 220 miles from Kuruman, he couldn't get away from the eyes of the Moffat family.

Edwards wasn't the only missionary with whom Livingstone had disagreements. David was impatient and aggressive, and older missionaries resented a newcomer telling them how to run things.

David did not feel he could speak with Mary about these disagreements. He wrote to a friend, "I tell you my sorrows although I have a wife," indicating that he did not feel he could share some of his deeper problems with her. It may have been, as some biographers have suggested, that he lacked confidence in her mental ability. More probably, however, it was because Mary didn't have a philosophical mind. She had more the soul of an artist than a scholar.

Problems between the Edwardses and the Livingstones continued to mount. Mrs. Edwards called David "shabby, ungentlemanly and unchristian" and Edwards called him "dishonest, dishonorable and mischievous."

Obviously, Mabotsa was not big enough for both couples. So, before the year was over, David and Mary Livingstone packed their bags and left their honeymoon cottage, heading farther northward into the African interior.

David halted his caravan at a spot he called "a blank on the map" and wrote friends that he was now the "most remotely situated missionary in southern Africa." The "blank on the map" was called Chinuone. A severe drought had begun to envelop the area even before David and Mary arrived, and during their twenty-month stay the famine got even worse. In those months, Mary bore two children and tried to get a school started for African children in her spare time.

Eventually, David realized that if Mary and the children didn't get some decent food, the results would be disastrous. So he sent them to his in-laws in Kuruman. When Mary arrived there the Africans hardly recognized her, because she had lost considerable weight. A few days later David arrived, and they taunted him, "How lean she is! Have you starved her?"

David decided he had better seek a new site for missionary endeavors. So shortly after they returned to Chinuone, he went with several Africans to seek a better location. Mary and the two children stayed behind in what was now a virtual ghost town.

She sent David a note. Life among the ruins of Chinuone was a bit dreary in the daytime, she wrote, but at least the nights wouldn't be boring. The lions were moving in to resume possession.

A month later, David finally returned to take her and the children to their new home in Kolobeng. The new home was actually not as good as the old one. It was a drafty, fly-infested hut of poles and reeds, insufferably hot in the daytime and amazingly cold at night.

Kolobeng was home for David and Mary for the next four years, their longest sojourn in any one spot. With all its problems and frustrations, it was probably the happiest time in Mary's life.

David describes an ordinary day: "The daily routine; up with the sun, family worship, breakfast, school, then manual work as required—ploughing, sowing, smythying, and every other sort. Mary, busy all the morning with culinary and other work; a rest of two hours after dinner; then she goes to the infant school with an attendance of from 60 to 80. Manual work for him again till 5 o'clock; then lessons in the town and talk to such as are disposed to listen. The cows are milked; then a meeting; followed by a prayer meeting in Sechele's house (the village chief) which brings him home about 8:30 too tired for any mental exertions. I do not enumerate these duties by way of telling you how much we do, but to let you know a cause of sorrow I have that so little of my time is devoted to real missionary work."

Mary had to make her own candles, soap, and butter. She ground her own meal and baked bread in ant-mud covered with hot ashes. When meat was scarce, they lived on caterpillars or roasted locusts. David didn't like boiled locusts, "but when they are roasted, I should much prefer them to shrimp," and then he adds, "though I would avoid both if possible."

Missionary work had been discouraging to him partly because he did not see results quickly enough. Only one African had declared his faith in Christ during David's six years as missionary. And when he looked at the efforts of other missionaries, it didn't seem as if they had much more to show for their labors. Even his in-laws, after thirty years of service, had not seen great success.

At one time he wrote, "God had an only Son, and He was a missionary and a physician. A poor, poor imitation of Him I am, or wish to be."

While David was having second thoughts about his aptitude as a missionary, he began to realize that perhaps his greatest contribution to the missionary cause would be to open up Africa's interior for other missionaries.

Three months after Mary gave birth to their third child, David took her to stay with her parents in Kuruman while he went on a four-month, six-hundred-mile trek to find a legendary lake, Lake Ngami, about which the Africans had told him. Several Europeans had previously tried to find it, but none had succeeded.

David Livingstone found it. He was more interested in what might lie on the other side of the lake, however. So the following year David was eager to make the trip again, this time going beyond the lake, and this time going with his family.

Taking his wife and children caused the tongue of almost every missionary in Africa to wag. On this extremely hazardous journey across a desert, a wide river infested with crocodiles, disease-ridden swamps, and unpredictable African tribesmen, David dared to take his family. Mary was five months pregnant, and she had three small children with her.

But the options were for Mary to stay with her mother again or for her to go exploring with David. She chose to go with David.

They arrived none too soon. A week later, Mary delivered her fourth child. The child, however, lived only a few weeks before succumbing to an infection.

Mary too became ill. She suffered from paralysis for several weeks. David wrote, "The right side of her face became motionless" and "the pain continually recurs and affects the right side and leg."

To give her time to recuperate, David took her to Kuruman, where they stayed with the Moffats for three months. Physically, it was a restful time for Mary. Emotionally, there was an air of an uneasy truce. As biographer Tim Jeal states, "It was a tense and disagreeable time."

The news leaked out that David was planning still another trip to Lake Ngami and beyond. Nobody wanted to talk about it or even to think the unthinkable—that David would want Mary and the children to go with him again.

Mrs. Moffat struggled to contain herself, and that wasn't easy. She normally spoke her mind on any subject. Three months later, she could restrain herself no longer. The Livingstones had returned to their station in Kolobeng. Mary was expecting another child. That was the good news. The bad news was that David still planned to have her accompany him on the next expedition.

Mrs. Moffat wrote a letter to her son-in-law as soon as she got the news. "My dear Livingstone," it began, and any letter that started like that sounded ominous. She warmed to her subject by stating that she should have had the courage to have a candid discussion when they had been together at Kuruman. Then she tackled it head-on. "Mary had told me all along that should she be pregnant you would not take her." Instead, Mary would let David go exploring by himself and she would bring the children with her to Kuruman. "But to my dismay I now get a letter in which she writes: 'I must again wend my way to the far interior.' . . . O Livingstone, what do you mean? Was it not enough that you lost one lovely babe, and scarcely saved the other, while the mother came home threatened with paralysis? . . . A pregnant woman with three children trailing about with a company of the other sex, through the wilds of Africa, among savage men and beasts. . . . The thing is preposterous."

Mrs. Moffat wasn't simply an overly protective mother. She had given birth to ten children in Africa, and she knew what it was like to live in primitive and hazardous conditions. She knew that God would protect his children if they were doing his will. But she was afraid that David and Mary weren't doing God's will when they were exploring instead of evangelizing.

In David's mind, however, was the notion that he could open up a continent for hundreds of new missionaries. Besides, he never liked people telling him what to do—least of all a mother-in-law. As one observer described him, he was "unaggressively obstinate."

Mrs. Moffat didn't realize that Mary agreed with David's thinking. At first, Mary thought she might remain at Kolobeng while David explored. But since Kolobeng was being threatened by the Boers and was still drought-stricken, the family was no longer safe there.

Should she return to Kuruman and stay with her parents again? Neither Mary nor David liked that option. Biographer George Seaver writes: "Mary could no longer feel happy in her parents' home; she would bale subject to their whim and treated as she had always been from childhood—as a child; but she was a child no longer; she was a wife and mother. And her husband was a human being with a sense of humor, a freedom-loving fellow-mortal, and she loved him."

And David loved Mary, too, though he often didn't express it. He enjoyed her company; she was a good traveler; and he would miss her if she weren't with him.

Staying at Kuruman would have presented other problems. If Mary were in Kuruman, she would be hearing all those breezes of gossip: "Why is he always leaving her? Can't they get along? Something must be wrong with their marriage." Mary had many reasons to leave Kuruman.

Besides, David was a physician. Where else should a pregnant woman be but at the side of her husband the doctor?

Seaver comments on this stage of Livingstone's life: "This journey was to prove the crux of his career. It forced upon him the realization that his aims as an active missionary and his duties as a husband were two things incompatible, and that one or the other must be sacrificed."

But why couldn't he wait another year or two for his exploration, at least until Mary had regained more strength? Livingstone was concerned that if slave traders reached Africa's interior before missionaries, the Africans would never again be open to the gospel message; instead they would fear anything that came from the white man. But if a missionary would come to them with his wife and children, they would recognize him as a man of peace. David was determined to be that man.

Soon David, Mary, and the children were leading a small caravan, exploring once again the interior of Africa. They investigated the wilds for the next seven months.

Their most significant discovery was the upper Zambezi River, which, if it proved to be navigable to the Indian Ocean, would provide missionaries an easy way to get to central Africa.

Returning, they stopped the caravan for eight days along the banks of the Chobe River. There, Mary gave birth to her fifth child. Then they moved on. This time the baby survived. Mary, however, once again suffered from paralysis, and it was more severe than before.

This frightened David. But it also confirmed a difficult decision. David had unfinished business in Africa. Until he found a better way for missionaries to reach the interior, he would not know if his exploration had accomplished anything for the cause of Christ. "I view the end of the geographical feat as the beginning of the missionary enterprise," he had written, but until he had crossed Africa from coast to coast he couldn't write *Finis* above the geographical feat.

Yet that was a trip that would take two years. Since Mary's paralysis had returned, it was obvious that she couldn't accompany him. Besides, their oldest son Robert would soon be six years old, and David wanted him to get some proper education.

To the mission board David wrote a long letter telling them his plans. What he needed, he said, were "two years devoid of family cares. . . . As we must send our children to England soon, it would be no great additional expense to send them now along with their mother. This arrangement would enable me to proceed alone and devote about two, perhaps three, years to this new region."

It wouldn't be easy to say good-bye to his wife and children and he knew it. He said that he felt as if he were "orphaning" his children. He said that it hurt as if he were tearing out his insides.

At another time he wrote, "Some of the brethren do not hesitate to tell the natives that my object is to obtain the applause of men. This bothers me, for sometimes I suspect my own motives."

Doubting his motives was not the only problem. He had no money to support his family while they lived in England. He told the mission board that they must find a way to provide for his family in England. Without waiting for the board to approve his plan to explore the Zambezi or to confirm their willingness to look after Mary and the children, he decided to go ahead anyway.

"So powerfully convinced am I that it is the will of our Lord I should, I will go, no matter who opposes. . . . I will open a way to the interior or perish."

It was a tearful parting at Cape Town, South Africa. David told his children to consider Jesus, rather than himself, as their father from then on. "I have given you back to Him and you are in His care." He wasn't sure that the mission board could provide for the family, but he was sure that Jesus could.

For a few weeks David stayed in Cape Town to get supplies. Almost every day he wrote to Mary.

In one letter he wrote, "My dearest Mary: How I miss you now, and the children. My heart yearns incessantly over you. How many thoughts of the past crowd into my mind. I feel as if I would treat you all much more tenderly and lovingly than ever.

"You have been a great blessing to me. You attended to my comfort in many, many ways. May God bless you for all your kindnesses. I see no face now to be compared with that sunburnt one which has so often greeted me with its kind looks. Let us do our duty to our Savior, and we shall meet again. I wish that time were now."

With his supplies purchased, David began his trek back into the interior. It was a difficult time for him emotionally, and he shared his feelings in his journal: "28th September 1852—Have I seen the end of my wife and children? . . . O Jesus, use me a little for thy glory. I have done nothing for thee yet, and I would like to do something."

While David battled loneliness, disease, drought, wild animals, and hostile tribesmen, Mary had battles of her own when she arrived in England. With four children in tow, she was a stranger in her own country. Africa was much more her home than England. Her first residence in Great Britain was with David's parents in Scotland. It was a small home to begin with, and David's two unmarried sisters were living there, but that wasn't the heart of the problem.

David's parents were strict and orderly, prim and precise. Mary's lifestyle and background were far different from theirs. Writes Jeal, "It is not hard to imagine the impact of the arrival of a strange daughter-in-law and four children, none of them older than seven, on a religious and meticulously ordered Scottish household."

She arrived in poor physical health, and before long her mental health was ailing.

She stayed with the Livingstones less than half a year, but for both parties it must have seemed far longer than that. She left in a huff, telling her in-laws that she didn't want to see them again, didn't want them running her life, and didn't want them telling her how to raise her children.

After that she wandered around England, living what Jeal terms "a wretched nomadic existence," staying sometimes in rented rooms and sometimes with some of David's old friends whom she knew only by name. It was a humiliating existence for her, and not always a happy one for David's old friends upon whose doors she unexpectedly knocked.

Her in-laws lost contact with her and didn't know if they should try to find her or not. David's father eventually wrote to the mission board: "Mrs. L. does not write to us, nor are we anxious that she should, neither do we wish her to know that we are inquiring about them. Yet we do love the children much. . . . Their mother was pleased to forbid all communication with us no less than three different times. . . . Owing to her strange behavior ever since we became acquainted with her, we have resolved to have no more intercourse with her until there is evidence that she is a changed person."

Mary was never reconciled to her in-laws, but a year later she felt that she had seen enough of England and resolved to go back to Africa. David was scheduled to return soon, and she wanted to go to Cape Town to meet him. But the leaders of the mission board refused to advance her money for the trip, and she was unable to go.

Things kept deteriorating for Mary. She became physically ill again and couldn't afford medical treatment. Unhappy with the mission board's lack of concern, she became bitter and started to spread scandalous rumors about the mission. She wrote an urgent letter to David, begging him to return, but she never knew whether he got the letter or not.

She began drinking, and this made her pleas to the mission board for money more desperate: "Be lenient with me. I don't attempt to justify myself. I may not have been so discreet in the use of my money."

Time dragged. David was supposed to have returned to England after a two-year expedition, but two years passed and he was still exploring Africa. Two years, then three, then four years.

His initial intention had been to go from the center of Africa westward to the Atlantic Ocean, but after he had been successful in that venture, he felt he needed to go eastward to the Indian Ocean, following the Zambezi River.

While Mary was sinking in despair, her husband was being hailed in absentia as a national hero. The Royal Geographical Society hailed his travel across Africa as "the greatest triumph in geographical research . . . in our times."

And when he finally returned to England in mid-December 1856, he received a festive welcome. It had been four and a half years since Mary had seen him.

When Mary got the official word that he would be landing in a few weeks, her clouds began to lift; her depression soon disappeared.

343

For the next six months, Mary and David were together in London. Even though David spent most of his waking hours penning his *Missionary Travels,* Mary was recovering her spirit again. It was a happy time for the Livingstone family. As David wrote, the children milled around, but he had the knack of shutting out all distractions, including children, while he was working. On weekends, David, Mary, and the children went on long walks in the woods together.

Published that fall, *Missionary Travels* was an overnight best-seller and added to Livingstone's stature as an international celebrity. Soon he was acclaimed as a saint as well as an explorer-scientist. He received honorary degrees from Oxford and was proposed to be a Fellow of the Royal Society.

London feted David with one banquet after another, and Mary usually accompanied him.

Sometimes honor was showered upon Mary as well. In fact, she heard Lord Shaftesbury (who no doubt didn't know her too well) praise "her spirit and her counsel" and also how she had endured her time in England "with patience and resignation, and even joy."

Few people knew the depths to which Mary had plunged only a year before. Now she seemed like a model wife, and David a model husband. One person in whose home they stayed said, "The doctor was sportive and fond of a joke and Mrs. Livingstone entered into his humor. Dr. and Mrs. Livingstone were much attached, and thoroughly understood each other. In society both were reserved and quiet. Neither of them cared for grandeur. It was a great trial to Dr. Livingstone to go to a grand dinner."

David said that he was uncomfortable with "lionizing"; along with Mary he looked forward to the day when they could return to Africa together.

When David spoke, he publicly thanked his wife for forgiving him for staying in Africa four and a half years instead of the two which he had promised. He spoke of how useful she would be on his next exploration. "She is familiar with the languages; she is able to work; she is willing to endure. . . . Glad am I indeed to be accompanied by my guardian angel."

And glad was Mary indeed to be going with him.

While in England, David severed his official ties with the mission. The mission directors tended to consider his explorations as secular rather than missionary. David was convinced that exploration was the only way to open Africa up for further Christian outreach. So he accepted a formal commission from the British government to serve as government consul and to command an expedition to central Africa, and in particular, the Zambezi River area.

David chose his own team, and it was understood that Mary would be a part of it. So after a whirlwind furlough in England of only fifteen months, he made arrangements to return to Africa.

When they embarked in February 1858, three of their children stayed behind for education; only the youngest, not yet seven, accompanied them. It seemed almost like a long-delayed honeymoon for David and Mary.

But on board the ship, Mary became seasick. At least, that is what David assumed at first. Soon they both realized that it was not seasickness; it was morning sickness. Mary was pregnant again. It was the worst news that Mary could imagine. It meant that she and David would be separated again. It meant returning to the tormented life that she had been living in England.

As soon as they arrived in Africa, Mary was detoured to Kuruman, where she would stay with her parents until the baby arrived. Then it would be back to England again, because Mary could not endure living with her mother indefinitely.

"It was a bitter parting with my wife, like tearing the heart out of one. It was so unexpected," David wrote. At another time he wrote that if he could have what he wanted most, it would be simply this: "I would like to be alone with my wife." Instead, he was alone with Africa, his second wife.

The baby, Anna Marie, was born that November. Shortly afterward, Mary returned to England to be with her other children. Her departure from Kuruman was hastened by the gossip of the other missionaries. "Her husband cannot live with her. That is why they are separated." It didn't take long for some of Mary's bitterness to return.

This separation from David proved no more pleasant than the previous one. The older children were now teenagers, and Mary was unable to cope with them. She wanted to leave them and join David, but that was impossible. Again, she felt trapped. W. Garden Blaikie writes simply, "Her letters to her husband tell of much spiritual darkness." Once again she was drinking heavily. She was given to "queer and disagreeable moods."

In 1861 a letter finally came from David, asking her to come and meet him in Africa. She didn't need to be coaxed. Her youngest child, only three, was left with David's sisters; the others were in school.

A contemporary writer says that Mary, now forty, had become "a coarse, vulgar woman" and extremely overweight.

Without David, she was nothing; with him, she was a queen.

But David was having problems of his own. As a lone explorer, he had been eminently successful. As a leader of an exploring team, he was a flop. The crew was almost mutinous. After four years, his Zambezi River expedition was an expensive fiasco. It had shown his weaknesses as a leader.

So he looked forward to Mary's arrival. As he made his way to the mouth of the Zambezi to meet the ship, he encountered one disastrous delay after another. "Always too late," he wrote sadly in his journal.

That's what Mary must have thought too when her ship arrived at the Zambezi and David was nowhere to be seen. In poor emotional health already, she didn't need another disappointment.

Not finding Livingstone, the captain of Mary's ship turned his craft around and headed for Mozambique, planning to return to the Zambezi a week later. But when the ship was caught in a tornado, its return was delayed for three weeks.

By this time, both Mary and David were distressed. But finally on February 1, 1862, the captain of the vessel spotted the hull of a small paddle steamer near the mouth of the Zambezi.

Despite the momentary joy of reunion after years of separation, there were problems. Mary wasn't the same woman David had known before.

At first she seemed the same. She could joke as she used to do when she was able to cheer him up regardless of the circumstances. In fact, once when he thought that others wouldn't understand their light-hearted jesting, he told her, "We old bodies ought now to be more sober, and not play so much."

But underneath her sometimes carefree exterior, David detected something that troubled him. Her bitterness was deeper now; her Christian faith was shaky. Once amiable, she now found it difficult to get along with anyone.

David faced other problems too. Because of the delays, they seemed likely to spend the malarial season in the lower Zambezi area, a notorious region for the disease.

Depression set in again. David tried to joke with her to break her despondency, but nothing altered her mood. The following week, she began running a high fever.

A member of Livingstone's party commented, "The state of her mind has been such as to predispose her to any disease, while her indiscretions in eating and drinking previously have been such as to undermine her health."

According to David, she lost her will to live. He tried what he could to reduce her fever, but even massive doses of quinine were ineffective. Her mind wandered; she rambled on about her children.

David stayed by her bedside. A friend described the scene: "The man who had faced so many deaths, and braved so many dangers, was now utterly broken down and weeping like a child."

Mary's breathing became labored, then irregular. He took her in his arms. "Are you resting in Jesus?" he asked, realizing that she probably couldn't understand what he was saying. Within a few hours, she breathed her last.

Though weary, David went through Mary's possessions to search for answers. He sought to be consoled about her spiritual condition. Recently, all he heard from her was bitterness and despair. When she emerged from gloom, she would joke and laugh. But he hadn't seen any evidence of spirituality since she had returned to Africa.

Then he discovered a prayer she had written. It was short, simple, and plaintive. "Accept me, Lord, as I am, and make me such as thou wouldst have me to be." He also came across a letter on which she had written: "Let others plead for pensions; I give my services in the world from uninterested motives. I have motives for my own conduct I would not exchange for a hundred pensions."

Under a large baobab tree in Shupanga, Africa, Mary Moffat Livingstone was buried. She was only forty-one years old.

David mourned deeply.

His journal entries display his grief: "It is the first heavy stroke I have suffered. . . . I loved her when I married her, and the longer I lived with her I loved her the more. Oh Mary, my Mary. How often we have longed for a quiet home. . . . Surely He has rewarded you by taking you to the best home."

Two weeks later he wrote, "For the first time in my life I feel willing to die."

He wrote to his mother-in-law and then to his children in England. "A right straightforward woman was she. No crooked way was ever hers, and she could act with decision and energy when required."

"Everything else that happened in my career," he wrote in another letter, "made the mind rise to overcome it, but with this sad stroke I feel crushed and void of strength. I try to bow to the stroke as from the Lord . . . but there are regrets that will follow me to my dying day. If I had only done so and so."

Mrs. Moffat penned a very understanding and insightful letter to David, in which she admitted that her daughter Mary could not be termed "eminently pious" (a remarkable understatement), but she went on to add that "the Lord knew that her heart was right. And while her life's voyage had been difficult and stormy, God had not allowed her to become a wreck."

Later David, with clearer vision, described Mary as a "sincere if somewhat dejected Christian."

David never remarried. For another eleven years he explored Africa, most of the time as a solitary figure, accompanied only by native Africans.

But like Mary's, his life was beset by disappointments.

Says biographer Seaver: "It must have seemed that all he had striven for had been failure; that over it all might be written one word: Disillusion. In everything he had failed: he had failed as a husband; he had failed as a father; he had failed as a missionary; he had failed as a geographer; he had failed most of all as a liberator. It was through his fault that his wife had died untimely, through his neglect that his children were orphaned." Indeed, he had failed to end the slave trade and failed to establish permanent Christian missions. He was painfully aware that he had not reached his goals.

All that is true. And yet it was through his death that Africa became such a focus of missionary activity that today Africa south of the Sahara is turning to Christianity. His efforts were not, in the long run, fruitless.

David was an intensely driven man who could push himself to super-human limits. Goal-oriented, he ventured all no matter how others viewed it. "He that loveth father or mother more than me is not worthy of me; and he that loveth son or daughter more than me is not worthy of me" (Matt. 10:37) was a verse he took seriously.

Mary too could push herself to surprising limits—when she had support. She needed approval; she required a place where she could be herself, a place where she could contribute meaningfully, a place where she was safe from the barbs of others. She found that place at David's side.

Bibliography

Blaikie, W. Garden. *The Personal Life of David Livingstone*. New York: Fleming H. Revell, 1890.

Campbell, R. J. *Livingstone*. New York: Dodd, Mead, 1930.

Jeal, Tim. *Livingstone*. New York: Putnam's, 1973.

Northcott, Cecil. *Livingstone's Missionary Correspondence, 1841–1856*. Berkeley: University of California Press, 1961.

Schapera, I., ed. *David Livingstone: His Life and Letters*. New York: Harper and Row, 1957.

A Union of Two Forgivers
Billy and Ruth Graham

We all know Billy Graham. Or do we?

So much has been written about this internationally famous evangelist that he is recognized immediately wherever he travels around the world.

But what is Billy Graham like when he's at home?

And Ruth Graham? What adjustments has she had to make in her marriage to a man who has become an international celebrity?

You know that there are no typical marriages. You can be sure that the Graham marriage isn't typical either. From it you can learn some lessons that will strengthen your own marriage relationship.

She was raised in a missionary compound in China, the daughter of a Presbyterian physician. At night she and her family read the classics and played games together.

He was raised on a dairy farm in North Carolina. His parents didn't talk much about religion. He was more interested in batting averages than in school, and probably thought Dostoevski was a rookie shortstop for the Cincinnati Reds.

In her family, women were outspoken; in his family, the men did the talking.

As a teenager she dreamed of becoming a missionary to an isolated outpost in Tibet. He wanted to be a major league first baseman, with a cud of chewing tobacco in his cheek.

The girl: Ruth McCue Bell. The boy: Billy Frank Graham.

Billy and Ruth Graham have become legendary figures around the world. For three decades he has been among the most admired men in America. One secular magazine called Dr. Graham the best-known man in the world. He has preached to more than 100 million people in person and many times that number by radio and television. He has visited presidents, prime ministers, and royalty, to say nothing of corporate executives and financial tycoons. Every book he writes is a guaranteed best-seller. Probably more than two million people have made decisions for Christ as a direct result of his ministry. That's Billy Graham.

Yet as one close observer remarked, "Half Billy is Ruth."

To which she says, "Nonsense."

She also says, "Nonsense," when Billy says, "Heaven is like being married to Ruth."

Billy sometimes veers toward the pious and pontifical; Ruth opts for the practical. Once when Billy preached a sermon on the Christian home, he asked his wife (as he usually does) what she thought of it.

She responded: "It was a good sermon except for one thing."

"What was that?"

"The timing."

"The what?"

"The timing. You spent eleven minutes on a wife's duty to her husband and only seven on a husband's duty to his wife."

That's the way Ruth is.

She has a mind of her own. Despite Billy's Baptist beliefs, she has remained a staunch Presbyterian.

"At the beginning of our marriage," Ruth recalls, "some very wise person told me that when two people agree on everything, one of them is unnecessary."

Billy and Ruth Graham do not agree on everything. She admits, "Life in the Billy Graham household is not a matter of uninterrupted sweetness and light."

With her evangelist husband away from home for months at a time, Ruth Graham has had to make some adjustments, but she says, "Although we don't have the usual family life, we have an interesting and fulfilled one."

One of the key reasons for this happiness is a favorite saying of Ruth's: "A happy marriage is a union of two forgivers." Another key reason is the sense of humor that both Billy and Ruth have. "If you don't take things too seriously," Ruth says, "disagreeing can even be a lot of fun."

Billy and Ruth are not at all alike. Billy may have been raised on a farm, and Ruth in a secluded Chinese compound, but she is a far better handyman than he is. A respect for the other's strengths, rather than a harping on the other's weaknesses, has made their marriage grow stronger through the years. In the first few years of marriage there was a lot of give and take, however.

They met as students at Wheaton College (Illinois) in 1940. She was a twenty-year-old sophomore; he was a freshman, but nearly two years older.

He had already come a long way from those days on the farm in North Carolina. In high school he liked to race cars and enjoyed the girls. He loved the excitement of the former and was actually somewhat shy with the latter. But at the age of sixteen, Billy saw an evangelist's finger pointed at him. "I remember a great sense of burden that I was a sinner before God and had a great fear of hell and judgment." Before long, he had walked the aisle and had committed his life to Jesus Christ.

During the rest of his high school days he was, according to his coach, "an interesting, challenging, and inspiring mixture of saint and devil, with a predominant measure of saint." After graduation, he enrolled in fundamentalist Bob Jones College. He lasted one semester. On the farm he had been footloose; the college's rigid schedule cooped him up. He couldn't stand the confinement. Besides that, school authorities had already scolded him a couple times for stepping over their boundaries.

So he enrolled in another unaccredited school, Florida Bible Institute. It was here that he began preaching. It was also here that he began going steady. By the end of his first year in Florida he was practically engaged. Four months later, however, his girlfriend announced to him that she was breaking their "understanding" because she wanted to marry another student. He was crushed. He wrote to a friend: "All the stars have fallen out of my sky. There is nothing to live for. We have broken up."

Shortly afterward, he made two decisions: one, to be more cautious about his involvement with girls in the future; and two, to zero in on one particular vocation. He wrote home: "Dear Mother and Dad: I feel that God has called me to be a preacher."

Then nearly twenty-two, he headed north to Wheaton College to prepare himself for the ministry. It was his third college, but he was still classified a freshman.

To Billy, whose North Carolina accent could hardly be understood by Midwesterners and who found the raw northern temperatures almost unbearable, Illinois seemed to be a foreign country. In fact, he considered dropping out. But before he could consider it seriously, he met a hazel-eyed brunette from China.

Although Ruth thought him somewhat of a "beanpole," it apparently was love after the first date for her. Just the way he raced up the stairs made her think that he knew where he was going and was in a hurry to get there. She admired that.

Billy was smitten, too, despite his resolution to take it slow with girls. After their first date, he wrote home to his mother that he "just could not believe anyone could be so beautiful and so sweet." Meanwhile Ruth went to her room and "told the Lord that if I could spend the rest of my life serving Him with Bill, I would consider it the greatest privilege imaginable."

Ruth McCue Bell had already lived an eventful twenty-one years. Her father and mother had been married in Waynesboro, Virginia (only a couple of hundred miles from Billy Graham's home near Charlotte), but Dr. Nelson Bell had taken his wife to northern China to serve God in a missionary hospital in 1916. It was there, four years later, that Ruth was born, the second of the three Bell daughters.

Those were turbulent days in China. Ruth reminisces: "I can never recall going to sleep at night without hearing gunshots in the countryside around the house." The children were never permitted to leave the mission compound without an adult. In that part of China, warlords, bandits, and kidnappers were all commonplace.

Despite the excitement, Ruth wasn't fearful. "I think the greatest tribute to mother's courage is that we children never sensed fear [in her] and so we ourselves never had any fear."

It was a missionary home full of good humor, books of all kinds—from detective stories to the classics—and enjoyable Bible study. The idea that Bible study should be enjoyable has been a slogan for Ruth.

Her sense of humor probably came from her father: "He could make a joke out of any situation," she says.

Ruth can't recall when she didn't love the Lord. "My earliest recollections are of deepest gratitude to God for having loved me so much that He was willing to send His Son to die in my place."

Despite their wholesome upbringing, Ruth and her older sister, Rosa, scrapped constantly. "We fought verbally and with our hands and feet, and the servants used to gather around, when our parents were at their afternoon clinic, and try to guess who was going to win." In the evenings they read the classics (Dickens and Scott were Ruth's favorites) and played word games, Carroms, or Flinch. Bible games on Sunday sharpened their grasp of Scripture facts.

Ruth's mother was concerned about her children's appearance. She didn't want them to look as if their clothes came from a missionary barrel. In agreement with her mother's philosophy, Ruth says, "Not caring about one's appearance goes against a woman's nature."

As Ruth approached teenage years, her mother wrote, "Ruth is growing fast and is somewhat scatterbrained." Maybe she was scatterbrained, but she was also dedicated. She told her sister that she wanted to be "captured by bandits and beheaded, killed for Jesus' sake."

When she dared to pray like that, her sister Rosa refused to say "amen." Instead, Rosa countered by praying, "Lord, don't listen to her." When she heard and read about the needs of Tibet, Ruth became interested in that exotic land, and decided that she was "called" to be an old-maid missionary to Tibet.

For junior high school, Ruth and Rosa, together with three other children, were taught by a tutor, Miss Lucy Fletcher, at their parents' expense. For senior high school she was sent to a mission school in Korea where she "excelled in Bible but not much else." Leaving her parents and going away to school was not easy for her to do. It was not easy on her parents, either. Her father said, "It is certainly the one hard thing that missionaries have to do—have their children so far away during these important years."

But at age seventeen, Ruth was on her way to America and to Wheaton College, where she would major in Bible and minor in art. Bible has always been a strong subject for Ruth. Her husband still considers her to be a better Bible student than he is.

Ruth didn't consider Wheaton College as spiritual a school as she needed and wanted to transfer to Prairie Bible Institute in Canada. Her father's blunt response was, "As long as I pay the bills, you go where I send you."

She stayed. Actually, after she met Bill (she never called him Billy), she was troubled because he seemed to be so serious. She liked the fact that "he knows where he is going," but he didn't seem to have fun doing it. "Every date we had was to a preaching service of some kind. He didn't have enough time to go to ball games." The first time she heard him preach, she wasn't impressed. His wild gestures embarrassed her, and he preached so loudly. *How am I ever going to sit through all this?* she asked herself.

When they were together, having recently been jilted by the girl in Florida, Billy guarded his emotions. Ruth interpreted this as coolness or even disinterest. Yet she knew that he had practically been engaged to one girl and had dated several others. She wondered if he could manage to maintain a relationship longer than a month or two. Opening her Bible at random to Proverbs, she discovered a Scripture verse which reinforced her misgivings. The verse said, "Meddle not with them that are given to change."

But Ruth kept meddling with him anyway. The biggest snag in the relationship was her commitment to return to Tibet as a missionary. She confided in her sister Rosa, who was also a student at Wheaton. Rosa advised her frankly: "You think the Lord is leading you to Tibet, but maybe He might have led you here to meet Billy."

Ruth still wasn't convinced. Even after she and Billy were engaged in the summer of 1941, she had second thoughts. She tried to persuade Bill to go to Tibet with her. He promised to pray about it, but he returned, telling her that he "just had no leading whatsoever" about going to Tibet. Finally, Billy put it this way: "If you believe that God has brought us together and if you believe that the husband is the head of the wife, then if the Lord is leading me, it's up to you to follow."

About the time that Ruth was finally convinced, Billy had some problems of his own. Ruth's father was a missionary with the Southern Presbyterian Church, a denomination Billy regarded as liberal. How could Dr. Bell be in the will of God and stay in such a denomination? Ruth was incensed that Billy doubted her father's spiritual consecration. Once again the engagement seemed tenuous. (Years later, Billy acknowledged that Ruth and her father were the greatest influences in making his ministry more church-centered.)

Ruth continued to have her doubts, but finally agreed to his proposal of marriage. Billy recalls, "She said she still wasn't sure that she loved me, but she felt led of the Lord that it was God's will for her life." Billy and Ruth were married at Montreat, the Presbyterian conference center in the mountains of North Carolina, in August 1943, two months after his graduation from college.

Biographer John Pollock aptly summarizes Ruth's contribution to Billy this way: "Ruth more than anyone broadened Billy's mind. She had no need to polish his manners or graces, as D. L. Moody's were polished by his wife, but she was cultured, traveled, with a love of art and literature. She saved his seriousness from degenerating into stuffy solemnity, and preserved from extinction the light touch, the slice of small boy. Moreover, Ruth and her family, loyal Presbyterians, eased Billy Graham from his outspoken conviction that a vigorous Scriptural faith could not dwell within the great denominations."

Another biographer, Stanley High, says, "It is her common sense and household-fashioned wit that help him, when in the clouds, not to get lost there; her unawed attitude is a safeguard, for him, against idiosyncrasies, pontifications, and most of all the sin of pride."

The adjustment to married life was not easy for either of them. Years later Billy admitted in an article in *McCall's* magazine, "We did have a difficult time adjusting to this new life and to each other."

Part of Ruth's problem was the transition from a campus life with literature, art, and Bible courses that she loved to the life of a home-maker with household chores. She made no claim to being a skilled cook, except perhaps of Chinese dishes "cooked with plenty of garlic, and Billy didn't care for garlic."

Then there was dishwashing. "I don't like dishwashing. There's no future in it, nothing creative," Ruth says. In high school someone had given her a small plaque which read, "Praise and Pray and Peg Away." She hung it over the sink, where it still is today.

Of course, there were other adjustment problems. She didn't see why Billy always left his desk so cluttered or why he couldn't break the habit of throwing used towels over the top of the bathroom door.

But those were the little irritations that vex every marriage. Billy acknowledges, "We had come from different backgrounds, and suddenly we were on our own. It was hard, and not just because of our different temperaments."

Ruth recalls those early days of marriage and says, "Happy marriages are never accidental. They are the result of good hard work."

And at times they did have to work hard at it. After their honeymoon, they returned to Western Springs, Illinois, west of Chicago, where Billy had just accepted the call to become the pastor of the local Baptist church. That was a problem for two reasons: first, Ruth had never been consulted on the decision, and second, Ruth was a Presbyterian. Ruth was annoyed that Billy would make such a decision unilaterally.

At first, it wasn't easy for Billy to counsel with Ruth on decisions, but as he grew to appreciate her wisdom, he did it naturally. After the first five years of married life, Billy made few significant decisions without getting Ruth's insight on them. She was the one who suggested the name for his radio broadcast, "The Hour of Decision." She was the one who urged him to go full-time into an evangelistic ministry. She was the one who did the major research for his first best-seller, *Peace with God*. And when the Billy Graham Evangelistic Association was formed,

Billy wanted Ruth to be on the five-member board of directors with him (and she consented).

However, the bigger problem in Western Springs was that the new pastor at the Baptist church had a wife who was a Presbyterian and refused to become a Baptist. It wasn't that she didn't consider it. She studied the Scriptures, but they didn't convince her that she needed to be rebaptized by immersion.

The situation was helped when the church leaders changed the name of the church to the Village Church, feeling it would have a wider appeal. Among other advantages, the change relieved Ruth of having to change denominations.

During the early days of their marriage, Billy was introduced to a widening circle of friends. Youth for Christ was just beginning and Billy felt privileged to be on the inside of this exciting evangelistic movement. A new radio program called "Songs in the Night," featuring a bass-baritone soloist named George Beverly Shea, was now being broadcast from Billy's church. Ruth helped write the weekly scripts.

Always full of ideas, Billy loved to discuss them with other ministers. While he was discussing and discoursing, Ruth was left alone in their upstairs apartment in Western Springs. It was another problem in their young marriage. Ruth didn't enjoy being taken for granted, and she told him so.

As Youth for Christ rallies spread across the country, so did Billy Graham's ministry. Traveling had always fascinated him, and the opportunity to win souls for Christ could not be refused. But it meant being away from home three-fourths of the time.

For Ruth, living in an apartment in a Chicago suburb far away from family and being separated from her husband of less than two years were not easy adjustments.

She recognized that God had given her husband the gift of evangelism, and that in itself would necessitate their being apart for long periods of time. She also recognized that Billy had a hard time saying no to any invitation to speak. And she couldn't do much about that just then, either.

Not being able to change his situation, she decided to change her own. She "simply packed her bags," and moved down to North Carolina where her parents, now home from China, were living. "I realized that it was going to be like this from now on," she explains, "and that he was going to be gone most of the time. In a case like ours, I believe the family is the Lord's business, but a husband should have his wife settled where she's going to be happy."

Living near her parents made it easier on Ruth, but for the girl who had aspired to a lifetime in isolated Tibet, loneliness seemed part of the divine game plan.

Billy says, "My wife and I have both had to be dedicated on this point—and Ruth has great gifts for it." She keeps a stiff upper lip and tries not to acknowledge pain of any kind—emotional or physical. She says of the frequent separations from Billy: "You get used to it. You keep busy. The best thing for any of us is keeping busy."

Speaking of her earlier desire to be a missionary to Tibet, Ruth wrote in *Ladies Home Journal*: "I think that the Lord must have given me that intense longing for a purpose, so that I could have the understanding and the sense of fulfillment that I receive now from Bill's work. I knew from the very beginning that I wouldn't be in first place in his life. Christ would be first. Knowing that, accepting that, solves an awful lot of problems right there. So I can watch him go with no regrets, and wait for him joyfully."

But when they have been together, Billy and Ruth have shared much and have contributed much to each other's lives.

Their children (Virginia, born 1945; Anne, born 1948; Ruth [nicknamed "Bunny"], born 1950; William Franklin, born 1952; and Nelson Edman, born 1958) made it difficult for Ruth to travel frequently with her husband even when his ministry had grown to such proportions that traveling was affordable.

Grandparents helped in the raising of the children, but Ruth, of course, missed having Billy around for many reasons. Much of the disciplining was left to her ("I played them like a xylophone," she says). And the young children did not provide the mental stimulation that Ruth's active mind craved. "There's nothing greatly stimulating about wiping noses or cleaning muddy shoes and the dirt they leave. A mother just must realize that God put her there."

As a homemaker in Montreat, North Carolina, she handled the family finances, did the carpentry (although she insists that her husband could hit a nail with a hammer if he put his mind to it), and even supervised the building of their new home when the first one became too much of a tourist attraction.

In the home, Ruth still keeps a Bible open on a special desk. "When Bill is away, I'm likely to have the Book open to Proverbs. It's got more practical help in it than ten books on child psychology."

Here are some principles of her home drawn from Proverbs: "Put happiness in the home before neatness. . . . In discipline be firm but patient. . . . Teach that right means behaving as well as believing."

Frequently Billy's letters stated, "If you were only here, I could talk over my sermon with you." He always knew he could get an honest evaluation from Ruth; he missed her perceptive insight.

On long crusades, Ruth tried to be with him at least one week of the meetings. But she never wanted to leave her children for long periods. "A mother, like the Lord, needs to be a very present help in time of trouble."

One time that Ruth did accompany Billy, however, was to Great Britain in 1954. It was Billy's second trip there, and he had toned down his Youth for Christ wardrobe, which had been characterized by bright socks and ties. Remembering what he had learned from his prior experience in England, he suggested to Ruth that she might not want to wear lipstick because most church people in London did not.

Ruth didn't readily accept the suggestion: "Don't you think that may be something on which the Lord expects us to help their understanding?"

In her diary Ruth recorded the incident: "Bill stooped from being a man of God to become a meddlesome husband and ordered my lipstick off. There was a lively argument—then I wiped it off. He got so busy getting the bags together I managed to put more on without notice." Later Ruth explained, "It doesn't seem to me to be a credit to Christ to be drab."

The British Crusades in 1954 and 1955 were monumental. At Wembley, despite almost continual rain, crowds of 50,000 to 80,000 gathered each night to hear the American evangelist.

More unnerving than the huge crowds, however, were the invitations to be guests of royalty. Ruth wrote home, "You should have heard all the titles and seen all the jewels and decorations—and me in a homemade number with zipper trouble." When they were invited to meet the Queen Mother, Ruth wrote a play-by-play description of the scene to her parents: "Our little tan Ford drove up to the gate at 11:45. . . . We all went to a side room where we talked about golf and the Cockrell-Marciano fight. Then suddenly the door opened: 'Her Majesty the Queen Mother will receive Dr. and Mrs. Graham.' . . . The Queen Mother came toward us with her hand outstretched, and I didn't know whether to curtsy first and shake hands later or shake hands first and then curtsy. I don't know which I did. Bill—the merciless wretch—said it looked as though I'd tripped over the rug."

During the London Crusade, Ruth wrote home, "I am the world's worst soul-winner," but night after night she was counseling those who came forward for salvation. One of those to whom she witnessed was British movie star Joan Winmill, who later said, "I didn't know then she was Mrs. Billy Graham. But the first thought that came to my mind when I saw her was how much sooner people like me might have been attracted to Christianity if we had met a few such attractive Christians."

Meanwhile, back in North Carolina, friends had been gathering funds to help the Grahams build a new home. Tourists had been overrunning their yard at the house on Assembly Drive. Sick at home one day, Ruth looked up to see a face pressed against the bedroom window.

Ruth immediately went to work on the planning of the new home. According to biographer John Pollock, "She scoured the mountains, buying old timber from disused cabins and brick from an ancient schoolhouse to build a place which fitted exactly into his background. Soon it looked a hundred years old, even to the split-rail fences."

Ever since 1955, this mountainside home has been a haven for Billy. Ruth describes it as "a kind of eagle's nest." Over the years a succession of loyal, faithful helpers have assisted the Grahams around the house and with the children. Each one has been special to the family and has contributed greatly to the children's development. With five children and an assortment of pets, Ruth used to describe it as "a Noah's ark of happy confusion."

But living in a mountain retreat didn't make the times of separation from Billy any easier. In the early years of marriage she sometimes went to bed with his "old, rough sports coat," because she missed him so much. The fact that she has had few close friends apart from her own parents may have aggravated the situation. Her daughter Bunny says, "I don't know if you can say Mother has a close friend. She doesn't confide in friends that much. Really, the Lord is her best friend."

As Billy Graham became a national figure, presidents courted his favor, his counsel, and sometimes his influence with voters. Ruth has always cautioned her husband against political involvement. Once, in 1964, she and Billy were invited to the White House to be guests of President Lyndon Johnson. At the dinner table LBJ asked Billy who he thought would make a good vice-presidential running mate for him in the forthcoming campaign.

Under the table, Ruth dug her shoes into Billy's shins, her way of reminding him to stay away from politics.

Billy, who always has delighted in teasing his wife, asked her with seeming innocence, "Why did you kick me?" She wasted no time in answering: "You're supposed to give advice only on spiritual matters."

For the moment, that ended the discussion, but as soon as Lady Bird escorted Ruth out of the room, LBJ asked the evangelist, "Now that they've gone, what do you really think?"

But away from the limelight of the crusades and the dinners with presidents and royalty, Billy and Ruth had concerns about their children. Billy realized that his children were having problems in growing up with an absentee father, and certain things in his personality made it hard to develop a closeness with his children.

Ruth prayed about it, then asked Bill to let her administer discipline in his absence, rather than letting it pile up for him to handle on his return. Otherwise, the children would grow to dread their father's coming home. Subsequently, there has always been mutual love and companionship.

It was their fourth child and eldest son who had special problems in growing up. "He was into everything you can think of," admits Billy.

His lifestyle was a concern to the parents, but they tried not to allow it to break their relationship with him. Eventually, the son returned to the Lord and became involved in Christian ministry himself.

But looking back on the darker days, Billy recalls, "During that time, we would hug each other when we met. You need to keep their love at any cost. Because when they come through it, they'll still have that there. When it was over with Franklin, there was no relationship to reestablish; it had been there all along."

The relationship between Billy and Ruth has grown stronger through the years. Daughter Bunny says that she has never heard a harsh word between them.

Ruth explains casually, "During the years, we really haven't had a chance to get tired of each other. So I think we'll just hang in there a little longer."

Teasing and kidding are a part of their sharing, but another part of it consists of serious discussions. Now that the children are grown, Ruth has more time than ever for reading as well as for poetry, painting, and sewing—all of which she enjoys. Over the years she read the writings of Dostoevski and Tolstoy and their biographies because she especially enjoyed these writers. They stretched her mind and gave her a new appreciation of history.

Billy enjoys her input. His sermon illustrations sometimes are derived from books that Ruth has shared with him. "You know how well-read Ruth is," he once said; "she seems to know everything about everything"—a remarkable accolade for a husband to give his wife.

Always polite, even to Ruth, Billy has grown in his ability to show his care and interest. "For some reason," Billy's sister says, "the older he's gotten, the freer and more expressive his body language has become." Other family members have noticed it, too. One said, "He used to just shake hands when he'd see me or another member of his family. But now he'll throw those long arms around us and just hug us."

As they have grown older, Billy and Ruth have each shown increasing concern for the other's health. Once when Billy was away on a crusade, Ruth had a small therapeutic pool built at the back of the house. When he returned, he was unhappy with the extravagance. All she said was, "It's cheaper than a funeral," and she walked away.

Both remain active people. In her book *Special People*, Julie Nixon Eisenhower asks with some degree of amazement, "How many other grandmothers take up hang-gliding in their fifties?" Ruth did. And the first time she jumped from a steep bank, she hit the ground hard. Later she fell out of a tree when she was putting up a swing for her grandchildren, resulting in injuries so severe that it was a week before she regained consciousness. Julie continued, "And how many grandmothers borrow their son's black leather jacket and go vrooming along mountain roads on a Harley-Davidson?"

Ruth smiles about her adventures and says, "There's no fool like an old fool."

Obviously Ruth is no stereotype of an evangelist's wife. Her view of marriage is not a chain of command in which the wife is directly under the husband, but rather a triangle with God at the top, and the husband and wife at the bottom. The husband, she says, "has certain responsibilities and final authority, but marriage is best characterized by mutual submission, not merely the submission of the wife to the husband."

Billy's view is not quite the same. Quoting the verse in Genesis, "He shall rule over thee," Billy says that injunction "has never changed. . . . The wife is to fit into the world of the husband."

In the Graham marriage you see both views from time to time. Ruth has certainly fit into the world of her husband, and she has been content with that. But Ruth's individuality is unflappable, and mutual submission is prominent in the household.

They've come from two different worlds; they live in two different worlds, but together they have built a strong relationship that has brought blessing to the world.

Billy's active life takes him to the masses. Ruth says, "I have an antipathy for platforms." She prefers books, and often keeps four with her: "One book to stimulate me. One book to relax me. One book for information and one book for conversation." And then Ruth says, "And I love nature. I just love to hear the wind in the trees. I love to hear birds. And mostly, I just love to listen to silence."

Ruth was asked to give advice to a young woman about to be married. Said Ruth: "Don't expect your husband to be what only Jesus can be. Don't expect him to give you the security, the joy, the peace, the love that only God Himself can give you."

Bibliography

Eisenhower, Julie Nixon. *Special People*. New York: Simon and Schuster, 1979.
High, Stanley. *Billy Graham*. New York: McGraw-Hill, 1956.
Pollock, John. *Billy Graham*. New York: McGraw-Hill, 1966.
————. *A Foreign Devil in China*. Grand Rapids: Zondervan, 1971.

19

I Must Venture All with God

John Bunyan and His Two Wives

John Bunyan, a seventeenth-century English Baptist, is best known for his classic allegory, *The Pilgrim's Progress,* which has outsold every Christian book except the Bible and has been translated into scores of languages. Unfortunately, not too many people know of its sequel, which tells of the pilgrimage of the pilgrim's wife.

But that is to be expected. After all, not too many people know about Elizabeth Bunyan either. And that's a pity, for her influence on the famous author was great. And the story of their marriage is a tale as engaging as anything Bunyan wrote.

As far as his married life was concerned, John Bunyan was a pilgrim who made progress. But, admittedly, a lot of progress needed to be made.

His married life—and he was married twice—was not a continual Celestial City. In fact, it started in a Slough of Despond and wallowed at times in a Valley of Humiliation.

John was one of those husbands who was never home. During the first thirteen years of married life with Elizabeth (his second wife), John was home for less than two years. Most of the time he spent in the county jail, not a very good way to maintain a marriage.

Yet the marriage turned out well, and was certainly far more happy than his first marriage.

It is not surprising that his first marriage was not particularly happy, for there was little in his upbringing that gave promise that he would amount to much. His father was a tinker who pushed his noisy cart along Bedfordshire's dusty roads and banged his kettle in front of prospective customers' doors. He was illiterate, his vocabulary pock-marked with curse words.

John called his father's house "the meanest and most despised of all families in the land," which was probably a slight exaggeration. It was a little thatched-roof cottage on the outskirts of the half-timbered hamlet of Elstow, a mile south of Bedford.

It was probably his mother who encouraged him to trudge to school at Bedford, where he learned "to read and write according to the rate of other poor men's children." But then his father called upon him to learn the tinkering trade and to help put food on the table for the family. John says he "almost utterly" forgot all he had learned in his school primer.

An active child, an English version of Huck Finn, he was addicted to athletics and curious about nature. His mother seemed delighted with his questioning mind. Then when he was fifteen his mother died. She was only forty. For the sensitive teenager, it was a crushing loss. A month later, perhaps from the same epidemic, his sister suddenly passed away. Only a year younger than John, Margaret had been his closest playmate and his best friend.

Less than a month later, John's father remarried. For John, a sensitive boy still grief-stricken by the sudden deaths of his mother and sister, the sudden marriage must have cut like a knife.

He tried not to let his hurt show. He swore more and didn't let anyone know that he was crying on the inside. And three months later, on the day he turned sixteen and became eligible to join the army, he became a soldier.

It was the time of England's Civil War, with the Parliamentary army and its rising star, Oliver Cromwell. John Bunyan never said what side he fought on, and his biographers have debated the issue ever since. But probably he was in the Parliamentary army, since the residents of

Bedfordshire were anti-Royalist. (Two years earlier they had petitioned the king, "Many are the miseries your subjects suffer and our fears are beyond our miseries.")

No doubt John took part in a couple of small skirmishes, although one that he didn't take part in was the one he remembered the longest. "When I was just ready to go, one of the company desired to go in my room. . . . He took my place, and coming to the siege, as he stood sentinel, he was shot in the head with a musket bullet and died." He later felt he had been preserved by God's providence.

In 1647, after thirty-two months of military duty, he returned to Elstow and became an apprentice tinker. Unhappy living in the same house with his stepmother, John wanted to move out. And the best way to do that was to get married.

Very little is known about his first wife. She was not a local girl. John may have met her when he was in the army, but more possibly he met her when he began his travels from town to town as a tinker. Because their first daughter was named Mary, biographers conclude that her first name may also have been Mary.

Basically, three things are known about Mary: She was just as poor as John was, if not poorer; she had a very religious father from whom she inherited two religious books; and she had a tendency to nag.

"We came together," recalls John, "as poor as poor might be, not having so much household stuff as a dish or spoon betwixt us both."

Her father, whom she idolized, had recently died. John could sincerely sympathize with Mary. He knew what it was to grieve over a departed parent. Perhaps that, more than anything else, is what attracted Mary to John. She needed sympathy and a masculine image in her life. John could provide both. On John's part, he needed someone to care for, a bird with a broken wing, someone who would look up to him.

Married at nineteen, John was one part little boy, one part rebellious adolescent, and one part big man.

But it didn't take Mary long to realize that John wasn't the spitting image of her father. She wanted to remake him, to reprogram him. "She would often tell me what a godly man her father was, and how he would reprove and correct vice, both in his house and amongst his neighbors; what a strict and holy life he lived in his day, both in word and deed."

John tried to be as virtuous as her father had been. He read to her—because she herself couldn't read—the two religious books her father had bequeathed her, *The Plain Man's Pathway to Heaven* and *The Practice of Piety.* He also became a good churchman.

"I fell in very eagerly with the religious practices of the times, to wit, to go to church twice a day . . . and there very devoutly both say and sing as others did, yet retaining my wicked life."

His wicked life consisted of his addiction to swearing and to Sunday sports. Neither of these bothered him until he read in one of his wife's books that swearing is "an evident demonstration of a reprobate" and until his minister preached one Sunday morning on the ungodliness of Sabbath amusements.

That afternoon John went out to play his usual Sunday afternoon game of tipcat (an early form of baseball) on the village green. As John took his turn at bat, "a voice did suddenly dart from heaven into my soul, which said, 'Wilt thou leave thy sins and go to Heaven, or have thy sins and go to Hell?'"

John stopped, looked up to heaven, and thought he saw Jesus looking down in displeasure on him. At first, he was stunned. But then, reckoning it was too late for him to change his ways, he picked up his bat again and returned to the game. "I resolved . . . to go on in sin. . . . I had as good be damned for many sins, as to be damned for few."

So John decided "to take my fill of sin, still studying what sin was yet to be committed, that I might taste the sweetness of it."

The sin in which John was most proficient was cursing, a habit picked up from his father. "One day as I was standing at a neighbor's shop window and there cursing and swearing, . . . there sat within the woman of the house, and heard me, who though she was a very loose and ungodly wretch, yet protested that I swore and cursed at that most fearful rate, that she was made to tremble to hear me."

He says that he hung his head "and wished with all my heart that I might be a little child again" and learn to speak without swearing.

John did make an attempt at reform. Now twenty-one, he had just become a father for the first time, and little Mary had been born blind.

John was deeply affected. He began to take life more seriously again. He did quite well at clearing up his speech. In fact, as he recalled, "I fell to some outward reformation."

His neighbors were impressed. "I loved to be talked of as one that was truly godly," he says, but "I was nothing but a poor painted hypocrite."

One day as he was peddling his wares through the streets of Bedford, he noticed "three or four poor women sitting . . . talking about the things of God." John, who was now priding himself on his new religious image, began chatting with them about his new hobby, religion, but when they referred to a new birth and the work of God in their hearts, John didn't know what they were talking about. Yet he saw that they had a contentment that he had never possessed.

He began attending the Baptist meeting in Bedford where these humble women went. "I could not stay away; and the more I went, the more I did question my condition."

John struggled. He felt there was a well that he could not get through. He wondered if the day of grace had passed for him or if he was not among the elect. He could not imagine that God loved him.

His sinfulness loomed like a monster over him. "I was more loathsome in my own eyes than was a toad. . . . I fell deeply into despair."

The pastor of the church, John Gifford, tried to help him, but Bunyan wallowed in his Slough of Despond. He would have times of spiritual insight into God's mercy, but then he would fall back into depression.

One Sunday, Gifford spoke on a text from the Song of Solomon: "Behold, thou art . . . my love." The text stuck with John. The next morning he felt like telling the verse "to the very crows that eat upon the plowed lands before me."

Then came another low period. "All my comfort was taken from me; darkness seized upon me, after which whole floods of blasphemies, both against God, Christ and the Scriptures, were poured upon my spirit, to my great confusion and astonishment." John thought he must be possessed of the devil or else crazy. Every time he thought of God, some blasphemous thought would come into his mind.

Pastor Gifford suggested that he read Martin Luther's commentary on Galatians. As John began reading, he was amazed. Luther seemed to have written the commentary directly to him. "This made me marvel," he said. Luther too had faced enormous temptations from Satan and had struggled with blasphemies.

It was a turning point for Bunyan.

He still had his ups and downs, but gradually Scripture, Luther's commentary, and Pastor Gifford's patient counsel began to bear fruit. "Mr. Gifford's doctrine was much for my stability," wrote John.

And then there were the Bible verses that kept coming into his mind as he plodded the streets. Sometimes they were a bit jumbled, and when he returned home, he couldn't find them in his Bible, but they gave him much to meditate on. "My grace is sufficient for thee. . . . Thy righteousness is in heaven. . . . Jesus Christ is my righteousness. . . . I will never leave thee nor forsake thee. . . . Him that cometh to me I will in no wise cast out."

Though his wife knew her Bible fairly well, she wasn't much help to John in his spiritual wrestling. The Church of England, the established church, had been good enough for her father; why wasn't it good enough for John?

It is significant that *The Pilgrim's Progress* begins with Christian expressing his spiritual concerns to his family. In response, his wife and relatives tell him to go to bed, get a good night's sleep, and perhaps he will feel better in the morning. No doubt the same thing had happened in the Bunyan household.

In *The Pilgrim's Progress,* when Christian continued to talk with his family about his struggles, "sometimes they would deride, and sometimes they would chide, and sometimes they would quite neglect him. Wherefore he began to retire himself to his chamber to pray for and pity them, and also to condole his own misery; he would also walk solitarily in the fields, sometimes reading, and sometimes praying, and thus for some days he spent his time." That was probably autobiographical as well.

Undoubtedly, John and Mary cared deeply for each other, but they weren't on the same wavelength during John's spiritual struggles. Mary simply couldn't understand what all the fuss was about.

Besides, Mary had problems of her own. Not only was she experiencing a difficult second pregnancy, but Mary, their blind daughter, was toddling now. That made life nerve-wracking.

For most of the past two years, John, now twenty-four, had been preoccupied with his sinful state. He had been walking to the Baptist church in Bedford every Sunday, while his wife and daughter continued to attend the Anglican church in Elstow where they lived.

Eventually, however, Mary's anguish broke through to him. She was in great pain; in fact, he feared that her life was in danger. He tells about it in *Grace Abounding*: "Her pangs . . . were fierce and strong upon her, even as if she would immediately have fallen in labor."

At the time John was questioning whether God existed, and, if he did, whether he cared for John and realized the turmoil he was now undergoing. As his wife lay groaning in pain, John prayed, "Lord, if thou wilt now remove this sad affliction from my wife, and cause her to be troubled no more this night, then I shall know that thou canst discern the secret thoughts of my heart."

No sooner had the prayer gone through his mind than Mary's pains were eased and she fell into a deep sleep. Once again John was assured that God existed and that he cared.

"At this time also," John writes, "I saw more in those words 'heirs of God' than ever I shall be able to express while I live in this world." Gradually he was getting his spiritual equilibrium.

By the time the second child, Elizabeth, was born in 1654, John had been baptized into the Baptist church in Bedford. Later the family moved to Bedford.

Why the Bunyans moved from Elstow to a small house on St. Cuthbert Street in Bedford in 1655 is not certain. John's business had been growing despite his personal turmoils, and Bedford would certainly have provided more opportunity for growth than Elstow. But John's move was probably prompted by spiritual concerns. No doubt he thought that by living in Bedford, Mary and the children might be influenced by John Gifford's preaching. Besides that, he himself had been spending an increasing amount of time counseling with Pastor Gifford, who had much to teach him, and a move would make such meetings easier. In addition, and John couldn't understand why, the church was calling on him to take more responsibility, including preaching on occasion.

It was quite a novelty to hear a tinker preach, so crowds flocked whenever a meeting was announced.

Though he was a lay preacher, some of his nagging temptations clung to him. He was sometimes tempted to pour out blasphemies in the middle of a sermon. But he had many other things besides spiritual concerns to occupy his mind.

Two sons—John and Thomas—were born during those busy years. And it may have been shortly after Thomas was born that John's wife became ill and died. The exact time or cause of her death is unknown, but since it is known that she had difficulty with her pregnancies, it is probable that after her fourth child she was too weak to withstand infection.

Mary's death left John with four small children, ranging from Mary, the blind daughter who was now eight, to Thomas, still a babe-in-arms.

The congregation, closely knit and caring, assisted John with his family. Doubtless they also let him know that it was his duty to find a wife without too much delay.

John describes himself as "shy" toward women. In fact, he says that he did not allow himself to "so much as touch a woman's hand." John never denied his vices, but being overly bold to the opposite sex was not one of them.

One of the younger church members to babysit for John was Elizabeth, still a teenager herself. There were several things about Elizabeth that interested John: She was a believer, she handled his children well, and, though she was young, she enjoyed talking with him about spiritual matters.

When John Bunyan married Elizabeth, she was only sixteen or seventeen. John was thirty-one. The wedding, simple as it was, took place late in 1659. That was also the year of the crackdown, the year when Englishmen were ordered to worship only in the Church of England, the established church; all other religious services were illegal. (Non-Anglican Protestants were known as Dissenters or Nonconformists.)

John Bunyan had already seen turbulent times. In 1658 his first wife had died; so had Oliver Cromwell, England's Lord Protector. Cromwell had extended toleration for Nonconformists, and when he died, it signaled the end of religious freedom for Baptists like John Bunyan. So the prospects for 1659 didn't look good. England was preparing for the return of a Stuart king, Charles II, to the throne. And the Stuarts had been notoriously hostile to Nonconformists.

But the bright spot in 1659, which made the year glow for the Bedford tinker, was Elizabeth.

Elizabeth was young, but she wasn't stupid. As a member of the Baptist church, she must have known what the probabilities were for her as the wife of a tinker who moonlighted as a Baptist preacher. And she knew what kind of man she was marrying.

Outwardly, he was a rather typical working-class Englishman. A contemporary describes him as "tall of stature, strong-boned though not corpulent, somewhat of a ruddy face with sparkling eyes, wearing his hair on his upper lip after the old English fashion; his hair reddish . . . his nose well set . . . and his mouth moderately large."

Yet inwardly, he was far from typical—and far from being well-adjusted. At times he was morbidly introspective. He was extremely sensitive because his mind was so burdened with fears and guilt. And he was a preacher associated with an outlawed religion.

She was, apparently, well prepared to be the wife of a man whose work kept him away from home. During the week, he carried a heavy anvil on his back, traveling to nearby villages and hamlets, mending pots, pans, and lanterns, and occasionally selling one as well. When he came home at night, he was weary.

On weekends he was on call as a lay preacher, even though it had now become illegal to preach to more than five people at a time, except in the established church. For John, weekends brought an exciting change of pace; for teenaged Elizabeth, weekends meant being alone with her four stepchildren in the two-room cottage they called home.

Despite the hardships, the first year of marriage was a happy one. He enjoyed sharing spiritual matters with his wife, and he was relieved to have found a good mother for his children.

But the following year was different. The Baptists in Bedford lost their minister by death and their property by confiscation, and it looked as if they would lose a lot more if Judge Francis Wingate had anything to do with it. (Apparently Judge Wingate had lost part of his estate when Oliver Cromwell was in power, and he seemed eager for revenge upon any Cromwell sympathizers.)

John was aware that his movements, especially on Sunday, were being watched. "I saw what was a-coming," he wrote.

On November 12, 1660, he was asked to preach in a house in Lower Samsell, about twelve miles from Bedford. Judge Wingate found out about it and issued a warrant for Bunyan's arrest.

"I could have escaped," John said, "and kept out of his hands." In fact, some of his friends had suggested that the meeting be canceled or at least that Bunyan flee before the constable came.

For John, the decision wasn't easy. He had been telling congregations to be strong even in persecution. If he should run away and play the coward, how would other Christians respond?

Yet at the same time John knew that imprisonment would mean separation from his young wife. "I was a man pulling down his house upon the head of his wife and children." After wrestling with all the options, he concluded, "I must do it, I must do it." So he walked to the front of his small congregation and opened the meeting in prayer.

That was as far as John got. The constable entered and placed him under arrest.

John was taken to the Bedford jail, and Elizabeth, who was pregnant at the time, was so shocked by the event that she had a miscarriage. After one year of marriage, she was left as a virtual widow with four children.

John's imprisonment was to last for three months. At the end of that time, he was to be released if he agreed to conform to the laws of the land. If he wouldn't conform, harsher punishment would be exacted. John feared hanging, but deportation was also a possibility.

Elizabeth and his children visited him every day. According to one tradition, his blind daughter brought him a jug of soup daily.

John agonized over whether he should continue to preach. Family visits did not make his decision any easier. Every time Elizabeth and the children closed the cell door and left him behind in prison, he agonized more. But how could he stop preaching?

375

He wrote, "The parting with my wife and poor children has often been to me in this place as the pulling of my flesh from my bones. . . . But yet I must venture all with God."

So when his first three months were completed, John refused to agree to stop preaching, and as a result he was imprisoned indefinitely. He had no desire to be a martyr—his family meant too much to him— but what choice did he have? He felt compelled to preach the Word of God.

A few weeks later the new king, Charles II, was crowned. In honor of the occasion, it was announced that hundreds of prisoners throughout England would be released.

As soon as the news got to Bedford, Elizabeth made plans to go to London to make an appeal for her husband. Still a teenager, she probably had never been to London before, but that didn't seem to daunt her. In London she presented her petition to the Earl of Bedford, asking for her husband's release. In turn, he brought the matter to the House of Lords, which quickly passed the buck to the Judges of Assize, who were scheduled to meet in Bedford later in the summer.

She must have grown impatient waiting for her chance to petition the judges. She had no knowledge of proper protocol, but she had heard that one of the judges, Matthew Hale, was known to be more lenient in his attitudes toward Nonconformists.

Hesitantly, she approached him. He answered that he was afraid he couldn't help her, although he would see if anything were possible.

The next day, she tried another angle, presenting her petition to a different judge as he rode by her in his coach. His response was cold and direct: John Bunyan had been convicted of a crime and could not be released until he promised to stop preaching.

Each rejection made Elizabeth more desperate in her attempts. She was just about ready to give up when a sheriff encouraged her to try one more time. The judges were scheduled to meet in the Swan Chamber of Bedford along with several other justices and leading gentry of the area. It would be her last chance.

She entered, she said, "with trembling heart." At first, she addressed Judge Hale, who she thought might be willing to listen to her. "My lord, I make bold to come once again to your lordship, to know what may be done with my husband." Hale answered that he couldn't do anything for John Bunyan. She tried to argue that her husband had been unlawfully convicted. But it was useless for a teenaged housewife to lecture judges about the law.

She told her story about how she had gone to London and had presented her petition to a member of the House of Lords and how he had told her that the judges would give it consideration. She begged them at least to consider the matter. They realized that she wouldn't be put off easily. One judge asked, "Will your husband stop preaching if he is released?"

They had not been married long, but Elizabeth knew what her husband's answer would be. "No," she answered. "He dare not, as long as he can speak."

"Then he is a peacebreaker."

"No, he is a peaceable man," she responded quickly. "He simply wants to pursue his calling so that he can feed and clothe his family." She paused and then began talking about the family. "My lord, I have four small children that cannot help themselves. One of them is blind. We have nothing to live on but the charity of good people."

"You have four children?" one judge asked incredulously. "You're too young to have four children."

She explained to the judges that she really was the stepmother to the children. Then she also added, "I was with child when my husband was arrested. . . . But I was so distressed at the news that I fell into labor and continued in labor for eight days. Then the baby was delivered, but it died."

It was a touching story, and a couple of the judges began to soften. Others said she was merely trying to sway them by pretending she was poverty-stricken. They charged that Bunyan made more money as a preacher than as a tinker.

When his occupation of tinker was mentioned, Elizabeth was defensive. "And because he is a tinker and a poor man, he is despised and cannot have justice."

They didn't answer her strong charge. Instead they pointed out again that if they released him, he would immediately start preaching again.

"He preaches nothing but the Word of God," Elizabeth interjected.

377

One of the justices scoffed, "He preaches the Word of God?" He moved toward her almost as if he were going to strike her.

Elizabeth took a step back and then begged them to send for her husband and let him answer for himself. "He can answer you better than I can. I've forgotten so many things."

During the entire time she had held up extremely well; finally she broke into tears. It was not, she says, "because they were so hardhearted against me and my husband, but to think what a sad account such poor creatures will have to give at the coming of the Lord."

Slowly, she moved out of the judicial chambers. Her efforts had been fruitless. But they were efforts that her husband would never forget.

For most of the next twelve years John was in jail. Biographer Ola Winslow writes, "The cruelest aspect of an imprisonment like Bunyan's was that it made an entire family destitute. The friends of the Bedford Meeting kept the Bunyan family out of a sense of religious duty, but the congregation was a poor one, and charity is a chancy sort of income; the hardships must have been considerable." To provide some income for his family, John made bootlaces in jail, but the income it provided was meager indeed. He also preached to the other prisoners and managed to write ten works, including his autobiographical *Grace Abounding*.

Released finally in 1672 under Charles II's Declaration of Indulgence (a general pardon for religious prisoners), John became pastor of the local church. He was now forty-three and Elizabeth was nearly thirty. He opened up his tinker's shop again because "his temporal affairs had gone to wreck," but more and more he was in demand as a preacher. He was playfully called "Bishop Bunyan," and his stand for principle had made him a folk hero throughout England's Midlands.

Four years later, his preaching got him into trouble again. He was returned to prison for six months. But what an eventful imprisonment that was! During that time he wrote much of *The Pilgrim's Progress*, which was published two years later and which made him a household name throughout the country. The two parts of this classic show how much Bunyan had learned to appreciate women and marriage.

In his writings John doesn't speak much about his marriage, but as he grew older, women and children become increasingly more prominent in them. John's earlier works, including Part I of *The Pilgrim's Progress*, focus on men. In Part I, Christian leaves his wife and children behind. The women who are depicted in it are incidental characters. Though John's sense of humor peeks through repeatedly, Part I is still a grim journey, filled with ominous people and places like Doubting Castle and the Giant Despair, the Valley of Humiliation and Apollyon, and the Slough of Despond.

But in Part II, written about nine years later, Christian's wife begins her journey to the Celestial City, and it has been termed "a smiling journey." In it the Valley of the Shadow is passed in the daytime.

The focus is now on Christiana, who is modeled after Elizabeth. "Christiana is not a dream woman," writes Monica Furlong. She is "believable." She does not battle monsters and ogres. She meets fascinating people like Mrs. Bats-Eyes, Mrs. Light-Mind, and Madam Bubble.

Part I is mostly a solitary pilgrimage. Part II is a family walking tour. It may seem humdrum compared to Part I, but it is gracious and good-humored. Part I shows John's own spiritual struggles and answers the question *What must I do to be saved?* Part II shows Elizabeth's characteristics of determination, grace, and tenderness and answers the question *How do I grow as a Christian?*

At times there is a gaiety, almost a frivolity in Part II, although Christiana's journey is taken just as seriously as her husband's was previously. When John writes about women in Part II, there is more refinement, as if in his mind women were associated with refinement.

Perhaps it is not strange at all that John should treat women so sympathetically. The poor women of Bedford had played a key role in his conversion when they engaged him in spiritual conversation, and women continued to be prominent in the church when he served it as pastor. His mother and sister were noble figures in his early years, and Elizabeth had been a tower of strength for him during his imprisonment.

John taught that a wife "is to be subject to her husband, but she is not to be her husband's slave; she is his yoke-fellow, his flesh and bones. . . . The husband, if his wife is a believer, should so love her that their life together may preach the marriage of Christ to his Church."

379

John's marriage brought him much satisfaction. So did the forward movement of the Nonconformist congregations. As pastor of the Bedford church and as an evangelist throughout the Midlands (even in places as far away as London), John saw the numbers of Baptists grow rapidly. It was said that when he went to preach in London "if there was one day's notice, the meeting house was crowded to overflowing."

But when Charles II died in 1685, and his brother James II took the throne, Nonconformists like Bunyan experienced another reign of terror. Once again, non-Anglican worshipers were hauled off to jail, and Baptists and others took special precautions to keep their meeting places unknown. Places of meeting were changed every few weeks; sentinels were posted to give warning; hymns were no longer sung because congregational singing would attract attention; more services were held in the evening.

For John, it looked as if another prison stay was inevitable. So John transferred all his property to his "well-beloved wife, Elizabeth."

To avoid detection as he traveled he disguised himself, once pretending to be a professional wagon driver, wearing a smock and carrying a whip in his hand. Stopped by a constable who asked if he knew "that devil of a fellow Bunyan," John replied, "Know him? You might call him a devil if you knew him as well as I once did."

But the persecution under James was short-lived. After 1688, the year Bunyan died, the new rulers, William III and his wife Mary II, did their best to promote religious toleration. Had he lived longer, John would never again have faced the prospect of prison.

When John was almost sixty, he was asked by a young man to see if he could mend the relationship between him and his father in the town of Reading. Doubtless remembering the problems that he had had with his own father, John went out of his way to make the journey on horseback. On his return he was caught in a driving rainstorm. He caught a cold, began running a high fever, and a few days later he died.

Elizabeth, who had inherited John's entire estate (which was worth only forty-two pounds), died less than three years later. She was only forty-six.

It is difficult to assess Elizabeth's influence on John, but undoubtedly she played a major factor in his maturing. At the age of twenty,

John had not been a strong personality. As one biographer put it, Mary (his first wife) seemed to have the stronger personality because John "was not yet sure where he wanted to go." His "daily conduct was observed and measured by the recording angel at home and to his humiliation he found that the standards admired in Elstow seemed tawdry and contemptible in the eyes of his wife."

The apostle Paul speaks of the law as a schoolmaster that brings us to Christ. Mary functioned as the law for John, but it was Elizabeth who helped him to mature in the grace of God.

The character of his preaching and writing changed because of Elizabeth's influence. Previously he had preached "against man's sins and their fearful state because of them." But about the time of his marriage to Elizabeth, "I altered in my preaching" because "the Lord came in upon my own soul with some staid peace and comfort through Christ, for he did give me many sweet discoveries of his blessed grace." Just before he met Elizabeth, he published a tract called "A Few Sighs from Hell, or the Groans of a Damned Soul." His first sermon published after he met Elizabeth was on the text "Ye are not under the law, but under grace."

Of course, God was doing much in the heart of John Bunyan apart from Elizabeth's influence, but God's timing of bringing Elizabeth into John's life was remarkably effective. John found in her a strength and consistent support that he had not known before.

In his twenties, he may have been mentally disturbed. Certainly he was self-centered and morbid. But in his forties and fifties, he became a well-balanced man with humor and grace, purpose and confidence, and he was sought out for his wise counsel.

Too little is known of Elizabeth. But one thing is sure: When she came into John's life, heavenly music started playing, and even twelve years of separation, while he was in prison, couldn't put a stop to it.

Bibliography

Bunyan, John. *Grace Abounding to the Chief of Sinners.* London: J. M. Dent, 1930. Many other editions in print.

Coats, R. H. *John Bunyan*. London: Student Christian Movement, 1927.

Day, Richard Ellsworth. *So Pilgrim Rang the Bells*. Grand Rapids: Zondervan, 1955.

Froude, James Anthony. *Bunyan*. New York: Harper and Brothers, 1880.

Furlong, Monica. *Puritan's Progress*. New York: Coward, McCann, and Geoghgan, 1975.

Harrison, G. B. *John Bunyan*. New York: Doubleday, Foran, 1928.

Loane, Marcus L. *Makers of Religious Freedom*. Grand Rapids: Eerdmans, 1961.

Winslow, Ola E. *John Bunyan*. New York: Macmillan, 1961.

Alike? But Oh, So Different

"Do you like chocolate chip cookies?"

"My favorite."

"Mine too. What about yogurt?"

"Can't stand the stuff."

"I can't either."

Conversations like that during courtship days are commonplace as fellows and girls try to determine whether or not they will be compatible in a future marriage.

Sometimes the discussions get more serious.

"Do you like classical music?"

"Do you like to travel?"

And the most serious of all: "Do you like kids?"

After considerable sparring, the couple decides if it's worth it to continue the relationship. After all, if the two have nothing in common, the following decades of married life are going to be dull at best, but more likely hotly contested tussles.

Today, couples sometimes find that the few things they enjoyed together during courtship days are hardly strong enough to preserve their relationship later. An interest in the Beatles or Elvis Presley may have brought happiness during the time a couple was dating, but five years later, when little children are screaming for attention, the Beatles will have lost their relevance.

But no matter how many things a couple enjoys together, there are always differences. Often these differences can add zest to the marriage. Sometimes they add problems.

Look at Francis and Edith Schaeffer, or consider two musicians like Johann and Magdalena Bach, or read through the chapter on Jonathan and Sarah Edwards, or compare stubborn Adoniram with independent Ann Judson. In many ways, the husband and wife were similar, with similar backgrounds and similar interests.

But oh, how enjoyably different they were, and that is what made these three marriages so successful.

How can differences enhance rather than destroy a marriage? How can differences be built upon so that both individuals retain their unique personalities, gifts, and strengths? The four couples in this section will give you some insight into how they did it.

20

The Companionship
of Walking Together

Francis and Edith Schaeffer

He was born on the other side of the tracks; she was born on the other side of the world.

But they happened upon each other one Sunday evening as they both took exception to a young man speaking on the subject, "How I know that Jesus is not the Son of God."

Francis and Edith Schaeffer were a fascinating twosome. No doubt about that. And neither would have been complete without the other.

Their lives were full of surprises.

For instance, neither of them claimed to be a great evangelist; yet the people they led to Christ are scattered among every nation in the world.

Francis didn't boast great academic credentials, yet evangelicals today acclaim him as one of the greatest minds in the twentieth century.

Neither of them claimed to be great writers, yet the thirty books that Francis and Edith wrote have sold millions of copies.

Undoubtedly, the surprising Schaeffers have made an indelible mark on the latter half of the twentieth century.

They spent much of their adult life in a little out-of-the-way village in Switzerland that you can't find on most maps. Yet L'Abri became a household word to Christians around the world, and young people from every background found their way there.

Until they were in their fifties, the Schaeffers were little-known outside their small denomination. But from 1964 to 1984, the year Francis died of cancer, the Schaeffers were a major influence on evangelical thinking.

In some ways these two remarkable people were quite different. Francis had come from a working-class family in Philadelphia. Books were a rarity in this home, and Francis had every intention of making his living by the sweat of his brow as his father did. Edith was born in China to missionary parents. Her father was a seminary graduate who enjoyed Hebrew and Greek as well as the intricacies of the Chinese language.

But in other ways, they were quite alike. Neither of them, for instance, was afraid of speaking out or of trying to win an argument. Such similarities have broken up many marriages.

Why, then, did the Schaeffers' marriage work?

And why did it enrich both of their lives and the outside world as well?

Seventeen years old, just out of high school, and quite interested in boys—that was Edith Seville. In fact, when she thought that a very handsome young man was attending a certain Christian Endeavor group on Sunday evenings, she decided that she would go there too.

Later she found out that the young man didn't attend, but by that time she had made a few friends and had become part of the group.

Edith needed friends. Her family had moved to Philadelphia from Toronto only a few months before, and during her senior year in high school she felt very much an outsider. It was difficult for her in other ways too. She felt almost detached from reality. "I was feeling an artificial quality about my words and actions," she recalls, "as if I were someone acting in an ongoing play, rather than being myself."

Francis Schaeffer, twenty years old, had just returned from his first year of college. He had started attending the church years before because it had a Boy Scout troop, not because of its evangelical commitment. Indeed, the church itself had played no part in Francis' becoming a Christian at the age of eighteen.

As he meandered into the Christian Endeavor meeting that Sunday evening, he wondered whether he might be the only born-again Christian there. The speaker was a former member of the church who had become a Unitarian. His subject was, "How I Know That Jesus Is Not the Son of God and How I Know That the Bible Is Not the Word of God."

When the speaker finished his presentation and threw the meeting open for discussion, Edith was first on her feet to challenge him. For all she knew, she was the only one in the room who might make a defense of Christianity.

Just as she was about to speak, she heard someone else's voice. It was a boy she had never seen before.

Edith slid back in her seat and in a whisper asked the girl next to her, "Who is that?"

"That," said her friend, who had grown up in the church, "is Fran Schaeffer."

When Fran completed his argument, Edith stood and made her case for the truth of the Bible.

Now it was Fran's turn to whisper to his neighbor, "Who on earth is that girl?"

After the meeting, Fran wasted no time in getting to know her better.

"May I take you home?" he asked.

"I'm sorry. I already have a date," she responded.

"Break it," he told her bluntly.

She did.

And thus the courtship began.

The two young believers did not have much in common in terms of upbringing. Edith had been born in 1914 to a missionary couple in China. Five years later the Seville family returned to America on furlough and then, because of health reasons, were not permitted to return. Edith's father, George Seville, became a pastor, then the assistant editor of the China Inland Mission's magazine.

By the time Edith arrived in Philadelphia in 1931 to begin her senior year in high school, she had lived five years in China, two years in

California, one year in Pennsylvania, seven years in New York, and two years in Canada. Obviously she was well-traveled, but she was also well-read and well-grounded in Christianity. And she wasn't afraid to argue with her high school teachers. Yet she knew she was talking on a higher spiritual level than she was walking.

Fran was born in 1912, the only child of Frank and Bessie Schaeffer, hardworking blue-collar people with little interest in books, religion, or life outside of Philadelphia. Wanting to become a handyman like his father, Fran lined up school courses like mechanical drawing, woodwork, and metalwork. After school, he worked with his father at sanding floors, laying brick, mending gutters, spreading cement, repairing electrical outlets, and hammering nails.

On Saturdays and during the summers he took odd jobs, selling fish, working in a meat market, and cleaning out steam boilers.

It was hardly the beginning you would imagine for a future intellectual or for the future husband of Edith Seville.

Because his parents didn't care what church he went to, Fran made his decision based on the Boy Scout troop. However, the turning point in Fran's life was not when he started going to church, but when, as a seventeen-year-old, he was asked to help a Russian count learn to read English. For some assistance, he went to a bookstore to find a beginner's English reading book. By mistake, he was given a book on Greek philosophy.

Rather than return it immediately, he began to read it, and as he read, his mind began stretching. He began asking questions about the meaning of life. As he grappled with these profound questions, he contemplated renouncing Christianity, because the church he attended was "devoid of answers." But before he threw it all over, he decided that, to be fair, he ought to read the Bible along with the Greek philosophers. As he read he was surprised to find that it made a lot of sense. "What rang the bell for me were the answers in Genesis," he said later.

Over the next few months, Fran "accepted Christ as his Savior, having come to an understanding directly from the Word of God itself." One evening during the following summer, not long after he had graduated from high school, he walked into an evangelistic tent meeting.

That night he scribbled in his diary, "Have decided to give my whole life to Christ unconditionally."

At first that didn't imply becoming a minister or a missionary. In fact, he intended to follow his parents' wishes and study mechanical engineering at Drexel Institute. But on his nineteenth birthday he dropped out of the school's engineering program in order to prepare for the ministry.

His parents opposed the switch. His hardworking father considered ministers to be drones. Fran's diary said, "Mother and Dad still hostile to my plan." The next night he wrote, "Worried all day over Mother and Dad's not being back of me for my life's work."

But that fall, despite parental objections, Fran left for Hampden-Sydney College in Virginia.

The morning of Fran's departure, his father told him, "I don't want a son who is a minister."

As an only child, very close to both parents, Fran didn't know whether he should change his mind. He asked his father to give him a few minutes to think about it. Down in the basement, Fran prayed about it one more time. Then after praying, he flipped a coin. Walking slowly up the stairs to face his father again, he tried to think of proper words to say. All he said was, "Dad, I've got to go."

The following June, at the beginning of his summer vacation, he met Edith.

His summer job was selling silk hosiery from door to door, but his major interest was developing a relationship with Edith. It was a busy summer. His diary tells of their walking the Atlantic City boardwalk together, attending concerts, and going to the art museum. It even tells of how he played tennis with her father.

When Fran headed back to school in Virginia, Edith was beginning her college career, commuting to Beaver College just north of Philadelphia. She fantasized about studying art in Paris, but she was a home economics major at a school only a few miles from home.

At college, besides pursuing a preministerial curriculum, teaching a black Sunday school class every week, and trying to develop into a hurdler on the track team, Fran wrote letters to Philadelphia. At first, he and Edith wrote twice a week, but soon they were writing every day.

Over the Christmas holiday, Fran began having second thoughts about it. He wasn't sure it was right. Edith recalls, "He had decided that he was growing too fond of me." Maybe God would call him to a place where a woman couldn't go.

So on New Year's Eve they broke up, promising to pray for each other.

Their breakup lasted, however, for only two hours. Then Fran phoned Edith, "I've been so miserable since I left you." Before the evening was over, she had promised that she would wait for him for the two and a half years before he graduated. After that they could get married.

Their correspondence began again. In her letters she usually called him "Franz" and signed her letters "Ede," but occasionally she would begin a letter with, "How are you, old squeedunk?" and he with "Dearest wonderful sweetheart."

Their letters were both romantic and deeply spiritual. For example, Edith would write, "Darling, I love you. I'm in Bible class and I've just had an argument about creation."

And Fran would write to her, "It is the strong but sweet Christian who really shows the Christian way of life." That combination of strong and sweet attracted him, but he confessed to her, "I am lacking in that sweetness." Then he added, "It is the wonderful sweetness, yet staunch standing for the uncompromising truth of belief and action that can best lead men to Christ."

After two and a half years of waiting, Fran and Edie were married, with her father performing the ceremony. Until the last minute it was not know if Fran's mother would even come to the wedding. She had been strongly opposed to the marriage.

Their honeymoon was spent in a tiny attic room at a Bible conference in Michigan, where they served as camp counselors. The small room had "two canvas cots narrower than anything we had ever seen" and two thin mattresses. The newlyweds put "two mattresses on one cot for a bit more softness." And then, Edith recalls, they slept "as pretzels, with my declaring I didn't mind sleeping with one hand braced on the floor to keep from falling out."

On the way back to Philadelphia, however, where Fran was to begin seminary, Edith was behind the wheel of the car when she bumped into the car in front of them. Fran's temper flared, and he berated his wife for her stupidity and inability to drive a car without hitting something. "If that's the way you feel," Edith responded, "I'll never drive a car again." It was a never-to-be-broken resolve; she never drove a car again. Thus, early in their married life, Edith learned that Fran had a temper that could easily flare, and Fran learned that Edith could be determined and strong-willed.

The next three years, 1935–38, were seminary years. Edith set up her sewing machine, and besides making dresses, she designed, made, and sold leather belts and buttons. Her training in home ec was also put to practical use as she designed a frugal menu to keep their food costs at five dollars a week.

With some difficulty she learned when Fran wanted to talk and when he wanted her to be silent. Hebrew was such an ordeal for Fran that at times she felt as if she were being replaced by a Hebrew vocabulary card. "Don't talk," he would remind her brusquely. "Can't you see I'm learning Hebrew? When I've finished seminary there will be plenty of time to talk."

Those times were difficult for a creative woman like Edith, whose mind was just as active as his, and who needed, even more than he, someone to share with. But despite his Hebrew vocabulary cards, they still found time to talk—and they had plenty to talk about.

They both were wrestling with problems. Edith was bothered when some faculty wives chided her for being specific in her praying. "God knows more about your needs than you do," she was told. Fran was bothered by the bickering between Christians, by the lack of love of men who were contending for orthodoxy.

Such problems caused Fran and Edith to transfer to a new seminary. He received his divinity degree from Faith Theological Seminary, then located in Wilmington, Delaware.

Though their first church in Grove City, Pennsylvania, had only eighteen members, Fran and Edith with their infant daughter accepted the opportunity eagerly. As a pastor's wife, Edith learned to pray for Fran while he preached. She continued the practice throughout his ministry, "even if we had just had a 'fight' of some sort before he spoke." She found it very possible to "forget anything personal" and "to listen to what was coming forth, and to be thankful that Fran was hearing this, as well as to hear it myself." In Grove City, Fran and Edith reached out to children. Though the church had no Sunday school and only eighteen attended the church service, seventy-nine boys and girls came to their vacation Bible school. Three years later, the church, now with 110 members, had a new building, a Sunday school, and an active youth ministry.

After three years in Grove City, Pennsylvania, and two in Chester, Pennsylvania, where Fran served as associate pastor of a larger church, a call came from a church in St. Louis.

Moves seemed more difficult to Edith than they were to Fran. As a pastor he saw exciting opportunities; as a young mother, she felt she was just getting to know people when they had to move on. Ever since her parents had returned from China when she was five, her life had been a series of moves. She hoped for a place where she could settle in. She was also concerned about her children, and when St. Louis beckoned, Susan was eighteen months and Priscilla was five years old.

While Fran felt the call to go to St. Louis, Edith was not so sure. In *The Tapestry*, Edith tells how "I knelt down beside my own big old chair and buried my face in the depths of the natural linen-covered cushion, making a damp spot with my very real tears. 'Oh Lord, I don't even know how to pray . . . but how can we be sure that we are right? And what about all these people?'"

Finally, in an emergency room of a hospital after a steam iron had exploded in her face, Edith confessed that it may have been stubbornness more than anything else that made her reluctant to move to St. Louis.

For Edith, the exploding steam iron was a never-to-be-forgotten experience. "Communication between the Heavenly Father and His children . . . is diverse. It is not always the exciting positive answer to prayer which other people can envy."

In St. Louis the Schaeffers again developed a successful children's ministry. It included home Bible classes, released-time classes, open-air work, a scouting program, a summer Bible school, and a camp program. Besides teaching a class for children in their basement, Edith used her creative talents making posters and working on advertising materials to augment Fran's organizational gifts. The work became known as "Children for Christ."

Soon the program was recognized throughout the Bible Presbyterian denomination and the entire American Council of Churches. Before long, Fran was involved in numerous committees and was traveling extensively.

Despite their busy and often hectic schedules—during one month Fran had only one free night—they felt it important for them to have time together, an evening alone.

In *The Tapestry*, Edith tells about it:

> Our "evening alone" started at midnight, or one o'clock, or whenever he got home. I would prepare some very special sandwich and a milk-shake, and in the summer we would eat together outdoors on the bush-surrounded patio, and in the winter, beside a fire in the fireplace. That meal was our most important, because it was our time to talk about whatever was uppermost in our thoughts. For a growing relationship, we believe such a planned time is important, at some regular moment of the day.

Edith says that if they had any secret for marital happiness to share, it was this.

In St. Louis, Monday was Fran's day off, and often Fran and Edith would take their children to an art museum or enjoy a picnic in the park. The Schaeffers worked to make those times creatively special for their children.

But Fran and Edith had no idea what lay ahead of them. Fran wondered if the Lord wanted him to go on for further theological education, perhaps to get a doctorate in theology in Edinburgh, Scotland. Another possibility was the mission field. On their bedroom wall they created a montage of various photos from Asia, and across it Edith had written, "Go ye into all the world." They looked to God to guide them.

In 1947, the Independent Board of Presbyterian Foreign Missions asked the thirty-five-year-old Francis Schaeffer to conduct a fact-finding survey of Europe. They asked him to investigate the condition of the European churches and find out how Christians in America could help. Specifically, they wondered whether European churches needed help in ministering to children, and that was an area of the Schaeffers' expertise.

That summer Fran whistle-stopped his way through thirteen countries, keeping some 180 appointments. Though saddened by the lack of evangelical fervor and biblical confidence in the state churches of Europe, he found in most every country a few churches which were committed to biblical authority and the importance of defending the faith.

It was a grueling itinerary. Arriving back in the United States, he was near collapse. Though the schedule had been hard for him to handle physically, it was just as trying emotionally.

In *The Tapestry,* Edith says, "That ninety days for Fran was a devastating time. He had real problems and struggles. . . . The putting aside of our physical oneness, as well as of our talking everything over together day by day, was extremely hard on him." Edith felt that the mission board, like many other Christian ministries, ignored "the fact that the Bible loudly states that sexual relationship, physical oneness in marriage, is meant to be an ongoing daily thing of fulfillment, as important to life in its own way as a balanced diet is to physical well-being."

Back in St. Louis, Fran nearly broke down. He said no to speaking engagements and refused to answer phone calls. He vowed never to buy another train ticket. When the mission board asked him to return to Philadelphia to make an official report on his three-month fact-finding trip, he was about to tell them he couldn't do it. But Edith said she would accompany him, handling all the details of the travel. Together they traveled to Philadelphia, and he made his report.

After the meeting, the board decided that someone should be sent to Europe on a permanent basis. Who should it be? "The consensus is that the only ones we should send would be you and Edith."

With Fran physically and emotionally drained and Edith enjoying the ministry in St. Louis, it wasn't an easy decision for them to make. But they had asked the Lord for guidance, and this was a clear request by the mission board.

In spite of some misgivings, they agreed to go. ("I am impressed," Edith wrote later, "by the constantly repeated opportunity in life to trust the Lord in a fog.") Apart from planning some meetings in Amsterdam, Fran and Edith had only a vague idea of where they should go or even what they would do. Fran would try to strengthen Bible-believing pastors in Europe. Occasionally he would have an opportunity to preach. And together they would seek to establish a ministry to children that could be used by churches in Europe.

One thing was certain: Because Fran would be writing many letters to pastors throughout Europe, he would need a secretary who could take shorthand, type, and work without pay. Only one person was available who could meet those requirements, so Edith enrolled in a secretarial school to learn shorthand.

Thus in 1948, Fran, Edith, and their three children sailed across the Atlantic, stopping first in Amsterdam where Fran set up the organizational meetings for the International Council of Christian Churches and then traveling to Lausanne, Switzerland, which was selected to be their base for future operations.

While Fran's mission may have seemed a bit murky, Edith's seemed downright dismal. It was her job to make a happy home out of two small bedrooms. The children's bedroom, filled with two beds and a crib, left no space to play. The parents' bedroom, also crowded, would have to double as Fran's office and as their Sunday school and church facilities on weekends.

Considering the size of the sanctuary, perhaps it was fortunate that the congregation was small, just the children and Edith at first, sitting in four chairs lined up on one side of a bed. But Fran took the charge seriously and prepared a series of sermons for his family as faithfully as if he were to speak to a large congregation.

That winter all three girls were felled by the flu, and two of them had pneumonia. A teacher suggested that the girls be taken into the Alps the next summer for their health. Fran and Edith liked the idea.

They expected to live in the Alps for only sixty days. But when the summer ended, the girls begged to stay. "Why can't we just live here?" And for the next thirty-two years they made their home in the Swiss Alps.

They had no long-range goals. All they knew was that God had opened up a chalet for them to live in. Fran continued to travel across Europe, talking to pastors and theologians on behalf of the International Council of Christian Churches. Frequently Edith and the girls would go along to present their special Children for Christ ministry, but their chalet in the Alps was home.

Near their chalet was a finishing school for girls, and one night a week the Schaeffers opened their home to the girls for "tea and discussion." In the afternoons Edith started a cooking class plus discussion for the girls.

Both Fran and Edith enjoyed chatting with these young people. He had an unusual ability to bring together facts from many different disciplines and explain what they meant in terms of the Bible.

But in spite of ministering through such personal contacts with the school, Francis and Edith were discouraged about other aspects of their work. The churches in Europe were cold and dead. Secularism and existentialism had captured the continent.

Fran was also discouraged by what he saw in his own International Council of Christian Churches. He was also discouraged with himself. One day he told Edith, "I really feel torn to pieces by the lack of reality. . . . in the Lord's people. . . . And I'm not satisfied with myself."

The only honest thing to do, he felt, would be to "reexamine the whole matter of Christianity. Is it true? I need to go back to my agnosticism and start at the beginning."

That's what he did. Retreating to a hayloft, he paced back and forth, back and forth, talking to himself, talking to God, trying to find reality.

Edith admits she was scared of what was going on in the mind of her thirty-nine-year-old husband. She didn't know how to help him or even if she should. It was his spiritual struggle, and she felt it would be wrong to interrupt.

Gradually, however, Fran came to a firmer conviction, not only that the Bible is true, but that God's truth applied to all aspects of life. In the hayloft he was no longer talking under his breath to God. Now he was singing songs of praise.

One day he came to Edith asking, "I wonder how much difference it would make to most churches and to most Christian work if everything concerning the Holy Spirit and everything concerning prayer were removed from the Bible."

He knew that objective truth was vital to Christianity and that the inerrant Word of God was crucial. But he wondered how a Christian could insist so vehemently on the truth of Scripture and yet at the same time neglect the Holy Spirit or the necessity of prayer. He was beginning to see that the experiential aspects of the Christian life are as important as the objective truths of the faith. Like many great Christian thinkers of the past, he found that thoughts and deeds must work together in the life of holiness.

A new day was dawning for Francis Schaeffer.

While Fran had been pacing in the hayloft, Edith had been making some spiritual discoveries too.

Now knowing exactly how to help her husband, Edith began writing her prayers to the Lord, "simply as one would write a note to emphasize something to another person in a more concrete way than speaking. For me, it was a more vivid way of communicating."

During this critical time, Edith's prayer life plumbed new depths. From that time on, she resolved to believe and to behave "as if it mattered, as if it would make a difference in history, if I acted upon the admonition to pray . . . 'on all occasions with all kinds of prayers and requests.'" She also resolved that she would not read a newspaper or magazine in the morning until she had spent time reading her Bible, praying, and writing her personal note to the Lord.

The life-changing ministries of the Schaeffers can be dated to those soul-wrenching days in late 1951 and early 1952.

They still weren't sure, however, what all of that soul-searching would mean to their missionary work, but a few weeks later, in February 1952, a number of young people—some of them friends of their daughters—began coming to the Schaeffer chalet to ask spiritual questions. That was only a trickle of interest compared to the rushing mountain stream that would follow, but it was the start of a new type of ministry.

During that year Edith bore her fourth child (and first son), Francis August Schaeffer V. Two years earlier, she had suffered a miscarriage, so this pregnancy was a time of special concern.

Then it was time for the Schaeffers to return to the U.S. for their missionary furlough. Fran had agreed to teach a course in pastoral theology at Faith Theological Seminary in Philadelphia. The position would give him a home base for his family, but it would also allow him some freedom to accept speaking engagements across the country.

Fran had been praying much for a place for his family to stay during the furlough, and when his Uncle Harrison offered his Philadelphia row home, Fran praised God for the answer.

However, when they arrived in Philadelphia and saw the size of their new lodgings, Edith was aghast. As she recalls, "To contemplate living here for sixteen months with four children . . . filled me with dismay. Yet how could I complain or even sigh too audibly, when Fran felt . . . that the provision of this house was one of the most vivid provisions of the Lord that he had ever experienced?"

While Fran was praising God for his provision, Edith was praying for special grace to endure. "We are not," Edith commented, "promised freedom from hardships on the basis of prayer."

Fran's hardships were of a different kind. Concerned with the lack of evidence of the work of the Holy Spirit in his own denomination, Fran faced major battles from some who had previously been close friends. He could see concern for biblical truth, but what he didn't see was a concern for brotherly love or for sanctification. And he said so. In eighteen months in America, Fran spoke 346 times, and frequently his emphasis was on sanctification. Later these messages were put in book form under the title, *True Spirituality*.

The small denomination was on the verge of splitting. The rift between Fran and denominational leaders was serious. Some accused Fran of making a power grab for denominational leadership.

At times Edith and Fran wondered if they should return to Europe at all. They seemed to be at odds not only with key leaders in their denomination, but with their mission leaders as well. If they returned to Europe without the blessing of the mission, what would they do?

On the other hand, if they remained in the U.S., they would be embroiled in the denominational battle.

"We didn't know what would take place in our work," Edith wrote later, "but we began to pray alone and together. . . . We were living in uncertainty."

One area of uncertainty was financial. They had no money to get back to Europe. Fran made reservations anyway, and the entire family prayed for the money to come in. "This will be a good way to find out what God wants us to do," Fran said. "If He wants us to go, He will send it in."

One daughter drew a thermometer poster and taped it on the refrigerator. Each day, as money arrived for the boat passage, she adjusted the thermometer a few degrees higher. Shortly before the deadline, the morning mail brought in the final check that was needed for the boat passage, and the mercury went through the top of the thermometer.

But that dramatic answer to prayer didn't place the Schaeffers on Easy Street. In the course of the next several months, little Franky contracted polio, the mission board urged supporting churches to stop giving to the Schaeffers, an avalanche almost wiped them out, and the Swiss government ordered them to leave the country because they were "having a religious influence in the village of Champery."

"What are we going to do?" Edith wondered. "How could all this be happening to us? Hadn't we been in God's will when we decided to return to Switzerland?"

Their problems were snowballing into another avalanche. Whenever God provided a way through one obstacle, a greater problem engulfed them.

"Time after time we were helped by people," Edith recalls, "but each encouraging thing was followed by a discouraging one. . . . And each mail brought letters urging us to leave Switzerland and come to be a pastor of a church in America or to teach in a seminary."

Perhaps the Schaeffers would have wondered if God was telling them to return to America had not L'Abri been starting to take shape.

The name L'Abri had been Fran's idea. On board ship, as they were returning to Europe, Fran suggested that they call their chalet by the name of "L'Abri," the French word for shelter. He thought of their home as a "spiritual shelter they can come to for help."

Edith was delighted with the idea. Quickly, she sketched a picture in india ink. Her rough drawing had pine trees, chalets, hills, and a few skiers, and underneath the sketch she scribbled, "L'Abri . . . come for morning coffee or afternoon tea, with your questions."

On board ship they weren't thinking that L'Abri would be their main ministry. After all, Fran had been having an effective ministry with European pastors during his first missionary term. But that ended abruptly. Shortly after they arrived in Switzerland, they discovered that letters had been written from the U.S. to European churches, warning pastors to avoid contact with the Schaeffers.

With fewer open doors to European churches the children's ministry would also be greatly limited, so it seemed that God was restricting them to serve him out of their Swiss chalet.

Then came the government edict that they were no longer welcome in the Swiss canton in which they had been living. At first the situation seemed hopeless; then the government ruled that if they could find another chalet in another village with the approval of the village and the canton authorities, then they could make a fresh application to stay in Switzerland.

Hunting for a chalet seemed hopeless too. But the day before the government's deadline, Edith found one in the village of Huemoz. The realtor, however, told her it was not for rent; it was for sale.

With no money for a down payment, no permit to stay in Switzerland, and less than twenty-four hours before the deadline, it seemed that their days in Switzerland were numbered. But Edith was convinced that God wanted them to have the chalet in Huemoz. However, when she returned home, she didn't have the nerve to tell Fran that it was for sale, not for rent. "I feared Fran would say it was no use going to look at a house for sale," she recalled. When she told Fran about an available chalet, he agreed to see it the next day, not knowing it was for sale only.

That night she talked to the Lord about it.

The next morning on the way to the train, they met their postman, who was coming on skis to deliver their mail to them. He gave them three letters, and a few minutes later when they had boarded the train, they opened them.

One of them contained a check for a thousand dollars, earmarked for "a house that will always be open to young people." With that encouragement, Edith told Fran the entire story, and in the next few hours they signed the papers to buy the chalet, then hurriedly went to a lawyer, the police, and the notary to process the papers, which were then sent to the president of the canton for his approval. His approval came just in time.

In the next three months, another eight thousand francs were needed to complete the down payment. Once again, the Schaeffers refused to send out a general appeal for funds, but instead talked to the Lord about it. Within ninety days, 8,011 francs were received, and just as importantly they also received their permit to remain in Switzerland.

L'Abri had begun, and the entire family was part of the ministry. Visitors enjoyed the family discussions.

"We had only one rule," writes Edith. "Discussions for our own family and for those who had joined us must revolve around ideas and not organizations or personalities—that is, people." So they talked about art, music, books, science, philosophy, medicine, law, world events, world religions, and more. Whatever was discussed was analyzed in the light of what the Scripture had to say.

Gradually, L'Abri grew. Other chalets had to be purchased, and soon new workers joined the Schaeffers in the ministry.

The secret of L'Abri was only partly Francis Schaeffer and his unique ability to fit any subject into a larger biblical framework. L'Abri was more than that. It was a place where people found a Christian family—a very extended family to be sure, but a family nonetheless, a loving and very human family.

As part of this very human family, Fran sometimes lost his temper. Edith sometimes walked out in a huff. "No," says Edith, "we were not politely bowing to each other, always saying the right thing in sweet tones of voice."

In *What Is a Family?* Edith tells of Fran losing his temper and taking it out on an ivy plant which grew in a red clay pot on the coffee table. Edith handled the flare-up calmly. "A broom, dustpan, and brush, another pot brought up out of the woodshed, some extra dirt added to the old, maybe a shot of fertilizer, a pail of sudsy water, and a cloth—and the room would be cleaner than before, the ivy repotted and back in its place." Although the ivy became a family joke (because the scene happened several times), "it was not a joke to talk about in front of Daddy."

Edith handled her anger and frustration differently. "When my adrenaline flows, my reaction is to try to get more done in the next hour than any human being could do."

Having an open home with young people walking in at any hour was often a challenge for Edith. "Often . . . I have said to the children, 'I can't face one more person today; I just want to run away.'"

But usually she couldn't run away. "After I had dished out the last of fifty-two desserts and said that, I heard a knock at the door." Someone else had discovered the Schaeffer chalet.

Although privacy in the Schaeffer home may have seemed to be a precious commodity, Edith and Fran both knew the importance of creating times to be alone. "We have a need, a responsibility, and a command to spend time alone in marriage," Edith wrote. "Some togetherness is needed so that the continual having of people around you does not become an escape from being together as a married couple or as parents with children." That is one reason why L'Abri never developed into a commune; it was a shared home, with privacy for those who lived there. The children had their own rooms for individual privacy as well.

Fran and Edith developed other ways to be together. When they were about sixty years old, they were both given cross-country skis as a gift. "We can go for miles and miles through woods and fields, around barns and across little bridges. . . . It is also an occasion for getting away and into the midst of nature, while there is the companionship of walking together."

Prayer life at L'Abri was usually organized by Edith. She made certain that every aspect of the work was bathed in prayer. On the kitchen wall she placed a chart with the hours of the day divided into half-hour periods. Anyone who wanted to could place his initials alongside a period and pledge to pray at that time, and Edith made sure that prayer requests were listed by the chart.

Edith couldn't imagine how L'Abri could accomplish anything without prayer and fellowship. And Fran couldn't think of L'Abri without truth and love. When you put truth, love, prayer, and fellowship together, you have the core of L'Abri.

Analyzing the success of L'Abri, Christopher Catherwood concluded that "the key . . . was love, not just as a concept, but as an emotion. . . . That was why Schaeffer insisted on dealing with each person as an individual. 'Love,' he said, 'means meeting people where they are.'"

But those who came felt not only the love of Fran and Edith for them as individuals, no matter how mixed up their lives might be, but they also sensed the love and respect that Fran and Edith had for each other and for their children.

Some visitors came and stayed at L'Abri, becoming long-term students. Others came for only a weekend, arriving on Friday night. The Saturday night meal was usually out-of-doors, the tables having been set by Edith, who also saw to it that classical music (perhaps Vivaldi's *Four Seasons*) was playing in the background.

For Edith table settings were just as much a work of art as classical music, and all was presented to the glory of God.

Catherwood says, "The number of people there could increase dramatically from thirty to one hundred thirty in a flash, but Edith Schaeffer would cope." Coping was something Edith learned by experience.

After the meal, Fran invited everyone to join him inside in the living room for hot drinks around the fireplace. Sitting informally in a red barrel chair, he would open up the floor for questions, and no questions were off limits. Young people were amazed at the breadth of Fran's knowledge, but even more than that, how he was able to dovetail everything into a Christian worldview. One person commented that "Schaeffer must have thought about every angle to life." Many came to faith in Jesus Christ after those evening question-and-answer sessions.

At times, however, Fran was frustrated by the fact that he was only reaching a handful in his Bible studies. Edith recalls that after a Saturday night study Fran would "hit his fist against the wooden wall until his knuckles would get red. 'Oh, Edith, I know I can help people. . . . But no one is ever going to hear. . . . no one . . . except a handful. A handful of people will understand something and then . . . forget. What are we doing? What are we doing?'" He wanted so badly to expand the L'Abri ministry beyond the walls of L'Abri itself.

When some suggested that copies be made of his remarks, however, he was reluctant to formalize the procedure for fear of spoiling it. When a tape recorder was sent from the United States to record his talks for friends in America, he refused to use it. He thought a tape recorder would inhibit the spontaneous interchange. So the recorder sat on a shelf for several months.

But one evening, with Edith's agreement, one worker set a small microphone in a potted plant while tea was being served. That began the tape ministry.

Before long, more of the Bible studies and lectures were taped, and these tapes found their way to places like Ghana, Hong Kong, Finland, and Singapore, as well as to every part of the United States. And then Fran began receiving invitations to speak at key colleges and universities in America.

At first, Fran turned down the invitations. The Schaeffer home was a significant part of L'Abri, and if Fran spent much time away from home, the L'Abri ministry might be hindered.

Edith, of course, enjoyed having him home, and she didn't know how to separate what was selfish from what was God's will for the ministry.

Late in 1954, when Fran and Edith had returned to Switzerland, they had what Edith called a "willingness for anything." But eight years later, she confessed that she had become interested in "something for myself." Family times were important, and the thought of losing some of them so that Fran could have a wider ministry was painful. In addition, L'Abri had been a ministry they shared as husband and wife. If Fran would travel extensively, she would have to make some major adjustments.

The turning point came in a Zurich apartment. Fran was surrounded by doctors, lawyers, businessmen, pilots, and airline hostesses. They fired questions at Fran, and he calmly answered each one. Soon skepticism changed to interest, and as Edith watched the faces, she could see the light dawn as Fran brought truth to bear upon confused thinking.

Before the evening was over, Edith prayed, "Lord, forgive me for my selfish prayers for a different life. . . . If you want Fran to do a much wider work, if You want what happened here in this room tonight to happen on a much wider scale, if You have people in other parts of the world who should hear what Fran has said tonight . . . then I am willing for whatever it takes on my part."

It was a difficult decision.

In 1965 Fran spoke at Harvard, at the Massachusetts Institute of Technology, and at other universities, and from these lectures came his first book, *The God Who Is There.* The following year Edith traveled with Fran to schools in the Midwest and the Far West. In 1967 he spoke at British universities. The schedule became more hectic. In her L'Abri "Family Letter," Edith wrote that she was tempted to cry out, "It's too much. . . . We can't go on."

In the following years the speaking engagements bred more tapes, books, and radio talks. In America Fran and Edith met with the president and with leading congressmen. And then came the film series *How Shall We Then Live?* and *Whatever Happened to the Human Race?*

During the filming of the second series, Fran lost twenty-five pounds. At first, he thought it was simply fatigue. At sixty-six, he could not be expected to keep up the pace he had maintained earlier. But soon it appeared that it might be more serious. Edith called a physician at the Mayo Clinic.

The day after he arrived at Mayo, his problem was diagnosed as a malignant cancer. It was lymphoma, a malignancy that could be treated only by chemotherapy. Doctors gave him six weeks to six months to live. Instead, because of two lengthy remissions, Francis Schaeffer lived almost six years more.

It was 11.4 percent of their married life, as Edith pointed out in *Forever Music.* It was also one of their most productive periods. Fran once said, "I feel I can accomplish more with this condition than I could without it." L'Abri conferences were conducted at Rochester, Minnesota, near the clinic; Fran wrote two more best-selling books, *A Christian Manifesto* and *The Great Evangelical Disaster,* and he continued to accept speaking engagements as often as he could, including a speaking tour to eleven colleges less than two months before his death. But it was also a time for family, with the four children and fourteen grandchildren, and a time "of greater honesty and recognition of the precariousness of relationships than ever before."

Late in April 1984, when Edith saw that his cancer was spreading rapidly and that his life was draining from him, she told the doctors at the clinic, "I want to take him home." She felt he should spend his final days surrounded by love instead of sterile hospital walls.

At their home in Rochester, Fran's bed looked out over a pleasant garden with geraniums and petunias. Edith had arranged for classical music to waft through the room. Bach, Chopin, Mendelssohn, and Handel—all favorites of Fran's—were played, but it was especially Handel's *Messiah* that he loved, coming into his deathbed room, thundering at full volume: "King of Kings, Lord of Lords, Hallelujah, Hallelujah."

After more than forty-eight years of marriage and partnership, they were separated by death. Fran died on May 15, 1984.

Not all marriages are partnerships, but certainly the Schaeffers' relationship was one. Fran had often talked of the necessity of balance in marriage, but he admitted that it is always a very complicated thing "with the man being the head of the home and yet the woman having at times more ability in leadership in certain ways than the man has. . . . Though always within the structure that God has given, the stress should be on partnership."

The marriage of Fran and Edith was a good partnership.

Bibliography

Catherwood, Christopher. *Five Evangelical Leaders.* Wheaton, Ill.: Harold Shaw, 1985.

Parkhurst, Louis Gifford, Jr. *Francis Schaeffer: The Man and His Message.* Wheaton, Ill.: Tyndale House, 1985.

Schaeffer, Edith. *Affliction.* Old Tappan, N.J.: Fleming H. Revell, 1978.

————. *Forever Music.* Nashville: Thomas Nelson, 1986.

————. *The Hidden Art of Homemaking.* Wheaton, Ill.: Tyndale House, 1971.

————. *L'Abri.* Wheaton, Ill.: Tyndale House, 1969.

————. *The Tapestry.* Waco, Tex.: Word, 1981.

————. *What Is a Family?* Old Tappan, N.J.: Fleming H. Revell, 1975.

Schaeffer, Francis. *Letters of Francis A. Schaeffer.* Westchester, Ill.: Crossway, 1985.

————, and Edith Schaeffer. *Everybody Can Know.* Wheaton, Ill.: Tyndale House, 1973.

Music and Family Go Hand in Hand

Johann Sebastian Bach and His Two Wives

Sebastian Bach had his problems as a church music director.

"He plays the organ too loudly," some charged. "If he continues to play this way, the organ will be ruined in two years or most of the congregation will be deaf."

"He puts in so many cadenzas and arpeggios that we don't know when to sing," others said.

"He shouldn't have called me a nanny-goat bassoonist," an instrumentalist moaned.

"He had no right to extend his vacation three months without telling us," one church council complained.

Let's face it. The man who wrote *Jesu, Joy of Man's Desiring* and *Sheep May Safely Graze* was not the ideal director of music for a local church. In fact, he had stormy relationships in most churches he served.

Johann Sebastian Bach, who has been called "God's greatest musical servant since King David," was renowned for his lack of patience and his short fuse. The composer of the *St. Matthew Passion* and the *Mass in B Minor* had a temper that, according to one biographer, "could assume violent proportions." And he never budged on his principles. This inevitably caused problems on the job.

But he had peace and quiet at home.

Well, not exactly.

For Johann Sebastian Bach, peace and quiet was when he, Anna Magdalena, and the ten children could retreat to the large music room on the first floor of their home. There the children would take their places at the six keyboard instruments in the room or tune up one of the dozen other wind and stringed instruments lying around. Then Anna Magdalena with her robust soprano voice would try to sing an aria that could be heard over the instruments.

For Sebastian, to be surrounded by his family singing and playing their praise of God was the closest thing to heaven that this world affords.

Why was it that Sebastian had problems outside, but at home enjoyed happy relationships?

Maybe you should ask Anna Magdalena, that delightful wife who liked to have songbirds and carnations adorn her home, who didn't object to loud music, and who didn't mind when traveling musicians dropped in unexpectedly to stay a night or two.

Anna Magdalena was one of a kind, even as Sebastian was one of a kind.

In eastern Germany during the seventeenth and eighteenth centuries the name of Bach was practically synonymous with musician. In fact, town musicians were often called *bachs,* because more than likely that was their name. And chances are that if you met a Bach his first name would be Johann. Between 1600 and 1750 more than forty Johann Bachs inhabited eastern Germany, and 90 percent of them were musicians.

Of course, the most famous of the Johann Bachs was Sebastian, born in 1685, two centuries after Martin Luther walked the streets of the same province, Thuringia. Sebastian's great-great-grandfather, a baker from Hungary, had fled to Germany to escape religious persecution. In Germany he found freedom to practice his faith. He also had freedom to practice his guitar while baking bread. From that time on, music leavened the Bach family, and the Bach family leavened the church music of Lutheran Germany.

So when the town musician of Eisenach, Johann Ambrosius Bach, and his wife Elizabeth named their fourth son Johann Sebastian, it was assumed that he too would become a musician. (His three older brothers were Johann Christoph, Johann Jakob, and Johann Nicolaus.) Sebastian learned how to play stringed instruments from his father and how to play the organ from his brother. But it was from the town of Eisenach that he learned how to sing.

In the northwest corner of the Thuringian forest, Eisenach was renowned for its singing. In every church of the area, plowboys formed the church choirs, singing in perfect harmony to the accompaniment of several violins. The singing was more polished than most professional choirs.

Students sang in the streets to pay for their tuition. People came out of their houses and gave them money for their singing. Luther had done it as a student at Eisenach's Latin school two hundred years earlier. Sebastian did it, too.

But Sebastian's music changed to a minor key; not long after his ninth birthday his mother died. A few months later his father remarried; shortly afterwards, he too became ill and died.

The new stepmother did not know what to do. In desperation she wrote to the city council. Would they employ her as the church music director? Her credentials were meager, but she had become a Bach by marriage and that should be enough to qualify her to direct the church music.

The council didn't like her idea. Instead, they employed someone else as the church musician. Unable to provide for the boys, she returned to her previous home, rejecting her stepchildren. Sebastian and an older brother moved in with Johann Christoph, their oldest brother, who had just married.

His brother's house was small to begin with. As babies were periodically added to the household, Sebastian got the idea that there wouldn't be room for him very long. Besides, Johann Christoph was the town organist, and town organists seldom had enough income to feed too many mouths.

So at fourteen, when he heard of a music school in northern Germany—two hundred miles away—a music school that gave scholarships to "offspring of poor people, with nothing to live on, but possessing good voices," Sebastian packed a bag and started walking north.

Though accepted first as a singer because of his boy soprano voice, his voice soon changed, and he had to count on his talents as a violinist and organist to keep him at the school.

Three years later, now seventeen, Sebastian began job hunting, and he took a position back in his home territory, only five or six miles away from where he had been raised.

As church organist of the smallest of the three churches in Arnstadt, he was charged by the town council "to cultivate the fear of God, sobriety, and the love of peace."

Whether Sebastian cultivated the love of peace in Arnstadt is debatable, but he did cultivate the love of Maria Barbara Bach. Barbara was living with an aunt and uncle at the Golden Crown, the same boarding house where Sebastian was rooming. They had much in common. A second cousin of Sebastian's, she too was an orphan; her father had been a church organist, and he had died in the same year that Sebastian's father had died, leaving her, like Sebastian, fatherless by the age of ten.

There was no doubt in Sebastian's mind that Barbara was the girl for him. They both needed each other. Everything seemed so unsettled for both of them. So they talked together of music and marriage as they strolled under Arnstadt's beautiful linden trees.

But they were both still teenagers, and since Sebastian never felt too secure—for good reason—about his job in Arnstadt, they thought it best to wait a bit. Barbara must have wondered, as month after month passed by, whether conditions would ever stabilize and whether Sebastian's job would ever be secure.

For one thing, Sebastian had perennial trouble with his choir. Choir directing hadn't been in his job description, and Sebastian waged a continuing battle with the council about it. He was an organist, not a choir director. For another thing, since the church was the smallest in Arnstadt, it got the dregs of teenaged singers. They had little ability in music, and even the city council admitted that they behaved "in a scandalous manner." For two years he ranted and screamed at the unruly mob of choristers, but they simply didn't share his devotion to music.

411

Finally, one dark night, a choir member whom Sebastian had nick-named a "nanny-goat bassoonist" met him on the street and called him a "dirty dog." Sebastian, who was never renowned for keeping his tem-per under control, whipped out a sword and slashed a few holes in his adversary's clothing before bystanders halted the fight.

Sebastian was called on the carpet by the council. A few weeks later he thought it might be advisable to request a vacation. He was tired of the constant wrangling with the council and his running feud with the choir. He didn't know what would happen if he saw that nanny-goat bassoonist out on the street again. The council must have agreed that a four-week vacation would be good for all parties concerned, because they readily consented.

Sebastian used his leave of absence to visit a famous church organ-ist at St. Mary's Church in Lubeck in northern Germany. It was a visit that he would never forget. Not only was the church organist magnif-icent, but the church also had an outstanding choir and a forty-piece orchestra. It was music that truly glorified God.

After he had played the magnificent church organ—and impressed the authorities—he was informed that he could become the successor to the church organist, who was ready to retire. All he needed to do was consent to marry the organist's daughter.

When Sebastian thought of his mediocre organ back in Arnstadt and the unruly teenagers that masqueraded under the name of a church choir, the offer must have been tempting.

But then he thought about Barbara, waiting for him. Of course, he recognized that many men in that day did not marry because of love. The most common motive for marriage was to get ahead in the world. Certainly, marrying an organist's daughter would qualify.

Should he stay in Lubeck and marry the organist's daughter? Or should he return to Arnstadt and marry an orphan girl?

Though she didn't know about Sebastian's opportunity, Barbara must have questioned whether he would ever return. The city council also wondered. The four-week leave of absence stretched into five, six, and seven weeks. Barbara doubted if he would have a job at all when (or if) he returned.

"It seems not unlikely," writes biographer Karl Geininger, "that her beloved was so engrossed by his tremendous artistic experiences that he did not even write to her."

Eventually, four months later, Sebastian did come back to Arnstadt. And he came back with all sorts of new musical ideas, none of which seemed to be appreciated by his congregation. "His improvisations between the verses never seemed to come to an end," and the congregation was "bewildered, outraged, and at times unable to stumble through the chorales."

In addition, Sebastian was more adamant than ever about leading the choir. It wasn't in his job description and he refused to do it.

So the running battle with the church council continued. When they objected to cadenzas between verses of hymns, he retaliated by making his preludes ridiculously short and plain. Throughout the year the council cajoled, admonished, and threatened. Then in the fall, he was summoned before his bosses again. This time, in addition to the perpetual problem with the choir, there was a new charge against Sebastian. The official records indicate that "he recently caused the strange maiden to be invited into the choir loft and let her make music there."

No doubt this "strange maiden" was Barbara. Since women were not allowed to sing in the choirs of that day, it was a serious offense to permit a woman to sing in the choir loft. Whether Barbara posed as a boy soprano and sang in a church service or whether she simply sang while Sebastian practiced on the organ is not known. Probably it was the latter.

Whatever it was, it was apparently the last straw. The whole year of 1706 had been one of friction with the town council. Sebastian had faced repeated complaints from parishioners and innumerable ultimatums from his supervisors. The joy had left his organ playing. Sebastian and Barbara agreed that Arnstadt was not the place to start their married life.

So that December, when Barbara heard, through a relative, that the church organist in the nearby town of Muhlhausen had died, she asked the relative to get her fiancé an audition for the job. By the following spring, Sebastian had a new position. And Arnstadt was not too sorry to see him go.

In the fall of 1707, Barbara and Sebastian, both twenty-two years old, were married in a little village church not far from Muhlhausen.

Sebastian enjoyed married life. Says one biographer, "If ever a genius was suited to the state of matrimony, it was Sebastian Bach." Many other great musicians had troubled marriages, but Sebastian found happiness in his home. He and Barbara were apparently much in love and quite compatible.

Not too much is known about Barbara. However, as one biographer states, "We can reasonably assume that someone who was descended from a line of outstanding artists as Barbara was, and who became the mother of Sebastian's most talented sons, was also a real helpmate to her husband in musical matters." She must have been a positive influence musically, for it was only after his marriage that Sebastian became serious about composing. In fact, only three months after his wedding, one of his earliest cantatas, *God Is My King*, was performed in the large Marienkirche of Muhlhausen.

Before long Sebastian was once again embroiled in controversy. This time it was a theological hassle. The theological issue in Muhlhausen was Pietism, and Pietists emphasized the importance of Christ dwelling within the believer. The formal, mechanical adoption of Lutheran creeds wasn't enough; the soul must have a personal experience with God.

Sebastian found much in Pietism with which he could agree. But when the Pietists, who stressed simplicity, wanted simplicity in music as well as in lifestyle, Sebastian thought they were carrying things too far. The mainstream of Lutheranism, looking back to Martin Luther himself, had always held that beautiful music was a means of glorifying God.

How could Sebastian develop his God-given talents in a Pietistic atmosphere?

Very diplomatically—or at least as diplomatically as Sebastian knew how to be—he penned his letter of resignation. He wrote that, though he and Barbara lived simply, they could "exist only in strained circumstances" on the salary he received. But he went on to express his real reason for resigning: His calling in life was to "establish a proper church music to the glory of God," and in Muhlhausen he saw "no hope that this might come some day."

So now at the age of twenty-three, he accepted the position as organist for the court of the Duke of Weimar, forty miles away. His salary was doubled, but though Sebastian always displayed an interest in the financial realities of life, the increased salary was not the real reason for going to Weimar. The real reason was that the duke was known to be a very religious man. All his servants attended daily devotions, and they took turns in reading the Bible aloud. Sebastian was certain that at Weimar he had at last found the place where he would be removed from theological squabbles and from petty town councils and where he could achieve "a properly established church music."

In a ducal court Sebastian and Barbara gained a new circle of acquaintances. However, they still preferred their old friends. When they chose godparents for their children, they usually selected friends from the past. And relatives were invariably camping on their doorstep.

Barbara's sister came to Weimar to live with them as a permanent resident, and nephews of Sebastian came for organ lessons and stayed on for free room and board. Though it was a full household, it was not as large as it could have been. In the first eleven years of marriage Barbara gave birth to seven children, but only four of them survived infancy. Still, running the home kept her busy enough.

Sebastian kept busy too. Each month he composed a fresh cantata, and in between he wrote "an abundance of toccatas, fantasies, preludes, and fugues." From Weimar his fame as an organist and composer began spreading across the continent.

But Weimar wasn't paradise. Far from it. Before long, Sebastian found himself once again snarled in a problem. The problem was that when the young prince of Weimar died in 1715, the eccentric (bordering on the insane) duke became increasingly unpredictable.

In 1716, after Weimar's choir director died, Sebastian assumed that he would be named—or at the least seriously considered—to be the successor. But, without explanation, he was passed over. Other actions taken by the reigning duke also seemed extremely arbitrary. In response, Sebastian decided that he would write no more new music in Weimar. There was, admits one biographer, "a definitely pugnacious streak in his disposition. Far from trying to avoid difficulties, he acted rather to provoke them."

Things had deteriorated rapidly.

After nine years in the court of Weimar, the Bachs were packing their suitcases and ready to move again. When an offer came to join the court of the small principality of Cothen, Sebastian jumped at the chance.

But Sebastian jumped too soon. His request to be dismissed from Weimar was not received kindly by the duke. In fact, the duke didn't like the idea at all, and soon he placed Sebastian in the Weimar jail "for too obstinately requesting his dismissal."

The duke, of course, had no intention of keeping his organist in jail the rest of his life. He simply wanted Sebastian to change his mind about leaving Weimar. So it became a matter of who was the most stubborn.

Sebastian won.

After a month, the duke reluctantly released his organist, and Sebastian and Barbara left town as quickly as they could, before the duke could change his mind.

In the court of Cothen, Sebastian was named court conductor, or kapellmeister. It was a great honor to be the kapellmeister of a court orchestra. Though Cothen was a small court, it was nonetheless the court of a prince.

With the job came some fringe benefits. Besides the generous salary that he received, Sebastian was also privileged to travel to various parts of Europe with Prince Leopold. The prince was a lover of the arts; sometimes he joined Sebastian's orchestra and played the viola. The seventeen-piece orchestra was not large, but in it were several able musicians who had been part of King Friedrich Wilhelm's band in Berlin.

Though Sebastian enjoyed his career at the court, he enjoyed his home even more, especially as his children were growing up. His children, as might be expected, showed an aptitude in music, and he took special delight in teaching them. He trained his eldest son, Wilhelm Friedemann, on the clavier, a pianolike instrument, and prepared a special clavier book for him which could be used with other pupils as well. Inside the book's cover he inscribed, "In praise of the Almighty's will, And for my Neighbor's greater skill."

The Bach children were being trained in other subjects besides music. Though the main church in Cothen was Reformed—Calvinistic—and not Lutheran, the prince had established "freedom of conscience" for his subjects. That meant that the Bachs could continue to attend a Lutheran church and send their children to a Lutheran school.

Most great composers did not enjoy teaching; Sebastian did. He even enjoyed working with beginners. However, as Geiringer notes, "He exhibited patience only with gifted pupils. Lack of talent and a lukewarm attitude towards the craft made his temper boil over. He was the perfect teacher for talented youths, but he was unable to put up with mediocrity." Fortunately, the Bach children were not mediocre musically. A few—notably Carl Philipp Emanuel and Johann Christian—became noted composers.

Late in 1718, Barbara bore her seventh child. In honor of the prince, they named him Leopold Augustus. At the baby's christening, three members of the prince's family, including the prince himself, a court counselor, and the wife of a court minister, all served as godparents for the child.

The Bachs were getting up in the world.

But about a year later everything began to crash around Sebastian's head. First, little Leopold Augustus died in September. Then the following July, while Sebastian was traveling with the prince, Barbara became ill. It happened so quickly that there was no time for Sebastian to be notified.

He returned home exhilarated by his trip. As he walked into his house he was informed that his wife had died and had been buried during his absence.

Sebastian was grief-stricken. But something else was disturbing him, too. As happy as he was in Cothen, as compatible as he was with the prince, as much freedom as he enjoyed to write music, there was something lacking. His mission in life, he felt, was to write music for the glory of God in the service of the church. God had called him to write church music, not court music.

Of course, Sebastian felt that any music could be written for God's glory. At Cothen he had composed many secular sonatas and concertos. The Reformed church in Cothen did not encourage special church music, so there was no motivation to write church music there.

Perhaps God wanted him back in a setting where he could concentrate on church music. Wasn't that his particular calling?

A few months after Barbara's death, when he received an invitation to compete for the position of organist at St. Jacob's Church in Hamburg, he eagerly accepted.

After hearing him play, the Hamburg council favored his appointment. But there was one little snag. It was customary for the appointee to make a handsome contribution to the church.

Out of principle, Sebastian refused. He looked on it as the payment of a bribe. In response, the Hamburg council turned down Sebastian and opted for a candidate who had been willing to make a sizable contribution.

Back in Cothen, Sebastian received another serious setback. He received word that his older brother Johann Christoph had died at the age of forty-nine.

Perhaps this was the lowest time in Sebastian's life. The cumulative effect of three deaths—a child, a dearly loved wife, and a brother who had been a second father to him—overwhelmed him.

He brooded. When his own father had died, Johann Christoph had taken him into his house. But now if Sebastian were to die—and many of the Bachs had died before they turned fifty—his children would have no one to take them in.

It wasn't customary in those days for a widower to wait too long before remarrying. Most remarried within six months. Sebastian was taking longer than normal; he had waited eighteen months.

In those days love wasn't a high priority in a second marriage. Often, it wasn't too high in a first marriage either. The first time you married for economic considerations; the second time you married a good housekeeper and mother for the children. But love is, of course, always desirable.

Enter Anna Magdalena Wilcken. She was the ideal person to bring him out of his despair. The youngest daughter of the "Court and Field

418

Trumpeter of the Music of His Highness the Prince of Saxe-Weissenfels," she had been trained in vocal music and had been appointed as "Royal Singer" of Prince Leopold's court ensemble. In fact, her soprano voice was so highly regarded by the prince that she was given a salary of two hundred thaler, half as much as Sebastian himself was receiving. A few months later, her salary was increased to three hundred thaler.

In December 1721, when Sebastian was thirty-six and Magdalena was twenty, the two were married.

The new wife was much more than a stepmother to his children; she was a companion in his labors. Painstakingly, she copied music for him, and he trusted her completely to do the work accurately. On some pieces of music, she obviously began the copying and he completed it, or vice versa. Each had a mutual respect for the other's musicianship.

She even began taking clavier lessons from Sebastian, and probably organ lessons as well.

Then, a few months after their marriage, news came to Cothen that the music director of Leipzig's St. Thomas Church had died. Leipzig was known as a bastion of the Protestant faith. If Sebastian ever intended to get back into church music, he had to consider this opportunity.

But he hesitated. For one thing, he didn't want to get embroiled in ecclesiastical politics again. Cothen's serenity was something he hesitated to give up. For another thing, it would mean a drastic cut in pay. Only if he played for enough weddings and funerals might he make more. For another, it would mean a step down the social ladder. (To be a conductor in a prince's court was valued much more highly than to be a music director of any church.)

And then there was Magdalena to think about. For Magdalena, Cothen was home. In Cothen she had a position as a court singer, and her second income supplemented his. In Leipzig, she would have to give up her career. Of course, she could sing her husband's music at home, but she would not be permitted to sing it as a soloist in church.

For many reasons, it didn't make sense to leave Cothen.

But for some reasons, it did make sense. The biggest reason may have been that he felt God wanted him to return to service in the church. Besides that, Sebastian also was considering his children. At Cothen, the Lutheran school was second-rate. In Leipzig they would not only receive a good preparatory education, but at the University of Leipzig they could receive a well-rounded classical education that was available in few other places.

It was not an easy decision. For six months, Sebastian and Magdalena mulled the pros and cons. Then Sebastian decided to send in his application.

But the job wouldn't be handed to him on a silver platter. After all, although Sebastian had become known as an organist, he was not famous as a music director. Furthermore, the city fathers of Leipzig thought that in their university town the music director should have a college education. Sebastian did not.

Sebastian was one of six candidates and, because of his dallying, one of the last to throw his hat in the ring. The city council had already offered the position twice to previous candidates, and both were unable to accept it.

Finally, it was offered to Sebastian, with one councilman mumbling, "Since we cannot get the best, we will have to be satisfied with a mediocre one."

So in 1723, "the mediocre one" and Magdalena moved from the prince's court to their new lodgings—a 170-year-old school building.

Actually, it was in the left wing of the school building. The rest of the building served as the dormitory for the church school, and it was inhabited by underprivileged children who were often wild and unruly. These students were the choir that Sebastian worked with.

Only a thin wall separated the Bachs' living quarters from the dormitory. No doubt, contagious diseases from the dormitory ravaged the Bach children. Seven of the thirteen children that Magdalena bore succumbed to disease before their sixth birthday.

Sebastian had an amazing ability to concentrate amid bedlam. In the next few years he turned out an assortment of church music, producing a cantata each month.

Not only was there noise from the rambunctious pupils in the dormitory, but, of course, the Bachs contributed some noise themselves. When they moved to Leipzig, Magdalena was only twenty-two, and her stepdaughter Catherina was fifteen. The three boys were thirteen, nine, and eight. Magdalena was carrying an infant only a few months old in her arms, and already she was pregnant with another. Shortly after they arrived, a nephew (the son of Sebastian's brother Christoph) joined them. He was sixteen. And that wasn't all. Visiting musicians dropped in unannounced. When relatives came, they tended to stay for weeks.

Though he had a tendency to take her for granted, Sebastian was proud of Magdalena. Men of his rank in society rarely had their wives sit for a painting, but Sebastian commissioned an oil portrait of Magdalena by a well-known painter. Because the painting has been lost, it is not known if he did this because of her beauty or because of his deep appreciation for her. Maybe it was both.

She was such a part of his musical career that he prepared two music books for her. The first was a small and simple oblong volume, containing his five French suites and several smaller pieces. This was Magdalena's clavier book.

The second book for Magdalena was an unusual volume in green and gold with her initials AMB and the year 1725 stamped on the cover. This one became a kind of musical family album into which Sebastian, Magdalena, and the children all entered songs, some original, some copied, some sacred, some frivolous.

In this second book Sebastian prepared three different musical arrangements for one special hymn. Evidently he thought that Magdalena needed to consider the message of the hymn very carefully. The hymn begins, "Fret not, my soul; on God rely." The book also contains some soprano arias apparently transposed into Magdalena's voice range. One of these was entitled, "Wherefore art thou so sad and why so crushed and broken, oh, much tormented soul" may also have been designed to lift her spirits.

One love song written by Sebastian for his wife was transcribed later in the book by Magdalena. Apparently, however, as Magdalena transcribed it, there were some discords in it; then another handwriting is seen correcting the discords. It was obviously the hand of Sebastian, who couldn't allow a discord to remain anywhere, not even in a scrapbook.

Farther along in the musical scrapbook are also found some wedding verses. These were written several years later, but still reflect Sebastian's love for her.

> Your servant, sweetest maiden bride:
> Joy be with you this morning!
> To see you in your flowery crown
> And wedding day adorning
> Would fill with joy the sternest soul.
> What wonder, as I meet you,
> That my fond heart and loving lips
> O'erflow with song to greet you?

In spite of such tenderness, life was not easy for Magdalena. Perhaps she would have preferred life in the court of Cothen, but her husband felt called to prepare church music and she had been willing to sacrifice for him.

Before their seventh wedding anniversary and her twenty-seventh birthday, Magdalena had borne six children. About this time Sebastian wrote a letter to a friend in which he shared a bit about his home situation:

> Now I must add a little about my domestic situation. . . . The children of my second marriage are still small, the eldest, a boy, being six years old. But they are all born musicians, and I can assure you that I can already form an ensemble of both vocalists and instrumentalists within my family, particularly since my present wife sings a good clear soprano, and my eldest daughter, too, joins in not badly.

Somehow, despite the deaths of so many of her children, Magdalena was able to keep singing. Bach's biographers depict her as "hard-working, warm-hearted, and highly musical," perhaps more interested in operatic music than Sebastian, because that seemed to be her training.

One person who helped cheer her was a colorful relative named Johann Elias Bach, who accepted board and room in exchange for tutoring the Bach offspring and serving as a secretary to Sebastian. He was also trying to finish a seminary education. He had come at Sebastian's suggestion; Sebastian was frugal, but he was also hospitable, and he did not begrudge having another mouth to feed.

Sebastian signed a contract with Elias, and Elias jumped into his responsibilities with enthusiasm. Especially when it came time to prepare the Bach children for Communion, this young theology student did his job thoroughly. Once he turned down a better position because he wanted to continue teaching the Bach children, who he felt were "in the greatest need of a solid and faithful instruction."

Elias was also a secretary, a PR man, and a family counselor. Elias's letters always raved about Sebastian's compositions, and quite possibly he felt he had a ministry of publicizing his relative's works. "My honored cousin," he once wrote a friend in a distant city, "will bring out more clavier pieces which . . . are exceedingly well composed, and they will doubtless be ready for the coming Easter Fair."

Elias had the heart of a good pastor. At times he saw that Sebastian was so wrapped up in his music that Magdalena was suffering. Since she didn't want to do anything that would disturb the musical genius at work, she suffered in silence. Elias was at hand to provide some comfort and cheer.

At the time that Elias moved into the Bach home, Sebastian was fifty-three and Magdalena was thirty-seven. Besides rearing her four stepchildren, Magdalena had herself borne twelve children, and by the time Elias had left, she had given birth to another. Their oldest child was feebleminded, and seven of their children had died.

Despite the household guests, the children, and the work around the house, she still continued to assist Sebastian by transcribing his music. Concerned about his failing eyesight, she took on even more responsibility in transcribing his music. After a while, her script so resembled his that scholars today are not able to distinguish which manuscripts were copied by Magdalena and which by Sebastian.

Their handwriting may have been close, but the two were often separated physically. Throughout his life, Sebastian liked to travel. The more frustrated he became with his problems in the churches he served, the more time he spent away from home.

Once while Sebastian was in Berlin trying to get an audience with the king, Magdalena became ill at home. When the king became more interested in waging a war than in hearing musicians, Sebastian's visit to Berlin became extended.

Back in Leipzig, a concerned Elias wrote his master a letter. "The most lovable Mamma [as he called Magdalena] has been ailing for a week now, and we do not know whether perhaps as a result of the violent throbbing of her pulse a creeping fever or some other evil consequence may arise."

Sebastian answered that he would be returning very soon. He still hoped the king would be able to see him.

It wasn't good enough for Elias, who responded that while he was glad that Sebastian had made plans to return, he wanted his master to attach more urgency to the situation. "Great as was the pleasure we derived from this, just so great must be the pain we feel about the increasing weakness of our more honored Mamma, for the latter has for a fortnight now not had a single night with an hour's rest and cannot sit up or lie down, so that during last night I was called, and we could not help thinking that, to our great sorrow, we would lose her."

Sebastian came home in a hurry, and Magdalena recovered.

Life in Leipzig was never dull. As usual, Sebastian had problems with the town council. In his inaugural he had addressed them as a "Noble and Most Wise Council." It was probably the nicest thing he ever said to them. He had financial complaints. They seemed always to be "nickling and diming" the Bachs out of what had previously been promised. He complained about the poor musical talent that he was given to work with, and he complained about the slurs and slights. He simply was not appreciated by the council.

They tried continually to put him in his place. They didn't think he was working hard enough; he wasn't submissive enough; he didn't have a university education. He had been hired as a teacher for the school as well as the music director for the town's churches. As teacher for the school, he had to teach Latin as well as music, and he resented it.

He was continually trying to finagle his way out of his schoolteaching responsibilities in order to spend more time on his church music responsibilities. The town council felt he already spent more time on church music and not enough on the school.

424

In 1730, after seven years in Leipzig, he was ready to quit. He wrote a friend about his problems. Basically, there were four major problems: (1) "this appointment is by no means as advantageous as it was described to me, (2) many fees [that he had previously received to supplement his salary] are now stopped; (3) the town is a very expensive place to live in and (4) the authorities are very strange people, with small love of music, so that I live under almost constant vexation, jealousy and persecution."

But he never left Leipzig. The city council continually tried to break his pride, and so did a new rector at the school, who minimized music and humiliated musicians. Whenever he saw a youngster practicing his violin, he would sneer, "So it's a pothouse fiddler you want to become."

In return, Sebastian increasingly neglected his school responsibilities.

But despite the obstacles, Sebastian wrote nearly three hundred cantatas there, plus such major works as the *St. Matthew Passion*. While at Leipzig he also wrote his *Mass in B Minor,* sometimes called his "greatest theological testament."

Besides writing his music, Bach spent time reading theological works. He studied Luther's monumental three-volume translation of the Bible intensively and corrected errors in the text and commentary, inserting missing words, underlining passages, and making personal annotations that reveal his personal spiritual concerns. One writer observed that Bach was "a Christian who lived with the Bible."

He often inscribed his compositions, "S.D.G."—*Soli Deo Gloria*—"To God alone be the glory." Occasionally, he would use the initials, "J.J."—*Jesu juva*—"Jesus, help me."

Bach was indeed a Christian. Though his temper was well known, he was actually humble. Once when he was complimented on his organ playing, he responded, "There is nothing remarkable about it. All one has to do is hit the right notes at the right time, and the instrument plays itself."

Strained by writing small musical notes by candlelight, his eyesight weakened. In 1750, the English oculist who had previously operated on Handel came to Leipzig and operated twice on Bach. Both operations failed.

On his deathbed he dictated his final chorale. Originally, he called it "Lord, when we are in direst need," but then he renamed it "Before Thy throne I now approach."

Sebastian was sixty-five when he died. Magdalena, then forty-nine, resolved not to remarry. But she did not anticipate the financial problems that she would face.

Since Sebastian had died without a will, the estate was divided up between family members. Magdalena got one-third, and the remaining two-thirds went to the children. In addition, the city council gave her half a year's salary, minus an excess payment they had discovered they had overpaid Sebastian and Magdalena twenty-eight years earlier.

Magdalena's own children were too young to help her and, for reasons we do not know, her stepsons did nothing. In the next few years, she had to sell everything—including Sebastian's music—to make ends meet. Reportedly, some of his music was even used to wrap garbage. Ten years later, Magdalena died at the age of fifty-nine. She had been reduced to an almswoman and was given a pauper's funeral.

It is said of Sebastian that he was "temperate, industrious, devout, a home lover, and a family man, genuine, hospitable and jovial. Frugality and discipline ruled in the Bach home, but so did unity, laughter, loyalty and love."

What made the marriage work? Why was there peace and laughter inside even though Sebastian brought storm clouds wherever else he was?

Partly it was the respect and admiration that both Barbara and Magdalena had for Sebastian, and also the respect and admiration that he had for them. Though town councils and church authorities may have engaged in long-standing feuds with him, both Barbara and Magdalena supported him at home.

They also shared his interest in music. His career was a family affair. He saw his own children begin illustrious musical careers, and he even helped them get their music printed and sold.

Music, of course, had top priority for the Bachs. Yet music wasn't the only thing in their lives. Family and loved ones, hospitality, theology, the little delights of carnations and linnets—these things kept them close together as well.

Sometimes it seemed that Sebastian was so wrapped up in music that he could have forgotten his marriage. But not for long.

Music and family went hand in hand, just as Magdalena and Sebastian did.

Bibliography

David, Hans T., and Arthur Mendel, eds. *The Bach Reader.* Rev. ed. New York: W. W. Norton, 1966.

Geiringer, Karl. *The Bach Family.* New York: Oxford University Press, 1967.

Neumann, Werner. *Bach: A Pictorial Biography.* New York: Viking, 1961.

Schweitzer, Albert. *J. S. Bach.* New York: Dover, 1966.

Spitta, Philipp. *Johann Sebastian Bach.* New York: Dover, 1952.

Wohlfarth, Hannsdieter. *Johann Sebastian Bach.* Philadelphia: Fortress, 1985.

A Most Uncommon Union
Jonathan and Sarah Edwards

You may remember Jonathan Edwards for three things: (1) he was the preacher of a sermon entitled "Sinners in the Hands of an Angry God," (2) he was a key figure in America's Great Awakening, and (3) he was a brilliant metaphysical philosopher.

None of those things made him a popular folk hero like Johnny Appleseed, and none of them gave him an inside track on being a good husband.

Maybe he wasn't a particularly good husband. Maybe the credit for the good marriage should go to his wife, Sarah.

I'll let you decide that.

In a day when marriages tended to be cold and formal, this one was warm and friendly.

What was it that made this marriage a success?

"A sweeter couple I have not yet seen." That was what evangelist George Whitefield of England wrote regarding Jonathan and Sarah Edwards.

In fact, after visiting their Massachusetts home for a few days, Whitefield was so impressed with the Edwards household that he resolved to get married when he returned home to England.

That may sound strange to you. After all, Jonathan Edwards is best known for his fire-and-brimstone sermon "Sinners in the Hands of an Angry God," in which he says: "The God that holds you over the pit of hell, much as one holds a spider, or some loathsome insect, over the fire, abhors you, and is dreadfully provoked."

Writer Samuel Hopkins visited the Edwards home and had to admire "the perfect harmony and mutual love and esteem that subsisted between them."

Somehow we find it difficult to imagine that Jonathan Edwards could compose one half of such an idyllic marriage. Besides being a revivalist and a theologian, Jonathan was also one of the greatest philosophers America has ever produced. He was a profound metaphysical, abstract theoretician. Does that sound like a person from whose home would come harmony, love, and esteem? To tell the truth, that home produced not only harmony, love, and esteem, but a study of 1,400 descendants of Jonathan and Sarah Edwards indicated that it also produced 13 college presidents, 65 professors, 100 lawyers, 30 judges, 66 physicians, and 8 holders of public office, including 3 senators, 3 governors, and a vice president of the United States.

Much, but by no means all, of the credit for the happy union goes to Sarah Edwards. Elisabeth D. Dodds titled her book on Sarah Edwards *Marriage to a Difficult Man,* and no doubt he was a difficult man. Lost in his own world, impractical, and moody, Jonathan Edwards must have been a challenge to live with.

To the outsider, Sarah looked as if she was the one who had it all together. She never seemed to lose her composure, except in times of religious revival. She seemed to manage household and family calmly. But Jonathan Edwards knew better, especially once when she seemed on the verge of a nervous breakdown.

It takes two to make a good marriage, and both Jonathan and Sarah spent time making it work. Both of them were fascinating individuals, so let's take a closer look at them.

On the surface, Jonathan Edwards had a lot in common with John Wesley. Both men were born in the same year—1703. Both were sons of ministers. Both were raised in remote country towns. Both were surrounded by doting sisters. Of course, Edwards was born in East Windsor, Connecticut, not Epworth, England, and his father was a Congregational minister, not an Anglican rector.

Jonathan Edwards had ten sisters. All of them were tall—so was Jonathan—and the father called them his "sixty feet of daughters."

A precocious child, Jonathan loved nature and God. At thirteen, he wrote an extraordinary essay on "flying spiders." But even earlier than that he and his playmates had built a hut in a nearby swamp, not as a clubhouse, but as a prayer house.

"I used to pray five times a day in secret," he wrote much later, "and to spend much time in religious talk with other boys, and used to meet with them in secret to pray together. . . . I with some of my schoolmates joined together and built a booth in a swamp, in a very retired spot, for a place of prayer. And besides, I had a secret place of my own in the woods, where I used to retire by myself."

He entered Yale to study philosophy when only thirteen. Admittedly, Yale wasn't the university that it is today, but without a doubt Edwards wasn't a typical teenager. Writer James Wood says, "Brilliantly gifted, Jonathan Edwards at the age of fifteen to eighteen could have become a scientist, a naturalist or a philosopher, ranging freely over the whole world of thought. He might well have become a major poet."

Instead, he became a theologian. At seventeen, he was converted. The Scripture verse which God used in his life was 1 Timothy 1:17: "Now unto the King, eternal, immortal, invisible, the only wise God, be honor and glory for ever and ever. Amen." That verse boggled Edwards's mind. After confronting that verse, Edwards says, "I began to have a new kind of apprehension and ideas of Christ, and the work of redemption and the glorious way of salvation by Him."

By the time he was nineteen he had his ministerial degree and was off to New York City for a brief pastorate in a Presbyterian church there.

Then he came back to join the faculty of Yale. It was not the best of times for Yale. Bickering, heresy-hunting, and internal dissension rocked the school. While everyone else seemed to be throwing mud, young Edwards frequently found himself trying to run the college. The task was too big for him. His inadequacy weighed him down. He was beset with "despondencies, fears, perplexities, multitudes of cares and distraction of mind," in his own words.

430

One distraction was thirteen-year-old Sarah Pierrepont, daughter of a prominent New Haven minister who had been a driving force in the founding of Yale. Sarah was seven years younger than Jonathan and totally unlike him. He was moody; she was vibrant. He was shy; she was outgoing. He was socially inept; she was a natural conversationalist. He was gawky; she was graceful.

And she played "hard to get."

On the social ladder, the Pierreponts were top-rung. Her mother was a granddaughter of Thomas Hooker, noted Puritan divine and New Haven's founding father. Though she was only thirteen, suitors were already standing in line. Almost all of them were more dashing, more suave than gangling Jonathan. And since most girls in colonial days were married by the time they were sixteen, Sarah's single days were numbered.

But she couldn't forget Jonathan. She liked nature and so did Jonathan. They walked and talked along the shore. She liked to read, too. One of her books on the nature of the Covenant deeply influenced Jonathan's theological thinking. He seemed to respect her mind; he liked to talk to her about deep things.

Despite all the pressures and distractions at the university, Jonathan usually had no trouble concentrating. But after he met Sarah, things changed. At the strangest times, she intruded into his thoughts. It took discipline to resist the temptations. He wrote: "When I am violently beset with temptation . . . [I resolve to do some study] which necessarily engages all my thoughts and unavoidably keeps them from wandering." Such as studying Greek grammar, for instance.

Obviously, it didn't always work. On the front page of Jonathan's Greek grammar book was found this ode to Sarah: "They say there is a young lady in New Haven who is beloved of that Great Being, who made and rules the world, and that there are certain seasons in which the Great Being, in some way or another invisible, comes to her and fills her mind with exceeding sweet delight, and that she hardly cares for anything except to meditate on him. . . . She has a strange sweetness in her mind, and singular purity in her affections; is most just and conscientious in all her conduct; and you could not persuade her to do anything wrong or sinful if you would give her all the world. . . .

She will sometimes go about from place to place, singing sweetly and seems to be always full of joy and pleasure; and no one knows for what. She loves to be alone, walking in the fields and groves, and seems to have someone invisible always conversing with her."

After three years of friendship and courtship, Jonathan pressed her for marriage with the words: "Patience is commonly esteemed a virtue, but in this case I may almost regard it as a vice."

Choosing the course of virtue, Sarah Pierrepont consented to marry the lanky young man, and on July 20, 1727, when he was twenty-three and she was seventeen, they were wed.

They were married for thirty-one years, until death parted them in 1758. Twenty-three of those years were spent in the west central Massachusetts town of Northampton. Jonathan had been called to take charge of a 600-member parish, stepping into the shoes of his grandfather Solomon Stoddard, who had finally decided to retire at eighty-three. It was the largest and most significant church outside of Boston.

Perhaps the young couple would have been more suited for a parish in Boston. He was an intellectual, not a frontier preacher. She had come from an aristocratic background, and her tastes had been properly cultivated. Yet they felt divinely directed to Northampton.

Jonathan always enjoyed writing more than preaching, so he wrote out all his sermons in the style of the day. His style was certainly not dramatic. According to one biographer, "Tall, slight, round-faced with a high forehead and a student's pallor, he spoke quietly and distinctly. His face was grave, his manner dignified. He used no gestures. He depended for effect on the earnestness of his speech, the clarity of his sentences and the skillful use of the pause." The style was Twentieth-Century Funeral Director.

His sermons, which later became famous, were written on scraps of paper, backs of bills from the general store, backs of his children's writing exercises, and backs of broadside ads. Biographer Ola Winslow writes, "Edwards saved scraps of paper just as he saved scraps of time. Both could be made to serve a useful purpose." Today, both sides of Edwards's sermon notes fascinate the historian.

Edwards rose early each day. He noted in his journal, "I think Christ has recommended rising early in the morning by His rising from the grave very early." He had a phobia against wasting time. "Resolved never to lose one moment of time, but to improve it in the most profitable way I can." But this didn't mean he spent all his time praying and reading his Bible. One hour each day was spent in physical work. Chopping wood was a favorite wintertime chore for him. Sometimes he spent more than that, but Sarah was the manager not only of the household but also of the garden and the fields. Edwards once asked, "Isn't it about time for the hay to be cut?" Sarah responded, "It's been in the barn for two weeks."

Samuel Hopkins wrote: "It was a happy circumstance that he could trust everything to the care of Mrs. Edwards with entire safety and with undoubting confidence. She was a most judicious and faithful mistress of a family, habitually industrious, a sound economist, managing her household affairs with diligence and discretion. While she uniformly paid a becoming deference to her husband and treated him with entire respect, she spared no pains in conforming to his inclination and rendering everything in the family agreeable and pleasant."

Jonathan loved to ride his horse, although he resented the time it took to travel. To make proper use of the time, he wrote notes as he was riding. So that he wouldn't forget his valuable thoughts, he pinned his notes to his coat. When he arrived home, Sarah would unpin all the notes and help him sort out the ideas.

To give Sarah some time away from the children, he would frequently go riding with her. It wasn't simply a respite from the cares of the family; it was more the fact that Jonathan enjoyed her companionship. So, about four o'clock in the afternoon, they often went horseback riding together. At such times he would discuss ideas with her and hash over parish problems.

Late at night, when everyone else was tucked in bed, Sarah and Jonathan would share a devotional time together in his study.

The "everyone else" began with a baby girl, born a year after their marriage, and concluded twenty-two years later with the birth of their eleventh child.

"She had an excellent way of governing her children," Samuel Hopkins eulogizes. "She knew how to make them regard and obey her cheerfully, without loud, angry words, much less heavy blows. . . . If

any correction was necessary, she did not administer it in a passion.
. . . In her directions in matters of importance, she would address herself to the reason of her children, that they might not only know her
will, but at the same time be convinced of the reasonableness of it. . . .
Her system of discipline was begun at a very early age and it was her
rule to resist the first as well as every subsequent exhibition of temper
or disobedience in the child . . . wisely reflecting that until a child will
obey his parents, he can never be brought to obey God."

Jonathan himself set aside an hour at the close of each day to spend
with his children. According to Hopkins, the seemingly stern preacher
of righteousness "entered freely into the feelings and concerns of his
children and relaxed into cheerful and animated conversations, accompanied frequently with sprightly remarks and sallies of wit and humor.
. . . Then he went back to his study for more work before dinner."

A little of Edwards's philosophy about the family is disclosed in his
books and sermons. "The whole world of mankind is kept in action
from day to day by love." And "Every family ought to be a little church,
consecrated to Christ and wholly influenced and governed by His rules.
And family education and order are some of the chief means of grace.
If these fail, all other means are likely to prove ineffectual."

In 1734, the Great Awakening began in Northampton's church after
Edwards had preached a series of expository sermons on love from
1 Corinthians 13. "Scarcely a single person in the whole town was left
unconcerned about the great things of the eternal world," said Edwards.
He was only thirty-one; Sarah (with four daughters by that time) only
twenty-four, and they felt they had a tiger by the tail. Emotions were
running wild. Even Sarah herself was caught up in ecstasy. The parsonage had become the most popular place in town. Skeptics who
investigated were converted. Edwards tried to impose ground rules to
control emotional outbursts, but he wasn't always successful. Some
three hundred people claimed to have been converted in the small
Massachusetts town during a six-month period.

Just as quickly as it had exploded, it faded away. Then came the letdown. Many of the townspeople who claimed a spiritual experience
returned to their old vices. Jonathan was discouraged. What amazed
him, however, is what he began to observe happening in Sarah. Nor-

mally the cool, calm manager, she began to be irritable, finicky, picky. Looking back on this period in her life, Jonathan later wrote that she was "subject to unsteadiness and many ups and downs . . . often subject to melancholy. She had," uncharacteristically for her, "a disposition to censure and condemn others."

Of course, an outsider like Samuel Hopkins didn't detect any change at first. "She made it a rule to speak well of all," he wrote and lauded her patience, cheerfulness, and good humor. Jonathan knew better.

Opposition to Jonathan Edwards had begun to build in Northampton, and Sarah didn't know how to cope with it. She had always been popular with everyone; she had no enemies, and wouldn't know what to do if she had them. Jonathan, however, had plenty of foes. Even some of his cousins were making life miserable for him. Sometimes he didn't sense the opposition as soon as Sarah did. He stayed in his study. She would be out on the streets, in the shops, meeting people. Clouds were gathering around Northampton. Sarah could often feel what Jonathan could not yet see. She didn't want to disturb him about some of the petty problems in his parish. So she tried to keep up a good front; underneath, however, it was becoming more and more difficult for her to handle.

Sarah was only thirty, but she had already been the lady of the manse for thirteen years when 1740 rolled around. And in the next two years, more seemed to happen than in the previous thirteen.

She had just given birth to her seventh child (and sixth daughter). Four days later, she was shaken by the news that her older sister had died. That spring there was more illness than usual among the children, and the financial needs of the Edwards household became critical. No doubt urged by Sarah, Jonathan went to the town council to ask for a raise in pay.

That fall, twenty-six-year-old evangelist George Whitefield came to town. He had already stirred up Philadelphia and Boston; Northampton, which had experienced an awakening five years earlier, was ripe for another one. So was Sarah. Her heart, she said, "was swallowed up in a kind of glow of Christ's love coming down as a constant stream of sweet light."

No less stirred was Whitefield himself. He was deeply impressed with the Edwards children, with Jonathan ("I have not seen his Fellow in all New England"), and especially Sarah. He was moved by her ability to talk "feelingly and solidly of the things of God." He was amazed at how much of a helpmeet she was for her husband. Because of Sarah he renewed his prayers for a wife. He was married the following year.

If the Revival of 1735 was Phase One of the Great Awakening, the spark kindled by Whitefield in 1740 was Phase Two. In New England, it was Jonathan Edwards who kept fanning the flames. Though by style and inclination he was an unlikely revivalist, he was called away from home for weeks at a time to conduct evangelistic services in other New England churches. It was during this time that his sermon "Sinners in the Hands of an Angry God" became famous.

During this time, Sarah was once again struggling with her inner stability. She didn't like it when her husband was away from home so much, and yet she knew she couldn't ask him to stay in Northampton. God was using him wherever he went.

Jonathan didn't accept all the invitations that came his way. Some he turned down saying, "I have lately been so much gone from my people." But in mid-January 1742, in one of the most severe winters of the eighteenth century, he was going away again, and Sarah as usual was left home with her seven children. Every even-numbered year since their wedding, a baby had been born in the Edwardses' home. In 1742, Sarah wasn't pregnant. "I felt very uneasy and unhappy. . . . I thought I very much needed help from God. . . . I had for some time been earnestly wrestling with God."

Just before Jonathan had left, he had criticized her for being too negative about a "Mr. Williams of Hadley" who had been preaching in Northampton. Her husband's criticism came when she was very vulnerable. She crumbled. "It seemed to bereave me of the quietness and calm of my mind not to have the good opinion of my husband." Not only was she afraid that she had lost the confidence of her husband, but she also feared that she had offended Williams.

In Jonathan's absence from town, a recent seminary graduate named Samuel Buell came to the church to preach. Sarah was emotionally down. Of course, she wanted the revival fires to burn through his preaching; yet she feared that Buell might prove to be a better preacher than her husband and in the process show Jonathan up.

Did she want revival to come back to Northampton even if it meant someone other than Jonathan would be God's instrument? Especially if it meant a flashy young preacher like Samuel Buell? It was difficult for Sarah; she struggled for spiritual victory over it. But at length she attended Buell's sermons and "rejoiced" at the "greater success attending his preaching than had followed the preaching of Mr. Edwards."

And then once again Sarah was encompassed with feelings of ecstasy. Her "soul dwelt on high, was lost in God and almost seemed to leave the body." Hymns ran through her mind and she had a difficult time to "refrain from rising from my seat and leaping for joy."

The next day she fainted from exhaustion in the middle of the day, and she "lay for a considerable time faint with joy." During the following days, she says that she had a "sense of infinite beauty and amiableness of Christ's person, and the heavenly sweetness of his transcendent love." She emerged from the time a renewed person. "I never felt such an entire emptiness of self-love, or any regard to any private selfish interests of my own. I felt that the opinions of the world concerning me were nothing." From this time on, she experienced "a wonderful access to God in prayer."

While Sarah no longer regarded "the opinions of the world," she did regard the opinion of her husband. And she was afraid that when he returned and found out what had happened, he might think that she had made a fool of herself. After all, he had been trying to keep emotional excesses out of the revival.

But Jonathan's reaction was sympathetic. He was very interested in her experiences and asked her to describe her emotions as carefully as she could. Like a psychologist, Edwards took her stream of consciousness down in shorthand. Later, he published this (though anonymously to keep from embarrassing her) as part of a defense of the revival.

He didn't care to use his wife as a guinea pig or to analyze her experience scientifically, but he felt he had to. He had been disappointed in the seemingly short-lived effects of the revival of 1735. Some people had been genuinely converted, but many had only been caught up in emotion. The question was: What would be the long-range result of Sarah's experience?

He didn't glorify emotional religious experiences—even the experiences of his wife. In almost every emotional experience, "there is a mixture of that which is natural, and that which is corrupt, with that which is divine."

Jonathan, who had observed certain changes in Sarah's cool and collected self in the previous two or three years, could have guessed that Sarah would soon have to have some emotional release for what she had kept bottled up. So part of her experience was natural, but another part of it was undeniably spiritual.

She had been converted as a child; Jonathan knew that. She had lived a good life; Jonathan knew that too. He also knew that this experience was not only emotional; it was also spiritual. Sarah had her thoughts focused on Jesus Christ.

A year later Jonathan wrote up the results of his scientific study. Sarah now had an assurance of God's favor that she didn't have before. She was at rest with herself as well as with God. Jonathan was amazed at her "constant sweet peace, calm and serenity of soul." Whatever she did, she was now doing for the glory of God, not for the admiration of men. In Edwards's words, she lived with a "daily sensible doing and suffering everything for God." To him, the "daily sensible doing" was the bottom line of religious revival.

Perhaps, without such a spiritual experience, Sarah couldn't have handled the coming problems in Northampton.

The first problem was finances. Northampton had been growing increasingly unhappy with the need in the Edwardses' family for more funds. On the one hand, both Sarah and Jonathan were quite frugal. They saved everything. On the other hand, Sarah had been raised in one of the finest homes in New Haven, and it showed. She was accustomed to go "first class." She dressed well and furnished the home in taste. The townspeople didn't understand why Jonathan needed to acquire so many new books. Why couldn't he be content with a few old commentaries? After all, he was preaching from the Bible, wasn't he? The fact that every two years there was another mouth to feed in the Edwardses' home didn't get much sympathy. Many families in the area were able to feed several more children on half as much income. History records "a great uneasiness in the town" about the way the Edwards family handled their finances. Finally, Sarah Edwards was asked to turn over the itemized family budget so that everyone could see exactly how they were spending their money.

Why in the world, asked the townspeople, did Jonathan need two wigs? Why did he spend eleven pounds to buy his wife a gold chain and locket? How did Sarah have the nerve to wear such a display of ostentation?

The town was aghast at the extravagance. How could Jonathan ask for more money from the poor church members who were eating off wooden trenchers while he and Sarah and the children were eating from pewter dishes? Jonathan could afford silver buckles on his black shoes, while most of his parishioners had to tie their shoes with common string. And it was obvious to all that Sarah's dresses were expensive.

The financial matter had been a petty irritant for years. When revivals occurred, it was put on the back burner for a while; but the problem was always simmering.

The other problem was that Jonathan had decided not to accept the "non-committed" into church membership. He had discussed it with Sarah, and both realized that this would be a major issue. Sarah reported that he "told me that he would not dare ever to admit another person without a profession of real saving religion and spake much of the great difficulties that he expected would come upon him by reason of his opinion." Why was it such a bone of contention? Because he would be reversing the practice begun by his beloved grandfather, Solomon Stoddard, who had been pastor of the church for more than fifty years. Edwards predicted that, as a result of this decision to reverse his grandfather's procedure, he would be "thrown out of business" and he and his family would be brought to poverty.

Yet Jonathan had to see it through. A college invited him to be its president. Its committee suggested: "You had better run away from these difficulties." According to Sarah: "Mr. Edwards replied that he must not run away."

439

If the years 1735–1740 were the troubled years for Sarah, the years 1745–1750 were Jonathan's bugbear. Most of his life he had bouts with headaches, colitis, and moodiness. Now he showed his irritation on insignificant matters in the church; even some of his supporters lost heart. A few years later Jonathan mused: "God does not call us to have our spirits ceaselessly engaged in opposition and stirred in anger unless it be on some important occasions." But the issue of a "committed" church membership was important.

In the middle of the unrest, Sarah was asked to go to Boston and take care of an elderly relative who had suffered a stroke. After she had been there a few weeks, Jonathan wrote her tenderly, addressing her as "My dear companion," and told her how the younger children were faring in her absence. Then, after requesting she bring some cheese with her from Boston, he concluded with the line, "We have been without you almost as long as we know how to be."

He often spoke of her as his companion, and never did he need a companion more.

In 1750, there were problems aplenty. Sarah had just given birth to her eleventh child, and two months later, physically and emotionally depleted, she was flattened by rheumatic fever. That spring, townspeople shunned the Edwards family, refusing to talk with them on the street. Church attendance was only a fraction of what it used to be. A petition was circulated, and two hundred church members signed it asking for Edwards's dismissal as minister. By mid-year Jonathan was unemployed.

After twenty-three years in Northampton, Jonathan, forty-six, and Sarah, forty, had to move on. The citizens of Northampton, said Paul Elmer More in the *Cambridge History of American Literature,* "had ousted the greatest theologian and philosopher yet produced in this country."

As strange as it may seem, it wasn't easy for Edwards to find another church—or another job of any kind. He was depressed and felt he was over the hill. "I am now thrown upon the wide ocean of the world and know not what will become of me and my numerous and chargeable family." He admitted that he was "fitted for no other business but study."

Northampton, too, had its problems. It couldn't find a minister to fill the shoes of Edwards. For a while, Jonathan filled the pulpit of the church which had boisterously evicted him. He preached without bitterness. Meanwhile Sarah and her daughters made lacework and embroidery and painted fans, which they sent to market in Boston. Those were not easy months for either Jonathan or Sarah.

Then a call came for Jonathan to be a missionary to the Indians in Stockbridge on the western frontier of Massachusetts. There was a small church there. The congregation, composed of several white families and forty-two Indians, was summoned to services by an Indian named David who "blew a blast with a conch shell."

It was a far cry from fashionable New Haven and even from Northampton, the largest church congregation outside of Boston. In primitive Stockbridge, Jonathan preached in a small stuffy room through an interpreter to a small congregation, mostly Indians who had covered themselves in bear grease as a protection against the winter cold.

Writing to his elderly father in Windsor, Jonathan explained: "My wife and children are well pleased with our present situation. They like the place much better than they expected. Here, at present, we live in peace: which has of long time been an unusual thing with us. The Indians seem much pleased with my family, especially my wife."

Jonathan didn't mind living in isolation from the civilized world. Having a smaller congregation gave him time to do some serious writing. His most famous piece of philosophical writing, *On the Freedom of the Will*, was written in Stockbridge.

Yet it was frustrating to both of them. Jonathan felt inadequate in preaching through an interpreter. He tried to gear his sermons to the level of the Indians, but he realized that there was both a language barrier and a culture barrier between them. Sarah, whose sons and daughters were marrying, found that her interests and concerns were not as much on the ministry at Stockbridge as they ought to be. In Northampton, she had had a ministry of hospitality; the Edwards home had practically become a hotel. In Stockbridge, not too many New Englanders came calling.

But things were not boring, especially when the French and Indian War started heating up in 1754. Jonathan's mission work was virtually halted. In his congregation had been Mohicans, Mohawks, Iroquois, and Housatonnuck Indians. Some of the Indians favored the French; some the British; and some were on the warpath against both.

Several whites were murdered nearby, and soon the Edwards home was turned into a little fort. For three years, the Edwards family lived in a state of siege. White settlers came from miles away to camp at the compound, and four soldiers quartered themselves in the Edwards house. Later, Sarah submitted a bill to the colonial government for 800 dinners and seven gallons of rum.

Daughter Esther, who had married a young college professor named Aaron Burr, returned to Stockbridge to visit her parents during this siege and had trouble getting away again. But while there, she talked to her father about some spiritual problems she was having. "I opened my difficulties and he, as he freely advised and directed the conversation, has removed some distressing doubts that discouraged me much in my Christian warfare. He gave me some excellent directions to be observed in secret that tend to keep the soul near to God as well as others to be observed in a more public way. Oh, what a mercy that I have such a father—such a guide."

It's hardly the picture that most people have of Jonathan Edwards.

The school that Esther's husband served as president was the College of New Jersey, a school that would soon play a part in Jonathan's future. Esther's infant son was named Aaron after his father, and he would play a part—albeit infamously—in America's future.

The French and Indian War finally cooled down, the Indians were returning peacefully to Stockbridge, and Jonathan and Sarah were ready to resume their missionary ministry, when suddenly they received word that their son-in-law, Aaron Burr, had died.

Five days later, another message came to Stockbridge. The board of directors of the school, which later became better known as Princeton University, had extended an invitation to Jonathan Edwards to replace his son-in-law as president.

Jonathan didn't think he should take the job. Things were just returning to normal in Stockbridge; besides, he had two books on the

442

drawing board that he wanted to finish. Physically and emotionally, he wasn't up to it. "I have a constitution," he wrote back, "in many respects peculiarly unhappy, attended with flaccid solids, vapid . . . fluids, and a low tide of spirits; often occasioning a kind of childish weakness and contemptibleness of speech, presence, and demeanor, with a disagreeable dullness and stiffness, much unfitting me for conversation, but more especially for the government of a college."

And if that didn't rule him out of further consideration, he admitted that he didn't know algebra and he was not very familiar with the Greek classics. Knowing that a president's job entails much public speaking, he added, "I think I can write better than I can speak."

Princeton's board of trustees was not deterred. They understood his reply to be a "Maybe" rather than a "No," and sent a delegation to Stockbridge to convince the local church council that Edwards was needed in New Jersey more than in Massachusetts' Wild West. Edwards was amazed that his own church council agreed.

So in January 1758, Jonathan left Stockbridge for New Jersey and was inducted as president the following month. His wife, Sarah, would be coming shortly, as soon as she was able to conclude the family's affairs in Stockbridge.

But in March, after a presidency of only a few weeks, Jonathan Edwards was stricken with smallpox. As he lay dying, he talked much about his wife and children: "Give my kindest love," he said, "to my dear wife and tell her that the uncommon union that has so long subsisted between us has been of such a nature as I trust is spiritual and therefore will continue forever. And I hope she will be supported under so great a trial and submit cheerfully to the will of God. And as to my children, you are now like to be left fatherless, which I hope will be an inducement to you to seek a Father who will never fail you."

Just before he died, he told one of his daughters who was at his bedside, "Trust in God and you do not need to be afraid."

Sarah, of course, was stunned by the news. What was God's purpose in the call to Princeton? Yet, as Hopkins reported, she "had those invisible supports that enabled her to trust in God."

Two weeks after Jonathan's death, she wrote to one of her children: "My very dear child: What shall I say? A holy and good God has covered us with a dark cloud. . . . He has made me adore His goodness that we had him so long, but my God lives, and He has my heart."

After thirty-one years of marriage, Sarah was separated from her husband by death. Her favorite verse of Scripture came to mean much more to her at this time: "Who shall separate us from the love of Christ? . . . For I am persuaded that neither death nor life . . . nor any other creature shall be able to separate us from the love of God, which is in Christ Jesus our Lord."

Six months later, just as suddenly as her husband had died, Sarah became violently ill with dysentery and died. She was forty-eight.

It had been, as Jonathan Edwards said on his deathbed, a most "uncommon union." One biographer called it "a rare companionship with rich happiness." As companions together, they took time for each other and made their marriage a success. They enjoyed each other's companionship and respected each other's gifts.

Biographers tend to praise Sarah for making the marriage so successful. Perhaps so. But Jonathan shared his ministry with her and thus gave her a larger role than many women of that time enjoyed.

It was an uncommon union indeed.

Bibliography

Dodds, Elisabeth D. *Marriage to a Difficult Man*. Philadelphia: Westminster, 1971.

Hirt, Russell T., ed. *Heroic Colonial Christian*. Philadelphia: J. B. Lippincott, 1966.

Miller, Perry. *Jonathan Edwards*. 1949. Reprint. Amherst, Mass.: University of Massachusetts Press, 1981.

Winslow, Ola Elizabeth. *Jonathan Edwards*. New York: Macmillan, 1947.

Wood, James Playstead. *Mr. Jonathan Edwards*. New York: Seabury, 1968.

23
Strong-Minded and Independent
Adoniram and Ann Judson

The foreign missionary movement in America stems from the day that Adoniram and Ann Hasseltine Judson set sail for the land of Burma in 1812.

It was their honeymoon. They had been married one week earlier. The ship was strewn with chickens, pigs, chicken coops, and pigsties, and Adoniram was fastidious to a fault. Hardly the way to spend a honeymoon.

Besides that, they were both strong-minded and independent; so their marriage seemed to have two strikes against it before it got started.

But instead of striking out, their marriage made a big hit. And you have to ask the question, "Why?"

Why did this marriage succeed and the marriage of the Careys fail?

Certainly Adoniram was not an ideal husband, and as for Ann, she would have driven another man to distraction.

What, then, made this marriage work?

As a teenager, Nancy had a penchant for getting into trouble and then charming her way out of it. The townspeople thought that her liberal-minded father had spoiled her. After all, he had converted a large second-floor room into a dance hall. The Hasseltine ballroom soon became the social center for the town's young people, and you could be sure to find fun-loving Nancy at the center of things. Friends said that where she was, "no one can be gloomy or unhappy."

Most girls at the beginning of the nineteenth century received a very limited education, but Nancy's parents were determined that she should go further. Nancy, though undoubtedly quick-witted, was not a natural student; her social interests always seemed to get in the way.

Since Nancy was the youngest of four daughters, maybe it was to be expected that she should be pampered a bit, and especially after an older brother had been lost at sea. One biographer candidly says, "She certainly had a determination to get her own way. . . . Punishments and restraints brought no reform, nothing but resentful grief."

Sometimes she would leave the house and be gone for hours. Her mother was once heard to remark, "I hope one day you will be satisfied with rambling."

That was Nancy the rambler, charming but spoiled.

Then there was Don. Don was impetuous, brilliant, sometimes moody, and a bit eccentric. He had phobias against getting dirty and against saying good-bye. The son of a New England minister, he had learned to read when he was three years old. Although he was a bundle of wound-up energy, he always preferred books to play.

In a way, he admired his father, yet he was always rebelling against him. It was almost as if he were competing with him. Cocky, independent, and stubborn—determination was a family trait, just as evident in the father as in the son—he finished at the top of his college class and headed to New York City to seek fame and fortune as an actor and/or writer. He had renounced his father's belief in a personal God; his education had taken him beyond such primitive notions. And prayer, of course, was meaningless.

About the same time that Don was saying he was too educated to believe in prayer to a personal God, Nancy was saying, "If I'm old enough to attend balls, I am surely too old to say prayers."

You wouldn't think that God could make anything out of either of them, much less make them a couple who worked together beautifully. But that's what happened.

You see, Don and Nancy were only their nicknames. More properly they were called Adoniram Judson and Ann Hasseltine Judson, intrepid American missionaries to the land of Burma. Unlike the Careys, Adoniram and Ann were truly a missionary team.

The marriage between fun-loving, spoiled Ann and impetuous, stubborn Adoniram was not unending bliss, but it was remarkably compatible. They were a working team more than they were lovers, but what an effective team they were! The first Christian material published in Burma was a tract by Adoniram called *The Way to Heaven;* the second was a doctrinal piece written by Ann called *Mrs. Judson's Catechism.*

Just as William Carey is known as the father of British foreign missions, so Adoniram and Ann became the pioneers of American foreign missions. Ann also became a role model for thousands of women missionaries, not a millstone dragged to the mission field unwillingly, nor a passive servant of a missionary husband, but a co-missionary, part of the missionary team.

In the year 1806, in suburban Boston, where both of them grew up, you would never have guessed that either of them would be role models for anything, and certainly not for anything Christian.

Then, while reading a book by British reformer Hannah More, Ann was struck by this sentence: "She that liveth in pleasure is dead while she liveth." Sixteen-year-old Ann didn't like to be scolded by anyone, so she threw the book down and picked up Bunyan's *Pilgrim's Progress.* Within a few months, Ann, in her own words, "had passed from death into life."

Adoniram's conversion was not quite so simple. It was two years later that he was seeking a theatrical career in New York City. He had joined a traveling dramatic troupe which led "a reckless, vagabond life, finding lodgings where we could and bilking the landlord where we found opportunity—in other words running up a score and then decamping without paying the reckoning."

But twenty-year-old Adoniram didn't feel right about it. That certainly wasn't the way he wanted to spend the rest of his life. Disillusioned, he headed back to his home in Plymouth, Massachusetts, stopping for a night at a wayside inn. Adoniram had trouble sleeping that night, because a man in the next room was critically ill and moaning and groaning in pain. Obviously, his neighbor in the next room was dying. In the darkness of his room, Adoniram thought about the possibility of his own death and whether he was prepared for it. At times during the long hours he thought about returning to the Christian beliefs of his father, but then he imagined what his college chum Jacob Eames would say about his father's doctrines. And he waited for morning to come so that the terrors of the night would be forgotten.

Early the next morning, Adoniram went to the innkeeper. "That poor old man in the next room. How is he?" he asked.

"He passed away early this morning," came the reply. "And he wasn't old at all. He was a young man, about your age."

For some reason, Adoniram asked, "What was his name?" It was a rather stupid question, because Adoniram certainly didn't know anyone in that section of the country.

The innkeeper replied, "His name was Jacob Eames."

There was no mistaking the name or the identity. It was the young college friend whose religious skepticism had turned Adoniram against the religion of his father.

Dazed, he returned to Massachusetts and to his father. Echoing through his mind was the old word *Lost.* But it took three more months of intellectual struggle before he "made a solemn dedication of himself to God." It was December 2, 1808.

Remember that date, because that's when things started to happen in Adoniram's life. His father wanted him to enter the ministry and take a church in Massachusetts. Adoniram didn't want to. But the following fall he read a sermon about the need for missionaries in India and a book about the country of Burma. The idea captured his mind; in fact, he could think of little else. Neither ridicule nor common-sense reasoning could dampen his enthusiasm. He was stubbornly determined to be a missionary to either India or Burma, preferably the latter.

Of course, there were a few obstacles: No American mission boards existed and no American had ever gone out as a foreign missionary. The nearest mission board was in England, and the War of 1812 was looming. But what are a few minor obstacles to a dedicated and determined young man of twenty-two?

Undaunted, he found six other young men, and together they presented themselves to the New England Congregationalists for missionary service. And it was precisely on that day that he met Nancy (or Ann, whichever you prefer) Hasseltine over a deep-dish chicken pie and fell madly in love with her. He was never lukewarm about anything.

A month later he asked Nancy's father for her hand in marriage. Obviously, Adoniram was in a hurry. His letter to Mr. Hasseltine displays his spirit:

> I have now to ask whether you can consent to part with your daughter early next spring to see her no more in this world; whether you can consent to her departure and her subjection to the hardships and sufferings of a missionary life; whether you can consent to her exposure to the dangers of the ocean; to the fatal influence of the southern climate of India; to every kind of want and distress; to degradation, insult, persecution, and perhaps a violent death.

It was a nineteenth-century version of "telling it like it is."

Surprisingly, Hasseltine didn't say no to Adoniram. Instead he left the decision to Nancy. And not surprisingly, the girl who had lived for pleasure only a couple of years earlier didn't find it an easy decision to make. In her diary she asked herself whether she would be able to commit herself "entirely to God, to be disposed of, according to His pleasure."

Her sisters told her what they thought of Adoniram, and it wasn't all good. They acknowledged that he was single-minded and very religious, but he was also "by nature ardent, impetuous, and ambitious, with the most unshaken confidence in his own judgment, irrespective of the advice of his elders."

It was a package plan. She couldn't marry Adoniram without becoming a missionary to India, Burma, or some such place. So it was difficult to separate one decision from the other. But by October 1810 she succumbed to his wooing, if you can call it that. She wrote: "Jesus is faithful; His promises are precious. Were it not for these considerations, I should sink down in despair, especially as no female has, to my knowledge, ever left the shores of America to spend her life among the heathen."

Nancy the rambler accepted the challenge.

Adoniram, who had just turned twenty-two, was ecstatic about Nancy's acceptance of his proposal, but he was discouraged by the slow progress the New England Congregationalists were making toward raising financial support. So by year's end he was on a boat to London, hoping that he could convince the London Missionary Society to pitch in a few shillings toward their support. Perhaps he was thinking that he could shame the Americans into missionary support. Without a doubt, he was impetuous.

On his way he wrote Nancy: "With my whole heart I wish you, my love, a happy new year. . . . May every moment of the year bring you nearer to God and find you more prepared to hail the messenger of death as a deliverer and friend. . . . May this be the year in which you change your name, in which you take final leave of your relatives and native land; in which you will cross the wide ocean, and dwell on the other side of the world, among a heathen people." Hardly a typical love letter to one's fiancée.

Eighteen eleven was a year when God taught Adoniram a lesson in patience, and that was not easy for him to learn. The British ship on which he was traveling to London was attacked by a French privateer, and the prospective missionary was taken prisoner to France. He knew Greek and Hebrew but not French, so he had difficulty convincing his captors that he was American, not British. Eventually he got to London where he found that the London Missionary Society would not consent to a joint venture with an American board. Perhaps if he and Nancy would become British missionaries instead of American missionaries, they could gain support in London.

Back in America that fall, Adoniram squabbled with his own board. "If you will not send me," he shouted at them, "I will become a British missionary." The ultimatum was not appreciated. But finally, one of the board members—there's always a peacemaker in every crowd—said that young Adoniram had an excess of self-reliance that got him into trouble working as a team member, but it would stand him in good stead on the mission field. And with surprising speed, the necessary support was raised.

February 1812 was the big month. In fact, it's difficult to imagine how Adoniram and Nancy could pack so much into a few days.

Wednesday, February 5, Bradford, Massachusetts: Adoniram Judson, twenty-three, and Ann Hasseltine, twenty-two, were married in the west room of Deacon Hasseltine's house.

Thursday, February 6, Salem, Massachusetts: Adoniram, along with four other men, were "publicly set aside for the service of God in the Gospel of His Son, among the Heathen." It was an emotional ordination service attended by nearly two thousand people. As the young men were being ordained, Nancy, wearing her new scoop bonnet, walked quietly down the aisle and knelt near her husband. She, too, was becoming a missionary.

Monday, February 10, Salem harbor: After a farewell service the previous night, Adoniram and Nancy boarded their ship for India. "It looks like Noah's ark," Ann said when she saw all the chicken coops and pigpens aboard. Due to weather delays it wasn't for another week, however, that the ship finally set sail. That week—their honeymoon—they spent waiting anxiously in the home of a friend in Salem.

During those few days in February, Nancy learned about some of her husband's idiosyncrasies—such as his phobia against saying good-bye. On the morning after their marriage he got her to leave her home in Bradford before dawn, so he wouldn't have to say good-bye to her family. On the night of the huge ordination service, he again tried to get away quickly; this time they were thwarted in their escape attempt and were brought back to shake hands with the crowd.

In Salem when they were finally informed that their ship was ready to embark, they were staying in a home filled with friends. "Without a word to anyone, he slipped quietly out of the house, walked alone down the snowy street to the wharf, found a boat and went on board the *Caravan*. Here he waited for Nancy," according to biographer Courtney Anderson, who also records, "Nancy was distressed. . . ."

You can imagine the emotions going through Nancy's mind as the ship left port. After two weeks of incredible excitement, it was an emotional letdown. On board ship she confessed that she "had many distressing apprehensions of death" and "felt unwilling to die on the sea, not so much on account of my state after death, as the dreadfulness of perishing amid the waves."

But then she began to enjoy the voyage. To get exercise, Adoniram and Nancy skipped rope and danced. Because of the crowded decks, they couldn't do much walking or running.

And she got better acquainted with the strange, impetuous, brilliant young man she had married. In her journal, she wrote that she had found Adoniram to be "one of the kindest, most faithful and affectionate of husbands."

But before long some problems developed.

It all started when Adoniram began studying his Greek New Testament and analyzed the Greek word for "baptism." As a Congregationalist he had in infancy been sprinkled with a few drops of water on his head. Now his study of the Greek language and his consideration of biblical practice increasingly convinced him that baptism should be by immersion.

When he shared his thoughts with Nancy, she was alarmed—and for good reason. They were Congregational missionaries sent out by the Congregational board. Church leaders had worked long and hard to raise enough money to support the Judsons. It would be thoughtless and downright impractical to change beliefs now. They would be left without a mission board. You don't change horses in the middle of the stream, and you don't change mission boards in the middle of the ocean.

"I tried to have him give it up," Nancy wrote later, "and rest satisfied in his old sentiments, and frequently told him if he became a Baptist, I would not." That shows that Nancy had a mind of her own.

"He, however, said he felt it his duty to examine closely a subject on which he felt so many doubts" and "was determined to read candidly and prayerfully, and to hold fast or embrace the truth, however mortifying, however great the sacrifice."

Even after their ship had landed in Calcutta, the discussion on baptism continued, and it didn't help Nancy's Congregational position to be living among British Baptists and to be hobnobbing with William Carey, the pioneer Baptist missionary.

But Nancy wouldn't go down without a struggle. To defend her own position, she spent two or three days comparing the Old and New Testaments on the subject. "I intend to persevere in examining the subject, and hope that I shall be disposed to embrace the truth, whatever it may be. It is painfully mortifying to my natural feelings to think seriously of renouncing a system which I have been taught from infancy, and respect and embrace one which I have been taught to despise."

Such psychological factors did not faze Adoniram, who cherished his independence, but gregarious Nancy was bothered about being isolated from relatives and friends, and especially from the missionary colleagues who had accompanied them to India. "If he should renounce his former sentiments," she wrote, "he must offend his friends at home, hazard his reputation, and, what is still more trying, be separated from his missionary associates." Nancy dreaded the implications.

It was early in August that Adoniram reached his decision to become a Baptist. Nancy struggled with the issue longer, but by the end of the month she, too, felt that the weight of the scriptural arguments were on the side of the Baptists. The next month Adoniram and Nancy were baptized by immersion by one of William Carey's associates. In her journal Nancy wrote what the decision meant emotionally: "We feel that we are alone in the world, with no real friend but each other, no one on whom we can depend but God."

The Judsons had other problems, too, the biggest of which was how to get to Burma from India. Their idealistic notions of Burma were dashed; the source book on Burma was found to be totally unreliable. The British missionaries in India told them bluntly that Burma would be both impossible to enter and impossible to live in.

To complicate the situation, the British authorities in India didn't like missionaries, especially American ones. The Judsons were ordered to be deported to England. Feeling they had a higher calling, the Judsons jumped ship and hitchhiked aboard another vessel to the island of Mauritius, a little French island about twenty-five miles square and 3500 miles southwest in the middle of the Indian Ocean.

The longer they were on Mauritius, the more they realized that being there wasn't their calling either. To add to their complications Nancy was pregnant.

Adoniram, whose moods sometimes got the better of him, was getting discouraged. They had left New England in February 1812; now it was June 1813, and they were still 4000 miles from Burma. Mauritius was not exactly Grand Central Station; boats going anywhere, much less to Burma, were a rarity. And, of course, with all they had heard about Burma, it must have crossed their minds that maybe the whole thing was an impetuous mistake. After all, Adoniram had made impetuous mistakes before.

And then a ship pulled into the harbor bound for—of all places—Rangoon, Burma. Now the complication was that Nancy was eight months pregnant. Should they pass up the opportunity and return to England as the British authorities had ordered? Some advised them to postpone their missionary debut for a few years: "A few years lost are better than losing all to no purpose in the living hell of Burma."

As always, Nancy and Adoniram talked it over. The old idealism of their youth had now evaporated; this was serious business. But she and Adoniram were still determined to go to Burma, come what may.

At this point Nancy was not expecting great results: "We cannot expect to do much, in such a rough uncultivated field; yet, if we may be instrumental in removing some of the rubbish, and preparing the way for others, it will be a sufficient reward. I have been accustomed to view this field of labor, with dread and terror; but I now feel perfectly willing to make it my home the rest of my life."

Adoniram was concerned about Nancy's physical condition, so he hired a European woman to serve as a nurse for her on the voyage to Rangoon. But as the nurse stepped aboard the ship, she slipped and fell to the deck and died.

After struggling unsuccessfully to save the woman's life, Nancy went into a state of shock herself. A few days out to sea, Nancy gave birth to her first child; it was stillborn. No physician or nurse was aboard; only Adoniram was available to attend his wife. Later, Nancy said that she owed her life to her husband.

When they arrived in Rangoon, Nancy was hardly in the frame of mind and certainly not in physical health to begin her missionary service. Their first impression of Burma, which they had dreamed about for so long, was that it was "dark, cheerless and unpromising."

Despite the circumstances, the Judsons began immediately to learn the language. At first the Hindu scholar who agreed to teach Adoniram refused to instruct Nancy because, as she put it, "it was rather beneath him to instruct a female. . . . But when he saw I was determined to persevere, and that Mr. Judson was as desirous that he should instruct me as himself, he was more attentive." Once that hurdle was over, they spent twelve hours a day in language study.

A year later she described her daily schedule this way: "My mornings are busily employed in giving directions to the servants, providing food for the family, etc. I have many more interruptions than Mr. Judson, as I have the entire management of the family. This I took on myself for the sake of Mr. Judson's attending more closely to the study of the language, yet I have found that it is the most direct way I could have taken to acquire the language; as I am frequently obliged to speak Burmese all day. I can talk and understand others better than Mr. Judson, though he knows more about the nature and construction of the language."

Besides the language, Nancy also picked up the local customs, even adopting the dress style of the local women. The one custom she never followed was wearing Burmese sandals.

The work was slow, hard, and lonely. There were no European or American women to be Nancy's friends, and it took three years for the first packet of letters from America to arrive. Adoniram had a very satisfying conversation with his Burmese teacher about Christianity, but there were still no converts. A child born in 1815 (named Roger Williams Judson) was a joy to Nancy and Adoniram. Then, suffering from a cough and fever, he suddenly died at eight months. The funeral had to be held within hours, and the small body was buried among the mango trees in the garden of the mission house.

In her sorrow, Nancy launched a school for Burmese girls, wrote a simple catechism in Burmese, and began translating the Book of Jonah because she thought it would be easy to translate.

Five years went by with still no converts. Plenty of tracts, catechisms, and portions of Scripture. Weekly classes and counseling sessions. But no converts.

If one Hindu would step over the line, Adoniram was sure that others would follow. But how to get that first one—that was the question. Perhaps if he could import a few Indian Christians who lived on the Burmese border, their example would provide the needed nudge. It would take only a few weeks of travel for Adoniram, a few weeks away from Nancy, to talk the Indian Christians into visiting Burma with him. At least, that's what he thought.

Not long after Adoniram left, Nancy was engulfed in trouble. First came word from the Burmese viceroy that all foreign teachers were to be banished; then came a cholera epidemic followed by the rumor that the British would soon invade Burma, a rumor that didn't endear missionaries to the Burmese officials.

A missionary printer and his wife had joined the Judsons by this time, but the printer now decided that he could do his printing more effectively in India. After Adoniram's absence had stretched to seven months, Nancy got word that his ship was missing at sea.

Should she join the missionary printer and his wife? What future was there for her in Burma?

She decided to board the next vessel for India. Then she changed her mind. If Adoniram should return and find her missing, what would he do? No matter what the printer did, Nancy intended to stay in Burma, keep on with her studies, and "leave the event to God."

It was a wise decision.

Not long afterward, Adoniram came home. The joy of his return, Nancy wrote, "more than compensates for the months of dejection and distress which his long absence has occasioned. Now I feel ashamed of my repinings, my want of confidence in God and resignation to His will. I have foolishly thought, because my trials were protracted, they would never end, or rather that they would terminate in some 'dreadful event.'"

Yes, Nancy was human.

In 1818 two new missionary couples arrived in Burma; one of the wives found the living conditions unbearable. What she meant was that she had a hard time living with Nancy. "It could well have been true," says one biographer, "that Adoniram and Nancy ran things with a high hand." The Judsons had survived in Burma for five years and had a few ideas on how a mission should operate. The idealistic neophyte missionaries would have to adjust.

Perhaps Adoniram was impatient or perhaps he was prodded by the presence of the younger exuberant missionaries, but when a new emperor took the Burmese throne in the legendary capital city of Ava, it was agreed that the time had come to ask for royal permission to teach Christianity to the king's subjects. If he said yes, the door would be wide open for the Judsons and others; if he said no, at least they could leave their writings behind as they sailed away.

But there was a disagreement in the Judson home. Adoniram thought he should be accompanied on the historic visit to the king by one of the male missionaries who had just joined them. Nancy disagreed. She felt she not only could speak the Burmese language fluently but could also use her demonstrated ability to twist potentates around her fingers. Maybe Nancy also remembered the last time her husband had left her on a trip that was supposed to have taken only a few weeks.

But Adoniram said no, and one day before Nancy's thirtieth birthday, her husband and his fellow missionary Colman began their trek to visit the emperor at Ava, the seat of the "Golden Presence," as it was called.

Maybe Nancy was right after all. Six weeks later Adoniram and Colman returned with their heads hanging low. They had failed to get the emperor's OK. Adoniram was glum: "I could moralize half an hour on the apt resemblance, the beautiful congruity, between the desolate state of our feelings and the sandy barren surface of this miserable beach. But 'tis idle all.' Let the beach and the sorrow go together. Something better will turn up tomorrow."

It did.

There were new converts now, and they were less discouraged about the news than Adoniram. He feared that they might fall away from the faith. Instead, their faith grew stronger and more new converts were added.

However, all was not so well with Nancy. A liver ailment grew progressively worse. The only place where she could receive adequate treatment was in America. So this time it was Nancy's turn to leave and Adoniram's turn to stay behind.

He was never good at saying good-bye. He tried to joke about it, but his true feeling for Nancy came through clearly: "It is said that man is prone to jest in the depths of misery; and the bon mots of the scaffold have been collected. . . . I feel as if I was on the scaffold and signing as it were my own death warrant. I have been occupied in making up my mind to have my right arm amputated and my right eye extracted . . . in order to prevent a decay and mortification of the whole body conjugal."

In her absence, he busied himself in translating the New Testament. When she returned twenty-eight months later, she was well again. In his words, she was "the Ann Hasseltine of other days." His happiness was "inexpressible."

They had a lot of news to share with each other. Nancy had spent time in London, Boston, Baltimore, Calcutta, and points in between; had finished a book manuscript, *An Account of the American Baptist Mission to the Burman Empire;* and had seen a myriad of old friends and relatives.

Adoniram's big news for Nancy was that he had visited the emperor in Ava once again and that the emperor had invited them to come and live in the capital city. Despite their attachment to Rangoon, the opportunity was too good to pass up. Two months later, they moved to a little three-room home in Ava. Though the house was built on stilts to allow air movement, the 108 degree (Fahrenheit) heat of the stifling summer was still unbearable.

But unbearable heat was the least of their problems. Just as they had completed their move, word came that the British army was preparing to invade Burma. This time it was no idle rumor. And the Burmese, most of whom had never seen a white man before, had trouble distinguishing between Americans and Englishmen.

Within six months of their move to Ava, Adoniram was hauled off to prison, where he was bound with three pairs of ankle fetters to a block of granite. In the windowless prison, he was overwhelmed with heat, and gagged on the indescribable stench. His clothing was shredded, his face was covered with mud, and for Adoniram, who treasured cleanliness next to godliness, it was traumatic.

Understandably, Adoniram was thrown into depression. Biographer Courtney Anderson tells what was going through his mind: "What had he brought to those who depended on him? Nothing but death. Death for his only son. Now death for himself, probably death for Nancy. And what was there to show for it? Eighteen converts in the twelve years since he had left Salem. Of those, probably only a few would remain faithful—if they survived. Eighteen souls for all those years and lives. And the Burmese New Testament. But most of that was in manuscript, in the little wooden house by the river. Almost certainly it would be destroyed or lost."

Enterprising Nancy was doing everything she could. First, she had been summoned before the magistrate and interrogated. He got nowhere with her. The next day Nancy was able to smuggle food into the prison and began a letter-writing campaign to the emperor's sister (Nancy had an "in" with her). She wrote a petition to the empress and then tried to get permission to visit her husband.

She finally accomplished the latter by bribing a prison official. She almost wished she hadn't been successful. A British prisoner who was in the same jail described the reunion: "Two days in prison had turned the most fastidious man she knew into a haggard, unshaven scarecrow, his usually spotless white starched neckcloth a filthy rag, his neat black broadcloth suit disheveled, torn and smeared with fragments of rotting plantain leaves. She could scarcely recognize him. She gave him one long horrified incredulous look and hid her face in her hands."

Nancy couldn't succumb to weakness now. She would need divine strength and wisdom to cope, for she couldn't let Adoniram down. She knew that soldiers would soon be at her house confiscating everything of value, including Adoniram's translation of the Bible into Burmese. He had spent years in preparing it; she couldn't allow it to be destroyed.

She went into her small backyard, dug two holes, and buried the family silver in one and the Burmese Bible in the other. A few hours later, the soldiers came and went away empty-handed.

Nancy's next priority was to rouse her husband out of his depression. He needed encouragement and something to occupy his mind. The way to provide both was to try to devise ways of communicating to each other without the prison guards knowing it. Sometimes Nancy wrote notes on little cakes that she buried in bowls of rice; at other times she put notes in the long nose of a teapot which she brought to the prisoners. Adoniram could never be sure when or how the next note from his wife might appear. In response, he devised a system of writing on tile which was invisible when the tile was wet, but was legible to Nancy when it dried off.

Of course, all of Nancy's hectic efforts were looked upon with extreme suspicion by the authorities. Frequently she was summoned to court.

Such occasions became a challenge for her, and God supplemented her natural gift of being able to think on her feet with wisdom of the Spirit.

She knew that Adoniram's Bible translation couldn't stay buried in her backyard for long. For one thing, her husband was worrying about it too much; for another, the dampness of the soil would soon start to affect it and it would soon rot. So, in a rather daring operation, she smuggled the hefty manuscript to Adoniram in prison. He had asked the guards for a pillow, and the next day Nancy came to the prison with his request. The pillow was a bit heavy, rather bulky, and too hard for the normal comfort of most people, but Adoniram rested easy upon it, knowing that it contained his Burmese manuscript.

About this time, Nancy, now thirty-four, discovered she was pregnant once again. Her frantic pace had to slow down, although not by much. And in January 1825, seven months after Adoniram's arrest, Maria Elizabeth Judson was born. Ten years before, she had given birth to Roger Williams Judson, who lived only eight months. The place and the time were less propitious than ever for a baby to be born.

Shortly after Maria Elizabeth was born, Nancy resumed both her daily walks to the prison (with her babe in arms) to smuggle messages to her husband and her regular visits to the governor's house to beg for her husband's release.

After eleven months in prison, Adoniram was moved. He thought he was going to be assassinated, but the move was to a new location about four miles away. Some of the prisoners, "skin-covered skeletons, clothed in rags," collapsed on their march. Adoniram survived, but on reaching the destination, he fell into an unconscious stupor. The first voice to rouse him the next day was Nancy's. She had discovered that the prisoners were being moved and so had come with little Maria as quickly as she could.

Barely conscious, Adoniram whispered, "Why have you come? I hoped you would not follow. You cannot live here."

But Nancy did. For months she and Maria lived in a little room nearby that also served as a grain bin.

When the British troops came and liberated them in November 1825, Adoniram was in better physical shape than Nancy. Smallpox and then cerebral spinal meningitis had taken their toll. Her hair had been shaved off; her head and feet were covered with blisters. The Burmese thought that she was dead, but she rallied.

The general of the liberating British army honored the Judsons with a ceremonial dinner, but shortly thereafter Nancy was stricken with another fever. This time she couldn't fight it. She died at the age of thirty-six.

Adoniram continued his work in Burma for twenty-four more years. His translation of the Bible was published, and sixty-three churches were established in his lifetime.

Eight years after Nancy's death, he married Sarah Boardman, the widow of another missionary. She was different from Nancy, "calmer, less dominant, with less fire, but perhaps more glow," but like Nancy she was intelligent and courageous. After eleven years of marriage and eight children, she died.

Judson's third wife was also a remarkable woman. Emily Chubbock, who wrote children's books under the pen name of Fanny Forester, was a high school teacher with wit, charm, and a spirited personality. Adoniram was nearly sixty when he met her, and she was not quite thirty. He had no intention of marrying her. He had contacted her about the possibility of writing a biography of his second wife, Sarah. He ended up marrying her. A storm of criticism mounted: why should a dedicated missionary marry a professional woman who wrote stories for secular magazines? But Judson seldom let criticism bother him. Together Adoniram and Emily, alias Fanny Forester, returned to Burma to serve as missionaries. Four years later, Adoniram completed his pilgrimage and went to be with the Lord.

All three of Adoniram's wives were strong, somewhat determined women, even as he was independent. But Ann Hasseltine Judson is the wife who set the pattern for future missionaries and who provided Adoniram with a strong dedicated co-worker whom he could count on and respect as an equal.

Maybe that was their secret. They respected and honored each other, despite their idiosyncrasies. Though they often worked as a team, each gave the other space to develop independently. They had no better friends than each other.

Each possessed character traits that could have torn the marriage apart. Instead, they worked together to make it strong.

Bibliography

Anderson, Courtney. *To the Golden Shore*. Grand Rapids, Zondervan, 1977.
Hefley, James C. *How Great Christians Met Christ*. Chicago: Moody, 1973.
Miller, Basil. *Ann Judson: Heroine of Ava*. Grand Rapids, Zondervan, 1947.

The Taming of the Bachelor

Every man is a bachelor until he gets married. But bachelors under thirty are altogether a different breed of the male species than bachelors over thirty.

A bachelor over thirty has considered himself single for a decade or more. More than likely, he has not had to consider the wishes and desires of others, as far as his personal living arrangements are concerned. He has been able to come and go as he pleases. He has been able to pour himself into his work with abandon. He has been able to travel without consulting anyone and delay his return home for a day or a week or a month or even a year without being considered thoughtless.

Then he is wed. At that point he must make adjustments. Sometimes that is a difficult job.

At the time of their marriages, seven men in this book qualified as bachelors over thirty. C. S. Lewis, wed at 59, thought he would never marry, and must be considered a "confirmed bachelor." John Wesley, married at 47, was never confirmed in his bachelorhood. He had fallen in love several times before he finally married a woman he found he didn't really care for.

Next in seniority was Martin Luther, married at 42. Though an unlikely candidate for marriage, he became a good husband and father, and his wife, Kate, will no doubt receive her reward in heaven for her role in her husband's maturation and reluctant mellowing.

John Knox, married at 41, Peter Marshall, at 33, John Calvin, at 31 (after a "talent search"), and David Livingstone, at 30, also took their time before saying their nuptial vows.

As you read about the following two marriages (and as you recall the marriages of the other bachelors), you will see once again that marriage dynamics have not changed much over the centuries.

Look carefully at those dynamics. Consider what unique adjustments a former bachelor and his wife have made (or should have made). See what could have been done by both husband and wife to make the marriage even better.

24

I've Got to Meet That Man

Peter and Catherine Marshall

An eighteen-year-old coed has a crush on a thirty-one-year-old bachelor minister. Puppy love?

He notices her; in fact, he's attracted to her. But what would the people in his fashionable congregation say if they knew their minister was thinking of dating a teenager?

The minister was Peter, the Scottish immigrant, a factory worker turned into a preacher-poet.

The girl was Catherine, or Kate, as he often called her, the minister's daughter from West Virginia, who was trying to get through college on a shoestring and a lot of determination.

One thing that they both had in common: They both knew what it was to be poor.

Another thing: They both liked to play 159 games—from Monopoly to Chinese checkers to Parcheesi. In fact, Peter was nicknamed "The G.G.P." or "The Great Game Player" because he played games with a vengeance or, as Catherine put it, "he relaxed hard."

As for Catherine, her college classmates nicknamed her "Calamity Catherine." A debater, she approached the world's problems with intensity and what she termed "blazing indignation." Catherine didn't like to be taken for granted; Peter had an annoying way of doing just that. Catherine liked to be involved; Peter enjoyed his independence.

465

Catherine was no slave to neatness; Peter was meticulously precise. Such differences certainly can keep a marriage from becoming dull.

Peter Marshall, of course, became the oft-quoted chaplain of the United States Senate as well as minister of Washington's prestigious New York Avenue Presbyterian Church, where he served until his death at age forty-six.

Then, after Catherine had passed through the valley of the shadow of her husband's death, she emerged from the shadows herself. A widow at thirty-four, Catherine published two best-sellers within three years of Peter's death: *Mr. Jones, Meet the Master,* a collection of her husband's sermons, and *A Man Called Peter,* her husband's biography. Afterwards, she wrote more than a dozen other books, all best-sellers.

Toward the end of her life and a second marriage, Catherine wrote, "Husbands and wives are basically incompatible. . . . That's why the home is His classroom for molding and shaping us into mature people." Her marriage to Peter Marshall proved this to be true.

In the spring of her freshman year at Atlanta's Agnes Scott College, Catherine first heard of Peter Marshall. He was the new minister in town, having just taken the pulpit of the moldering Westminster Presbyterian Church, an hour's ride away from campus by streetcar, but well worth the trip.

Peter was certainly worth hearing—and, for coeds, worth seeing. A dramatic and poetic preacher, he spoke with a Scottish burr. As a literature major, Catherine was enchanted. But more than that, it was obvious that Peter knew the Lord in a very personal way and had a knack of bringing his congregation with him into a circle of divine friendship. This moved Catherine, who was spiritually restless at the time because her own relationship to Jesus Christ seemed "abstract."

The girls of Agnes Scott were also impressed with the physical aspect of Peter Marshall.

Broad-shouldered, tall, curly-haired, ruggedly handsome—and single—Peter seemed to be the answer to every coed's dream.

Born near Glasgow, Scotland, Peter had lied about his age to join the British Navy. He was only fourteen, and he wanted to fight in World War I. His naval career lasted about forty-eight hours before his fraud was discovered. Too proud to return to his high school and face his classmates, he enrolled in a technical school to study mechanical engineering, and at fifteen, he became a machinist.

But God had other plans for Peter's life.

Major influences on Peter were: (1) a praying mother, who reminded him, "Long ago I pit ye in the Lord's hands"; (2) Olympic medalist Eric Liddell (portrayed in the film *Chariots of Fire*), who challenged him to missionary service; and (3) a never-to-be-forgotten incident that took place one jet-black night as he was walking across the moors. As the wind howled around him, Peter thought he heard something or someone calling. He slowed his steps to listen more carefully. Suddenly he stumbled and reached out to break his fall. There was nothing there. He had fallen on the edge of an abandoned limestone quarry. One more step would have taken him over the precipice.

Shaken by this experience, he dedicated his life to serve the Lord. In 1927 he emigrated to America in order to study for the ministry. To earn money, he worked at a blast furnace and on a pipeline. Though he had no college degree, he was admitted to seminary and three years later graduated magna cum laude.

Then at the age of thirty-one he accepted the call to the pulpit of Atlanta's Westminster Presbyterian Church. The church services were sparsely attended when he came, but before long his sermons packed the sanctuary, forcing the deacons to stand out on the sidewalks in order to listen through open windows. Students from Georgia Tech, Emory, Oglethorpe, and Agnes Scott flocked to hear him.

From the moment he arrived in town, the matchmakers of Atlanta began working. Some of the young women didn't need any help. The "In" box in his study was often stuffed with letters and anonymous poetry from interested parties.

Meanwhile, Catherine floundered. In her sophomore year she wrote, "I am lazy spiritually. I would like to know God really—not in the abstract. But I don't seem to want to badly enough to do anything about it."

A few weeks later she wrote, "I have had no real, vital religious experience. God does not seem real to me. I believe in God now mostly because of people I know—like Peter, to whom religion is a vital, living thing."

As a child she had been profoundly stirred by evangelist Gypsy Smith's preaching, and shortly afterwards, she walked forward as her preacher father gave a gospel invitation. But now that decision seemed far away.

As she says in *A Man Called Peter,* "I . . . was groping to find my way out of an inherited Christianity into a spiritual experience of my own."

She was now attending Peter's church every Sunday, had shaken hands with him frequently, but had never really talked to him. In her journal she wrote, "I have never met anyone whom I so want to know as Mr. Marshall."

Her letters to her parents in West Virginia started mentioning this young minister: "I have never heard such prayers in my life. It's as if, when he opens his mouth, there is a connected line between you and God. I know this sounds silly, but I've got to meet that man." In another letter, she pined, "He doesn't even know I exist." After another paragraph, she concluded, "I wish I'd stop thinking about this man."

It was silly, she knew, but during the following summer, she read everything she could about Scottish history, eventually developing a bibliography of thirty-seven books. But by the time she returned for classes in her junior year, she had come to her senses and decided it was ridiculous for her to get moonstruck about a man who didn't even know she existed.

She decided to get interested in some college fellows her own age. In addition, she resolved to dedicate herself to her studies.

She even felt a bit relieved when she heard a rumor that Peter was engaged. That, she thought, would get him off her mind.

But the fellows she dated seemed so shallow; her mind kept going back to Peter. "Why must the embodiment of all my ideals be twelve years older than I and as remote as the South Pole?"

Then it happened. In the spring of her junior year, she, as a college debater, was asked to join—of all people—Peter Marshall and speak at a Prohibition rally. Her intensity on the platform had earned her the nickname of "Calamity Catherine," and she had debated subjects from Nazism to America's economic collapse. It wasn't hard for her to become intense on the subject of Prohibition.

On the way to the rally, Peter assured her that he definitely was not engaged. "Don't believe everything you hear, my dear girl." But on the way back, he said that he would like to take her bowling sometime. "I've wanted to know you for a long time."

It was more than Catherine had dreamed. She had simply wanted to get to know him better. Now he had actually asked her for a date.

But the date didn't materialize.

She saw him at church socials and "he overflowed with warmth toward me," and frequently he would drive her back to school afterwards. After one such get-together, he said, "I'll be in touch with you this week."

But he didn't get in touch. And a few weeks later, when summer vacation began, Catherine went home to West Virginia, more puzzled than ever about her dream man. She asked herself, "Why did he always seem so interested in me when I was with him, but then never follow up with a note or telephone call?"

He wrote a couple of times during the summer, but the correspondence seemed cold and formal, almost businesslike. He closed one card with "Regards, Peter Marshall," hardly the complimentary close of someone interested in romance.

Once again, Catherine resolved during the summer to forget about Peter Marshall. It wasn't easy, because the memories of their times together stuck in her mind. "I must forget Peter Marshall," she determined and decided to reinforce it by not going to his church in the fall.

Her resolve lasted six weeks. On her first Sunday back at Westminster, he shook hands with her and remarked that it was the first time he had seen her that year. She was somewhat surprised that he had even noticed that she hadn't been attending. Then he said that he would get in touch with her. That night she wrote in her journal, "I shan't hold my breath until he does."

When they were together, he continued to express his enjoyment of her company, but he never pursued the relationship. Catherine couldn't figure him out.

Peter had reasons for not being too obvious about the relationship. As a thirty-three-year-old minister of a rapidly growing congregation, he didn't want to be aggressive in his display of affection for a college girl.

The turning point for Peter came near the end of Catherine's senior year. She had been asked to review a book on prayer at the church's fellowship hour preceding the evening service. As she spoke, she honestly confessed her own failings in prayer. She admitted her superficiality and expressed her hunger to know God better. It was a time of intense catharsis for Catherine, especially so since she knew that Peter was listening to every word.

The church's evening service followed. By the time Catherine entered, it was late and the only available seats were in the front of the church. As the church service progressed, Catherine started feeling ill. At first, she thought she could last through the service, but then she felt sicker and sicker. Finally Catherine had to walk out from her third row seat.

Something happened to Peter as he watched Catherine leave the church. From then on, she had his undivided attention. Catherine's journal took on a different mood; it recorded steady progress in the relationship:

"Terribly solicitous . . .

"I believe now he wants to be serious . . .

"I think Peter is in love with me . . .

"He kissed me . . .

"We talked until three in the morning . . .

"He proposed."

She took a few days to pray about the proposal. It seemed strange to delay an answer, but she needed to be certain whether her dreams were just girlish fantasies or in keeping with God's will. As Catherine later wrote, "I saw how wrong it is to go after what we want and then—with considerable audacity—later ask God to bless it." But by graduation day, the question was answered. She said yes.

That summer was far different from the previous two. Letters flew back and forth, combining passion, spirituality, and humor. "Darling, I am so happy! I love you so much," Peter now wrote.

Initially, they had planned to wait a year for marriage; Catherine would teach school. But Peter couldn't wait, and he talked Catherine into a fall wedding in her father's church in West Virginia.

When Peter came to visit Catherine at her home that summer, he earned his nickname, "The G.G.P." (The Great Game Player). Catherine enjoyed games too, but she admitted, "I thought he was carrying it a bit too far when, thirty minutes before our wedding ceremony, he was so busy pushing his initial advantage in a game of Chinese checkers with my little sister that he still had not dressed."

The first night of their married life they honeymooned in Washington, D.C.—for good reason.

Peter had agreed to meet with the pulpit committee of Washington's New York Avenue Presbyterian Church the following morning. He apologized to Catherine for having to leave her before breakfast. "Take your time dressing," he told her. "When the men want to see you, I'll telephone."

Only twenty-two, the bride was terrified to meet the auspicious committee of seven men and one woman. She prayed silently, "Please, Lord, don't let me embarrass Peter."

Apparently she didn't, because Peter received a call to the Washington church.

The question was: Should he accept the call? The answer didn't come easily. He told Catherine: "I do not sincerely feel that I am equipped for what they would need. I lack the poise, the balance, the preparation, the academic standing, the confidence, the discretion and the grace to be bridled in my pulpit utterances." In addition, the church in Atlanta had just added a balcony to accommodate the crowds that were coming to hear him preach. He couldn't leave Atlanta until the balcony was paid for.

So he turned down the call, and the newlyweds set up housekeeping in Atlanta. But a year later, the New York Avenue Presbyterian Church of Washington renewed its call, and this time, after much prayer, Peter answered yes.

For the Scottish immigrant who had been working in a Glasgow factory only a decade earlier, it was frightening. "Catherine, I'm scared to death," he admitted. "Suppose I can't deliver the goods?" Catherine was scared too. Only eighteen months earlier she had been on a college campus wondering what life was all about. Now she was the wife of the minister of one of the most prestigious churches in the nation. The church was known as the church of presidents; eight presidents, including Lincoln, had worshiped there. She took a crash course in Washington protocol to help her through the maze of official niceties.

In Atlanta they had lived in a pleasant cottage. In Washington their manse was a ponderous red brick, three-storied house with ten rooms, including six bedrooms.

It didn't take long before the home reflected Peter's taste. As Catherine wrote, "To step into the living room of our home was like entering a marine museum. Seascapes were everywhere—Peter had seen to that."

Neat and methodical, Peter trained Catherine in his ways.

When she left the top off the toothpaste or failed to close a dresser drawer, he let her know about it.

He was proud of how quickly his bride was becoming a good housewife. After Catherine had successfully cooked a Christmas turkey, he wrote his mother in Scotland: "Catherine is managing quite nicely. We are all proud of her. It amazes me the way she has taken hold and manages like a veteran. It was a proud moment for me to sit at that table, so tastefully laid out, and look at Catherine at the other end, and serve turkey, which I carved myself, believe it or not."

Peter had some definite ideas regarding the role of a wife, and in theory Catherine had no trouble accepting them. He believed that a woman's place, no matter what education or talents she might have, is in the home. In one sermon he spoke of marriage as "a fusion of two hearts, the union of two lives, the coming together of two tributaries which after being joined in marriage, will flow in the same channel in the same direction . . . carrying the same burdens of responsibility and obligation."

Catherine had some reservations about his strong views; even before their marriage, she wanted to check on them. He assured her, "Darling, it is not that your life and love and gifts will be poured into my coffer . . . but that we both shall be poured into that new vehicle—and our joint lives—our blended hearts and fused souls—now one in the sight of God."

It sounded good to Catherine in theory. In practice, there were problems.

Ever since she began thinking of marriage to Peter, she had wondered how difficult it would be for him to adjust from his comfortable bachelor life to marriage. She thought that it might be better for him to remain a bachelor. "He seems to be altogether self-sufficient, independent, and perfectly happy that way."

Besides having an independent streak, Peter was a workaholic. He never took a day off. He worked long hours, usually attended committee meetings in the evening, and for diversion accepted frequent out-of-town speaking engagements.

The out-of-town speaking engagements certainly bothered Catherine, but even more troublesome to her was Peter's inability to share his thoughts. Maybe it was his Scottish reticence; more likely it was that he had never had to do so before. When he talked about their lives being poured into a new vehicle, it sounded good, but Peter continued to operate his vehicle as he had always done before, with no help from Catherine.

Catherine was perfectly willing to subjugate her desire to use her talents of writing and speaking and to throw herself into helping Peter as a minister. But she wanted Peter to share his ministry with her, and for the first few years of marriage he seemed incapable of doing it.

He had a divine call. His ministry came first. As she puts it, he was "at the beck and call of thousands of people," and all these thousands seemed to have priority over his wife.

That was a fact of her married life that she tried to accept. But resentment began to build. And at times she didn't know if she should be resentful against the church members, against Peter, or against God. The out-of-town speaking engagements were almost the last straw.

From his viewpoint, he was being charitable; after all, he received scores of invitations to speak and accepted only a relatively few of them. He thought she should appreciate the fact that he turned down many opportunities. She thought he still accepted far too many. He thought she was being self-centered and jealous of his ministry. She thought that he was being thoughtless and uncaring.

Despite the problems, the Marshalls had a good marriage. "We early discovered," Catherine writes, "that the important thing was not the differences between us, but the will, the determination to work them out. After all, every couple has difficulties. No two lives are fused into perfect oneness without a certain amount of painful adjustment."

Problems were dissolved sometimes by humor, sometimes by the deep love and respect they had for each other, and sometimes, perhaps most importantly, by their custom of praying with each other every day.

Even though she was frequently frustrated with him, Catherine enjoyed Peter. She liked the way he laughed and the way he sang with such gusto. She even liked the way he dressed up in his kilt and entertained church socials with "Roamin' in the Gloamin'." He was fun to be with. And of course, she also enjoyed his penchant for games, from Monopoly to baseball.

"One might wonder how a busy minister could find so much time for game playing," Catherine writes. "The answer was that Peter stole the time from sleep."

Gradually, Peter made attempts to share. One way he did this was by reading his Sunday morning sermons to Catherine on Saturday night. For him it was a warm-up; for her it was an enjoyable preview. One Saturday night, as Peter reached the middle of his practice sermon, Catherine interrupted him. She hated to do it. But she had to tell him something important. She was having labor pains. And shortly before nine the next morning Peter John Marshall was born.

Peter was at the hospital for his son's birth; then he returned to church in time to teach the young people's Sunday school class at ten and preach his half-rehearsed sermon at eleven. To his congregation he never said a word about the excitement that had occurred in his household a few hours earlier. Some people mentioned to him that he seemed tired that morning, almost as if he had been up all night. He still admitted nothing. Then as he was shaking hands with his parishioners at the close of the service, one woman asked him about Catherine, who she had observed was absent that morning. Peter finally had to divulge the reason for Catherine's absence.

It had always been a policy for Peter not to mention his wife or his home life in his sermons. After Peter John was born, that policy was quickly forgotten. Peter John provided too many colorful sermon anecdotes to be neglected.

Peter enjoyed his son; there was no doubt about that. He felt guilty because his church responsibilities often kept them from spending more time together.

To work out a practical solution, the family purchased a summer home far away from the demands of a church and the endless stream of speaking engagements. Located on Cape Cod, it was close to the sea that Peter loved. Of course, Peter immediately had to paint the green shutters of the cottage his favorite Chatham blue. The cottage gave Peter a chance to spend more time with his son, to plant a garden of hybrid tea roses, to build some furniture, and to listen to the sound of the ocean. Catherine enjoyed antiquing on the Cape most of all. There was a lot of family togetherness. Peter and little Peter John would go blueberry picking together, and then Catherine would make deep-dish blueberry pies and blueberry muffins. At night Peter would read a book to his son and tuck him into bed.

Peter wasn't a scholar by nature. He was a poet, an artist with words. For instance, he likened doubt to cobwebs in the corners of our rooms. Our brooms of faith can't get into those corners. Only God's divine grace can. "The use of the right word is the difference between a pencil with a sharp point and a thick crayon," he once said.

He told a group of seminarians, "If when you write your sermons, you can see the gleaming knuckles of a clenched fist, the lip that is bitten to keep back tears, the troubled heart that is suffering because it cannot forgive, the spirit that has no joy because it has no love, if you can see the big tears that run down a mother's face, preach for them—and get down deep."

Peter got his sermon ideas from anywhere and everywhere, and he took great care in selecting the titles. Since the church bulletin was prepared on Thursdays, he often discussed the subject of his sermon with Catherine at the Wednesday night dinner table. Sometimes, even though he had only a sketchy idea for a sermon, he would give a title to it with faith that sometime between Thursday and Sunday the sermon would become fully developed. Seldom could Peter develop sermon outlines more than a few days in advance.

Peter's responsibilities kept increasing. As the church grew, he began preaching identical sermons to two services on Sunday mornings. But still the crowds overflowed; people had to be turned away because the church could hold no more.

Catherine stayed behind the scenes, playing the role of a supportive wife. As she says in *A Man Called Peter,* she was expected to be "gracious, charming, poised, and equal to every occasion." And she fulfilled her role well.

Then when Peter John was three years old, Catherine was stricken by illness. At a church meeting she nearly fainted. Medical tests disclosed that she had contracted tuberculosis.

Because it was not infectious, she was allowed to remain home, but complete bed rest was required. She was not allowed to do work of any kind.

She lay in a large front bedroom. The room was pleasant enough, with five windows letting in the sun's rays. She propped herself up in bed and started filling her notebooks with her thoughts. She scribbled that some day she wanted to "become a writer who will make a real contribution to my generation and to the world."

At first, it was thought that Catherine would be well within three or four months. And, she says, "the first three months were the worst. Every muscle in my body ached in protest." But when the time stretched month by month beyond that, the x-rays showed the same spots, and Catherine's discouragement verged on depression. Nor did she appreciate what she felt were trite words from her husband. "Catherine, you know perfectly well that all discouragement is of Satan." He also reminded her, "Some day you will look back with gratitude on these bleak days as some of the richest of your life."

Later she acknowledged that although she had resented his comments at the time, those "bleak days" had indeed proven to be some of the richest of her life. In them she found a relationship with Jesus Christ that she hadn't known before. For the first time in her life she developed an interest in the Holy Spirit. Understandably, she also became intrigued with the subject of healing. She struggled to understand what the Bible taught. Frequently her experiments with faith ended in dead ends, thus frustrating her further.

Peter seemed sympathetic and caring; yet she was uneasy. She was concerned that he might lose interest in a wife who was an invalid. She dreaded that "someone else will usurp my place in Peter's heart." How could a virile man like Peter not become bored sooner or later with a "useless" wife? Especially when he traveled, she worried.

In late summer of 1944, after Catherine had been bedridden for seventeen months, the family situation was more desperate than ever. During her illness, the Marshalls had been served by fourteen different maids. It was the World War II era, and Washington, D.C., had plenty of high-paying jobs available; the Marshalls couldn't compete with the salaries the government offered. As a result, they couldn't keep a maid very long. Peter John was obviously feeling the effect of it; so were Peter and Catherine, not to mention their broken china and ruined linen.

The only alternative seemed to be to send Peter John to stay with Catherine's parents, for Catherine to go to a rest home, and for Peter to stay in a hotel until Catherine recovered—however long that might take.

Peter and Catherine prayed together fervently for some resolution to the problem. "If You want us to stay together, Lord, then we will trust You to send someone to take care of the household." It was with considerable difficulty that they also prayed, "Thy will be done."

On the deadline day, a young woman from Kansas came to the manse, saying, "I don't really want the job, but here I am." She volunteered to help out for a few months, and they accepted her offer. She ended up by staying with them for four years.

In an article in *Presbyterian Life* Peter referred to this incident saying, "The greatest answers to prayer in our family have come at times when our faith was so small almost to expect the worst. Until we took hands off and really turned the problem over to God, He could not help us."

The final lesson that Catherine learned through her illness was obedience. As she committed herself to learning this lesson, she began seeing some physical progress as well.

Her healing was not instantaneous, but she had no doubt that it was divine. It seemed to accompany a mystical experience in which she felt the presence of Christ as she never had before. "Why it should have happened to me, I had no idea. But I also knew that what I had experienced was real."

The years of Catherine's poor health taught both of them much. Peter worked to be more communicative, and she, no longer able to be involved in church activity, learned how to encourage him and to give him the understanding he needed.

They collaborated on writing projects, developing a Bible study on the Letter to the Ephesians, and also preparing two issues of the devotional magazine *Today*. They discovered that they enjoyed writing together.

Peter involved her more with his sermons. Her convalescence gave her time for more reading. As she read she discovered fresh ideas to pass along to her husband. She often did research for him—"the spadework," she called it—and he did the final writing. Frequently, they talked through the sermon together before he gave it. Sometimes he would even phone her from the church office and ask for her help. "I'm stuck," he would admit, and he valued the creative suggestions that she offered.

He told friends, "My most effective sermons have been the ones Catherine and I have worked on together."

Her writing career and her natural desire to develop as a separate individual were set aside. As she put it in *To Live Again*, "All the ideas I possessed, all energy, all creativeness, were poured into the marriage partnership, and no effort was made to channel any part of it in other directions." She acknowledges that Peter's "strong views on the role of women in marriage" might have caused conflict if she had been unwilling to put aside any personal goals. She testifies that in thus losing her life in his, "I found it again in a fulfillment of every shred of femininity in me."

She also recognizes that her years of poor health "had given me a special kind of training in the quiet life."

Then one Sunday morning in the spring of 1946, halfway through his first Sunday morning sermon, Peter felt sharp pains in his chest. He clutched at his heart, stopped his sermon, and asked, "Is there a doctor in the house? If there is, I'd like to ask his help." He quickly pronounced the benediction and was helped off the rostrum.

At the age of forty-three, he was having a coronary attack. He was rushed to the hospital, where he was given a fifty-fifty chance to survive.

When Peter saw Catherine at his bedside, he took her hand in his and said, "You shouldn't have come, Catherine. You're not up to it." She was still recuperating from her illness, but this was a time that Peter needed her, and she had to come to his side.

She phoned a few choice friends who would spread the message that Peter needed prayer. Soon thousands across the country were praying for Peter. And in the following weeks, Peter gradually recovered. After ten weeks in the hospital, two weeks at home and then twelve at the cottage on Cape Cod, Peter was back in his pulpit again in September.

Catherine thought that he might slow his pace a bit, and for a couple of months he did seem to be more cautious. But soon he resumed his usual hectic pace. "He had no desire to flirt with death," Catherine said. He really didn't know any other way to live. Along with a number of close friends, she tried reasoning with him. "But nothing really changed as a result of our talks. . . . It was like reasoning with a closed door," Catherine said. Peter didn't want a limited life.

More than anything else, Catherine wanted him to cut back on his out-of-town speaking engagements. The first year after his attack, he did; he took only ten of them. But the second year, he accepted twenty. "You should see the number I turn down," he told her. She had heard the same line before.

Then a few months later, much to his surprise as well as hers, he was elected chaplain of the United States Senate, a job he added to his regular church responsibilities.

In this capacity, he served as a personal chaplain to many of America's political leaders. His unique prayers became famous across the country.

Once he prayed, "Our Father in Heaven, help us to see that it is better to fail in a cause that will ultimately succeed than to succeed in a cause that will ultimately fail. . . . May Thy will be done here and may Thy program be carried out, above party and personality, beyond time and circumstance for the good of America and the peace of the world. Through Jesus Christ our Lord. Amen."

Peter's schedule was soon busier than ever. Yet he had no symptoms such as shortness of breath, dizziness, or swelling ankles. So he hadn't seen any reason to take it easy. Besides that, he didn't know the meaning of the words, "Slow down." Catherine feared what was coming.

Early in 1949, in the middle of the night, Peter called to Catherine, "I'm in great pain. Call a doctor." She wasted no time in calling for help. As the ambulance was ready to take him away, she whispered to him, "Darling, I'll see you in the morning."

By nine the next morning Peter had died. He was forty-six; he left his widow, thirty-four, and a nine-year-old son.

The church was packed for the funeral; people had to be turned away. *Time, Life,* and *Newsweek* all paid tribute.

The following Sunday, Catherine attended church as usual. On the surface she seemed strong. People remarked about how well she was taking it. Underneath, however, she was crumbling.

She should have taken better care of her husband, she told herself. After all, she had ample warning. He had had a heart attack three years earlier. Had she been a failure again?

After blaming herself, she heaped some of the blame on the church. After all, it was the congregation, no matter how loving the people seemed at times, that kept requiring more of him. *How selfish can human beings be?* she wondered.

Eventually, she got around to blaming God. "If God has the power to help us, why didn't He do something about Peter's heart?"

It was all part of the grieving process through which she had to work.

"I was a particularly ill-equipped widow," Catherine admits in *To Live Again.* She had never liked to face death. Peter had once said to her, "You act, Catherine, as if death can be avoided by willing it away."

But she was ill-equipped in other ways, too. Peter had handled not only the major decisions of their married life but the details as well. As a widow she was being called upon to make all sorts of decisions, and she felt uncomfortable about it. "My ideal inner image of woman's role in the world—formed partly by the femininity with which I was born, partly by a Southern heritage and partly by the years of my marriage—was definitely not that of the career woman. . . . Yet now circumstances which I had not sought were thrusting this genuinely distasteful role upon me."

While Catherine was struggling to know how to pick up the pieces, three different book publishers wrote and asked her to compile and edit a book of Peter's sermons and prayers.

She couldn't say no. She had long dreamed of becoming a writer. Now, by putting her beloved husband's messages into print, she had the opportunity. That fall, *Mr. Jones, Meet the Master* was published. The first printing of ten thousand copies sold out on the first day. The book hit the best-seller list quickly and remained on it for a year. Less than two years later, the biography *A Man Called Peter* was published. It reached the best-seller list in ten days and stayed there for three years.

Overnight, it seemed, Catherine had become a nationally recognized writer. Twentieth Century-Fox released a film version of Peter's life in 1955. It too was successful.

During her long illness she had learned to write in bed, and despite the disadvantages of writing that way, she continued the habit. In *To Live Again*, she describes her unconventional style: "A woman propped up in bed writing, with scrapbooks and papers cluttering the bed and the floor; pencil smudges on her face and hands; on the floor beside her a cocker keeping sleepy sentinel. On one side of the bed was an olive-green filing cabinet; in a corner, a dictating machine. Sometimes the woman would jump up out of bed to get a cookie or an apple; at other times, to search the file for a missing paper."

But Catherine's life as a widow was not as idyllic as it might sound, especially after her son Peter John left her for a prep school and then Yale. Despite her best-sellers and her fame, Catherine was very lonely.

After Peter's death and during the time that she was writing his biography, she was convinced that she would never marry again. "This would violate something very precious," she said, "that my husband and I had had together."

She waged a "running battle with self-pity" for a while, and talked herself into the idea that sooner or later she would get adjusted to this "doubtful state of single blessedness" and "inner peace will come."

Not too many months later, her journal indicates some wavering. "God has made me the way I am; he has made me for happiness and love. I do not believe that he means or wants me to stay by myself for the rest of my life."

There was no shortage of men. Several were interested in this attractive widow, now in her early forties. During one year she turned down three proposals of marriage. None of them measured up. "Somewhere there is a man whose life needs this lavish giving," she penned in her journal.

Loneliness increased. "I have felt defeated and frustrated," she wrote in her journal. "The zest has gone out of everyday life."

"It is especially lonely," she wrote in *To Live Again*, "when there is no one with whom to share what the world calls success."

Through her books she had become famous and had touched the lives of more people in less than a decade than Peter had done in two decades of pulpit ministry. Yet, she had to admit, "As a woman I was not impressed with any accomplishment of mine. . . . I felt drained, empty."

In 1957 she had to confess, "My personal answer to whether or not a woman can replace marriage with a career and find it satisfying was— no, definitely not. The career left the woman still wanting to be—only a woman."

Then one day in early 1959, *Guideposts* editor Leonard LeSourd asked her if he could discuss an article idea with her over lunch. To her it seemed like only a business lunch.

But a few months later, in the summer of 1959, Len asked her for a date. "I'll pick you up in the morning in my car and we'll just take off to the beach or to the mountains or whatever."

Catherine suggested the mountains, and off they went. "We had an open, honest communication at a deep level," she reported.

This began a new relationship, a relationship totally different from the one she had had with Peter. When she was with Peter, he was the leader, the decision-maker. He had all the spiritual answers too. With Len, it was different. "We were both seekers," she says. And on their second date, he proposed marriage.

As she analyzed him, she had to admit, "I liked what I saw. He was a caring man, affectionate, comfortable to be with, mature. He approached problems calmly. He had a father's heart."

Yet on the other hand, marrying Len would mean moving to New York and raising his family of three young children—a daughter, ten, and two sons, six and three. Catherine's own son was now in college, and she didn't know whether she wanted to take on the challenges of a young family again. What the decision boiled down to was this: She could stay in her sheltered, lonely existence and be comfortable, or she could make the difficult adjustment into Len's life and the tensions of involvement with a young and active family.

She chose involvement; she and Len were married in November.

A methodical man, Len kept a notebook for prayer requests and answers. He listed the date of the request and the date of the answer alongside each request. One of Len's first entries in his little brown notebook was the prayer request "That household help be found so that Catherine can continue the writing of her novel *Christy*."

That prayer was answered when a housekeeper was found. Soon Catherine was back at work on her novel. But it still took a while for her to complete it. In 1967, *Christy*, her first novel, was finally published. The public thought it was worth waiting for; 250,000 hardcover copies and 4,000,000 paperback copies were sold.

The following year she and Len founded the book publishing firm known as Chosen Books, which developed a reputation for producing carefully crafted Christian books.

By the time of her death in 1983 at the age of sixty-eight, Catherine had written or edited nearly twenty books; the sales of her books exceeded 18 million copies. She endeared herself to her readers because she wrote from the heart and expressed herself honestly, clearly, and conversationally.

Catherine, of course, was a different woman at the age of forty-five when she married Len LeSourd than she was when at twenty-three she married Peter Marshall. At twenty-three she was fresh from the campus, awed by the Peter Marshall mystique. At forty-five she was a best-selling author, known to Christians and non-Christians alike because of her books and the movie, *A Man Called Peter.*

Her first marriage lasted only eleven years before Peter Marshall was taken from her in death. Her second marriage was more than twice as long before she was taken from Len in death.

Catherine Marshall was a strong woman. She used her strength in ways that reinforced the men in her life. And that made for two good marriages.

Bibliography

Marshall, Catherine. *Beyond Ourselves.* New York: McGraw-Hill, 1961.

———. *A Man Called Peter.* New York: McGraw-Hill, 1951.

———. *Meeting God at Every Turn.* Lincoln, Va.: Chosen, 1980.

———. *To Live Again.* New York: McGraw-Hill, 1957.

Marshall, Peter. *Mr. Jones, Meet the Master.* New York: Fleming H. Revell, 1949.

Not One of Those Insane Lovers
John and Idelette Calvin

You know about John Calvin, but you've probably never heard of his wife, Idelette.

Although theologian John Calvin was the "brains" behind the Protestant Reformation in Switzerland and France, he had a few things to learn about marriage and about raising children.

Frankly, he disliked people problems, and marriage inevitably brought problems. But it also brought him some delightful benefits.

The John Calvin you know about may seem stern and bullheaded. But there's another John Calvin, the husband that Idelette knew.

What was it that softened this brilliant thinker?

How well did the marriage between John of the Reformed Church and Idelette the Anabaptist succeed?

Bookish, reticent, determined, and quick-tempered, John Calvin was still a bachelor at thirty-one. But he thought it was time to change the situation.

His encyclopedic mind was like a file of three-by-five cards. Anything he catalogued in it would be preserved forever. He envisioned himself as a scholar and author. Intellectual problems could be readily solved; people problems were an intrusion into his goal-oriented life.

In 1540 he was in Germany—this Frenchman who became best known for his Reformation ministry in Switzerland. That posed some problems in seeking a wife. He had strong views about predestination, but he was no fatalist about marriage. The right woman wouldn't appear on his doorstep; he would have to go out and find her.

He knew what he wanted, and he told his associates (who were even more interested in finding him a wife than he was) what those requirements were: "Always keep in mind what I seek to find in her, for I am none of those insane lovers who embrace also the vices of those with whom they are in love, where they are smitten at first sight with a fine figure. This only is the beauty that allures me: if she is chaste, if not too fussy or fastidious, if economical, if patient, if there is hope that she will be interested about my health."

The search committee worked for a year and a half. Their first recommended candidate was a wealthy German woman in Strasbourg. Her brother, an ardent supporter of Calvin's teachings, conducted a vigorous campaign. Since John Calvin desired to live the life of a scholar, he said, it would be helpful to have a wealthy wife underwriting his labors. You can't live on the royalties from the sales of theological books.

It made sense to Calvin's aides, but not to Calvin. The first problem was that she spoke no French. "A minor problem," said the searchers, who returned to the woman to talk her into trying to learn French. She wasn't very excited about the idea, but if it was the only way for her to marry John Calvin, she would consent to try.

John saw another problem. He described it to his friend William Farel. "You understand, William, that she would bring with her a large dowry, and this could be embarrassing to a poor minister like myself. I feel, too, that she might become dissatisfied with her humbler station in life." He could imagine her looking back to the "good old days" of prosperity and excitement.

Farel wrote back that he had a woman in his congregation who spoke French and who would make a suitable wife for Calvin. She was in her mid-forties, about fifteen years older than Calvin, and was a devout Protestant. She had never been married, and Farel hoped that Calvin wouldn't hold that against her.

Apparently Calvin did; he never pursued the matter.

The third choice came from the search committee and apparently interested Calvin. She didn't have any money, so he wouldn't be accused of marrying her for her dowry. He had never met her, for she lived in another city, but her reputation seemed to match Calvin's requirements for a wife. His brother Antoine told him, "Indeed, she is mightily commended by those who are acquainted with her." She sounded good to Calvin, and being the logical man that he was, he was sure that if she met his list of qualifications, she must be the right mate for him. He wrote Farel to get ready for a wedding on March 10, and he dispatched Antoine to bring her to meet him.

It's hard to say what went wrong. Calvin's writings don't disclose any great faults in the woman. And yet the more that John Calvin knew the woman, the more he disliked her. He would have given the word to cross her off the list, but a problem developed. The problem was that the intended bride had now fallen madly in love with John. What was intended to have been a very nonemotional arrangement was now laden with intense feeling.

When he had written to Farel earlier, Calvin had told him, "I make myself look very foolish if it should so happen that my hope fall through again." But it did fall through again. March 10 came and went, and John Calvin was still a bachelor. And the theologian who disliked people problems was ensnared by one.

The intended bride was not only trying to "overwhelm me altogether with her kindness" as Calvin put it, she was also pressing for marriage. Calvin was as determined not to marry her as she was resolved to be his bride. He wouldn't marry her "even if the Lord had altogether demented me," Calvin said, and he prayed, "Most earnestly do I desire to be delivered out of this difficulty." The job of "delivering him out of the difficulty" was delegated to brother Antoine, who had arranged the meeting in the first place. John couldn't do it by himself.

With three disappointments, John Calvin wasn't sure whether he should put himself into a vulnerable position again. Maybe God wanted him to stay single. He wrote, "I have not yet found a wife and frequently hesitate as to whether I ought any more to seek one." At this point, the search committee seems to have disbanded, either because of John's discouragement or its own inability to find additional candidates.

Then John remembered a widow in the small congregation which he pastored. With his encyclopedic mind why hadn't he recalled her before? Idelette de Bure Stordeur was his age, thirty-one, and from his station in life. She had cared lovingly for a sick husband, who had died in the plague a few months earlier.

John had converted both of them to the Reformed faith only a year before. She was an intelligent woman who spoke her mind, yet at the same time she had been very supportive of her husband. Besides, she was attractive. For John Calvin that was frosting on the cake.

In less than a month, he had written once again to William Farel to come and officiate at a wedding; within two months John and Idelette were married.

Like Luther, John Calvin can easily be caricatured, but such characterizations are seldom accurate. He was stubborn, quick-tempered, and bookish, but he was also friendly, conciliatory, and kind. You always knew where you stood with John Calvin. A man of iron self-discipline and definite principles, he was still more willing than Luther to work with other Protestants whose views were a shade different from his own.

Born in 1509 in the old cathedral city of Noyon, sixty miles from Paris, he was the son of Gerard Calvin, who worked as business manager and part-time attorney for the Catholic church. John's mother died when he was three; all he could remember was what he had been told about her. There was a stepmother, but John didn't like to talk about her.

John's father, a shrewd man, was determined to get his son the best education his influence could finagle. First, he got John, while still only a boy, appointed to the church office. Technically, it was illegal, but after all, the Archbishop of Rheims received his office at five and the Bishop of Mainz when he had just turned four, so it wasn't too hard for Gerard Calvin to get his son a minor chaplaincy appointment at the age of twelve, especially since the authorities knew that John would be training for the priesthood.

Two years later, at age fourteen, still receiving an honorarium as chaplain, young John went to Paris to attend college. He spent three years in a liberal arts college and one in a school of theology which was noted for its whippings, lice, and rotten eggs. Calvin survived and at age eighteen received a master's degree.

It was 1527, and Luther's writings were infiltrating the corners of France. Jacques LeFevre, a Parisian, had just been evicted from the Sorbonne for his Protestant-sounding books; Calvin's cousin Olivetan had embraced the new teachings. Young John Calvin, however, was not easily swayed.

Then his father got in trouble with the archbishop. Accusing him of mishandling an estate, the archbishop demanded that the elder Calvin open his books and reveal the financial records. Stubbornly, Gerard Calvin refused. As a result, he lost his job. Angrily, he wrote his son in Paris, urging him to transfer from theology to law. No longer did he want his son to be studying for the Catholic ministry. Obediently, John did what his father had bidden him to do.

Three years later, however, when his father died, John switched again. Now he had decided to become a classical scholar. Within a year he had published a learned commentary on the Roman philosopher Seneca, written properly in polished Latin.

Nobody bought it, though people said nice things about it. Calvin tried to promote its sales himself, but commercially it was a flop.

It was a blow to the up-and-coming scholar. Previously he had been successful in all his academic pursuits, but as he looked at the interests in his life, all he saw was confusion. He didn't know where to turn. Though he was still defending it, he was becoming increasingly disillusioned with the Roman Catholic church; the legal profession did not excite him; and his attempt in classical scholarship had fizzled.

Calvin didn't know what was going on, yet God did. Calvin later wrote: "God by a sudden conversion subdued my heart." It probably happened in 1533, when John was twenty-four years old, and it was preceded by a string of turbulent events.

A close friend had been made rector of the University of Paris and as part of his responsibility was called upon to make the annual All Saints Day address. Having received his training in medicine, the rector felt a bit insecure as he prepared his address for the older and more distinguished professors of philosophy and law at the Sorbonne.

In recent months the rector had become quite evangelical in his thinking, and so he had some strong things to say to the Sorbonne. Yet he needed the assistance of a scholar, someone who could support his arguments by the proper classical quotations and references to the church fathers. His friend John Calvin, though not yet convinced about the rector's Protestant leanings, would be glad to help him.

The speech was effective, perhaps too effective. The rector was run out of town, and John Calvin—when word got around that he had helped prepare the speech—became a hunted man as well. As the police were coming to John's apartment, he escaped through a back window on a rope made out of bedclothes. Seeking refuge, he found the home of a former classmate; probably at this time he had his conversion experience.

Calvin told it this way: "Whenever I descended into my soul or raised my mind up to Thee, extreme terror seized me, such terror as no expectations or satisfactions could cure. And the more closely I examined myself, the sharper the stings with which my conscience was pricked, so that the only solace left to me was to delude myself by trying to forget it all. . . . At last I saw in what a pigsty of error I had wallowed, and how polluted, and impure I had become. With great fear and tremblings, I could do no other than at once to betake myself to Thy way." Since his native France was no longer safe for him, he escaped across the border to Basel, Switzerland, where he wrote the first edition of his most famous work, *The Institutes of the Christian Religion*. He completed it when he was twenty-six years old, within a year or two of his conversion.

Finally Calvin had found his career, or so he thought. He would be a Protestant scholar-theologian. As he wrote later, "The summit of my wishes was the enjoyment of literary ease, with something of a free and honorable station." Pictures of Calvin at this period depict a rather dapper young man with a well-tended forked beard and a large ring on his left hand. Holding embroidered gloves, he appears the image of a well-bred Frenchman with a concern for his appearance.

In 1534 he had written, "I have learned from experience that we cannot see very far before us." He had already changed career goals four times in the previous eight years. In 1536 he would face another change.

Traveling through Geneva, Switzerland, he was halted by William Farel, a fiery Genevan cleric, who asked him to stay and assist in the reformation of the church there. Calvin knew better. Geneva had a bad reputation. Reforming it would be akin to reforming Sodom and Gomorrah. So Calvin told Farel that he was approaching the wrong man. Calvin was too shy to do what Farel was asking. He was a behind-the-scenes man, a scholar, not a fiery evangelist. His home was a library, not a pulpit.

Farel wouldn't take no for an answer. He responded: "You're using your studies as an excuse; you're being selfish and self-willed. If you don't stay with me in Geneva, God will curse you, for you will be seeking your own honor instead of Christ's."

Believe it or not, that began a lifelong friendship. Calvin stayed. He explained: "I felt as if God from heaven had laid his mighty hand upon me to stop me in my tracks." In one of his commentaries Calvin described the scribe of Matthew 8:19, probably describing himself as well: "He wants to fight in the shade and at ease, untroubled by sweat or dust, and beyond the reach of weapons of war." Farel put Calvin on the front lines.

And it was a battle, especially for someone like John Calvin, whose headaches and stomach upsets flared up in times of stress. The city council referred to him coldly as "that Frenchman," and most of the town boycotted his daily lectures on Paul's Epistles.

When the council began referring to him by a name, he was called the Protestant pope. John's temper flared. In the middle of a sermon he called the city fathers a "council of the devil," and that didn't help matters. Later he confessed, "I have been too hasty; I have tried to do too much too quickly."

Shortly after Easter 1538, Farel and Calvin were given three days to get out of town. A contemporary reporter said that it was a special miracle that they were able to get out before blood was shed.

Calvin resolved never again to return to Geneva and never again to get mixed up in church affairs. People problems caused his headaches. From now on, he would be engaged in scholarly pursuits. But hardly had he unpacked his books in Basel when he received an urgent letter from a pastor in Strasbourg, Germany, urging him to come and help with a church of French refugees. Naturally, Calvin turned him down. "I shall retire in Basel," he wrote. He was not quite twenty-nine years old.

But the Strasbourg leader Martin Bucer came back with a stronger letter. It pulled no punches. "God will know how to find the rebellious servant, as he found Jonah, if you try to run away from Him." It almost sounded like William Farel talking, and Calvin didn't know how to turn down orders like that. Hurriedly, he headed for Strasbourg.

The congregation of French refugees, though growing, was small, and so Calvin took on additional responsibilities as professor of theology at the newly formed University of Strasbourg. Neither job provided him with much income.

At first Calvin stayed in Bucer's home. Bucer was not only a happily married man, but he considered it one of his callings in life to get his assistants married as well. Once after Calvin had lost his temper, Bucer suggested, "John, you ought to have a wife." Calvin wasn't quite sure how the two things were related, but he told Bucer that he would consider it.

Because Calvin needed money to live on, he sold part of his library and rented a large house which he turned into a dormitory for students. "My poverty is so great that at present I do not even have a sou," he wrote Farel. But he soon discovered that running a boarding house was full of people problems, which aggravated his headaches and caused stomach upsets as well. So he hired a cook-housekeeper with a sharp tongue and slovenly housekeeping habits. Though he tried to stay as far away from her as possible, there was no room in the house that wasn't pierced when she began screaming at a tenant. Calvin was trying to revise the second edition of the *Institutes* at the time and didn't know what to do with her. On the other hand, he didn't know what he would do without her either. Maybe if he had a wife, she would know how to handle people problems like that.

Idelette de Bure had already lived a full life at thirty-one. A native of Gelderland, Holland, she had married Jean Stordeur of Liege when she was sixteen or seventeen. Two children were born—Jacques and Judith—and then Idelette and Jean were converted by Anabaptist missionaries.

Conversion to Anabaptist beliefs meant persecution. Idelette wasn't concerned for herself, but she was concerned for her children. If she and her husband were martyred, what would become of Jacques and Judith?

In the Low Countries of Belgium and the Netherlands, thousands of Anabaptists were slain; some historians have put the figure as high as 30,000. Menno Simons wrote about it: "Some they have hanged, some they have punished with inhuman tyranny and afterward garroted them with cords, tied to a post. Some they have roasted and burned alive. Some, holding their own entrails in their hands, have powerfully confessed the Word of God still. Some they beheaded and gave as food to the fowls of the air. Some they have consigned to the fish. They have torn down the houses of some. Some have they thrust into muddy bogs. . . . They must take to their heels and flee away with their wives and little children, from one city to another—hated by all men, abused, slandered, mocked, defamed, trampled upon." Little wonder that Idelette was concerned for her children.

Throughout Europe, Strasbourg was known as a free city, a refuge from religious oppression. Some of the earlier Anabaptists had believed that Strasbourg was the city where God would set up a new Jerusalem. Probably Idelette and Jean came simply to find a place where they could raise their children in peace. They followed other refugees to the church in which John Calvin ministered. His preaching was so biblical, so clear, so logical, so convincing that soon they were convinced, along with many other Anabaptist refugees, that Calvin's views of Scripture made sense.

In the small congregation where new members were catechized, Calvin must have taken some special interest in the spiritual progress of these new converts, the Stordeurs. And he must have sorrowed when he heard that Jean Stordeur had become ill.

God had preserved Jean Stordeur from the flames of martyrdom in Holland, but not the pestilential plague in Strasbourg. And there, not much more than a year after they had arrived, he was buried. No doubt it was one of the first funerals that Calvin conducted in Strasbourg. He couldn't have helped noticing the attractive, gentle woman dressed in black who looked too young to be the mother of the twelve-year-old son and six-year-old daughter who walked behind.

By this time Calvin had become a bit discouraged in his quest for a wife. However, he was still in the market for one. After all, three of the men that he respected most—Farel, Bucer, and even Luther's friend Philip Melanchthon—had urged him to consider it. Often the major moves of Calvin's life had been because of such urgings of friends and family. His father had told him to change from theology to law. Farel had stopped him in Geneva. Bucer had called him to come to Strasbourg; and now Bucer, Farel, and Melanchthon had all ganged up on him to get married.

Prior to Strasbourg, Calvin hadn't had many models of marriage. He knew little about the relationship of his mother and father. In Geneva his closest friend had been Farel, a fifty-year-old bachelor. So it wasn't until he had arrived in the home of Bucer in Strasbourg that he saw a Christian marriage. A deep love and warm camaraderie were evident. Elizabeth Bucer was a good mother, a hospitable homemaker, and her husband's best critic. Bucer regarded the last point as the most important. But visitors to the home, as John Calvin had been, noticed most of all the way Elizabeth Bucer opened her home to refugees. One visitor wrote: "For seventeen days after my arrival, I was entertained in Bucer's home. It is like a hostel, receiving refugees for the cause of Christ. In his family during the entire time I saw not the least occasion of offense but only ground for edification. I never left the table without having learned something."

In Strasbourg the senior minister was Matthew Zell, whose wife was the remarkably outspoken Katherine Zell. Her husband, who had been a priest, was roundly criticized for marrying her. He refused to reply to the criticisms, but she wasn't hesitant. She penned a biblical defense of clerical marriage, as well as a defense for herself, a woman writing to instruct theologians: "I do not pretend to be John the Baptist rebuk-

ing the Pharisees," she wrote. "I aspire only to be Balaam's ass, castigating his master." Like Elizabeth Bucer, she housed refugees in her
parsonage. At one time eighty found a haven there.

Once she wrote a letter to Luther urging him to reach an agreement
with other Protestant leaders, and once when John Calvin had a temper tantrum in their home, it was Katherine who mollified him. The
marriages of the Bucers and the Zells must have influenced John.

Just at the time when Calvin was beginning to think of marriage,
he met Philip Melanchthon, Luther's associate. They became good
friends. Melanchthon, who had now been married for nineteen years,
was one of those who encouraged Calvin to follow suit, no doubt sharing his personal testimony with him. Mrs. Melanchthon, who had a
rollicking sense of humor, took good care of Philip both physically and
emotionally. Melanchthon's one complaint was, "She always thinks
that I am dying of hunger unless I am stuffed like a sausage."

Thus, when Calvin began noticing Idelette, the attractive widow in
his congregation, his concept of marriage had evolved a bit from the
mechanical checklist of requirements with which he had begun his
search.

Farel, who had been alerted at least twice before to an impending
marriage, found that this was no false alarm. Idelette and John were
both ready for marriage. Farel took delight in performing the ceremony.

The biggest problem in their marriage soon became evident; it was
a health problem. Both of them had frequent bouts with illness. Hardly
had Farel pronounced them man and wife when both of them became
ill. A week or two later, Calvin sent a thank-you note to Farel from his
bed: "As if it had been so ordered, that our wedlock might not be over-
joyous, the Lord thus thwarted our joy by moderating it."

They had barely recovered from that illness when another string of
events confined them both to bed again. It started when Calvin's tart-
tongued housekeeper insulted his brother Antoine, who was staying
at the Calvin dormitory. Antoine walked out, vowing never to return
as long as the housekeeper remained. To Calvin, it was the last straw,
and his temper almost erupted against the surly housekeeper. Knowing that the volcano was soon to blow, the housekeeper quit after
preparing the evening meal. Trying to control himself, Calvin was still

seething. "I am wont," he explained later, "when heated to anger, or stirred by some greater anxiety than usual, to eat to excess . . . which so happened to me at that time." The next morning he had a severe digestive attack but carried on his preaching and teaching duties anyway. By evening he was running a fever, and he fainted from his weakened condition. That put him in bed, after which Idelette got the bug. "While I was still suffering under the weakness, my wife took a fever. The last eight days she has been so exhausted . . . that she can with difficulty sit up in bed."

Though Calvin did not share as much of his home life in his writings as Luther did, you get from Calvin's letters a glimpse of Idelette as one who cared deeply for John's well-being and for her children. At times she accompanied him on trips; sometimes John mentions their entertaining guests in their home. Calvin's biographers refer to her as "a woman of some force and individuality," and John himself describes her as "the faithful helper of my ministry" and "the best companion of my life."

During the first ten months of their marriage, however, companionship wasn't the hallmark of their relationship. It's true, of course, that they were companions in sickness during the first two months after their wedding. Then Calvin was urged to attend an important theological gathering in Worms, Germany. He wasn't eager to go, for several reasons, primarily because he didn't want to leave Idelette and because he was still weakened by his recent illnesses. But he felt he had no choice in the matter.

About a year earlier, Emperor Charles V, ruler of the Holy Roman Empire, had summoned the leading Catholic and Protestant scholars to a summit conference. The emperor wasn't really concerned about theological matters; what bothered him was the fact that the Turks were menacing his empire, and with the Catholics and Protestants squabbling among themselves, he couldn't form a united military front against the Turks. Therefore, he proposed a unity conference.

Most of those attending were German theologians, and Calvin, a thirty-one-year-old Frenchman, was flattered to be asked. But he remarked candidly, "I expect little from it." His expectations were accurate. Prior to his marriage two of these meetings had already been held.

Neither had accomplished much. The third was scheduled for November 1, 1540, in Worms.

Calvin soon had second thoughts about his decision to attend. The duke who was to chair the conference didn't show up until December 1, and then it took six weeks of arguing to agree on the agenda and the form of the debate. The debate itself lasted only a week. During all this time, Idelette the newlywed was home in Strasbourg, taking care of John's boardinghouse and her two children.

John got back home late in January, 1541. After one month back home, he headed to eastern Germany for the last of the series of conferences. "I am dragged most unwillingly to Ratisbon," Calvin wrote. But he went.

Several hundred miles from home, he received news that a plague was ravaging Strasbourg. Calvin was worried. "Day and night my wife has been constantly in my thoughts," he wrote. The previous plague had taken Idelette's first husband; this plague could easily take Idelette, who was already weakened by recent illness. He wrote advising her to leave town. But Idelette had taken matters into her own hands and had accompanied her children to her brother's home.

Idelette stayed out of town for several weeks, but not as long as her husband stayed at the emperor's theological conference. The gathering, which had begun in March, was still going strong four months later in June when John Calvin walked out and headed home to Idelette. By the end of June, Calvin had been married forty-five weeks and had been away from home for thirty-two of them.

But more than Idelette was on his mind. It had been three years since he had been kicked out of Geneva, and for the past two years he had been getting letters begging him to return. At first the letters had come from private citizens: "Everyone sighs for you," or "Come, come that we may rejoice in God our Redeemer." To put it mildly, John was not eager to return. "I would rather face death a hundred times" than return to Geneva, he wrote. When a pastor in Lausanne urged him to return to Geneva and mentioned that the climate would be good for his health, Calvin retorted by calling Geneva a torture chamber and asking how the good pastor could have an interest in his health and still urge him to return.

497

For Calvin, Geneva was the last place in the world in which he wanted to live. No doubt his concern for Idelette contributed to his strong feelings. She had known as much suffering as he had, probably more. If a second sojourn in Geneva would be anything like his first two years there, the problems would be endless. Strasbourg was a haven, even though it had its problems, too. But problems in Strasbourg could be faced and forgotten. Geneva's problems were perpetual. Looking at himself and his own talents, he realized that God had given him the gifts of a scholar, not the cast-iron stomach of a barroom brawler. It made no sense to him to consider returning to Geneva.

But the letters from Geneva became more insistent and sounded more desperate. Now they were coming from the city council itself. And even William Farel was begging him to return. He hated it when Farel turned his guns on him.

Calvin roared back: "You have deeply distressed me with your thundering and lightning. Why do you make me look so bad and feel so guilty? Do you want me to renounce your friendship? . . . If I had a free choice, I would prefer doing anything else in the world." Two months after his marriage, an official Geneva delegation came to Strasbourg, just after Calvin had gotten off his sickbed and gone to the conference in Worms. Undeterred, the delegation continued to Worms to deliver their message.

Calvin read Geneva's official invitation and then burst into tears. "The very thought of Geneva is agony to me." Sometime early in 1541, his decision was made. "It is difficult to overcome my soul and control it, but I know that I am not my own master. I offer my heart to the Lord in sacrifice." Then in the month of September, Calvin headed to Geneva. Some scholars feel that Calvin may have hoped that he could settle some matters there in a few weeks and then return home. But most feel that he was testing the sincerity of the council's invitation. At any rate, Idelette stayed behind in Strasbourg until John found out whether or not Geneva would be safe for her.

The city council did their best to accommodate the Calvins. They were promised a handsome salary (some of which was to be used to entertain prominent guests). The council also purchased a house for the Calvins and guaranteed their safety. Furthermore, they sent an escort to bring Idelette and all the family furniture to Geneva. John concluded that the "natives" might be friendly after all.

During their first summer back in Geneva, Idelette bore a son prematurely. Little Jacques died when only two weeks old. For both John and Idelette, it was a severe emotional blow. John wrote a fellow pastor, "The Lord has certainly inflicted a bitter wound in the death of our infant son. But He is Himself a father and knows what is good for His children." Three years later, a daughter died at birth, and two years after that, when both John and Idelette were thirty-nine, a third child was born prematurely and died. Idelette's physical problems worsened. Coughing spells dragged her down.

Idelette, of course, had two children by her first husband. Her son stayed in Strasbourg to complete his studies. Her daughter, who grew more rebellious in teenage years, became part of the Calvin home in Geneva.

Their Geneva home was at Number 11, Rue de Chanoines. The city council had loaned them furniture to help fill it. It had three bedrooms upstairs, and a living room, study, and kitchen downstairs. At the top of the short street was a water fountain where Idelette could wash clothes and draw water for the family.

The home wasn't large, but there was always someone staying in the third bedroom. For much of the time it was John's brother Antoine and his wife, and this was a help to Idelette. Behind the house was a garden, sloping down to the city walls. Herbs and flowers scented the air, and John enjoyed showing his guests where Idelette grew vegetables.

John's schedule was exhausting. He preached two Sunday sermons, conducted weekday services every other week, and on Tuesdays, Thursdays, and Saturdays gave theological lectures. Thursday was also his day to conduct elders' meetings, and on Friday he had a Bible study with the other preachers in town.

When Idelette was well enough, she accompanied her husband in visiting the sick and those in prison. She had a deep concern for those who were suffering. In John's spare time he wrote letters. In fact, he wrote so many of them that his home became a branch post office.

Amazingly, John was able to keep to this schedule even though his health was poor. Migraine headaches, stomach ulcers, asthma, and pleurisy were among his problems. The feeling that he was being constantly thrust into people problems, which he disliked, aggravated his physical maladies.

A timid man, he is described by John T. McNeill as "one of those scholarly and highly sensitive persons whose talents mark them for prominent leadership, and who shrink from but dare not shirk the duties involved. Such persons may become assertive even in overcoming an inclination to retirement."

"God thrust me into the game," Calvin once said, and Calvin played games seriously. At home he liked to play games when time permitted. His favorite were quoits (a sort of ring-toss) and bowls (indoor bowling), as well as a key-toss game. John Knox reported that, when he called at Calvin's home one Sunday afternoon, he found him playing bowls.

But the game into which God had thrust him in Geneva wasn't that much fun despite the early promises of the city council. Calvin had as many enemies in the city as he had friends, and they made life miserable. They called their dogs "Calvin." What angered John more, however, was to hear Idelette insulted; because of her Anabaptist background, Calvin's enemies called her first marriage an illegitimate one.

Despite her ill health, Idelette did a good job of keeping John on an even keel. Friends noticed that John seemed better able to control his temper since he had become married, in spite of the continuing provocations.

Idelette's health went steadily downhill. In August 1548 Calvin wrote, "She is so overpowered with her sickness that she can scarcely support herself." It was probably tuberculosis.

She never wanted her health problems to burden her husband. He had enough problems in Geneva without her adding her physical problem to them. But in 1549 Idelette lay dying. She was only forty and had been married to John for only nine years. As she neared death, she asked John to care for her two children. She hated to add to his load. "I have committed them to the Lord," she told him in short gasping phrases, "but I want you to promise that you will not neglect them." He promised.

Three days later, Idelette was still lingering, but John knew that death was only a few hours away. Her last words were "O glorious resurrection." Then when she was unable to speak any longer, John spoke to her about Christ's love, about eternal life, and about the blessings of their nine years together. An hour later, Idelette was gone.

Calvin was grief-stricken. A week afterward he wrote to a pastor friend: "Truly mine is no ordinary grief." And to his friend Farel he wrote, "I do what I can to keep myself from being overwhelmed with grief. My friends also leave nothing undone that may bring relief to my mental suffering. . . . May the Lord Jesus . . . support me under this heavy affliction, which would certainly have overcome me had not He who raises up the prostrate, strengthens the weak and refreshes the weary, stretched forth His hand from heaven to me."

In a few weeks one of his friends wrote back: "I know, friend, your innate tenderness. So I write to you a letter of congratulations rather than one of condolence. . . . With admiration, I experience the power of God's Spirit who works in you and shows Himself in you as Comforter. How well do I know how deeply this had wounded you, for nothing more difficult could have happened to you. How you must feel, you whom the grief of others moves so deeply."

Calvin, though only forty, never remarried. A year after Idelette's death, he spoke of her uniqueness and pledged that he intended henceforth "to lead a solitary life." He lived fifteen more years, shaping the city of Geneva, revising once again his masterpiece, *Institutes of the Christian Religion,* and preaching verse by verse through thirty books of the Bible.

His public life seemed busier than ever, but his home life remained solitary.

It is unfortunate that more is not known of the marriage of John and Idelette. The marriage was short—only nine years—and was hampered by bouts with poor health. But it was a good marriage for both of them.

For Idelette, it brought a meaning and purpose to life, and it provided a father for her children.

And for John, who was somewhat of a hypochondriac in addition to suffering from real ills, God provided someone to care for and to love. John had been looking for someone who could care for him, and God sent him someone to care for.

What marriage did for John was to evoke from him a more tender side than the world normally saw. John is perhaps best known for his theological emphasis on God the Father as Sovereign of the world. Through Idelette, John came to appreciate the ministry of the Holy Spirit as Comforter in the home.

Bibliography

Bainton, Roland. *Women of the Reformation.* Minneapolis: Augsburg, 1971.
Hyma, Albert. *The Life of John Calvin.* Grand Rapids: Eerdmans, 1943.
Johnson, E. M. *Man of Geneva.* Carlisle, Penn.: Banner of Truth, 1977.
Martin-Taylor, Duncan. *God's Man.* Grand Rapids: Baker, 1979.
McNeil, John T. *The History and Character of Calvinism.* Fair Lawn, N.J.: Oxford University Press, 1954.
Parker, T. H. L. *Portrait of Calvin.* Philadelphia: Westminster, 1954.
Van Halsema, Thea. *This Was John Calvin.* Grand Rapids: Zondervan, 1959.

William J. Petersen, editorial director of Fleming H. Revell and Chosen Books, was formerly editor of *Eternity Magazine* and *Evangelical Newsletter*, as well as editorial director of *Christian Life* and *Christian Bookseller Magazine*. Dr. Petersen has also served as president of the Evangelical Press Association. He and his wife Ardythe are the parents of three grown children. He has written more than twenty books.